Women's Experience of Modernity, 1875–1945

Women's Experience of Modernity, 1875–1945

EDITED BY

Ann L. Ardis and Leslie W. Lewis

THE JOHNS HOPKINS UNIVERSITY PRESS

Baltimore and London

The Johns Hopkins University Press
2715 North Charles Street
Baltimore, Maryland 21218-4363
www.press.jhu.edu

Library of Congress Cataloging-in-Publication Data

Women's experience of modernity, 1875–1945 / Ann L. Ardis and
Leslie W. Lewis, editors.
      p.   cm.
Includes bibliographical references and index.
   ISBN 0-8018-6935-8 (pbk. : acid-free paper)
      1. American literature—Women authors—History and criticism.
2. Modernism (Literature)—United States. 3. Women and
literature—United States—History—20th century. 4. Women and
literature—United States—History—19th century. 5. Women and
literature—Great Britain—History—20th century. 6. Women and
literature—Great Britain—History—19th century. 7. English
literature—Women authors—History and criticism. 8. Modernism
(Literature)—Great Britain. 9. Feminism and literature. 10. Sex
role in literature.   I. Lewis, Leslie W., 1960–   II. Ardis,
Ann L., 1957–
   PS228.M63 W66 2003
   820.9 9287'09034—dc21   2001008647

A catalog record for this book is available
from the British Library.

CONTENTS

ACKNOWLEDGMENTS

Recent scholarship recognizes collaborative writing as a feminist act of empowerment. And so we take this moment to acknowledge the pleasures as well as the intellectual use value of our labor together over this collection of essays on women's writing practices at the turn of the twenty-first century. Coming to this project with our respective interests and expertise in British and (African) American literature, our collaboration as editors has been a crucial means of securing the transatlantic scene we envisioned. Listening to each other's responses to our contributors' work has been, alternately, a reassuring confirmation of our own individual assessments and an occasion for further education. Sharing the work of corresponding with all of our authors certainly moved this project more quickly toward publication, while sharing a sense of excitement about the success of our contributors' responses to challenges and requests for revision has punctuated the relentless everydayness of pulling this manuscript into final shape. These essays speak thoughtfully to one another because of the desire to listen, as well as the desire to be heard, shared by us all. Our thanks go thus: to each other; to the Johns Hopkins University Press editors and our thorough and insightful reader; to our contributors, for their excellent work through all stages of this anthology's production; to Rita Felski, whose afterword provides a model reading of the collection. Additionally, Leslie would like to thank the College of Saint Rose for generous support of her work with this collection, and Ann would like to thank both the University of Delaware's Undergraduate Research Program, for supporting Christina Taneyhill and Laura Grodzecki's work on our contributors' earliest drafts, and the Office of the Vice Provost of Academic Programs and Planning, for supporting Anne Thalheimer's copyediting of the final manuscript. Finally, we both owe a debt of enormous gratitude to Holly Laird, much larger than we can name, for her enthusiastic involvement with this project, and for both her wisdom and her understanding.

Women's Experience of Modernity, 1875–1945

Introduction

This collection of original essays on women's history and literary production at the turn of the twentieth century rises to the challenge posed
in Rita Felski's recent study *The Gender of Modernity* (1995). "How
would our understanding of modernity" be changed, Felski asks, "if instead of
taking male experience as paradigmatic, we were to look instead at texts written primarily by women? And what if feminine phenomena, often seen as having a secondary or marginal status, were given a central importance in the
analysis of the culture of modernity? What *difference* would such a procedure
make?"[1] This collection marks that difference by exploring women's varied experiences of modernity, experiences that include cultural practices such as selling and shopping, travel and world expositions, political and social activism,
urban fieldwork and rural labor, and radical discourses of feminine sexuality,
as well as experiments with literary form.

In her important essay "Experience," Joan Wallach Scott has accused historians of taking entirely for granted as a primary category of analysis a concept
such as "experience," which is defined either as "an expression of an individual's being or consciousness" or as "the material upon which consciousness
then acts."[2] The problem with "talking about experience in these ways," Scott
argues, is that it "leads us to take the existence of individuals for granted (experience is something people have) rather than to ask how conceptions of
selves . . . are produced" (27). By making "individuals the starting point of
knowledge," categories such as "man, woman, black, white, heterosexual, or
homosexual" are naturalized, treated as "given characteristics of individuals,"
rather than being understood as products of history in and of themselves (27).

What Scott would have historians do instead, which she characterizes as "reading for 'the literary,' " is to attend to the history of this category. "Experience is not a word [historians] can do without," she concedes. But we must "analyze its operations and . . . redefine its meaning" (37). "Experience is at once always already an interpretation *and* in need of interpretation; it is always contested, always therefore political" (37, emphasis in original). Experience, therefore, must be treated as not "the origin of our explanation, but that which we want to explain" (38).

Although Scott's critique is aimed at historians, her argument, paired with Felski's challenge to literary critics, provides a useful point of departure for this collection of essays by literary scholars for several reasons. "Woman's experience" was an important rallying cry for feminists during this period, a means of making a variety of claims for women's right of access to the public world—as voters, as paid laborers and professionals, as political activists functioning in a (feminist or black counter-) public sphere, as both the subject and the creators of high, low, and middlebrow art. At the same time, however, "woman's experience" was also a source of great divisiveness among women, as these same claims about the universality of "woman's experience" were unraveled to reveal the classism, racism, and Eurocentrism of various feminist organizations and activists. The taylorization of industrial production, the bureaucratization of modern life, the rise of consumerism and commodity capitalism's economic hegemony: all of these sociohistorical phenomena that distinguish the turn of the twentieth century have been praised for epitomizing the Enlightenment values of efficiency, good management, rationality, and "modern" progress. Yet this same spectrum of phenomena has also been identified as a source of social alienation and cultural anomie, while the severest critics of modernity foreground the "complicity of rationality with the practice of white supremacist terror."[3] As a particularly powerful articulation of contemporary feminist standpoint theory, Scott's suggestion that we "rea[d] for 'the literary' " by treating all categories of analysis as "contextual, contested, and contingent" thus not only invites us to treat turn-of-the-twentieth-century representations of "woman's experience" as constructs, interpretations in need of interpretation and historical contextualization. Paired with Felski's challenge, Scott's work also urges us to attend to the gendered dimensions, and contradictions, of "modern" life.

Additionally, Scott's work provides a useful frame of reference for this collection because her recommendations parallel efforts being made within the discipline of English studies to read literature as history: to treat "the literary" itself as a historically contingent category and to understand the role(s) that literature—defined by Lyn Pykett as "aesthetically self-conscious and culturally valued" writing[4]—has played in the dissemination of social practices and cultural values. In all other regards, the theoretical debts registered in these essays are both many and hugely varied: to feminist and African American theorists' critiques of Jürgen Habermas's influential work on the organization of the bourgeois public sphere as an arena of disembodied, rational, discourse; to theorists of mass culture and the everyday such as Michel de Certeau and Laurie Langbauer; to theorists of modern spectatorship ranging from Walter Benjamin to Janet Wolff and Jonathan Crary; to sociologists of "the modern" such as Bruno Latour and postcolonialists such as Homi Bhabha. One of the assumptions that the contributors to this anthology do indeed share, however, is that, like other social practices, literary texts participate in the making of history rather than existing at one remove from it. Thus, the chapters that follow "explore and analyze a range of different kinds of writing, and not just that writing that has been filtered through the sieve of those definitions of the literary which emerged with the development of institutionalized literary studies in the twentieth century" (Pykett, 5). They look at "historical questions through the reading of literature . . . and "look at writing in general, and 'literary' . . . writing in particular as part of history" (ibid.). To borrow Scott's phrasing again, they read "for 'the literary' " by treating both literary and nonliterary writings as discursive events that organize and orchestrate our understanding of the historical real.

Because of our contributors' commitment to historicizing the literary field and attending to the contemporary theoretical concerns informing their recovery of women's literature and history, this volume both does and does not contribute to "new modernist studies," the revisionary scholarship on literary modernism that is currently reenergizing turn-of-the-twentieth-century studies.

On the one hand, by attending to the material specificity of women writers' negotiations in the literary marketplace, the chapters on Alice Meynell, Pauline Hopkins, Jane Addams, Rebecca West, H.D., Radclyffe Hall, and Opal Whiteley in Part I, "Negotiating the Literary Marketplace," contribute to a strong new vein of research on the marketing of literary modernism carved out recently by scholars such as Kevin Dettmar, Stephen Watt, Joyce Piell Wexler, and Lawrence Rainey.[5] On the other hand, by inviting our readers to consider "Edwardian" middlebrow essayists, "Georgian" pastoral poets, fin de siècle urban ethnographers, and a best-selling child diarist alongside a relatively familiar set of modernist women who alternately collaborated with and challenged the "men of 1914" and male leadership of the Harlem Renaissance, the essays in this section, and in the volume as a whole, challenge classic modernist "narratives of rupture" separating high from low culture and the Victorian from the "modern" period.[6]

Felski has suggested that modernism is "only one aspect of the culture of women's modernity" rather than the main vehicle of its articulation (25). The essays in this first section flesh out this line of argument by building on, and occasionally redirecting, a strong tradition of feminist scholarship on the "gender of modernism."[7] But the juxtaposition of modernist and nonmodernist figures and material in this section also renders suspect any lingering assumptions we might still harbor that literary modernism rose naturally or inevitably to the forefront of the cultural landscape at the turn of the twentieth century, or that the best way to map what Michael Levenson, in his introduction to the recent *Cambridge Companion to Modernism,* has termed a "richer, thicker" history of the period is by expanding the category "modernism" to include reference to women and other minorities excluded from that original coterie.[8] Scholars such as Peter Nicholls, Michael North, and Marjorie Perloff have joined Levenson in objecting to the ideological homogeneity of a "straw-man modernism" and opt instead for pluralizing the term.[9] By contrast, our contributors follow Felski's lead instead and retain the specificity of the term "modernism" as a "designation for . . . texts which display . . . formally self-conscious, experimental, [and] antimimetic features. . . while simultaneously questioning the assumption that such texts are necessarily the most important or representative works of the modern period (Felski, 25). If modernism was in fact one aspect—but only one aspect—of women's modernity, then what other aesthetic modes and venues of literary and/or cultural production, our contributors ask, did women explore and exploit? How were women such as Alice Meynell and Jane Addams, for example, deploying "conservative" literary forms and Victorian ideals of femininity as tactics of feminist critique, activism, and social experimentation to which modernist notions of "experimental writing" cannot begin to do justice?[10] What difficulties were faced by modernist and nonmodernist women alike in negotiating the "rhetorics of sexuality[, race,] and the modern in a changing world"?[11]

The contributors to our second and third sections move the discussion of women's experience of modernity even further beyond the parameters of modernist literary studies per se as they drawn on anti- and postdisciplinary work in gender and cultural studies that challenges us to "start imagining a larger discursive and highly politicized field of inquiry—a field wherein the 'literary' [is recognized as] only one of many newly specialized discourses struggling for legitimation"—in the early twentieth century.[12] Not all the essays in, respectively, Part II, "Outside the Metropolis," and Part III, "The Shifting Terrain of Public Life," focus exclusively or even centrally on literary matters. Instead, they roam more freely across a broader array of textual materials— photographic journalism, periodical essays, political pamphlets, sexual advice manuals, gynecology textbooks, and psychological treatises—as they investigate women's responses to a range of sociological phenomena that uniquely characterize the turn of the twentieth century. These include (to supplement the list provided earlier): the rise of commodity culture, the development of new modes of urban transportation, visual innovations in the mass-market newspaper industry, middle-class women's entrance into both the labor force and the public sphere, and the intensified eroticization of racial and class differences generated, in the United States, by massive waves of immigration and post–Reconstruction era problems of the color line and, in Britain and its ex-colonies, by "growing recognition of colonial subjectivity as separate from— and hostile to—English subjectivity."[13]

This volume's concern for women's participation in these profound and far-reaching transformations of the social order also dictates its attention to outposts of the English-speaking world such as South Africa, India, and the Asian subcontinent. While literary modernism itself is commonly recognized as a transnational phenomena, turn-of-the-twentieth-century studies more generally continue to be marked by what Benedict Anderson characterizes as the "limited" imaginings of national identity.[14] To compensate for the covert as well as the overt nationalism directing literary histories of the period, this volume not only deliberately juxtaposes American and British materials in each of its three sections.[15] The second section in particular also presents this "female Atlantic" in the larger context of the global diaspora of European feminist thought and its complex relationship to the history of Anglo-American colonialism at the turn of the twentieth century.

In his posthumously published work *The Politics of Modernism: Against the New Conformism,* the late Raymond Williams urged us to seek, "from time to time," a view "from the deprived hinterlands, where different forces are moving and from the poor world which has always been peripheral to metropolitan systems," rather than accepting the "metropolitan interpretation of its own processes as universal."[16] Taking a cue from him, our second section invites consideration of what lies "Outside the Metropolis." In essays about Toru Dutt's brief but spectacular literary career, Olive Schreiner's representations of Boer women, Edward Tilt's and Bram Stoker's colonialist women with "tropical ovaries," Emma Dunham Kelly-Hawkins's Christian conversion fiction, and a Hakka Chinese woman whose experience of modernization included "migration, illiteracy, a life of hard physical labor, and a driving commitment to her children's acquisition of an education,"[17] our contributors teach us about the nonglobalization of modernity, the nature and meaning of "progress" in the modern world, and the productive politics of "in-between" positions along the continuum between "tradition" and Westernization/modernization.[18] The attention paid here to the marketing of Indian women's writing to a fin de siècle British audience, to Olive Schreiner's efforts to "place her metropolitan women readers in a position where they are unable to avoid identification with the aspirations, and the plight, of ['backward'] Boer women,"[19] and to Kelley-Hawkins's strategic deployment of her African American women characters' whiteness, returns us to many of the issues raised in the first section about the material history of women's experience in the literary marketplace at the turn of the twentieth century. But by reminding us that "the bodily impact on women of modernization" is not to be "equated with scholarship on modernity," these essays also call attention to our own "confine[ment] in literacy" when we grant a priori value to literacy and to written (let alone, more narrowly still, "literary") artifacts.[20] Khun Fa's spoken words, translated and transcribed in English in Part II's final chapter, but available electronically in both Hakka and Thai to a world of women "who are still not going to read and write, with or without modernity,"[21] are, additionally, a humbling reminder of the "information borders" upheld even by collections such as this one that call attention to the global as well as the national economies in which women's words, bodies, artifacts, and labor circulate.[22]

The chapters in Part III, "The Shifting Terrain of Public Life," move the discussion of women's experience of modernity at the turn of the twentieth century still further outside of literary studies, as this field has been traditionally, and most narrowly, defined around modernist aesthetics.[23] What happens to our map of the period when, rather than focusing exclusively on aesthetic objects, our project of historical recovery targets not only the labor, both literal and discursive, that produced "new social actors"[24] at the turn of the twentieth

century but also the changing technologies of public transportation that facilitated women's access to the public sphere? How has "the gendering of intel-
lectuality"[25] shaped the terms of women's entrance into, or their relationship
to, newly professionalized discourses such as sociology and sexology, dictating
their continued deployment of literary forms deemed to have a more appro-
priately "female" cultural capital? In the face of strongly negative associations
of female "appetite" with the lures of modern commodity culture, how did
feminists such as Ida B. Wells, Amy Levy, Rebecca West, and Djuna Barnes develop and circulate raced and gendered readings of everyday life? Wells's sensitivity to the practices of exclusion undergirding the liberal democratic ideals of
the (white) bourgeois public sphere; Levy's euphoric representations of the female omnibus traveler as a figure of modernity; Barnes's much more darkly in-
flected exploitation of the new visuality of turn-of-the-century mass-market
newspapers; West's equally canny efforts to carve out space for a radical and
sexualized understanding of women's reading, buying, and eating habits in the
pages of the *Clarion,* the *Freewoman,* and the *New Freewoman;* Marie Stopes's
phobic representations of working-class discourses of sexuality in her enormously popular sexual advice manual, *Married Love;* Mass-Observation diarists' attempts to "write back" to the professional social investigators they
idealized as "young men who do things":[26] essays on these figures and phenomena in Part III demand our attention to the historical specificity of print technology, the solidification of "modern" disciplinary distinctions, and the impact
of new media and new modes of social observation between 1875 and 1945.

What is at stake in this volume is thus not the recovery of some sort of "lost
continent of [a] female tradition rising like Atlantis."[27] What is at stake here, to
borrow the words of one of our contributors, is "the narrative function of 'the
modern' within our histories, and the possibility not merely of assembling a
parallel or alternative gendered text of modernity, but of telling an entirely different kind of story," a story written "outside the terms and tropes of the so-called
'Great Divide' [between] modernist high seriousness and everyday life."[28] Col-
lectively, these essays about women's experience of modernity not only show us
that the categories "modernism" and "modernity" are "always an interpretation
and in need of interpretation," as Joan Scott has suggested regarding the category "experience" (Scott, 37, emphasis in original). They also enhance our understanding of "what modernity might mean for women and other subaltern
groups" by pursuing the vein of research on women's difference Rita Felski first
theorized so provocatively in *The Gender of Modernity* (192).

NOTES

1. Rita Felski, *The Gender of Modernity* (Cambridge, Mass.: Harvard University Press, 1995), 10. Subsequent citations of this source are given parenthetically in the text. While the term "modernity" has been used to refer to earlier historical periods, Felski uses it, and we shall be using it here, to refer to "a wide range of sociohistorical phenomena—e.g., the rise of commodity capitalism, urbanization, the development of new technologies of visualization as well as the taylorization of industrial and domestic production, and the development of the welfare state" (9)—that distinguish the turn of the twentieth century as a period of large-scale social transformation. While this collection builds in many obvious ways on recent scholarship that is bringing the turn of the twentieth century into the critical limelight, it also is fairly unique (at least in the context of British, if not American, cultural studies) in stretching back as far as the 1870s in doing so; as the chapters by Alpana Sharma and Piya Pal-Lapinski show, this historical stretch is required for an adequate treatment of issues related to the history of British imperialism.

2. Joan W. Scott, "Experience," in *Feminists Theorize the Political,* ed. id. and Judith Butler (New York: Routledge, 1992), 26, 27. Subsequent citations of this source are given parenthetically in the text.

3. Paul Gilroy, *The Black Atlantic: Modernity and Double Consciousness* (Cambridge, Mass.: Harvard University Press, 1993), 118.

4. Lyn Pykett, *Engendering Fictions: The English Novel in the Early Twentieth Century* (New York: Edward Arnold, 1995), 5. Subsequent citations of this source are given parenthetically in the text.

5. See *Marketing Modernism: Self-Promotion, Canonization, Rereading,* ed. Kevin Dettmar and Stephen Watt (Ann Arbor: University of Michigan Press, 1996); Joyce Piell Wexler, *Who Paid for Modernism? Art, Money, and the Fiction of Conrad, Joyce, and Lawrence* (Fayetteville: University of Arkansas, 1997); Lawrence Rainey, *The Institutions of Modernism: Literary Elites and Public Culture* (New Haven: Yale University Press, 1998).

6. "Men of 1914" is Wyndham Lewis's phrasing to describe James Joyce, T. S. Eliot, Ezra Pound, and himself. For a useful gloss on the importance of this characterization for the canonization of modernism, see Bonnie Kime Scott, *Refiguring Modernism: The Women of 1928* (Bloomington: Indiana University Press, 1995), xxxvii–xxxviii. "[T]he idea of rupture is a rhetorical commonplace in modernist texts," Tamar Katz notes in *Impressionist Subjects: Gender, Interiority, and Modernist Fiction in England* (Urbana: University of Illinois Press, 2000), 206. Other recent scholarship that invites us to rethink the period by challenging modernist period distinctions includes *High and Low Moderns: Literature and Culture, 1889–1939,* ed. Marie diBattista and Lucy MacDiarmid (New York: Oxford University Press, 1996); *Women Artists and Writers: Modernist (Im)positionings,* ed. Bridget Elliott and Jo-Ann Wallace (New York: Routledge, 1996); Jonathan Freedman, *Professions of Taste: Henry James, British Aestheticism, and Commodity Culture* (Stanford: Stanford University Press, 1998); Cassandra Laity, *H.D. and the Victorian Fin-de-Siècle* (New York: Cambridge University Press, 1996); Michael Levenson, *A Genealogy of Modernism: A Study of English Literary Doctrine*

1908–1922 (New York: Cambridge University Press, 1984); *Outside Modernism: In Pursuit of the English Novel, 1900–30,* ed. Lynne Hapgood and Nancy L. Paxton (New York: Macmillan, 2000); and Talia Schaffer, *The Forgotten Female Aesthetes: Literary Culture in Late-Victorian England* (Charlottesville: University of Virginia Press, 2000).

7. "The gender of modernism" is, of course, Bonnie Kime Scott's phrasing in *The Gender of Modernism* (Bloomington: Indiana University Press, 1990), and I use it here to gloss an entire field of revisionary feminist research on modernism that has transformed modernist studies in the past fifteen years.

8. Michael Levenson, "Introduction," in *The Cambridge Companion to Modernism* (Cambridge: Cambridge University Press, 1999), 1.

9. Marjorie Perloff, *Radical Artifice: Writing in the Age of Media* (Chicago: University of Chicago Press, 1991), 202. See also Peter Nicholls, *Modernisms: A Literary Guide* (London: Macmillan, 1995), 1–5; and Michael North, *Reading 1922: A Return to the Scene of the Modern* (New York: Oxford University Press, 1999).

10. Michel de Certeau's phrasing, as used in *The Practice of Everyday Life,* trans. Steven Randall (Berkeley: University of California Press, 1984).

11. Claire Buck, " 'This other Eden': Homoeroticism and the Great War in the Early Poetry of H.D. and Radclyffe Hall," 77 below.

12. Deborah Jacobs, "Feminist Criticism / Cultural Studies / Modernist Texts: A Manifesto for the '90s," in *ReReading Modernism: New Directions in Feminist Criticism,* ed. Lisa Rado (New York: Garland, 1994), 288–89.

13. Pamela Gilbert, "Ouida and the Other New Woman," *in Victorian Women Writers and the Woman Question,* ed. Nicola Diane Thompson (Cambridge: Cambridge University Press, 1999), 173–74. What is *not* included here: detailed treatment of women's incursions into science studies, of cinema's role in the invention of modern life, and of the full spectrum of technological innovations transforming the human experience of time and space at the turn of the century. For these one must look elsewhere: to anthologies such as *Natural Eloquence: Women Reinscribe Science,* ed. Barbara Gates and Ann B. Shteir (Madison: University of Wisconsin Press, 1997); *Cinema and the Invention of Modern Life,* ed. Leo Charney and Vanessa R. Schwartz (Berkeley: University of California Press, 1995); *Viewing Positions: Ways of Seeing Film,* ed. Linda Williams (New Brunswick, N.J.: Rutgers University Press, 1995); and *Virginia Woolf in the Age of Mechanical Reproduction,* ed. Pamela Caughie (New York: Garland Press, 1999).

14. Benedict Anderson, *Imagined Communities: Reflections on the Origin and Spread of Nationalism* (London: Verso, 1983), 16.

15. Nancy Paxton discusses the "covert" nationalism "direct[ing] the 'invention' of literary modernism . . . [and] the national literary canon of which it is an important part" in her introduction to *Outside Modernism,* ed. Hapgood and Paxton (6). Recent collections such as *Criticism and the Color Line: Desegregating American Literary Studies,* ed. Henry Wonham (New Brunswick, N.J.: Rutgers University Press, 1996), and *Subjects and Citizens: Nation, Race, and Gender from Oroonoko to Anita Hill,* ed. Michael Moon and Cathy N. Davidson (Durham, N.C.: Duke University Press, 1995), redefine "nation" more inclusively in the context of American studies. Anthologies such as *High and Low Moderns,* ed. diBattista and MacDiarmid, *Cultural Politics at the Fin-de-Siècle,* ed. Sally Ledger and Scott McCracken (New York: Cambridge University

Press, 1995), and *Outside Modernism* have certainly widened the lens of British turn-of-the-century studies by addressing issues of race and empire, high and low culture. Yet even as these scholars rethink not only the period but also our fundamental categories of analysis in important ways, these volumes reinscribe national literary boundaries. The fact that the MLA divisions in Late Nineteenth-Early Twentieth-Century American and English Literature held their first ever joint sessions, on the topic "Transatlantic Crossings," at the 2001 convention suggests the timeliness of this volume's resistance to a nationally defined focus in turn-of-the-twentieth-century studies.

16. Raymond Williams, *The Politics of Modernism: Against the New Conformists* (New York: Verso, 1989), 47.

17. Lynn Thiesmeyer, early draft of "Two Talks with Khun Fa."

18. Alpana Sharma, "In-Between Modernity: Toru Dutt (1856–1877) from a Postcolonial Perspective," 99 below.

19. Carolyn Burdett, "Olive Schreiner and the Costs of Modernity," 143 below.

20. Thiesmeyer, "Two Talks," 168, 176 below.

21. Ibid., 176 below.

22. I borrow phrasing here from Valentina Stoeva, "Women Against the Information Borders," in *Women, Information and the Future: Collecting and Sharing Information Worldwide*, ed. Eve Steiner Moseley (Fort Atkinson, Wisc.: Highsmith Press, 1995), 12.

23. See Bruce Robbins, *Secular Vocations: Intellectuals, Professionalism, Culture* (New York: Verso, 1993); Thomas Strychacz, *Modernism, Mass Culture, and Professionalism* (New York: Cambridge University Press, 1993); Gail McDonald, *Learning to be Modern: Pound, Eliot, and the American University* (New York: Oxford University Press, 1993); and Suzanne Clark, *Sentimental Modernism: Women Writers and the Revolution of the Word* (Bloomington: Indiana University Press, 1991).

24. Judith Walkowitz, *City of Dreadful Delight: Narratives of Sexual Danger in Late-Victorian London* (Chicago: University of Chicago Press, 1992).

25. Clark, *Sentimental Modernism*, 3.

26. Julian Yates, "Shift Work: Observing Women Observing, 1937–1945," 286 below.

27. Elaine Showalter's phrasing in *A Literature of Their Own: British Women Novelists from Brontë to Lessing* (Princeton: Princeton University Press, 1977), 10. I borrow her phrasing here because the 1999 reissue of her 1977 study is a useful reminder of how this volume diverges from the project of gynocriticism she first charted. As I have argued elsewhere, although *A Literature of Their Own* is a landmark in the history of feminist criticism, as a study that legitimized scholarship on women's writing and brought feminist criticism onto the center stage of debate in the discipline of English studies, her implicit endorsement of a modernist standard of literary value resulted in her very negative valuation of turn-of-the-twentieth-century women writers (See *New Women, New Novels: Feminism and Early Modernism* [New Brunswick, N.J.: Rutgers University Press, 1990], 6–7). Significantly, Showalter overturns this earlier judgment in her introduction to the reissued volume, noting now that the turn of the century was a "major period for women writers" ("Introduction: Twenty Years On: *A Literature of Their Own* Revisited," in *A Literature of Their Own: British Women Novelists from Brontë to Lessing* [Princeton: Princeton University Press, 1999], xxviii).

28. Yates, "Shift Work," 272 below.

Part I ❧ *Negotiating the*
Literary Marketplace

Writing a Public Self

Alice Meynell's "Unstable Equilibrium"

Alice Meynell was among the most famous female poets in England at the turn of the century and was also renowned for her ambitious prose essays, yet it has been difficult to accommodate her in traditional categories of literary history. Most modern criticism of Meynell has worked hard to reconcile her overpoweringly Victorian ladylikeness with her very abstruse, demanding, and feminist writing.[1] Alice Meynell managed to keep these roles in a complex balance, and this was the achievement in which her early-twentieth-century readers most delighted.

In this chapter, I focus on Meynell's own literary milieu, rather than reading her as progressing toward some sort of climactic modernism. Lynne Hapgood explains: "The modernist sense of rupture was, of course, deliberately constructed. In their determination to challenge the power of the past in formulating views of history and of literature, the early modernists were anxious to establish a starting point for the modern and innovative. In their desire to put a distance between themselves and the literary milieu they rejected, they set up a literary chronology and literary categories which complemented their perception of their own originality."[2] Consequently, we have inherited the notion that the period was divided between admirably experimental modernism and residually Edwardian popular literature. Within the past decade, however, a cadre of new modernist scholars has radically rethought this opposition.[3] They have not only shown that canonical modernist texts are intricately connected to aspects of "low" culture, such as film, jazz, and popular novels, but have also made a convincing case that Edwardian texts actually rival modernist ones in their hybridities, complex engagements with realism, and invigorating political stances. (Indeed, as John Lucas has pointed out, work excluded from modernism may actually be more radically experimental.)[4] In short, modernists are more historically based, and popular authors are more ambitiously experimental both socially and formally, than the "rupture" myth of canonical modernism would suggest. Alice Meynell's complicated work confirms the need to remap the period. Her particular contribution: bringing the late Victorian conventions of aestheticism to bear on political issues around gender.

Meynell's essays in the "Wares of Autolycus" column of the *Pall Mall Gazette* reveal the way some turn-of-the-century women were both allured by, and afraid of, recent innovations in women's roles. The essays sketch the sense of pure liberation that a fearless public life could give but frame this fantasy in warnings about loss, pain, and suffering. In this respect, although she was writing as an author traumatized by Oscar Wilde's fate, she was also consciously positioning herself as a spokesperson for women in the early years of the twentieth century. Both an active suffragist and a highly visible embodiment of the Angel in the House, Meynell was uniquely positioned to express women's anxieties about the many different and contradictory roles available to them.[5] Indeed, I suggest that her difficult, condensed language is actually a kind of experimental diction, which works to bridge apparently competing gender ideas, thereby representing the kind of work other female aesthetes performed during this period. Like her friends in the aesthetic movement, Meynell adopted deliberate archaisms, dense description, and self-consciously artificial styles. The presence of such specialized argot in her prose destabilizes its claims to journalistic clarity, instead forcing us to read it as a highly crafted art form.

Meynell herself constantly negotiated between her public persona and the imperative needs of her private identity. As a professional writer, her job was to publish tidbits that fed her readers' hunger for autobiographical information. As a Victorian lady, however, her duty was to keep her personal life sacrosanct. Obsessed with the notion of self-revelation, yet deeply wedded to the idea of self-concealment, Meynell artfully promised perpetual exposure, which she perpetually and pleasurably deferred. Turn-of-the-century critics often believed women's writing was inherently autobiographical, but the evident artifice of Meynell's language dissuaded readers from assuming that the essay was an unmediated, transparently personal revelation.[6] Her deliberately oblique prose protected Meynell from scrutiny.[7] In other words, I read the obliqueness of Meynell's prose, not as a trace of an underlying crisis of self-identity or a failure of feminist consciousness, but rather as the product of a richly complicated new form of identity shared by many women between about 1890 and 1920 and articulated through aesthetic diction. Through close analyses of two major essays, "The Colour of Life" (1896) and "The Woman in Grey" (1896), we shall see how Meynell's diction produces a finely balanced mediation between competing visions of her own identity. These pieces form an interesting comparison with Meynell's feminist literary criticism. Finally, I end by exploring the way Meynell's work both influenced and challenged Virginia Woolf's version of feminist history.

IN ONE OF HER MOST IMPORTANT ESSAYS, "The Colour of Life," Meynell imagines both the excitement and the terror of exposing herself to the urban crowd. The essay posits one transcendent moment of pure self-revelation, but frames it in warnings about the shame, pain, danger, and punishment Meynell associated with such a violation of taboos. Meynell regarded this temptation with such intense feeling that it seems to have done some violence to the very structure of the essay; the piece consists of abrupt juxtapositions of apparently unrelated material, while the governing ideas can only be recovered through close attention to the absences and allusions in the prose.[8]

"The Colour of Life" begins with a startling assertion: "Red has been praised for its nobility as the colour of life. But the true colour of life is not red. Red is the colour of violence, or of life broken open, edited, and published."[9] Publication is analogous to death; there could hardly be a stronger warning about the dangers of writerly self-revelation, particularly in a book published so soon after Oscar Wilde's trials. She continues: "The true colour of life is the colour of the body, the colour of the covered red, the implicit and not explicit red of the living heart and the pulses. It is the modest colour of the unpublished blood" (171). The beauty of the body consists of the vital secret remaining hidden, just as the beauty of Meynell's writing is its private component. Just as blood moves through the body, so too privacy circulates through her prose, animating, feeding, and coloring the essays. Furthermore, the image of the "implicit" blood is self-referential: the essay's crucial elements are hidden beneath the surface, pounding below the skin.

The central vision of "The Colour of Life" appears when Meynell celebrates "the London boy" who strips to bathe in the Serpentine, sloughing off his dusty, sooty garments to become a delicate, bright line of color, a figure celebrated with mystic and highly charged images, emotive language, and strong biblical associations (172). "So little stands between a gamin and all the dignities of Nature" that the boy, naked, is "clothed now with the sun" and "crowned by-and-by with twelve stars as he goes to bathe, and the reflection of an early moon is under his feet" (172). Apparently, nothing could be further from Meynell's Angel persona than the London street boy. Julia Saville has discussed the literary and artistic depictions of the naked boy during this period, arguing that fin de siècle writers like John Addington Symonds displaced erotic admiration into abstract meditations on color and form.[10] Meynell similarly uses literary allusions to make the bodies even more remote and abstract. Her description of the boy amidst the stars and moon seems to owe something to two famous late-nineteenth-century descriptions of ideal womanhood: Ruskin's rhetoric "the stars may be only at her feet" and Dante Gabriel Rossetti's "the stars in her hair were seven."[11] In that sense, the subtext of this essay continues to engage issues that were crucial to Meynell personally: idealization, femininity, rulership, sainthood. She also associates the boys with herself by giving descriptions of their skin usually reserved for lovely maidens: "Old ivory and wild rose in the deepening midsummer sun, he gives his colours to his world again" (173). The boy here unconsciously functions as a stand-in for Meynell. By transferring ivory, roses, and stars to a boy—and a homeless boy at that—Meynell parodically rewrites the Pre-Raphaelite ideal, just as Meynell revises the romantic "shepherdess" ideal in her poetry, according to Sharon Smulders.[12]

On the surface level of the text, however, something has shifted. For the reader hardly recollects that our narrator is a woman calmly watching "hundreds" of naked boys (172). We neglect the disturbing fact that she is staring at naked male bodies because she has lulled us into seeing them as pure color, milk, earth, sunset, lilies, gold, ivory (171–72). In the original version of this essay, published in the *Pall Mall Gazette* on June 28, 1895, Meynell flatly de-eroticizes the boys' bodies, insisting that "it is a most maternal pleasure to watch these children of the town" and noting that she watches "from a decorous distance," protected by police.[13] But in the more famous final version, Meynell relies solely upon the lush vocabulary of aestheticism to distract the reader. She induces us to follow Wilde's advice to derive pleasure from a well-crafted description without worrying over whether its subject is moral or immoral.[14]

What is also odd is that, in an essay about the beauty of the human body, the viewer erases our awareness of her body altogether. In a startling reversal of all literary tradition, Meynell hymns the sturdy, dirty, despised, street boy's body and neglects her own delicate, pale, much-adored woman's body, the usual object of desire. Nor is the reader aware of this switch, for two main reasons. First, the two identities (gazer and object of gaze) get conflated in an abstract consideration of colors—a technique used by Symonds too, as Saville explains. Second, a subtle series of allusions (a kind of bloodline) keeps us half-consciously aware that Meynell is really describing her own body all along.

But the gamin's blissful flight is too tempting, and Meynell hurls increasingly violent images to bring him down to earth. The essay ends with a fiercely controlled account of the guillotining of Olympe de Gouges:

See the curious history of the political rights of woman under the Revolution. On the scaffold she enjoyed an ungrudged share in the fortunes of party. Political life might be denied her, but that seems a trifle when you consider how generously she was permitted political death. . . . Women might be, and were, duly silenced when, by the mouth of Olympe de Gouges, they claimed a "right to concur in the choice of representatives for the formation of the laws"; but in her person, too, they were liberally allowed to bear political responsibility to the Republic. Olympe de Gouges was guillotined. Robespierre thus made her public and complete amends. (Meynell, "Colour," 175-76)

In this terse account, Meynell can bring back the image of publicly spilled blood, can warn graphically and bitterly about the dangers of trying to participate in political life. The body, so powerfully exalted in the "gamin" scene, is now subject to painful destruction. Meynell represents her omnipotent self in the nude, unconscious, supremely self-confident male body, but describes her terribly vulnerable self in the uncomfortably public, speaking, female body of Olympe de Gouge.

It is hard not to read Oscar Wilde behind this vision of public humiliation and destruction. "The Colour of Life" was probably written during or immediately after Wilde's trials, since it was published a month after his conviction. Yet, interestingly, the original *Pall Mall Gazette* version has no mention of martyrdom at all. Meynell contrasts the boys' ivory bodies, not with the horrifying spectacle of a publicly tortured writer, but with—bonnets: "The colours of the fashion are the most edited and published colours of all. They give to the light the intensities that life makes a secret of. They show and spill the blood of colour, and in doing so they expose something far stronger, sharper, more stinging, and more exaggerated than the private red of human blood. The colours of the mode at their worst are really deadly. They all have exceedingly definite, and generally vulgar, names" (Meynell, "Wares of Autolycus," 4). The essay ends by criticizing Frenchwomen for having gracelessly short necks. This version seems bizarrely flippant to anyone acquainted with the powerful political conclusions of the revised "Colour of Life" (although perhaps when Meynell reread her description of Frenchwomen's inferior necks, she remembered how many Frenchwomen had bared those necks for the guillotine). It is tempting to imagine that the revision reveals a deeper fear, a deeper identification with Wilde, than Meynell could admit at the time of his trial.[15] If in 1895 the worst vision she had was of an aniline-dyed bonnet, by the time she revised the piece for publication in 1896, she was thinking deeply about the way the government might torture and destroy an intellectual.

Thus the final version of "The Colour of Life" moves from a description of "edited" blood to an aesthetic paean about lads, and ends with an angry description of the martyrdom of Olympe de Gouges. What do these topics have in common? They share a continuous but suppressed theme: the problematic public/private status of Alice Meynell. Her feelings about her public exposure get negotiated through the metaphor of the body, a body that is alternately violated, empowered, transfigured, and destroyed. In a final complexity, the essay itself is a body, its own structure being a skin stretched over its hidden circulatory system.

The beginning and end of the essay express a terror of a violent world ready to break open, to publish, the inmost modesties of women. This fear literally frames the tentative central dream of pure, unashamed self-revelation. That enticing image of delightful exposure is doubly shrouded, first by embodying it in a figure that Victorian readers would find almost laughably inappropriate (the gamin), and second by offering a distracting set of different allusive descriptions (ivory, stars, colors). It is as if Meynell cannot even discuss self-revelation in an open way, but must complicate and alter it as well—as if her fearful pleasure in self-exposure is so great that she cannot expose it. If "The Colour of Life" was indeed inspired by Wilde, that origin is equally enshrouded and mystified. It is true, indeed, that Meynell did not like her "life broken open, edited, and published" (171).

A rather different approach to the problem of self-revelation appears in an essay entitled "A Woman in Grey." Like "The Colour of Life," "A Woman in Grey" offers two bodies, one representing joyful self-revelation, and the other recalling dangerous public vulnerability. But whereas "The Colour of Life" associated female public exposure with nakedness and bleeding wounds, "A Woman in Grey" engages a less violent, but more pervasive, sense of failure. Here, the narrator, who is clearly meant to be read as Meynell herself, calmly, completely, and irrevocably dissociates herself from a momentary glimpse of liberty.

Like "The Colour of Life," "A Woman in Grey" has a kind of frame narrative. Meynell begins and ends by gently mocking the fallacy of those who assume "that women derive from their mothers and grandmothers, and men from their fathers and grandfathers."[16] While the men were winning on the playing fields of Eton, Meynell writes, there were losses somewhere else—and here the essay grows somewhat oblique: "While the victories were once going forward in the playground, the defeats or disasters were once going forward in some other place, presumably. And this was surely the place that was not a playground, the place where the future wives of the football players were sitting still while their future husbands were playing football" (210). What defeats or disasters? What place that was not a playground? Instead of explaining these points, the essay moves into its central image: "this is the train of thought that followed the grey figure of a woman on a bicycle in Oxford Street" (210). Meynell has doubly complicated the inquiry, first, by refusing to specify its subjects, and, second, by reversing its chronology, so that the "train of thought" comes before, not after, the vision that incited it. These circumlocutions act like barriers, defending the emotive center of the essay from readers' invasive scrutiny.

The vision in the middle of this essay is of a woman in grey, riding a bicycle in the midst of a complicated stream of miscellaneous traffic in multiple streams and currents, including "an enormous and top-heavy omnibus at her back" (210). But the woman in grey is alert, composed, and steady. "The woman was doing what nothing in her youth could well have prepared her for," Meynell notes (210). The woman in grey is clearly a New Woman, first because she is doing something daring and independent, and second because she is associated with the great symbol of female progress of the 1890s, the bicycle. The title of the essay calls the reader's attention to the rider's "bicycling costume"; her practical grey outfit invokes the whole movement away from frilly, heavy Parisian fashions toward "rational dress" designed for the newly mobile urban woman.

Meynell's evaluation of the bicycle rider is worth quoting at length:

She, none the less, fled upon unstable equilibrium, escaped upon it, depended upon it, trusted it, was 'ware of it, was on guard against it, as she sped amid her crowd. . . . She had learnt the difficult peace of suspense. She had learnt also the lowly and self-denying faith in common chances. She had learnt to be content with her share—no more—in common security, and to be pleased with her part in common hope. . . . To this courage the woman in grey had attained with a spring, and she had seated herself suddenly upon a place of detachment between earth and air, freed from the principal detentions, weights, and embarrassments of the usual life of fear. She had made herself, as it were, light, so as not to dwell either in security or danger, but to pass between them. She confessed difficulty and peril by her delicate evasions, and consented to rest in neither. She would not owe safety to the mere motionlessness of a seat on the solid earth, but she used gravitation to balance the slight burdens of her wariness and her confidence. She put aside all the pride and vanity of terror, and leapt into an unsure condition of liberty and content. (Meynell, "Woman," 211-12)

It is tempting to see this passage as Meynell's own motto, for it sums up the way she hoped she lived. To move on an edge, to balance on an "unstable equilibrium"—this is what Meynell's writing does, as it rides delicately between revelation and concealment.

But Meynell's prose is not quite as balanced as the rider. The passage emphasizes all the dangers the woman does not see. Meynell mentions many disadvantages to bicycle-riding: "detentions, weights, and embarrassments," "life of fear," "danger," "difficulty and peril," "wariness," "the pride and vanity of terror." On the other side of the balance, there are fewer positive words, and half of them are modified by negatives that reduce their value: she has no more than "common security, she "would not owe safety," and she experiences "an unsure condition of liberty and content." Clearly, Meynell cannot share the confidence she recognizes in the woman in grey.

Furthermore, the rich leisure of Meynell's philosophy—the philosophy that has made her writing famous—depends upon her retaining her secure seat. If she were to ride a bicycle, she would have to be like the woman in grey, "limiting not only her foresight, which must become brief, but her memory, which must do more; for it must rather cease than become brief" (212). Recollect that Meynell has framed this whole vision in "a train of thought," thus enlisting the reader on her side. We want her to have more of these trains of thought, which would, apparently, be impossible if she lived the momentary and thrilling life of the bicyclist.

At this moment it might be relevant to ask where the speaker is located. She has not disappeared, as she did in "The Colour of Life." On the contrary, she is observing Oxford Street, most probably in the overcrowded omnibus that Meynell describes as bearing down upon the rider. Meynell's situation introduces two new considerations. First, it means that, much as Meynell admires the New Woman, she will not join her. The woman in grey is violating every aspect of the Victorian doctrine of separate spheres; she is on the street instead of at home; she is confronting danger instead of being sheltered from it; she is defying male drivers instead of requesting their protection; she is, perhaps most fundamentally, *going* somewhere instead of sitting still at home. She is in a public space because she wants to be there. But Meynell shows little disposition to emulate her. Second, the omnibus on which she sits is "enormous and top-heavy." It could fall and crush the bicyclist. Thus Meynell depicts herself in a position that threatens the woman in grey, and becomes herself one of the many dangers that she admires the woman for evading.

Ana Vadillo's chapter in this collection argues that the woman omnibus rider was a figure of poetic and social transgression, defiantly claiming her right to occupy a non-eroticized public space. Interestingly, however, by rendering the omnibus as a threat to the independent rider, Meynell here produces a very different urban street scene than contemporaries such as Amy Levy: "She had an enormous and top-heavy omnibus at her back. All the things on the near side of the street—the things going her way—were going at different paces, in two streams, overtaking and being overtaken. The tributary streets shot omnibuses and carriages, cabs and carts—some to go her own way, some with an impetus that carried them curving into the other current, and other some making a straight line right across Oxford Street into the street opposite" (210). In Meynell's view, mass transit conspires to destabilize, threaten, and isolate the vulnerable woman. Omnibuses and carriages are projectiles, like bullets, "shot" at her from all directions—hardly sites where other dramas of female courage and independence might be staged. Indeed, the pathos of this essay lies in Meynell's supposition that the only assertive woman on Oxford Street is the one surrounded by terrifying traffic, and that this woman's courage is itself a kind of unprecedented and irreproducible phenomenon.

Just as "blood" is the metaphor for the essay in which it appears, so too "riding" constitutes the self-referential metaphor for "A Woman in Grey." Meynell is taking us on a "train of thought," the transportation metaphor a particularly apt one. By reading the essay, we too become riders upon the "train of thought," in parallel motion with the omnibus and bicycle that the essay's subjects occupy. The essay, too, swerves, recovers, and balances. For as the train of thought moves on, the essay changes, mimicking the physical change as the woman in grey and the omnibus separate in traffic. A essay drives along too, putting the woman in grey behind. "Idle memory . . . shortens life," warns Meynell, and she perforce ceases to remember the bicyclist (212). Instead, she returns to her original concern, those mysterious "defeats or disasters." We can now see that the topic of "women's failures" has been acting like the bicyclist, for it has been threading its way between obstacles and disappearing into the crowd. As the bicyclist herself disappears, however, the equally fleeting and daring topic she had displaced reemerges into the daylight.

The essay ends with a return to the frame narrative, the argument that men inherit from their mothers as well as their fathers. "Brutus knew that the valour of Portia was settled upon his sons" (212). The link between this argument and the woman in grey is obvious, and Meynell assumes the reader will see it: if women are trained to be courageous, steady, and self-reliant, like the woman in grey (or Portia), their sons will inherit such qualities.

The argument is convincing; the example is memorable. The only problem is that the example actually disproves the argument. For Meynell argues that the woman in grey was not trained to be self-confident at all. "The woman was doing what nothing in her youth could well have prepared her for," she asserts (210). This slippage indicates how much the woman in grey is a fantasy projection of Meynell's. Although it ruins her main point, she cannot help but ascribe to the rider the same sort of childhood she and her readers had, so we can imagine that we, too, might achieve this self-reliance. Though Meynell rejects the woman in grey, here she unconsciously and wistfully identifies with her.

At the end of "A Woman in Grey," then, we still wonder: what were those "defeats or disasters"? Clearly, the woman in grey has nothing to do with any defeats. She is a living symbol of victory over an adverse upbringing and an unpromising environment. The woman in grey has won. The woman who has lost is the speaker. It is Meynell herself who recollects "defeats and disasters," who recognizes "the pride and vanity of terror," who knows just what dangers lurk all around the confident rider, and who sits silently in her omnibus, while she watches another woman compete, balance, and race around her. The carefully complicated prose of that passage comes from Meynell's reluctance to acknowledge that she is too frightened to emulate the New Woman. And so, as the bicyclist triumphantly rides off upon her perfect equilibrium, Meynell shares with her reader a soberer ride upon a train of thought, a top-heavy omnibus, the vehicle of slow, dependent, ladylike conventionality from which she does not dare to disembark. Levy might have described that omnibus as a space within which the woman in grey's revolution continues, but Meynell sees her own vehicle only as a threat to the woman she most envies.

In both "The Colour of Life" and "A Woman in Grey," Meynell constructs substitutes for herself, figures who can embrace the public space she both desires and flees. To be completely, confidently, unselfconsciously exposed to the public gaze—this, for Meynell, is a state of ecstatic transcendence, which she represents by an almost supernatural flight ("between earth and air") or a visual transfiguration (as in "The Colour of Life"). This is the crux of both essays, the successful realization of a state of rapture at a perfect self-revelation, at being entirely exposed without being remotely vulnerable. But in both essays, the central vision is framed by arguments about weak, irrational, uneducated women ("Woman") or bleeding, murdered women ("Colour"), as if to remind Meynell of how dangerous this fantasy of public self-confidence might be. On the whole, the essays are relatively balanced. Although the voice of cautious, private warning gets both the first and last words, the visions in the middle of the essays are so vivid and passionate that they overwhelm the frame narrative in the readers' remembrance.

Thus the essays can be said to stage a battle between Meynell's two drives: the need to stay safe, protected, and private, and the equally importunate wish to publish her strongest emotions. Though these were clearly personal psychological imperatives for Meynell, they also represent the paradox of being a woman writer at the turn of the century. The essays come out of the tension between the two, and, at their best, the essays balance on the "unstable equilibrium" between both states, between "earth and air."

However, Meynell found a more direct outlet for her frustrated passions. Whereas Meynell's prose essays celebrate solitude and silence, Meynell's feminist literary criticism is full of women's discourses, quarrels, and pleadings.[17] Throughout her life, Meynell wrote innumerable articles about women of the past. In essays published between 1896 and 1926, she helped shape what we would today call feminist literary historiography, the recovery and reassessment of neglected writers from the past. Her subjects included Arabella Stuart, Mrs. Dingley, Joanna Baillie, "Steele's Prue," "Mrs. Johnson," "Marceline Valmore," "Mrs. Thrale," Olympia de Gouges, "The Lady of the Lyrics," "The Swan of Lichfield" (Anna Seward), "Mary Wollestonecraft's Letters," "Elizabeth Inchbald," "Joanna Baillie," "Madame Roland," the Brontës, Christina Rossetti, and Elizabeth Barrett Browning.

Meynell's feminist essays reveal a sophisticated sense of the way language constructs experience, revealing Meynell's participation in aestheticism's historical nostalgia. The aesthetes enjoyed recovering older words that had fallen into disuse, not only for the sake of their sound and their associations, but also because they testified to the aesthetic author's wide and detailed reading.[18] The movement's emphasis on historical alterity, cultural sensitivity, and rhetorical subtleties served Meynell well in her feminist criticism.

"Arabella Stuart," for instance, describes how Renaissance epistolary style shaped the writers' personal emotions and political affiliations. Meynell discusses Stuart's remorseful letters to her king: "By these forms of ignominy did men and women rule, not their phrases only, but, apparently, their very thoughts. Such declarations were much more than a courtesy due to kings or the decorum of a style in letter-writing. Hearts beat hard to that most grotesque tune; those were real self-reproaches; they banished real sleep, human sleep, afflicted real consciences, set the tears of men running, and squandered and scattered to waste that human treasure, humility."[19] Meynell resists the temptation to declare Stuart's entreaties either hypocritical or incomprehensible, instead entering the Renaissance mentality as much as possible and revealing that the letters do express a real emotion, albeit one inaccessible to modern readers.

The bulk of "Arabella Stuart" is composed of extended quotations from Stuart's letters, with her pleas for favor, her assurances of continued loyalty, her hopeless expressions of love. This reliance upon quotations accomplishes three things. First, it introduces readers to Stuart's own words, thus encouraging a renewed appreciation of Stuart's writing. Second, it transports the reader into a semi-Renaissance atmosphere, making us respect the period's cultural alterity instead of reading and judging Stuart through a turn-of-the-twentieth-century lens. Third, the quotations lull the reader into the sad, gentle, loving mood of the letters. Indeed, even when Meynell uses her own voice, she modulates it to fall into archaic rhythms and language, harmonizing with Stuart's rhetoric: "Ill fortune set all the times, tides, and winds wrong on that unhappy adventure" (184). This softened tone heightens the contrast with the essay's unexpected last paragraph, a damning indictment of Stuart's enemies, which leaps out with a particularly violent effect. "Her King and Queen and country sent her civilization into solitude, gagged her classics, disproved her poetry, and thrust her 'expanded mind' into the inner darkness" (185). The active verbs, direct subject-verb-object construction, and uncompromising vocabulary are particularly harrowing, juxtaposed with the gentler, more passive, more indirect language of the previous pages. The last paragraph stands as Meynell's own voice, all the angrier because it had previously been subdued to accord with its gentle subject, and all the more outraged because Meynell must denounce enemies for a woman who, during her life, was not able to articulate her own anger.

In "Arabella Stuart" and her other feminist articles, Meynell was criticizing the literary canon while it was still in process of formation. She was among the first professional literary critics to argue that literary historians harbored biases against women. "No one else in literary history has been so defrauded of her honours," Meynell declares in defending Mrs. Dingley.[20] When showing that nineteenth-century critics unfairly make fun of Steele's Prue, she points out that "every creature has a right to security from the banterings peculiar to the humorists of a succeeding age."[21] And Meynell fulminates against nineteenth-century scorn of Samuel Johnson's wife, "Tetty": "No slight to him, to his person, or to his fame could have had power to cause him pain more sensibly than the customary, habitual, ready-made ridicule that has been cast by posterity upon her whom he loved for twenty years, prayed for during thirty-two more, who satisfied one of the saddest human hearts, but to whom the world, assiduous to admire him, hardly accords human dignity."[22] In this passage, Meynell adopts the Johnsonian periods, the dignified and balanced sentence full of latinate words, which her subject seems to demand, just as she modulated her prose to suit Arabella Stuart's courtly rhetoric.

I would like to suggest that Meynell herself was codifying the critical standards she sensed might be required to revive her own reputation. In her customarily oblique style, she wrote about herself by writing about women of the past. When Meynell insists on sensitivity to different cultures' gender roles and rhetorical customs, surely she wishes the same attention to be given to herself—particularly since she wrote many of these essays in the 1920s, when she could perceive that her own career, her own standards, and her own style, already seemed outmoded. As Hapgood notes, the modernists' dismissals of realist writers "persuaded later critics to see the novelists of the early twentieth century in chronologically linear terms which emphasized the movement from the old to the new (Edwardian/Georgian; traditional/modern; Victorian/modernist) despite the actual contemporaneity of realist and modernist writers and the synchronicity of many of their literary productions."[23] Meynell was to be relegated to the wrong side of this divide. Her feminist criticism provides a rare case of a self-aware writer fighting against her contemporaries' literary judgment even as it solidified and settled around her. I am not suggesting that Meynell's feminist historiography was simply disguised self-interest. Rather, it worked the other way: her fears for herself enabled her to develop an unusually sophisticated and sensitive technique for feminist criticism. And her desire to recover lost women writers, her respect for their different cultural situations, and her outspoken anger at critics' biases against them, were matched only by Virginia Woolf.

In fact, though, Virginia Woolf had a highly ambivalent reaction to Alice Meynell, whom she knew and whose work she reviewed. Woolf was revolted by the genteel ladylikeness Meynell struggled so hard to preserve, but which Woolf found hypocritical, regressive, and artificial.[24] Yet both women were interested in recovering forgotten female writers to form a women's literary tradition, and Woolf, consciously or unconsciously, learned much of her craft from Meynell. Gillian Beer argues that "Woolf did not simply reject the Victorians and their concerns, or renounce them. Instead she persistently rewrote them."[25] Woolf incorporated the characteristic discourses of crucial nineteenth-century writers, only to exaggerate, parody, and infiltrate their words, thereby claiming them for herself. In fact, as Barbara Green has shown, Woolf performed this sort of rewriting as a feminist tactic. During the Edwardian period, she collected, preserved, juxtaposed, and commented upon others' texts as an alternative to the more spectacular performances of the suffrage movement. This complicated appropriation and subversion of the past—along with a corresponding attempt to erase that relationship—was fundamental to modernist self-fashioning.[26]

Woolf constantly rewrote Meynell. Both Woolf and Meynell wrote about Mrs. Dingley, the companion of Swift's beloved Stella. Both insist, in almost the same words, that "MD" stood for Stella and Dingley together, never Stella alone, though they come to opposite conclusions regarding whether Swift loved Dingley. "Dr. Burney's Evening Party" and "Mrs. Thrale" justify Mrs. Thrale's marriage to Piozzi exactly the same way Meynell does in "Hester," by depicting Piozzi as charming and cultivated and Mrs. Thrale as a kinder, wittier woman than was usually believed. Woolf's "Mary Wollestonecraft" follows the structure of Meynell's "Mary Wollstonecraft's Letters," for both essays begin by sketching the miserable marriages of Wollstonecraft's mother and sister, and both cite her avowal that she prefers the term "affection" to "love." Both wrote articles on Ruskin and George Meredith.[27] There were also more indirect and complex influences. Anyone reading "A Woman in Grey" might well wonder if Woolf had it in mind when she wrote the famous scene in *Mrs. Dalloway* in which Elizabeth balances like a rider, in perfect freedom, balance, and self-control, atop an omnibus threading through the traffic. That scene in *Mrs. Dalloway* may owe something else to Meynell's influence; in 1929 Woolf recollected how she saw Meynell in 1909: "there she was ecstatic in an omnibus."[28]

Perhaps the most interesting example of Woolf's reluctant discipleship occurs in the case of their reactions to Charlotte Brontë. In 1917, Woolf reviewed Meynell's new collection *Hearts of Controversy* for the *Times Literary Supplement*. The review shows a respect for Meynell's work: "Mrs. Meynell is a true critic, courageous, authoritative, and individual." However, Woolf complains that Meynell is sometimes overcritical: "Mrs. Meynell['s] sense of right and wrong in these matters is so clearly defined that she can make the question of Charlotte Brontë's use of English in the earlier books a cause of controversy. She wrote 'to evince, to reside, to intimate, to peruse'; she spoke of 'communicating instruction,' 'a small competency,' and so on. It is quite true, and, to us, quite immaterial."[29] Woolf is rejecting Meynell's complaint that Brontë abandoned her own perfectly dramatic voice to use Gibbon's colorless Latinate terms. Yet twelve years later, Woolf would make precisely the same critique of Brontë's writing style in *A Room of One's Own*, where she announced: "That is a man's sentence; behind it one can see Johnson, Gibbon, and the rest. It was a sentence that was unsuited for a woman's use. Charlotte Brontë, with all her splendid gift for prose, stumbled and fell with that clumsy weapon in her hands."[30]

Meynell was one of the earliest and most influential critics to delineate a tradition of women's writing and to insist on the repressive conditions and inappropriate rules that crippled women's writing. *A Room of One's Own* was, in part, enabled by Meynell's work. It was precisely because of the extent of this debt that Woolf did not like to acknowledge it. Had Meynell been silenced by the requirements of bearing and raising her seven children, Woolf might have described Meynell as another potentially great woman writer lost to posterity. Meynell did not have a room of her own; she locked herself in the bathroom to get privacy for writing, while her obstreperous son hammered and screamed at the door. Nor did she have five hundred pounds a year of her own; continually in financial straits, she desperately tried to earn enough money for her enormous family. Yet Meynell succeeded in writing under these apparently impossible conditions, a feat that made Woolf feel simultaneously envious and appalled.

Consequently, Woolf excludes Meynell from the literary history of women writers. More, she constructs a history of women writers that argues that women such as Meynell could not have existed. *A Room of One's Own* makes its eloquent plea for freedom and security on the grounds that no writer could have worked under conditions such as Meynell's. Its feminist argument depends upon the suppression of such counterexamples. Thus we have the irony that the first great book of feminist historiography excludes its own immediate foremother.

Meynell's prose deserves the same kind of careful, culturally sensitive readings she herself showed us how to perform. What Woolf's modernist imperative condemned as ladylike indecisiveness or outmoded gentility can be read as an interestingly complex mode of mediating amongst competing female identities at the turn of the century.[31] Meynell's aestheticism—her archaisms, her jagged and fragmented prose, her submerged connections, and her half-buried allusions—made her writing express far more than it showed. Meynell's essays open up new ideas about turn-of-the-century women writers' rhetorical strategies for representing their experiences, and teach us that these women's oblique prose, the "unstable equilibrium" of the bicycle rider, may have been the most useful way to keep themselves in balance after all.

NOTES

I would like to thank Ann Ardis, Maria Frawley, and Sally Mitchell for their useful suggestions, and the University Press of Virginia for permission to reprint material that appeared in an earlier version in *The Forgotten Female Aesthetes*.

1. This struggle is particularly evident in Angela Leighton, *Victorian Women Poets: Writing Against the Heart* (Charlottesville: University Press of Virginia, 1992); Sharon Smulders, "Feminism, Pacificism and the Ethics of War: The Politics and Poetics of Alice Meynell's War Verse," *ELT 36*, 2 (1993): 159–77; Maria Frawley, "'The Tides of the Mind': Alice Meynell's Poetry of Perception," *Victorian Poetry* 38, 1 (Spring 2000): 62–76; Talia Schaffer, *The Forgotten Female Aesthetes: Literary Culture in Late-Victorian England* (Charlottesville: University of Virginia Press, 2000); and Schaffer, "A Tethered Angel: The Martyrology of Alice Meynell," *Victorian Poetry* 38, 1 (Spring 2000): 49–61. Other relevant work includes Jon S. Anson, "'The Wind is Blind': Power and Constraint in the Poetry of Alice Meynell," *Studia Mystica* 9, 1 (Spring 1986): 37–50; Beverly Ann Schlack, "The 'Poetess of Poets': Alice Meynell Rediscovered," *Women's Studies 7*, 1–2 (1980): 111–26; and biographical material by June Badeni, *The Slender Tree: A Life of Alice Meynell* (Padstow, Cornwall: Tabb House, 1981); Viola Meynell, *Alice Meynell* (London: Jonathan Cape, 1929); and Vita Sackville-West, "Introduction," in *Alice Meynell: Prose and Poetry, Centenary Volume* (London: Jonathan Cape, 1947).

2. Lynne Hapgood, "Transforming the Victorian," in *Outside Modernism: In Pursuit of the English Novel*, ed. Lynne Hapgood and Nancy L. Paxton (London: Macmillan, 2000), 23.

3. These include *High and Low Moderns: Literature and Culture 1889–1939*, ed. Marie DiBattista and Lucy MacDiarmid (New York: Oxford University Press, 1996); *Outside Modernism*, ed. Hapgood and Paxton; Thomas Strychascz, *Modernism, Mass Culture, and Professionalism* (New York: Cambridge University Press, 1993); Ann Ardis,

New Women, New Novels: Feminism and Early Modernism (New Brunswick, N.J.: Rutgers University Press, 1990; Cassandra Laity, *H.D. and the Victorian Fin de Siècle: Gender, Modernism, Decadence* (New York: Cambridge University Press, 1996); Rita Felski, *The Gender of Modernity* (Cambridge, Mass.: Harvard University Press, 1995); and Jane Eldridge Miller, *Rebel Women: Feminism, Modernism, and the Edwardian Novel* (London: Virago, 1994).

4. John Lucas, "From Realism to Radicalism: Sylvia Townsend Warner, Patrick Hamilton and Henry Green in the 1920s," in *Outside Modernism*, ed. Hapgood and Paxton, 203–24.

5. Regarding Meynell's identification with the Angel in the House, see Schaffer, "Tethered Angel" and *Forgotten Female Aesthetes*.

6. One influential exponent of this theory was W. L. Courtney, *The Feminine Note in Fiction* (London: Chapman & Hall, 1904).

7. In *The Uses of Obscurity: The Fiction of Early Modernism* (London: Routledge & Kegan Paul, 1981), Allon White argues persuasively that modernist writers employed obscurity to defend themselves against "symptomatic readings": readers' propensity to interpret the text as evidence of the writer's neuroses. Obliqueness, I would like to suggest, worked just as well as obscurity for this purpose.

8. This analysis is indebted to Smulders's argument that Meynell's writing works by subtexts and relies on unspoken key terms; see Smulders, "Feminism, Pacificism, and the Ethics of War."

9. Alice Meynell, "The Colour of Life," *Essays* (New York: Scribner, 1914), 171–75, 171. Revised version first published in *The Colour of Life* (1896). All subsequent citations of this essay are given parenthetically in the text.

10. Julia Saville, "The Romance of Boys Bathing: Poetic Precedents and Respondents to the Paintings of Henry Scott Tuke," in *Victorian Sexual Dissidence*, ed. Richard Dellamora (Chicago: University of Chicago Press, 1999), 253–77.

11. John Ruskin, "Of Queens' Gardens," in *Sesame and Lilies* (New York: H. M. Caldwell, 1871), 152; Dante Gabriel Rossetti, "The Blessed Damozel," in *The Norton Anthology of English Literature*, 5th ed. (New York: Norton, 1982), 2: 1489.

12. Sharon Smulders, "Looking 'Past Wordsworth and the Rest,'" *Victorian Poetry* 38, 1 (Spring 2000): 35–48.

13. Meynell, "Wares of Autolycus: The Colour of Life," *Pall Mall Gazette*, June 28, 1895, 4. Subsequently cited parenthetically in the text.

14. Oscar Wilde, "Preface," in *The Picture of Dorian Grey* (1891; Oxford: Oxford University Press, 1981), xxiii.

15. Indeed, when Wilde was convicted, Meynell commented that "while there is a weak omnibus horse at work or a hungry cat I am not going to spend feeling on Oscar" (as quoted by Badeni, *Slender* Tree, 115).

16. Meynell, "A Woman in Grey," in *Alice Meynell: Prose and Poetry* (London: Jonathan Cape, 1947), 208–12; 209. Revised version first published in *The Colour of Life* (1896). Subsequent citations of this essay are given parenthetically in the text.

17. For more on Meynell's celebrated solitude and silence, see Frawley, "Tides of the Mind."

18. See Linda Dowling, *Language and Decadence in the Victorian Fin de Siècle* (Princeton: Princeton University Press, 1986).

19. Meynell, "Arabella Stuart," *Alice Meynell: Prose and Poetry* (London: Jonathan Cape, 1947), 181–85; 183. First revised version published in *The Second Person Singular* (1921). Subsequent citations are given parenthetically in the text.

20. Meynell, "Mrs. Dingley," *Alice Meynell: Prose and Poetry*, 185–89, 186. Revised version first published in *The Spirit of Place* (1898).

21. Meynell, "Steele's Prue," in *Alice Meynell: Prose and Poetry*, 189–93; 192–93. Revised version first published in *Essays* (1914).

22. Meynell, "Mrs. Johnson," in *Alice Meynell: Prose and Poetry*, 193–97, 197. Revised version first published in *Essays* (1914).

23. Hapgood, "Transforming the Victorian," 23.

24. Virginia Woolf, *The Diary of Virginia Woolf*, vol. 3: *1925–1930*, ed. Anne Olivier Bell (London: Hogarth Press, 1980), 250–51 and app. 2, 352–53.

25. Gillian Beer, "The Victorians in Virginia Woolf, 1832–1941," in *Arguing with the Past: Essays in Narrative from Woolf to Sidney* (London: Routledge, 1989), 138–58, 140.

26. Barbara Green, *Spectacular Confessions: Autobiography, Performative Activism, and the Sites of Suffrage 1905–1938* (New York: St. Martin's Press, 1997).

27. Woolf's essays appear in *The Common Reader: Second Series* (London: Hogarth Press, 1935) and *The Captain's Death Bed, and Other Essays* (New York: Harcourt, Brace, 1990).

28. Woolf, *Diary of Virginia Woolf*, 3: 251.

29. Woolf, "Hearts of Controversy," *Times Literary Supplement*, October 26, 1917, 515.

30. Woolf, *A Room of One's Own* (1929; San Diego: Harcourt Brace Jovanovich, 1989), 76–77.

31. I treat Woolf as a representative modernist inasmuch as she produced influential narratives of modernist "rupture" with the past. Of course, there are other contexts in which Woolf's relation to canonical modernism is much more problematic, as Nancy Paxton explains in "Eclipsed by Modernism," in *Outside Modernism*, ed. Hapgood and Paxton, 8–9.

Towards a New "Colored" Consciousness

Biracial Identity in Pauline Hopkins's Fiction

White men's children spread over the earth—
A rainbow suspending the drawn swords of birth,
Uniting and blending the races in one
The world man—cosmopolite—everyman's son!

He channels the stream of the red blood and blue,
Behold him! A Triton—the peer of the two;
Unriddle this riddle of "outside in"
White men's children in black men's skin.
          —Georgia Douglas Johnson, "The Riddle"

In Frances E. W. Harper's famous speech at the World's Congress of Representative Women at the Columbian Exposition in 1893, she posits that while "the fifteenth century discovered America to the Old World, the nineteenth century is discovering woman to herself."[1] Calling for "fairer and higher aims than the greed of gold and the lust of power," she declares this moment at the end of the nineteenth century to be "the threshold of women's era" and predicts that "women's work" will be "grandly constructive."[2] In making this pronouncement about a new era centered upon women's work, Harper defines modernity through a gendered construction of the "new" that is also implicitly racialized. Drawing from the collective vision of numerous black women of the late nineteenth century, who formed clubs dedicated to cooperative efforts that would give "causes dear and vital to humanity the valuable aid of organized intelligence," Harper points to efforts that attempted to define a new morality focused on the idea of "uplift," a moral imperative tied both to liberation theology and racial solidarity.[3] Significantly, many of the women involved in uplift work knew that the attention of the world focused upon them as women. It was with this knowledge that the Woman's Era Club was formed in Boston in 1873, and that a journal titled *The Woman's Era* (edited by Josephine St. Pierre Ruffin) was published during the mid 1890s. Early black women's clubs like the Women's Era Club seem to have grown out of established, predominantly white women's clubs as more specific interests warranted. They were not exclusively black, however; the Woman's Era Club, for example, upon its founding had several white members. When racism within the white women's club movement forced black women to organize their own federation in 1895, which they called the National Conference of the Colored Women of America (later the National Association of Colored Women), the women who attended the federation's organizing conference refused to define themselves by race or color. Because these women had been excluded from white women's organizations, they would not prohibit from membership anyone "who could share the aims and ideals of the movement." The president of the Woman's Era Club who called the conference, Josephine St. Pierre Ruffin, stated: "We are not drawing the color line; we are women, American women, as intensely interested in all that pertains to us as such as all other American women."[4]

The National Association of Colored Women determined to call itself "colored" during a time of great argument against the use of this term as too general and not racially specific. Self-identification as "colored" (rather than "Negro" or "Afro-American") at the turn of the twentieth century was sometimes dismissed as the consequence of class bias or intraracial prejudice, an unjustified simplification of the term's mediative use, particularly with regard to black female experience. "Colored" suggests that black women leaders at the turn of the century understood their mission and their collective identity to be integrally connected to both black and white life, to be, in other words, significantly focused on the interconnections between the races. Pauline E. Hopkins, who edited and wrote for the *Colored American Magazine*, is at the center of these formations of "colored" identity. While her career with the *CAM* was cut short by a change in publishers and a new editorial mission influenced by Booker T. Washington's ideology, Hopkins's work nevertheless represents a significant contribution to modern theoretical explorations of race and racial identity. Through the *CAM*, Hopkins develops a female-centered "colored" consciousness that in and of itself is a complex and fascinating precursor to the turn-of-the-twenty-first century *mestiza*, or borderland, transformative identity described by Gloria Anzaldua and now paradigmatic in American Studies.[5]

Further, what might be termed Hopkins's "new colored" consciousness also plays a significant role in the development of "new Negro" identity, particularly as it is manifest in literary production of the 1920s and 1930s and characterized by Alain Locke as a new race pride.[6] Specifically, Hopkins's fiction continues a literary tradition established by Frances Harper that transforms slavery's stories of female victimization into the foundation of strong and positive mother identity at once both racialized and racially transcendent.

Postbellum African American fiction, coincidentally with the development of a race politics that establishes a firm color line between black and white, focuses on the presentation of biracial characters. The earliest readings of the "tragic mulatto" see this character's near-whiteness as a device with which to arouse white readers' sympathies.[7] Hazel Carby's refiguration, however, which allows that the "dominance of the mulatto figure in Afro-American fiction . . . has too often been dismissed as politically unacceptable without a detailed analysis of its historical and narrative function," presents the mulatto "as a vehicle for an exploration of the relationship between the races."[8] I would also argue that such characters function as affirmations of race consciousness, because when these characters are light enough to pass for white, they often choose not to, thus rejecting whiteness and affirming a distinctive racial identity. It is most significant that the post-Reconstruction South focused its efforts on legal segregation, and that the U.S. Supreme Court established the doctrine of "separate but equal" through the 1896 *Plessy v. Ferguson* case, while at the same time the number of "mulattoes" dramatically increased from 11.2 percent of the black population in 1859 to 20.9 percent in 1910.[9] Consequently, the very existence of biracial peoples contradicts the claim made by Booker T. Washington in his 1895 Atlanta Exposition Address that in all things "purely social we can be as separate as the fingers" (*Up from Slavery*, 221–22). Or, as the strongly worded "Furnace Blasts: Black or White—Which Should Be the Young Afro-American's Choice in Marriage" from Pauline Hopkins's *Colored American Magazine* remarks, "Shall the Anglo-Saxon and the Afro-American mix? They have mixed."[10]

The *Plessy v. Ferguson* Supreme Court case, often referred to as the case that established "separate but equal" doctrine, was also responsible for making the so-called "one drop" rule the law of the land, thus complicating race consciousness, as a question of personal identity, history, and memory, with a strictly dichotomous legal definition. As social historians who focus on black life within the African diaspora have shown, the legal rules of race with regard to citizenship privilege as constructed in the United States are unique: in no other country is the status of the racially mixed population the same as the lower-status parent group.[11] When Homer Plessy sued for the right to ride on a train in Louisiana in seats reserved for whites, he argued that because he was only one-eighth Negro and could pass for white he was entitled to consideration as a white man. As part of the argument against this position, the Supreme Court took judicial notice that a person is considered a Negro, or black, as a consequence of any black ancestry.[12] This superstructure of racial definition constructed by the judiciary system has held as precedent to this day; thus, in modern American life the category "white" implies racial purity while "black" means everyone else. Historically, then, black families incorporate within them people of various racial genealogies, and, as we might expect, ideals of domesticity presented by African American writers reflect this multiracial reality.

Claudia Tate makes the point that, unlike their twentieth-century readers, Frances Harper and Pauline Hopkins "regard mulatto as a generic term for designating the emancipated population and their heirs."[13] Neither author, in Tate's words, intended to present "racially ambivalent African Americans who rely on their light skin color to bolster their self-esteem and bourgeois ambitions," a common late-twentieth-century reading of these authors' texts.[14] Frances Harper's novels *Minnie's Sacrifice* and *Iola Leroy; or, Shadows Uplifted* present white-skinned biracial characters as affirmations of race (that is, black or African American) consciousness; only because Harper's characters are able to pass for white can they choose not to do so, thus rejecting whiteness and affirming their own racial identity. Harper's stories of very light-skinned protagonists who grow up believing they are white until some event occurs that forces the realization of their true identity are more than melodrama. In both *Minnie's Sacrifice* and *Iola Leroy*, these events allow Harper to make connections between matrifocal knowledge, racial identity, and a higher or "new" consciousness. As the more mature formulation of these ideas, Harper's *Iola Leroy* returns again and again to the figure of the slave mother, not in acquiescence to the sentimentality of the age, but because race consciousness is born of slave mothers: the extent to which characters identify with the race is in direct proportion to the extent with which they refuse to forsake their mothers. By choosing formerly enslaved mothers over white, often powerful, fathers, these characters demonstrate a system of values in deep contrast with, yet clearly superior to, dominant America's. As Harper presents it, the African American community formed from the choice to stand in opposition to America's "arrogance, aggressiveness, and indomitable power" is comprised of first-generation freed men and women endowed with a potentially world-transforming new consciousness.[15]

Pauline Hopkins's fiction suggests that early twentieth-century black women defined African American identity based on an understanding of the past that acknowledges a racially mixed heritage. As Hazel Carby has argued, Hopkins's work with the *Colored American Magazine* was intended to fulfill the call by black women intellectuals for "race literature" that would establish "good, helpful, and stimulating" examples of African American values and achievements.[16] An editorial in the first issue of the *Colored American Magazine* states that the magazine proposes "to offer the colored people of the United States, a medium through which they can demonstrate their ability and tastes, in fiction, poetry, and art, as well as in the arena of historical, social and economical literature."[17] As the first "general purpose" African American magazine, the *CAM* seems to have been under Hopkins's control from its inception in May 1900 until June 1904, and as such it seems particularly focused on a reading audience inclusive of African American women. During the first four years of its existence, Hopkins's imprint on the magazine is undeniable, and her own writing dominates many of the magazine's issues. The first issue of the magazine notes that Hopkins will be the editor of a "department devoted exclusively to the interest of women and the home" beginning in the next issue, but her influence seems to quickly expand. In the second issue of *CAM* there is the promised "Woman's Department," presumably written by Hopkins, that reports news from black women's clubs, but by the third issue of *CAM* (August 1900) this function has been folded into the editorial column "Here and There" and the magazine as a whole is very obviously gender-inclusive: photographic images present professional black women, and three works of fiction are written by women (including Angelina Grimké and, it seems, Anne Spencer).[18] By September 1900, Hopkins's own novel *Contending Forces* is advertised with a two-page spread, including an order form.[19] In addition to *Contending Forces*, which was published separately from *CAM* but by the same publishing company, and her editorial work with *CAM*, Hopkins also wrote prodigiously for the magazine; under her own name or the pseudonym Sarah A. Allen she published three serialized novels, seven short stories, the series "Famous Men of the Negro Race" in twelve parts, the series "Famous Women of the Negro Race" in eleven parts, and twelve additional articles. Additionally, there is good evidence to suggest that she published under other pseudonyms, including J. Shirley Shadrach.[20]

The *CAM*'s opening editorial also states, after naming its purpose in terms of demonstrating the colored American's "ability and tastes" in "fiction, poetry, and art," that its mission is to "above all ... [aspire] to develop and intensify the bonds of that racial brotherhood, which alone can enable a people, to assert their racial rights as men, and demand their privileges as citizens."[21] Advertisements in the *CAM* for *Contending Forces* use similar language and make it clear that the *CAM*'s goal, in particular, is to strengthen "brotherhood" through the fiction it presents. In the prospectus of *Contending Forces*, for example, after asking the question, "Of what use is fiction to the colored race at the present crisis in its history?" the claim is made that "it is the simple, homely tale told in an unassuming manner which cements the bond of brotherhood among all classes and all complexions."[22] Again according to this prospectus and additional advertisements for *Contending Forces*, the novel presents incidents that "have actually occurred" and while the story is told impartially, "both sides of the dark picture—lynching and concubinage" are included. "Lynching" and "concubinage" are, as Hopkins presents them, both intertwined with issues of racial mixing.

Contending Forces is a novel of some four hundred pages; its range is broad and its story intricate. In order to demonstrate the significance of the multiracial roots of African American families for Hopkins, however, we need only focus on the subplot that presents the story of Sappho Clark, where Hopkins addresses "accusations that miscegenation was the inmost desire of the darker races of the earth" by reconstructing miscegenation "as white male rape."[23] Sappho Clark is herself, as the daughter of parents who are each biracial, the product of miscegenation. We discover that as a fourteen-year-old girl she was abducted from her Catholic private school in New Orleans by her white uncle, raped by him, and kept imprisoned in a house of prostitution for three weeks until her family managed to rescue her. She leaves this past behind her in the form of a son, Alphonse, until forced through blackmail into a confrontation with her past. In the chapter titled "Mother-Love," Sappho decides not to run from her past any longer, and weeps bitter tears yet feels peace. Looking on her sleeping child, she "fold[s] him in her arms" and when he awakes she feels "new-found ecstacy [sic] at the rosy face." According to the narrator, while "her feeling of degradation had made her ashamed of the joys of motherhood, of pride of possession in her child ... all that feeling was swept away."[24] For the first time, Sappho tells the child that she is his mother and promises him that she will always be with him. Thus, with this reunion, Hopkins demonstrates that the significant miscegenation issue in American society is the way in which mothers lift and carry into the black community their biracial children conceived through acts of white male rape.

By acknowledging her son Alphonse, which Hazel Carby argues is the "necessary transition" that precedes "the final transformation into wifehood and marriage," Sappho becomes, in a sense, sanctified.[25] Like her predecessor, the title character in Frances Harper's novel *Iola Leroy*, the psychic pain Sappho experiences brings her to a new consciousness. By accepting her son as her own, however, Sappho literally overcomes the basest form of white male aggression, transforming it into an object worthy of love. At this point, Sappho begins to see herself and her suffering as part of a larger purpose and, says the narrator, will in the future learn "to value the strong, chastening influence of her present sorrow, and the force of character it developed, fitting her perfectly for the place she was to occupy in carrying comfort and hope to the women of the race" (347). As she is spiritually transformed, Sappho also becomes psychologically ready for the work of racial uplift, and ready, as well, to marry her intended, Will Smith. When the two meet again, they are quickly reunited. They marry, and together plan "to bring joy to hearts crushed by despair," presumably by speaking from their own experiences (401). At the conclusion of the novel, the reconstructed African American family stands on the deck of a ship bound for Europe. They have become rich through reparations paid as a consequence of a lawsuit against the United States, and these riches will be shared with all the family's members, including Sappho and her son, Alphonse, who is accepted as one of their own.

While keeping this concluding image in mind, when we reconsider the claim made by the advertisements for (and preface to) *Contending Forces* that its story will "cement the bond of brotherhood among all classes and complexions," we discover a new image of the racially subscribed subject. Sappho, our exemplar, clearly demonstrates that her choice of mother-love, her choice to claim her child, plays the significant role in establishing race consciousness. Furthermore, the family does not move forward, cannot form itself anew, until its members revisit and reconstruct the trauma buried in consciousness. All black women, Hopkins implies, no matter their past experiences, make the claim of the racial subject and so define the race. In this context, Anna Julia Cooper's famous statement, "Only the Black Woman can say, 'when and where I enter, in the quiet, undisputed dignity of my womanhood, without violence and without suing or special patronage, then and there the whole *Negro race enters with me,*'" applies not to the privileged few but to each and every black woman.[26] This image of inclusion correlates with the mission of the black women's club movement in its intent to reach out to all women regardless of their pasts; furthermore, traditional judgments concerning women's morality become clearly inappropriate. When family is defined matrilineally, and uplift is defined through a mother's choice to lift her child into her arms, as Sappho's claiming of her son Alphonse suggests, the bond of brotherhood depends upon embracing and being embraced by a common mother.[27]

In June 1904, the *CAM* announced for the second time that it was "under new management" and became editorially controlled by Fred R. Moore, acting in the interest of Booker T. Washington. Historical scholarship published as early as 1928 suggests that Hopkins's editorial stance was incompatible with Washington's views. Under Hopkins's editorship, the masthead proclaimed, "Devoted to Literature, Science, Music, Art, Religion, Facts, Fiction and Traditions of the Negro Race" and then, still under Hopkins's editorship, simply "Devoted to the Interests of the Colored Race." Under new management, Moore explains, the magazine now "seeks to publish articles showing the advancement of our people along material lines, believing that the people generally are more interested in having information of the doings of the members of the race, rather [than] the writings of dreamers or theorists."[28] By extending Arnold Rampersad's argument in "Slavery and the Literary Imagination" about the nature of the disagreement between Du Bois and Washington to Hopkins, we can see that more than the role of imaginative work is at stake. In Washington's *Up from Slavery*, according to Rampersad, the institution of slavery is treated as something whose "evils, insofar as they existed, were to be acknowledged briefly and then forgotten."[29] Relying on a vision of the African American as a black Adam, Rampersad explains, Washington refigures slavery as the fortunate fall whereby "Africans gained the skills and the knowledge needed for the modern world." In Washington's view, then, there is no blame to be placed on white America for slavery's debilitating effects; furthermore, as with all Adamic stories, the point is that the individual himself must, as Washington has, build himself up into a "powerful, fully realized human being."[30] While this vision of slavery is obviously problematic on many levels, it becomes even more so when the role of women is considered. Rampersad suggests that, for Washington, the slave himself must be responsible for his fall, but Adamic myth would place that blame on enslaved women. This Adamic mythologizing of slavery, then, is particularly pernicious in its effects on women because it twists black female experience so that, for example, white male rape becomes black female seduction. Given Washington's presentation of slavery in this manner, it is not surprising that Pauline Hopkins's fiction, with its focus on female experiences of victimization, was incompatible with his ideology and that she was released from editorial responsibilities when the *CAM* fell under Washington's influence.

According to most accounts, Hopkins was released as editor of the *CAM* because she was too outspoken. In the November 1904 issue, however, the "Publishers' Announcements" say only that: "On account of ill-health Miss Pauline Hopkins has found it necessary to sever her relations with this Magazine."[31] By this point, the aim of the magazine had completely changed. It was no longer a cooperative venture asking for a member's contribution of one dollar, but instead incorporated and selling stock at five dollars a share. In addition to its focus on "the doings of the race along material lines," it had become much more exclusively male, adding, for example, a "Masonic Department." Nevertheless, reports that Hopkins parted company with the magazine for other than ideological reasons persisted. In a 1912 issue of the *Crisis*, W. E. B. Du Bois explains that Hopkins was not "conciliatory enough" for the new management. Furthermore, in a 1928 article on African American magazines, Charles S. Johnson notes that because Hopkins made "no attempt to modify the magazine's expressions out of consideration for the white persons from whom most . . . support was obtained" she was removed by people who believed "that there was greater usefulness in a more conciliatory policy."[32] Combined, these comments point to a particular conflict that occurred in 1903 between Hopkins and Cornelia Condict, a white subscriber to the *CAM*, recorded through the letters to the editor of the magazine.

Referring to Hopkins's serialized novels *Hagar's Daughter: A Story of Southern Caste Prejudice, Winona: A Tale of Negro Life in the South and Southwest*, and *Of One Blood, or, The Hidden Self*, Cornelia Condict wrote to complain that "without exception [the serialized novels] have been of love between colored and whites." Furthermore, she states, "the stories of these tragic mixed loves will not commend themselves to your white readers and will not elevate the colored readers."[33] In her response published with Condict's letter in the March 1903 issue of the magazine, Hopkins boldly replied:

My stories are definitely planned to show the obstacles persistently placed in our paths by a dominant race to subjugate us spiritually. Marriage is made illegal between the races and yet the mulattoes increase. Thus the shadow of corruption falls on the blacks and on the whites, without whose aid the mulattoes would not exist. And then the hue and cry goes abroad of the immorality of the Negro and the disgrace that the mulattoes are to this nation. Amalgamation is an institution designed by God for some wise purpose, and mixed bloods have always exercised a great influence on the progress of human affairs.[34]

After making this statement, Hopkins continues by claiming that the letter shows that "white people don't understand *what pleases Negroes* [emphasis in original]," thereby suggesting that these stories of relationships that cross color lines were profoundly important to her African American audience.[35] While Condict has misread the stories' purposes as insinuations that sexual relations with whites are advantageous in uplifting the race, Hopkins instead focuses on the spiritual crisis her characters face through sexual victimization and implies that her fiction speaks to needs springing from group trauma.

Hopkins's attitude towards "amalgamation," that is, consensual marriage by people of different races, is presented in detail in an earlier short story, "Talma Gordon," published in the October 1900 issue of the *CAM*.[36] In that story, during a discussion among the most elite class of men in Boston, the renowned doctor at whose home these twenty-five men are dining takes the surprising position of believing in the inevitability of intermarriage among people of different races. In order to make his "meaning clearer with illustration," Dr. Thornton tells the story of the Gordon family, one of the founding families of New England ("Talma Gordon," 52). Through various twists in the narrative we discover that none of the family are who they appear to be: the patriarch of the family is really a pirate who has made his fortune at the expense of others; the mother who died after childbirth is proven by her dark-skinned child to be an "octoroon" herself; and the daughter, Talma Gordon, who has been accused of the murder of her father, stepmother, and half-brother is innocent of any crime.[37] While Dr. Thornton's story of the Gordon family, in itself, presents a common story of accidental racial intermarriage, the flourish of "Talma Gordon" occurs as Dr. Thornton finishes his tale. "'But what became of Talma Gordon?'" one of the listeners asks. In answer to that question, Hopkins adds the final line of her own story: "'Gentlemen,'" says Dr. Thornton, "'I shall have much pleasure in introducing you to my wife—née Talma Gordon'" (68). This racial intermarriage, clearly no accident, is presented as the deliberate action of a most sophisticated and brilliant man of social position. Furthermore, with this conclusion to her own story, Hopkins counters the more popular opinion that intermarriage, if it takes place at all, will only take place "among the lower classes."[38]

Hopkins's final novel, *Of One Blood, or, The Hidden Self*, which was being serialized when Cornelia Condict wrote her complaint about the preponderance of stories in the *Colored American Magazine* focused on "tragic mixed loves," also presents a racially tangled familial lineage. This novel's point, however, is in its title phrase, repeated throughout the text: "His promises stand, and He will prove His words, 'Of one blood have I made all races of men.'"[39] Going much further than even "Talma Gordon's" claim of the inevitability of racial intermarriage, *Of One Blood*, with its focus on the Africentric roots of Egyptian civilization, strikes at the heart of Eurocentric claims of racial superiority. Hopkins, in this novel of race pride, attempts to write the supernatural into reality in order to show America's racial problems as foreshadowing the world's future. She begins with her claim: there is a real yet hidden city in Ethiopia whose riches prove it the true birthplace of "all the arts and cunning inventions that make . . . modern glory" (*Of One Blood*, 560). It is to this civilization that the African American Reuel Briggs returns as the long-awaited king. This Pan-African vision does not, however, mean that Hopkins was making a black nationalist argument.[40] In the final image of the novel, Reuel is waiting in the Hidden City "with serious apprehension, the advance of mighty nations penetrating the dark, mysterious forests of his native land."[41] Given that the conversation about the inevitability of amalgamation presented in Hopkins's "Talma Gordon" began as discussion of the subject: "Expansion; Its Effects upon the Future Development of the Anglo-Saxon throughout the World," we can safely assume that racial purity will have no place in the modern future that Hopkins envisions ("Talma Gordon," 49).

In *Of One Blood*, as in Frances Harper's novels *Minnie's Sacrifice* and *Iola Leroy*, transformative knowledge is passed matrilineally, from Aunt Hannah to her granddaughter, Dianthe Lusk.[42] Jennie Kassanoff points out that "Aunt Hannah administers the healing antidote of narrative—of decoded genealogies [and] descriptive histories."[43] Aunt Hannah's knowledge of true identities springing from events of slavery is disruptive yet restorative; while sharing her knowledge ends some lives and changes others, it is necessary to a true preparation for the possibilities of the future. For readers, believing her means acknowledging the authority of the woman known as "the most noted 'voodoo' doctor or witch in the country" (*Of One Blood*, 603). Furthermore, this authority is matriarchal: Aunt Hannah knows, through her own sexual experiences, the patrimony of her own daughter; and presumably, through her daughter's confidences, she knows who has fathered her grandchildren. But

Aunt Hannah has acted to obscure identity, as well. It is through an act of her own deception that one of her grandchildren thinks of himself as a white man when this is not true. Judging from this tangled genealogy, then, in general we might say that Hopkins wants us to understand that full knowledge of identity can be obtained only after consultation with black matriarchs; and this would be as true for "white" men as for black women.

In August 1904, just after Fred R. Moore had taken control of the *Colored American Magazine*, the magazine ran an essay by T. Thomas Fortune, editor of the *New York Age*. Fortune's essay, titled "False Theory of Education Cause of Race Demoralization," stressed as ridiculous an education that focused students' attention on "building up . . . the character and material well-being of . . . the race, as the first rule of action."[44] According to Fortune, students should be building up "individual character and material well-being," following the example of Booker T. Washington. "The Negro and Indian are the only race elements of the American citizenship who are taught that their chief mission in life is to lift up their race," he notes, while continuing by suggesting that success lies in "individual initiative and selfishness, with no conscious thought of benefiting the race or nation, as the case may be" ("False Theory of Education," 474–75). Fortune's philosophy could not be more antithetical to the prevailing ideal of the "colored" women's club movement, focused on women as they define themselves through racial subjectivity. This concern for the individual as expressed by Fortune entirely disregards black women's experiences at the turn of the century. At the center of Fortune's criticism of the education he received at Howard University, for example, is the charge that it did not offer "the proper sort of education in manliness and self-respect and self-interest" that would make "strong and useful men" ("False Theory of Education," 476). Here the "race" is the men, born of themselves or their own will to power. This vision of black manhood allows no room for any reminder of the crucible of slavery, nor for black matriarchs or mother-love. And yet, read against the ethos of Pauline Hopkins's *Colored American Magazine*, Fortune's position is overdetermined in its emphasis on black masculinity, and his revisionist definition of the race points to the significance of Hopkins's "colored" vision.

Alain Locke claims that "Negro genius" of the 1920s "relies upon the race-gift as a vast spiritual endowment from which our best developments have come and must come."[45] He also claims that the New Negro is a "changeling" who has not been "swathed" in the formulae of "the Sociologist, the Philanthropist, the Race-leader," thereby implying that the New Negro's conception and infancy have not yet been rightly identified.[46] Indeed, what the sociologist, philanthropist, and race-leader fathers cannot explain, the mothers can. The "changeling" identity marked by race pride that defines a new generation of writers and artists is, according to Pauline Hopkins and Frances Harper before her, both possessed and passed on by black women. Thomas Fortune's "strong and useful men," following the exemplary Booker T. Washington, must ignore the "race-gift" conveyed by black women in order to become black "individuals" rather than "race men." As individuals, they are the ideological, if not literal, children of white fathers. Yet Georgia Douglass Johnson's 1922 poem "The Riddle," the epigraph to this essay, speaks of these men who claim individual rather than race identity: men who are "white men's children in black men's skins" but, when so posited as children, also identified as children of "other" mothers, of "colored" mothers. Johnson's "cosmopolite" is the modern everyman, characterized by her as the son of white male aggression and empire building "over the earth." Yet he is not Locke's "changeling," not a child switched at birth, not a white stepchild. The image Johnson uses in place of "changeling" is "Triton," creature of two identities, literally both/and—in Johnson's words "peer of the two," in Hopkins's work, "colored." Perhaps, then, women's "colored" experience lends itself to a subjectivity that blends rather than doubles the racialized selves, and so provides an other, rather than a double, new race consciousness.

NOTES

Epigraph: Georgia Douglas Johnson, "The Riddle," in *The New Negro*, ed. Alain Locke (1925; reprint, New York: Atheneum, 1970), 147.

1. Harper was one of only six African American women to address the international delegation during the three-day forum. See Hazel Carby, *Reconstructing Womanhood: The Emergence of the Afro-American Woman Novelist* (New York: Oxford University Press, 1987), 3–6, for a contemporary account of this event.

2. "Woman's Political Future," in *World's Congress of Representative Women*, ed. May Wright Sewell (Chicago: Rand McNally, 1894), 473.

3. Pauline Hopkins, "Club Life Among Colored Women," part 9 in a series titled "Famous Women of the Negro Race," *Colored American Magazine* 5, 4 (August 1902): 273. For a detailed discussion of "uplift," see Kevin K. Gaines, *Uplifting the Race: Black Leadership, Politics, and Culture in the Twentieth Century* (Chapel Hill: University of North Carolina Press, 1996).

4. See Carby, *Reconstructing Womanhood*, 17, where she quotes Elizabeth Lindsay Davis, *Lifting as They Climb: The National Association of Colored Women* (Washington, D.C.: National Association of Colored Women, 1933), 19.

5. See Gloria Anzaldúa, *Borderlands/La Frontera: The New Mestiza* (San Francisco: Aunt Lute Books, 1987).

6. Alain Locke, "The New Negro," in *The New Negro*, ed. Alain Locke (1925; reprint, New York: Atheneum, 1970), 3-16.

7. See Barbara Christian, *Black Women Novelists: The Development of a Tradition, 1892-1976* (Westport, Conn.: Greenwood, 1980), 26, and Deborah McDowell, "'The Changing Same': Generational Connections and Black Women Novelists," *New Literary History: A Journal of Theory and Interpretation* 18, 2 (Winter 1987), 284–85.

8. Carby, *Reconstructing Womanhood*, 89.

9. See F. James Davis, *Who Is Black? One Nation's Definition* (University Park: Pennsylvania University Press, 1991), 54. As Davis makes clear, these numbers are undoubtedly too low, since the "mulatto" designation depended upon visible white ancestry.

10. *Colored American Magazine* [henceforth cited as *CAM*] 6, 5 (March 1903): 349.

11. Davis, *Who Is Black?* 82.

12. Ibid., 8.

13. Claudia Tate, *Domestic Allegories of Political Desire: The Black Heroine's Text at the Turn of the Century* (New York: Oxford University Press, 1992), 146.

14. Ibid., 146.

15. Frances E. W. Harper, *Iola Leroy; or, Shadows Uplifted* (1892; Boston: Beacon Press, 1987), 260.

16. Carby, *Reconstructing Womanhood*, 120.

17. *CAM* 1, 1 (May 1900): 60.

18. *CAM* 1, 3 (August 1900) includes Angelina Grimké's "Black Is, As Black Does (A Dream)," 160–63, and part one of "Beth's Triumph," 152–59, by Anne Bethel Scales, presumably Anne Spencer. Spencer was Annie Bethel Bannister prior to her marriage to Edward Spencer in May 1901, but since her mother was Sarah Scales, she could also have referred to herself, in public as well as in writing, as Anne Bethel Scales prior to her marriage.

19. *CAM* 1, 4 (September 1900): 195–96.

20. For a list of Hopkins's publications, see Malin LaVon Walther, "Works by and about Pauline Hopkins," in *The Unruly Voice: Rediscovering Pauline Elizabeth Hopkins*, ed. John Cullen Grueser (Urbana: University of Illinois Press, 1996), 221–24. Additionally, there is good reason to believe that the author of "Furnace Blasts I. The Growth of the Social Evil Among all Classes and Races in America" (*CAM* 6, 4 [February 1903]: 259–63) and "Furnace Blasts II. Black or White—Which Should be the Young Afro-American's Choice in Marriage" (*CAM* 6, 5 [March 1903]: 348–52), J. Shirley Shadrach, is a pseudonym for Pauline Hopkins herself (and certainly an article titled "Furnace Blasts" written by "Shadrach" is pseudonymous). Comments made and quotations used in the "Furnace Blasts" editorials are also found in writing attributed to Hopkins. For example, there are language similarities between "Furnace Blasts II" and the novel *Of One Blood; or, The Hidden Self*, serialized in *CAM* as "Furnace Blasts II" was pub-

lished. Furthermore, we know Hopkins wrote under other pseudonyms, e.g., as Sarah A. Allen. Finally, the article "Charles Winter Wood; or, From Bootblack to Professor," advertised in a preview of the next issue's table of contents lists Sarah A. Allen as its author, but switches authorship to J. Shirley Shadrach in the issue when published—another indication that Allen and Shadrach are one and the same. See *CAM* 5, 4 (August 1902) advertisement and *CAM* 5, 5 (September 1902): 345.

21. *CAM* 1, 1 (May 1900): 60.

22. *CAM* 1, 4 (September 1900): n.p.

23. Carby, *Reconstructing Womanhood,* 141.

24. *Contending Forces,* 345. Subsequent citations of this novel are given parenthetically in the text.

25. Carby, *Reconstructing Womanhood,* 143.

26. Anna Julia Cooper, *A Voice from the South,* Schomburg Library of Nineteenth-Century Black Women Writers (New York: Oxford University Press, 1988), 31.

27. My thanks to Marjorie Pryse for helping me to clarify this and related ideas.

28. *CAM* 7, 9 (November 1904): 693.

29. Arnold Rampersad, "Slavery and the Literary Imagination: Du Bois's *The Souls of Black Folk,*" in *Slavery and the Literary Imagination,* ed. Deborah E. McDowell and Arnold Rampersad (Baltimore: Johns Hopkins University Press, 1989), 106.

30. Ibid., 110.

31. *CAM* 7, 9 (November 1904): 700.

32. See W. E. B. Du Bois, "The Colored Magazine in America," *The Crisis* 5 (November 1912), 33, and Charles S. Johnson, "The Rise of the Negro Magazine," *Journal of Negro History,* 13 (January 1928), 13. For an excellent overview of Hopkins's difficulties with Booker T. Washington, and his role in the publishing of the *CAM,* see Abby Arthur Johnson and Ronald M. Johnson, "Away from Accommodation: Radical Editors and Protest Journalism, 1900–1910," *Journal of Negro History* 62 (October 1977): 325–38.

33. *CAM* 6, 5 (March 1903): 399.

34. Ibid.

35. Ibid.

36. "Talma Gordon," in *Short Fiction by Black Women, 1900–1920,* ed. Elizabeth Ammons, Schomburg Library of Nineteenth-Century Black Women Writers (New York: Oxford University Press, 1991), 49–68. Subsequent citations are given parenthetically in the text.

37. Hazel Carby's analysis of "Talma Gordon," part of her larger discussion of Hopkins's views on imperialism, has shaped my summary presentation of this story. See Carby, *Reconstructing Womanhood,* 135–36.

38. In "Talma Gordon" one of the characters, a college president, had responded earlier to the inevitability of amalgamation as argued by Doctor Thornton, saying, "Among the lower classes that may occur, but not to any great extent" (51). This same college president, ironically, is the listener who asks about Talma Gordon's fate.

39. See *Of One Blood; or, The Hidden Self* (1902–03), in *The Magazine Novels of Pauline Hopkins,* Schomburg Library of Nineteenth-Century Black Women Writers (New York: Oxford University Press, 1988), 621. Further references to this novel are

documented parenthetically in the text. "Furnace Blasts: II. Black or White—Which Should Be the Young Afro-American's Choice in Marriage," by J. Shirley Shadrach, was also published in the same issue with the serialized *Of One Blood* and Cornelia Condict's letter of complaint about Hopkins's serialized fiction. "Furnace Blasts: II" also points to the inevitability of interracial relations, and concludes by saying: "The grand finale of this racial drama is about to begin, the key-note of which lies in the affirmation: 'Of one blood have I made all nations of men.' Today we can say how wonderfully the law of evolution is fulfilling old Bible prophecies!" (*CAM* 6, 5 [March 1903]: 352). If J. Shirley Shadrach is one of Hopkins's pseudonyms, her position on amalgamation is even clearer.

40. Jennie A. Kassanoff makes this argument for Hopkins's nationalism in "'Fate Has Linked Us Together': Blood, Gender, and the Politics of Representation in Pauline Hopkins's *Of One Blood*," in *The Unruly Voice: Rediscovering Pauline Hopkins*, ed. John Cullen Gruesser (Urbana: University of Illinois Press, 1996). Her claim, with which I disagree, is that "although *Of One Blood* explicitly argues for a brotherhood of man, subtexts . . . dispute this claim" (171).

41. The sexual connotation of this description suggests an analogy between white male rape of African American women and the expansionist forces of colonization as they enter Africa.

42. Elizabeth Ammons has noted the implications of Hopkins's use of female names with classical ties, exploring, for example, Dianthe as virgin goddess of the hunt (*Conflicting Stories: American Women Writers at the Turn into the Twentieth Century* [New York: Oxford University Press, 1992], 218). It is also significant that Dianthe Lusk is the exact name of the famous abolitionist John Brown's first wife. Certainly, this is no accident on Hopkins's part.

43. Kassanoff, "'Fate Has Linked Up Together,'" 176.

44. *CAM* 7, 6 (July 1904): 473.

45. "Negro Youth Speaks," in *New Negro*, ed. Locke, 47.

46. Locke, "New Negro," 3.

The Authority of Experience

Jane Addams and Hull-House

E "Experience," a concept crucial to the development of pluralist and feminist discourse, has come under increasing scrutiny in recent years.[1] Joan Scott, for example, writes that the concept has been useful for "historians of difference" because it fits so comfortably within disciplinary paradigms whereby old narratives are displaced "when new evidence is discovered" (24). Such success, however, also reveals the concept's limitations. Histories that use experience as evidence, Scott argues, tend to "take as self-evident the identities of those whose experience is being documented and thus naturalize their difference" (25). Experience becomes a "foundational concept," posited as working in "a realm of reality outside of discourse" (32). As a result, says Scott, "critical examination of the workings of the ideological system [of difference] . . . and of its historicity" is precluded, thereby reproducing rather than contesting that system (25). Like many critics of "experience," Scott concludes that experience is "not a word we can do without," but she argues we need to deny all foundational concepts and turn our attention instead to the history of such concepts (37).

This chapter draws on Scott's critique of "experience" in order to analyze the emergence of a foundational concept of experience in the turn-of-the-century writings of the progressive reformer Jane Addams. It extends Scott's insights, however, by focusing not on the history of Addams's concept of experience, but on why the concept might have been constructed as it was, what kind of work it may have done for Addams and her readers, and what kind of work it still does today. I show that Addams's powerful version of experience, one that has been formative for pluralism and feminism, depended on the narrative conventions of literary realism to figure itself (to borrow Scott's phrasing) "outside of discourse" (32)—and therefore irreducibly real. The need for a foundational concept of experience, I argue, is the result of political and ideological struggles within the "culture of professionalism" that has been seen as dominating both the Victorian and modern periods.[2] For the first generation of college women, like Addams, who had been both invited to join and barred from the professions, "experience" provided the grounding for an expertise that authorized their work within the professional culture that excluded them. "Experience" did not authorize only the work of women or "others" within the culture of professionalism; after all, "experience" has been useful to professionals across gender, race, and ethnic divides.[3] Nonetheless, "experience" was of particular use to those who could not (and cannot) make claims to institutionalized forms of authority.

In focusing on the culture of professionalism, I am highlighting (like many other critics today) the continuities rather than discontinuities between the Victorian and modern periods. In recent years, aesthetic developments of the Victorian period, such as sentimentalism and realism, have been convincingly linked to professional culture, as have those of the modern period, such as naturalism and radical experimentation.[4] The culture of professionalism did not remain static over time; however, by focusing on the continuities between its discourses, I am insisting that if we are to understand the complicated gender politics of modernism, we need to read against its rhetoric of a "break" with the Victorian past. Hence, I read literary realism, often associated with Victorian culture, as part of a modernism that constructs itself as professional by defining itself against a putatively feminine, amateur Victorian past, even though it is closely connected to that past. Addams's writings, read in the context of these gendered cultural dynamics, suggest that a notion of experience as transparent reality is connected, as supplement and alternative, to professionalism, often seen as transparent abstraction. In other words, this essay shows that when we recover women's contributions to the debates that constituted modernity, our understanding of these debates will change; however, that recovery does not entail making claims to the essential difference of women's "experience" of modernity—claims that duplicate precisely the history we need to examine, not assume.

∾

IN A LETTER written to Addams in 1909, William James writes, "The fact is, Madam, that you are not like the rest of us, who seek the truth and try to express it. You inhabit reality, and when you open your mouth truth can't help being uttered."[5] James describes Addams as a kind of prophet—living, embodying, and transparently relaying the truth that is reality. Reading Addams's work, however, one realizes that her skill at inhabiting "reality" and uttering "truth" was consciously and carefully developed. For example, in "Cassandra" (1881), Addams's graduation speech at Rockford Seminary, she criticizes precisely the notion of woman as transparent relayer of truth upon which James relies. Addams describes "the tragic fate of Cassandra—always to be in the right, and always to be disbelieved and rejected."[6] Eight years before the founding of Hull- House, Addams argues that Cassandra's fate was that of all women, who while gifted with "intuitive perception" have "failed to make themselves intelligible," who "have not gained what the ancients call *auethoritas*, right of speaker to make themselves [sic] heard" (37). Addams claims the problem of authorization for women can finally, however, be solved: "There is a way opened, women of the nineteenth century, to convert this wasted force to the highest use . . . a way opened by the scientific ideal of culture" (38). If women were to combine their intuition with nineteenth-century scientific knowledge, Addams argues, the "story of Cassandra will be forgotten, which now constantly meets and stirs us with its proud pathos" (39). No longer can the "brave warriors laugh . . . to scorn the beautiful prophetess and call . . . her mad" (37). In other words, a prophetess requires "training" to make truth intelligible to her audience (38). While such training apparently does not alter the truth, if it is lacking, tragedy ensues.

It is not surprising, then, that Addams's writings depend on important intellectual discourses of the time to compel and convince her audience. What links these discourses together is literary realism. At its simplest level, realism is seen as making a claim to and about reality. More specifically, critics argue, it represents an important development in the modernist rebellion against Victorian culture and its supposedly sentimental, Christian-influenced, "feminized" ideology. Realists imagined themselves as modern professionals, representing society more fully and objectively than their amateur predecessors had. They claimed to undermine democratically the genteel pretensions and prevarications of Victorianism, thereby revealing the real workings of society.[7] While literary realism is a professional discourse, critics in its time as well as ours have pointed out that it is in no way an objective account of reality. Amy Kaplan, for example, argues that realism is an attempt to manage rather than neutrally depict a reality that was seen as chaotic and threatening. While realists did democratize representation to a degree by depicting many of the competing perspectives within American society, they insisted on fitting all those perspectives finally into an imagined "social whole."[8]

Addams's formulation of pluralist convictions demonstrates her reliance on narrative themes and techniques important to literary realism, as well as the benefits and problems that ensue. In the wake of the Spanish-American War, for example, Addams sought to strengthen the case for pacifism and anti-imperialism through her conception of "cosmopolitanism" or "internationalism." Her 1906 book *Newer Ideals of Peace* systematizes this conception. She argues that the "older dovelike" ideas about peace were based on two appeals: "sensibility and . . . prudence."[9] The "feeble," "passiv[e]," and "goody-goody" (8) ideals of peace of the Victorian era were "dogmatic" and therefore largely ineffectual (7). By contrast, the "newer, more aggressive ideals of peace" are not based on dogma, but on real experience (3). More specifically, these newer ideals can be found in "the poorer quarters of a cosmopolitan city," where because immigrants from all nations and religious backgrounds are forced together, "they are really attaining cosmopolitan relations through daily experience" (11, 18). Addams also argues that because immigrants in a cosmopolitan city must commingle despite differences, they "are forced to found their community of interests upon the basic and essential likenesses of their common nature; for, after all, the things that make men alike are stronger and more primitive than the things that separate them" (17). Because commonality becomes a lived experience (rather than a dogma), she writes, "We may predict that each nation quite as a natural process will reach the moment when virile good-will will be substituted for the spirit of warfare" (26).

Addams's narrative about "cosmopolitanism" clearly depends on the dynamics of literary realism. She opposes sentimental dogma to the truth of real experience. The unrealistic, elitist, and feminized past must give way to a realistic, democratic, and masculinized present. The "newer ideals of peace" are being formed in the lived and daily experiences of the most despised and oppressed classes. This democratization, however, must finally be contained imaginatively. Experience of difference, for Addams, as for realists, leads to commonality rather than conflict. The irreducible reality of experience leads to the melting of difference, to the real that is real because it is also universal.

In pointing to Addams's use of literary realism to construct a notion of "cosmopolitanism," I do not wish to deny the deep and radical appeal of her formulation. Nor do I wish to denigrate her committed and brave pacifism. I am suggesting, though, that we need to pay careful attention to the way her argument relies for its force on concepts of experience and reality that are foundational, holistic, and inextricable from each other. In Addams's view, reality is experience, and experience is reality (and so in referring to Addams's writings, I shall use the terms interchangeably). Ideological, institutional, and economic factors, however, all trouble Addams's version of a transcendent, holistic, experiential real.

It is this same version of the experiential real that Addams appeals to in her carefully presented feminism. Addams's call to vocation illuminates the way she relies on a foundational reality to make her case for feminism both powerful and unthreatening. In Addams's autobiography *Twenty Years at Hull-House* (1910), her vocation emerges out of a vision of "reality" she has and as an attempt to live, rather than simply observe, that reality. Taken on a tour of the East End of London by a city missionary, Addams sees for the "first time the overcrowded quarters of a great city."[10] The shock of this sight makes her feel that everything is "unreal" except the poverty she has just seen (42).[11] As a result she gradually reached a conviction that the first generation of college women had taken their learning too quickly, had departed too suddenly from the active, emotional lives led by their grandmothers and great-grandmothers; that the contemporary education of young women had developed too exclusively the power of acquiring knowledge and of merely receiving impressions; that somewhere in the process of "being educated" they had lost that simple and almost automatic response to the human appeal, that old healthful reaction resulting in activity (44).

Influenced by her feeling that college women have left reality behind as they have become educated, Addams creates Hull-House as an attempt to regain reality: "I gradually became convinced that it would be a good thing to rent a house in a part of the city where many primitive and actual needs are found, in which young women who had been given over too exclusively to study, might restore a balance of activity along traditional lines and learn of life from life itself" (51). As in her formulation of cosmopolitanism, Addams seeks to engage with a democratized "real," with "life itself," a life that in its multiplicity can be somehow accessed through, though also contained in, the "house." Addams relies here on the conventions of literary realism to formulate an implicitly feminist critique of domesticity and to reimagine the supposedly private home as a public space.[12] Curiously, however, her critique also relies for its force on the notion that to engage with "life itself," college-educated women should return to the "lives led by their grandmothers," to "activity along traditional lines," in other words, to domesticity. I shall discuss this peculiar nostalgia in a moment.

James's letter illustrates Addams's success at using literary realism to make an appealing case for both pluralism and feminism at the turn of the century. The recent explosion of scholarly studies on Jane Addams and the circle of women reformers with whom she worked at Hull-House suggests that her appeal has been renewed.[13] This contemporary interest in Addams has a number of related causes. At a theoretical level, the call to deconstruct the public/private binary used to theorize women's history,[14] as well as the reevaluation of turn-of-the-century women's contributions to modernity,[15] have made figures like Addams newly important. At a political level, Addams's writings, which document the need for and possibilities of democratic, nationally supported social reform, are becoming more available in a period when such forms of reform have been vigorously attacked. Similarly, these studies about Addams have appeared during a much-discussed "crisis in the humanities." As funding for public education decreases, criticism of "tenured radicals" (who are said to promote political correctness or pluralism and feminism) has grown. The desire to find models of effective critical work that address social inequality has clearly fueled the renewed interest in Addams and is evident in the ways in which her work is figured in contemporary academic texts. Charlene Haddock Seigfried's impressive and provocative *Pragmatism and Feminism* perhaps best demonstrates why Addams's foundational notion of experience and reality have a continuing appeal. In turn, this continuing appeal helps shed light on why Addams constructed "reality" as she did.

In *Pragmatism and Feminism*, Seigfried seeks to recover the important and unexplored connection between pragmatism and feminism through an examination of the turn-of-the-century dialogue between the two. At the center of her analysis is the concept of "experience." Despite their differences, Seigfried argues, pragmatism and feminism share the notion that "Experience and theory are intricately, dynamically interrelated."[16] The commitment to experience, Seigfried says, enables both pragmatism and feminism to resist narrow specialization and professionalization. Feminist scholars implicitly and pragmatist scholars explicitly attack professionalization, which Seigfried defines as "favor[ing] mere verbal solutions, abstractions, and pretended absolutes over concrete analyses of the human condition" (11).

While Seigfried defines "experience" early on in the book as a pragmatist construction, the constructed aspect of it slowly gives way in her account until it becomes a foundational reality placed in opposition to an unreal "professionalism." Particularly, experience becomes foundational to Seigfried when she discusses Addams and the women of Hull-House, her models of pragmatist feminism. The women of Hull-House, Seigfried writes, "refused in principle to subordinate flesh-and-blood human beings, in all their diversity, to the requirements of any theory, program, or institution" (263). They preferred an outcome that "actually bettered the lives of individuals" to a "theoretical victory" (262). This means, says Seigfried, that the "women of Hull House were not only constructing new professional roles for themselves but were providing new exemplary models of professionalization, ones that directly challenged the dominant modes of professionalization and practice that were elitist and oppressive" (265). The pragmatist/feminist theory of knowledge and experience, in Seigfried's analysis, transparently enabled Addams and Hull-House to deal with "flesh-and-blood" human beings whose lives are "actually bettered." By contrast, the abstract work of professionals, Seigfried argues, is disengaged from "flesh-and-blood" people and therefore fails to better anyone's life.[17] This is not merely a historical issue to Seigfried. It is also a distinctly contemporary one:

Increasingly feminist research has become more narrowly specialized along disciplinary lines, more distanced from community involvement, and more single-mindedly theoretical. It has reproduced the ideological divides of the scholarly community, and litmus tests for feminism often depend on how closely one adheres to the standards set by postmodernist, socialist, lesbian or queer, black, Latina, or noncolonialist theories. Meanwhile, what changes? What difference does it make to the world outside of higher education what version of feminism one adheres to when feminism itself is under attack and many of its causes are losing ground? (266)

This is a deeply problematic analysis of contemporary women's studies, with its stark contrasts and its divisive rhetoric. For the purposes of this chapter, however, I want to focus only on what Seigfried's accusations might tell us about her reading of Addams and Hull-House. On the one hand, in Seigfried's view, lies the past and Hull-House where lived experience led to effective community-based activism, consensus, and social change. On the other hand, there is the present and professional academic feminism where lived experience has given way to old patriarchal forms of authority, private and individualist inaction, ethnic and racial conflict, and hence retrenchment from the "real world." What is most noticeable here is that Seigfried depends, as Addams did, on the conventions of literary realism to make her argument. As in Addams's notion of "cosmopolitanism," Seigfried claims that through the transparent experience of "reality," interethnic [feminist] conflict ceases and a social whole is attained that betters the world. Equally striking is Seigfried's nostalgia. As in Addams's vocational moment when she praises women's domestic past and criticizes contemporary college education, so Seigfried praises Hull-House to excoriate contemporary academic feminism. Why this reliance on similar narrative techniques and nostalgia in these two texts written a century apart?

Bruce Robbins's notion of the professional "allegory of vocation" is helpful here. Robbins defines such allegories as "critical works which, while doing whatever other interpretive tasks they set themselves, also perform a second, most often implicit function: they invent and arrange their concepts and characters so as to narrativize and argue for the general value and significance of the intellectual vocation they exemplify."[18] Allegories of vocation often authorize themselves, Robbins argues, through a kind of secular jeremiad (19), which is a response to debates within and outside of a given profession (xi). In such a jeremiad, the professional criticizes the current fallen state of a discipline or profession, as opposed to its prelapsarian form, in order to prove the disinterestedness of the version of professionalism s/he espouses (19–21). Robbins claims that the jeremiad reveals "how disciplines work, how they manufacture vocations for themselves, how they shift from one vocation or paradigm to another" (21). Robbins wants neither to deny nor decry the self-interestedness of professionals in analyzing their jeremiads, but instead to insist on their worldliness. The disinterested autonomy we often imagine our predecessors possessed, he argues, depends structurally on a gendered division of labor, on an imagined separation of public (corruption) and private (purity): "[W]e have to stop positing spaces of freedom which, like domesticity[,] . . . inevitably mask someone's servitude. . . . Not disembodied freedom, but diverse embodiedness and incomplete servitude have to become the common sense view of intellectual work" (10).

Addams's work contains in it what Robbins calls a professional allegory of vocation; and in turn, as Seigfried's book reveals, Addams's allegory has become a site upon which we debate and construct our own professional allegories of vocation. That Addams's jeremiad, with its binaries of experience/education and reality/professionalism, is duplicated in recent analyses of her suggests that experience imagined as a "realm of reality outside of discourse" is linked historically to the emergence and consolidation of professionalism (Scott, 32). The duplication of jeremiads furthermore shows that in a democratic culture there is continuing ambivalence about professionalism, an ambivalence exacerbated by gender issues.[19] In the late nineteenth and early twentieth centuries, professional knowledge was increasingly relied on and yet largely forbidden to women. At the same time, it was (and is) at times criticized by professionals themselves for its disconnection from reality and its elitism. In such a context, Addams relied on a foundational concept of experience she borrowed from literary realism to both authorize her claim to a kind of transcendent professional expertise *and* to defuse, even deny, such a claim.

While Addams's reasons for relying on a foundational version of "experience" make sense, there nonetheless remain the problems with it that Scott has mapped out for us and that Seigfried and others elide. Importantly, however, at various moments in her work, Addams herself recognizes these problems. Her recognition is particularly evident in the way she acknowledges that "experience" makes an ineffectual claim to authority if it is not carefully shaped historically for its audience. This is an Addams we need to be more attentive to as we think through the role gender plays in the construction of modernity. One of her favorite essays, "The Devil Baby at Hull-House," exemplifies the thinking of this Addams.

∽

ADDAMS PUBLISHED "The Devil Baby at Hull-House" three times during her life. It first appeared in the *American Journal of Sociology* (July 1914). Addams made minor changes to it and reprinted it in *The Long Road of Women's Memory* (1916); and then, finally, she revised it again for *The Second Twenty Years at Hull-House* (1930). I shall focus on the third version, since it highlights Addams's awareness of shaping experience for a changing audience. In this essay, Addams specifically analyzes "woman's" relation to narrative— what work it does, what desires it represents for both a narrator and an audience. At the same time, the essay can be read as a reflection on Addams's own relation to narrative. Experience is indeed central in this essay and is to some degree juxtaposed to a kind of professionalism. Experience's power, however, is shown to lie not in itself but in its narrativization, which not only undermines experience's foundational status but also links nonprofessionals and professionals in the work they can potentially do.

In 1913, Addams tells us, a rumor sweeps through the immigrant communities in Chicago that Hull-House is sheltering a devil baby. Different immigrant groups have different versions of the devil baby's genesis and parentage, but all the versions agree that he is the result of a husband's cruelty to his wife and their unborn child. For six weeks, on the basis of this rumor, "thousands of people"[20] from all over Chicago make the trek out to see the devil baby. Addams positions the Hull-House residents as neutrally, if repeatedly, denying the story, despite the immigrants' "acrimonious" asseverations (52). Addams describes herself as at first viewing the phenomenon somewhat neutrally as well, seeing it as "a case of what the psychologists call the contagion of emotion" added to an "aesthetic sociability," but her neutrality gives way as the days pass, and she is soon "quite revolted" by "such a vapid manifestation of even an admirable human trait" (53). However, when she hears "the high eager voices of old women," who "really seemed to have come into their own" during the devil baby phenomenon, Addams becomes "irresistibly interested" (53). The rest of the essay is structured, as so many of Addams's works are, in the alteration of the old women's narratives of their lives and Addams's speculation as to their larger meaning.

The lives that Addams narrates are, she emphasizes, lives of extraordinary hardship, especially gendered hardship: "these old women had struggled with poverty and much childbearing, had known what it was to be bullied and beaten by their husbands, neglected and ignored by their prosperous children, and burdened by the support of the imbecile and shiftless ones" (55). These women are honest about "life's misery," being "long past the stage of make-believe" (54), and they have "no word of blame" for anyone, perhaps because, Addams theorizes, "they had obtained, if not renunciation, at least that quiet endurance which allows the wounds of the spirit to heal" (55). The old women's realism, however, is juxtaposed in Addams's narrative to their belief in the devil baby and the way the baby represents "retribution for domestic derelictions" (63). In the space between the women's realistic narration of their life stories and their belief in the supernatural devil baby, Addams analyzes what she sees as the relation between experience and narrative.

First, she argues that the devil baby story is "an unconscious, although powerful, testimony that tragic experiences gradually become dressed in such trappings in order that their spent agony may prove of some use to a world which learns at the hardest" (61). Experience must be transformed before it can be used. It is as a story that experience becomes "an instrument in the business of living" (62). The devil baby story supports "the theory that woman first fashioned the fairy story" to create "a crude creed for domestic conduct, softening the treatment men accorded to women" (64). And these stories, while shaped from experience, do not directly or transparently reflect the real experience: "Because such stories, expressing the very essence of human emotion, did not pretend to imitate the outside of life, they were careless of verisimilitude and absolutely indifferent to the real world" (64).

Second, Addams argues that while women's experiences reshaped into narrative have "a restraining influence," they are also an idealistic attempt to imagine a world outside this one (64). It is "probable," writes Addams, that "the [devil baby] story itself, like all interpretive art, was one of those free, unconscious attempts to satisfy, outside of life, those cravings which life itself leaves unsatisfied" (67). A foundational version of "experience" and "reality" here is undermined by her notion of narrative. If the old women's experiences have made them realists, it has not made their narratives so; and it is their narratives that do the work of making their world more bearable and of creating a different, more equitable one. It is only through shaping or transforming the "real" that reality itself can be transformed. This idea is applicable not just to the old women but also to Hull-House itself.

As noted above, the essay begins with the residents of Hull-House playing the role of neutral professionals to the old women's excitement about the devil baby. Then, midway through the essay, Addams undermines this opposition, explicitly linking the devil baby phenomenon to the work of Hull-House. A group of men offers to pay to see the devil baby, "insisting that it must be at Hull-House because 'the women had seen it.'" When Addams asks them if they think she would display such a baby for money, they reply, "'Sure, why not?' and 'it teaches a good lesson, too.'" The latter statement, Addams says, apparently is "a concession to the strange moral standards of a place like Hull-House" (63). The men see both the old women and the residents of Hull-House as engaged in disciplining family and social life to create "moral standards." This explicit link between the devil baby phenomenon and Hull-House, however, is one of failure. The old women's claim to the reality of the baby, to its visible materiality, undermines the lesson they seek to teach, just as Addams must also undermine their story, albeit at times with deep ambivalence (56–57, 59–60). The transhistorical claim about women's use of narrative to discipline family life is placed in dialogue with one about the failure of old stories to work in new contexts. Similarly, while the "real" life stories of the old women are crucial in the essay, "realism's" appeal to transparency, to visible materiality, is associated with failure.

In this regard, Addams's republication of "The Devil Baby" for a third time in *The Second Twenty Years at Hull-House* seems particularly suggestive. The essay feels out of place since it does not easily fit into the book's somewhat chronological account of Hull-House's political activism and of the generational shift after World War I that, Addams argues, has led to the decline of the Progressive movement. Moreover, while Addams used and reused material, she rarely commented publicly on that fact. Here, she does by saying that the story best illustrates an important aspect of life at Hull-House (50), "the great revelation of tragedy . . . which has power in its own right to make life palatable and at rare moments beautiful" (79). In the context of the book's larger argument about a generational shift, one can also read the essay as a reflection on the tragic dismantling of Hull-House's work during the 1920s. Addams's *The Second Twenty Years at Hull-House* insists on the power of shaping experience into narrative to create change. As she writes late in the book, "The human power for action mysteriously depends upon our capacity to throw into imaginative form that which we already know, upon a generous impulse to let it determine our needs" (148). Here is Hull-House's story, Addams suggests. Like the devil baby, it is a story that is no longer as convincing as it was. The challenge, therefore, is to write a new, more convincing one. The essay becomes a kind of rallying cry, one that encourages the continuing construction of progressive narratives to counter the reactionary ones currently being deployed. "The Devil Baby," in 1914, but even more so in 1930, suggests that Addams saw her work as shaping "experience" and "reality" into "imaginative form," into a transformed and transformative narrative. It also suggests that she saw that work as continuous. If literary realism was a narrative form that no longer worked as it had, it might well be the moment to shape a new kind of narrative.

∾

I   H A V E   A R G U E D   that a modern, foundational concept of "experience" developed in dialogue with a "modern" culture of professionalism. Connected to literary realism, experience was figured as transparent reality and therefore could be used to authorize the ideas and work of those individuals who were and are, to greater and lesser degrees, excluded from the professions. The continuing resilience of this transparent notion of "experience" attests both to this exclusion and to an ambivalence about professionalism that can itself paradoxically be seen as a product of professionalism. My point is not that the culture of professionalism determines all modern claims to authority, nor simply that the professions need to be opened up. Rather, it is to insist, like Scott, that all authorizing strategies need to be examined historically, and that experience's claims were and are linked to the claims of professionalism.

William James's 1909 letter to Addams provides an illuminating angle on these links. While he describes her as "inhabit[ing] reality" and therefore speaking "truth," he also signs his letter "your faithful colleague and pupil in sociology."[21] The transparent relayer of truth, the prophet, is also here the professional sociologist. In other words, James places Addams in woman's traditional symbolic role of immanence (experience), as well as in an untraditional role of transcendence (professionalism). This paradoxical formulation depends on James's assumption here that experience and professionalism are connected as forms of authority by their transparency. James's assumption highlights how important it is to read any claim to transparency as constructed, whether it is of experience or professionalism, or as in this case, of both.

At the same time, we need to think through why claims to transparency are used and what kind of recognition is implicit in those claims. Addams makes a similar point in a speech, "Social Workers and the Other Professions" (1930), which she delivered at the National Conference of Social Work. This speech, which traces the history of the professionalization of social work, argues that both professionals and nonprofessionals work toward "scientific detachment" but that both are inevitably grounded in a mixed social reality that affects how they describe their work.[22] On the one hand, she insists on and celebrates the "professional standard" (51) that social work has finally attained. On the other hand, throughout the talk, she refers to social workers as "laymen" (51–53) and cites their achievements as "pioneers in certain [reform] movements" (51), behind which the professions trailed (51–53). Similarly, she criticizes the professions for their exclusivity and timidity, arguing that they constitute a "socially unified group" and so "all see alike" (54). At the same time, however, she does not idealize the "lay" social worker, who she says has had to convince "the prosperous members of the community . . . that . . . [the social worker's] services were both necessary to the social good and were well done . . . against the very denials and shrill outcries of the recipients themselves" (50). The "layman" social worker has had to engage in "all those activities so close to advertising . . . so associated with quackery that no real profession tolerates them" (50).

This is an "allegory of vocation" worth thinking about. If the "layman" is juxtaposed to the "professional," real experience to objectivity, neither position is seen as pure. Each represents struggles with the social and institutional forces that shape, constrict, and enable change. Addams's negotiations with these forces are the ones that we must continue to historicize, criticize, and renegotiate in order to analyze and understand our predecessors' work, as well as our own.

NOTES

I would like to thank Ann Ardis, Leslie Lewis, Ari Kelman, Jean Gregorek, and especially Josh Piker for their suggestions and comments on this essay.

1. See, e.g., Teresa De Lauretis, "Semiotics and Experience," in *Alice Doesn't* (Bloomington: Indiana University Press, 1984), 158–86; Chandra Talpade Mohanty, "Feminist Encounters: Locating the Politics of Experience," in *Destabilizing Theory*, ed. Michele Barrett and Anne Phillips (Stanford: Stanford University Press, 1992), 74–92; Joan Scott, "Experience," in *Feminists Theorize the Political*, ed. Judith Butler and Joan W. Scott (New York: Routledge, 1992), 22–40. Subsequent citations of Scott are given parenthetically in the text.

2. "The culture of professionalism" is Burton Bledstein's phrase in *The Culture of Professionalism* (New York: Norton, 1978).

3. In Addams's time, for example, the male pragmatists at Harvard and Chicago clearly relied on the concept of "experience." Brook Thomas links these men's notion of "experience" to professional culture in suggestive ways that complement and also diverge from my account of Addams's concept. See his *The New Historicism and Other Old-Fashioned Topics* (Princeton: Princeton University Press, 1991), 80–89.

4. For the relation between aesthetic developments and the culture of professionalism in the United States, see Mary Kelley, *Private Woman, Public Stage* (New York: Oxford University Press, 1984); Nancy Glazener, *Reading for Realism* (Durham, N.C.: Duke University Press, 1997); Christopher Wilson, *The Labor of Words* (Athens: University of Georgia Press, 1985); and Thomas Strychacz, *Modernism, Mass Culture, and Professionalism* (New York: Cambridge University Press, 1993). Important overviews of the development of professionalism in the nineteenth and twentieth centuries include Bledstein, *Culture of Professionalism*; Thomas Haskell, *The Emergence of Professional Social Science* (Urbana: University of Illinois Press, 1977); *The Professions in American History*, ed. Nathan Hatch (Notre Dame: University of Notre Dame Press, 1988); Magali Sarfatti Larson, *The Rise of Professionalism: A Sociological Analysis* (Berkeley: University of California Press, 1977); and Rosalind Rosenberg, *Beyond Separate Spheres: Intellectual Roots of Modern Feminism* (New Haven: Yale University Press, 1982).

5. William James to Jane Addams, December 13, 1909, in *Jane Addams Papers*, ed.

Lynn McCree Bryan (microfilm), 5: 963. Hereafter this microfilm is abbreviated as *JAPP*.

6. Jane Addams, "Cassandra," *JAPP*, 46: 267. Subsequent citations of this source are given parenthetically in the text.

7. The genesis, features, and values of literary realism have been topics of extensive debate. Recent studies that inform my account of realism include Donna M. Campbell, *Resisting Regionalism* (Athens: Ohio University Press, 1997); Glazener, *Reading for Realism*; David Shi, *Facing Facts* (New York: Oxford University Press, 1995); Michael Davitt Bell, *The Problem of American Realism* (Chicago: University of Chicago Press, 1993); June Howard, *Form and History in American Literary Naturalism* (Chapel Hill: University of North Carolina Press, 1985); Amy Kaplan, *The Social Construction of American Realism* (Chicago: University of Chicago Press, 1988); and Wilson, *Labor of Words*.

8. Kaplan, *Social Construction of American Realism*, 11.

9. Jane Addams, *Newer Ideals of Peace* (New York: Macmillan, 1906), 3, 7. Subsequent citations of this source are given parenthetically in the text.

10. Jane Addams, *Twenty Years at Hull-House* (Urbana: University of Illinois Press, 1990), 41. Subsequent citations of this source are given parenthetically in the text.

11. Allen F. Davis, *American Heroine* (New York: Oxford University Press, 1973), 34–35, says that Addams's letters to family and friends on this trip to London do not reflect any sense of crisis and that the crisis was created retrospectively for her autobiography. I would argue not only that crisis can occur privately, but also that it can occur retrospectively. Nonetheless, Davis's larger point, that Addams was a brilliant image maker, is helpful and well proven.

12. Addams's call to vocation obviously deserves more analysis than I have given it here. For in-depth analyses of this call, see Mina Carson, *Settlement Folk: Social Thought and the American Settlement Movement, 1885–1930* (Chicago: University of Chicago Press, 1990); Davis, *American Heroine*; Mary Jo Deegan, *Jane Addams and the Men of the Chicago School* (New Brunswick, N.J.: Transition Books, 1988); Robyn Muncy, *Creating a Female Dominion in American Reform* (New York: Oxford University Press, 1991); and *Gender and American Social Science*, ed. Helene Silverberg (Princeton: Princeton University Press, 1998).

13. Among the important recent studies on Addams and the Hull-House circle are Carson, *Settlement Folk*; Kathryn Kish Sklar, *Florence Kelley and the Nation's Work* (New Haven: Yale University Press, 1995); Elisabeth Lasch-Quinn, *Black Neighbors: Race and the Limits of Reform* (Chapel Hill: University of North Carolina Press, 1993); Rosenberg, *Beyond Separate Spheres*; Eleanor Stebner, *The Women of Hull-House* (Albany: State University of New York Press, 1997); Judith Ann Trolander, *Professionalism and Social Change* (New York: Columbia University Press, 1987).

14. See, e.g., Linda K. Kerber, "Separate Spheres, Female Worlds, Woman's Place: The Rhetoric of Women's History," in *Toward an Intellectual History of Women* (Chapel Hill: University of North Carolina Press, 1997), 159–99.

15. See, e.g., Ann Ardis, *New Women, New Novels* (New Brunswick, N.J.: Rutgers University Press, 1990); Desley Deacon, *Elsie Clews Parsons: Inventing Modern Life* (Chicago: University of Chicago Press, 1997); Tamar Katz, *Impressionist Subjects: Gender, Interiority, and Modernist Fiction in England* (Urbana: University of Illinois Press,

2000); *Gender and American Social Science*, ed. Silverberg; Christine Stansell, *American Moderns* (New York: Metropolitan Books, 2000).

16. Charlene Haddock Seigfried, *Pragmatism and Feminism* (Chicago: University of Chicago Press, 1996), 8. Subsequent citations of this source are given parenthetically in the text.

17. Seigfried is not alone in relying on this binary; her work simply dramatizes most clearly the way experience is posed against professionalism in recent studies of Addams, including this one.

18. Bruce Robbins, *Secular Vocations: Intellectuals, Professionalism, Culture* (New York: Verso, 1993), 190. Subsequent citations of this source are given parenthetically in the text.

19. For a succinct analysis of these ambivalences, see Elvin Hatch, "Introduction," in *Professions in American History*, 1–11.

20. Jane Addams, "The Devil Baby at Hull-House," in *The Second Twenty Years at Hull-House* (New York: Macmillan, 1930), 52. Subsequent citations of this source are given parenthetically in the text.

21. William James to Jane Addams, *JAPP*, 5: 963.

22. Jane Addams, "Social Workers and the Other Professions," *JAPP*, 48: 1324. Subsequent citations of this source are given parenthetically in the text.

"This Other Eden"

Homoeroticism and the Great War in the
Early Poetry of H.D. and Radclyffe Hall

One evening in 1918 at the Usher Hall in Edinburgh, a war-blinded Captain MacRobert invited an audience of 3,000 to join with him in singing "The Blind Ploughman," a poem by Radclyffe Hall that had, like so many other of her lyrics, achieved popularity as a concert hall ballad. Mignon Nevada, a singer and clairvoyant who attended the concert reported the scene to Hall in the following terms: "Over the audience's head a grey haze that as it ascended higher gradually went from blue to violet, and then to pink, then to a dazzling yellow-white which seemed to be full of moving forms. Some looked like spirits—and over the whole building there seemed a wonderful feeling of Peace and Harmony."[1] The Edinburgh crowd singing Hall's poem, as well as the spirits hovering above, articulated a complex of wartime emotion concerning the damage done by the events of World War I to both the wounded soldier's body, epitomized by singer and ploughman, and English national self-confidence. "The Blind Ploughman" invokes heroic endurance: "Set my hands upon the plough,/My feet upon the sod;/Turn my face towards the East,/And praise be to God," sings the wounded man. It invokes the healing powers of an indestructible English pastoral world: "Every year the rains do fall,/The seeds they stir and spring." And it marries this pastoralism to a powerful Christian rhetoric in which the body has to be wounded for the soul to be redeemed: "God has made his sun to shine. On both you and me;/God who took away my eyes/That my *soul* might see".[2] A London *Times* reviewer of Hall's poetry had summed up the dominant register as nostalgic, "marked by that faint spirit of melancholy which seems inseparable from the modern ballad."[3] The melancholic nostalgia for English pastoralism is essential to the poem's wartime role of speaking to the wounds of war. The assurance that the wounding leads to a better life has to be underwritten by the melancholic register in order to express the losses that the lyric also binds up.

"The Blind Ploughman" was originally published in Hall's 1913 collection *Songs from Three Counties*. Hall's only wartime collection, *The Forgotten Island*, published in spring 1915, was in fact scheduled to appear in the autumn of 1914 and was delayed by the onset of the war itself.[4] Prior to the war, Hall had earned a reputation as a very successful writer of lyric verses, which were frequently set to music by contemporary composers such as Robert Coningsby Clark, Easthrope Martin, and Lisa Lehmann and performed in concert locations. For example, her "Ode to Sappho" was sung at the Queen's Hall in London on October 2, 1910.[5] *The Forgotten Island* was her last collection, and between 1915 and her death, she published fiction including, of course, her scandalous *The Well of Loneliness,* banned soon after its publication in 1928 for its representation of homosexual love. The war's main impact on Hall's poetry seems to have been to put a complete stop to it. Her biographer Michael Baker suggests that "[t]he poems were out of step with the patriotic spirit that prevailed in 1915," and another critic, Lovat Dickson, writes that "[t]he poetry dried up because after 1915 the Georgian love lyric was crushed beneath the tremendous events of the World War."[6] For Dickson, and many other of Hall's critics, the popularity of her poetry is of only passing interest, since the focus of their work is on the 1920s and the trial of *The Well of Loneliness.* Almost inevitably, the scandal that attended Hall's attempt to write the novel of female inversion makes her later fiction the main event. *The Well of Loneliness,* however, was not Hall's first attempt to write a major literary work with inversion at its centre. *The Forgotten Island* represented a sustained attempt to present female homosexual desire in lyric verse, but one that has been difficult for later critics to take seriously. In the period after its publication, the emergence of modernism as the dominant aesthetic and critical paradigm narrowed the kinds of formal experimentation that could be linked to progressive work on gender and sexuality. Rather, the poetry of both the late Victorians and the Georgians looked from the perspective of the English modernist Osbert Sitwell like "the last dead grisly remains of a once vital movement of poetry . . . as infinitely pathetic as the excavated final joint in the tail of some huge but extinct monster."[7]

The Forgotten Island had been a new departure for Hall. It was composed in blank verse and organized according to a sapphic theme, rather than representing sapphic love in occasional single poems, as in the case, for example, of

"Ode to Sappho," which appeared in her collection *A Sheaf of Verses*.[8] Hall was ambitious for her poetry at this period, sending the proofs to Arthur Quiller-Couch at Cambridge University, who was soon to be appointed King Edward VII Professor of English Literature, and writing with pride that "with me [he] thinks that there is a great future for this style in English lyrical poetry."[9] History was not on Hall's side here, and her collection appears anything but forward-looking from the other side of modernism. Hall's poetry, and particularly her efforts to make Victorian sapphism express Edwardian female inversion, has become a footnote in literary history. At the time, with her idea of "a great future" for blank verse, Hall can be seen as responding to the ferment stirred up by the Georgians, who were declaring a renaissance in modern English poetry.[10] However, while her verse shares some of the attachments of the Georgians, for example, in its imitation of A. E. Housman's pastoral ballads, Hall's use of Victorian sapphism puts her at odds with the Georgians. Swinburne was one of the poets that the Georgians repudiated, and according to Harold Monroe, "the numbing effect of the Victorian period [seemed] finally to have relaxed its pressure on the brain of the rising generation."[11] Yet, in the prewar period, neither unambiguously Georgian nor modernist, Hall's poetry was recognized as peculiarly of its moment, capturing an audience that valued her writing for both its English pastoralism and its sapphic exoticism. *The Scotsman* praised *Poems of the Past and Present* (1910) for "a certain Southern, almost Oriental atmosphere" that allowed for "a happy licence of imagination."[12] And even though *The Forgotten Island* was received with minimal interest in 1915, the Edinburgh concert of 1918 suggests that aspects of Hall's poetry were still able to speak to an English wartime culture and a rhetoric of Englishness essential to patriotism.

However, the coincidence between that 1918 patriotism and her prewar English pastoral ballads represented a problem for Hall's early efforts to forge a poetics of sapphic lesbianism. Because of the war, Hall's verse came to seem old-fashioned; elegiac in form and attitude, it looked backward to a time and place that was gone. The question of why Hall abandoned poetry after 1915 and turned to fiction as a vehicle for her ambition is ultimately unanswerable. But, I want to explore this moment in greater detail in this chapter in order to argue that Hall's turn away from lyric sapphism concerns her efforts to link the female homosexual to an idea of the modern. In order to make this argument, I shall compare *The Forgotten Island* to H.D.'s *Sea Garden* (1916), a work that also appeared during the war, the year following Hall's collection, and which also made explicit use of Victorian homoerotic aesthetics in the interests of representing a transgressive sexual desire, but within a modernist frame.[13]

Hall and H.D have each been significant figures for twentieth-century literary and cultural criticism. Feminist critics in the 1970s put H.D. at the centre of a challenge to the gender politics of Anglo-American high modernism. H.D. went from being a minor female player in the history of modernist poetics to the representative of a radical poetics of female transgression, which co-opted modernist textual experimentation for the representation of female subjectivity and sexuality antithetical to the masculine aesthetics of high modernism. Hall, as the author of *The Well of Loneliness*, has been more important within the history of sexuality than feminist literary criticism. Hall has gone from being the political icon of a pre-stonewall butch lesbianism to being assimilated to a history of transgendered sexuality. H.D.'s and Hall's positions within these different fields make it difficult to consider the relationship between their parallel efforts to use Victorian Hellenism and fin de siècle sapphism to represent female homoeroticism. The dominance of literary modernism, with its claims to define both the modern and modernity, creates a picture in which H.D.'s linking of sexuality with textual experimentation necessarily supersedes Hall's apparent formal conservatism. Considered together, however, the two writers demonstrate the pressures on late nineteenth-century homoerotic poetics as they are enlisted in the representation of early twentieth-century female homoeroticism.

Hall's *The Forgotten Island* is a poem sequence memorializing a love affair that has already ended. The island is Hellenic, and Aphrodite appears both as presiding goddess and speaker: "Rich is the fruit of my loving, O mortal,/Sweet to the taste as a drop of gold honey."[14] The collection makes use of the male pronoun in the first lyric, allowing the verse to be read as a woman poet's version of heterosexual love poetry. Indeed, her earlier poetry had been reviewed in the *Daily News* as illustrating the particularity of a female point of view on love.[15] Hall's use of a sapphic setting doesn't necessarily undercut this heterosexual reading. Yopie Prins demonstrates in *Victorian Sappho*, that "[i]n Victorian England . . . Sappho of Lesbos emerges as a proper name for the Poetess."[16] Sappho's very name genders lyric poetry as a feminine genre. However, Thaïs Morgan's attention to the operations of what she terms "the ambiguous expression of aesthetic minoritizing discourse" rather than a fixed homosexual code in Victorian criticism, usefully indicates the double-voiced possibilities of

Hall's collection.[17] The poetry can be both heterosexual and homosexual. Indeed, this would seem to be an essential perspective if we are to understand the cultural and social context in which Hall could attend a public concert performance of her "Ode to Sappho" with her woman lover, Mabel Batten, and Batten's husband and sister-in-law.[18]

The poems of *Forgotten Island* can be read as both a passionate declaration of the erotic nature of love between women, something generic conventions could not allow in Hall's later naturalistic fiction, and a passionate rendering of heterosexual love by women. The polyvocal possibilities of the text emerge through the relay between Hall as author and her speaker. The woman poet's feelings are ventriloquized through the male speaker, so that the speaker's passion can at once be familiarly heterosexual and express the poet's passion for another woman. The author's name, Radclyffe Hall, is poised between the feminine and the masculine and articulates a style associated with new womanhood. Thus, reference to the author leads us to a marking of gender and sexuality that is associated with the woman who has moved beyond the conventional feminine. The dedication of the volume to Mrs. Gordon Woodhouse adds to this effect by linking the volume to an actual woman who may or may not be the object of these love poems. To a coterie reader, the dedication might suggest something improper, since Violet Gordon Woodhouse was a woman with a reputation. Suffragist, musician, and friend of Ethel Smyth, Woodhouse ran a musical salon of "cultish status" and was known for her sexual promiscuity. According to Hall's biographer Diana Souhami, Hall at the very least engaged in a short flirtation with Woodhouse (Souhami, 90). Both Hall's dedication and her authorial signature confirm Prins's point that the sapphic voice adopted by a woman poet does not securely anchor an identity or desire.

By contrast with *The Well*, the legibility of lesbian sapphism in *Forgotten Island* is a function of the collection's relationship to late Victorian and Edwardian minoritizing discourses of homosexuality, so that the collection's polyvocalism is arguably an essential condition of its publication.[19] This is in some sense obvious but becomes significant if we examine another marker of the volume's sapphism, the island setting. The island is Lesbos—home of Sappho—and according to Souhami, one of the factors that shaped Hall's interest in the subject was the experience of listening to Winaretta Singer, princesse de Polignac, read aloud from her manuscript about travels to Lesbos (Souhami, 60).

Hall's version of Lesbos is carefully located as a utopian and idyllic world no longer available to the lovers. It is a forgotten island rediscovered in the register of nostalgic melancholy by the poet/lover. The first lyric, for example, addresses a lover who has forgotten the power of their passion:

Thou who hast so much forgotten
Who may stir thy sleeping senses
To the memory of thy lover
And the island of his dreaming?

Yet it was a happy island,
Filled with sound of running water,
And the scent of wind, blowing southward
Through the spice-trees in thy garden.[20]

This opening lyric, together with title of the collection, defines both the location and the passion as available only through the medium of memory and hence of loss. The narrative of the volume is conventional, charting the progress of the affair from expectation, to fulfillment, to a decline in which the speaker's love is spurned. Hall's speaker pledges himself to Aphrodite and to desire itself; "where may I hide from this destroying rapture?" sings the lover after the end of the affair. But the affair never does end, in that the sequence uses the trope of loss to express an endless desire. The lover's role is to memorialize desire in the face of one who "hast forgotten how to love." In lyric liii, Hall writes: "Canst thou look up and behold/The whiteness of shaken stars/ And know not desire?"[21] The poem's island setting defines this demand on the lover to remember sexual desire as a call to return to a sapphic mode of desire that has been lost to both the fictional lovers and to the contemporary England of author and reader.

The island setting defines the mode of desire as sapphic, but it also relegates that desire to the past, making fulfillment unattainable in contemporary England. However, the delay that makes Hall's volume a wartime publication transforms the discursive location of the collection with particularly significant consequences for the meanings of its geography. In her essay "The Island and the Aeroplane: The Case of Virginia Woolf," Gillian Beer provides the framework for seeing Hall's island precariously located here between Lesbos and a long history of an English cultural imaginary organized by the motif of the island.[22] This other island is famously defined by John of Gaunt in Shakespeare's *Richard II* as this "sceptred Isle . . . this other Eden, demy Paradise."[23] Beer focuses on the moment at which the island metaphor can no longer sustain the idea of defined and defensible borders with the coming of the airplane. Among a number of examples, she cites H. G. Wells, whose character Bert Smallways in *The War in the Air* (1898) declares that "the little island in the silver sea was at the end of its immunity."[24] World War I foregrounds a patriotic discourse in which England is the island nation, standing firm against German aggression, whose story is told in the popular children's history book *Our Island* Story.[25] At this period, the identification between Englishness and the island is self-confident.

Writing about the war in newspapers and journals of the World War I period refers routinely to Britain as "these islands," and "an Island Empire," and the British as "an island people."[26] One of the distinctions that was made between the German and the English at the time was that the English character was strengthened by its island environment. But writings about naval policy during the war are striking both for the degree to which they assume the basic premise of England's national integrity being defined by its ability to sustain its spatial boundaries as an island, and for their recognition that the new technologies of war are redefining the space in which that island is located. For example, a commentator in the *English Review* wrote that "what we, as an island people, are to-day faced with is the introduction of a new element, or rather two new elements in naval warfare." The elements are the submarine and the Zeppelin, which fight the sea war from underneath and above, leaving the "surface sea a No Man's Land." The signs of a shift from an easy confidence in this island identity to an anxiety about the integrity of that national identity is already apparent.[27]

The island of Hall's poetry is by definition always other to England, identified with Lesbos and with the past. But the use she makes of memory and nostalgia forges a link between the reader, in the present, and the forgotten island. The speaker appeals to a contemporary "you" who has forgotten both the island and the desire experienced there, asking the loved one to remember the past. The reader is placed in the same structure that defines the relationship with the past in terms of nostalgia. The reader can effectively recreate the conditions of Lesbos in the present world by reading the poems. It is this nostalgic construction of Hall's forgotten island that allows it to be overtaken by a discourse that links Eden, the island, and the effects of World War I together, that is, the imagining of prewar England as an Eden that will never come again. The war alters among many other things England's temporality—Eden after 1914 is always prewar.

This Edenic image is explored a few years later by Rebecca West in *Return of the Soldier* (1918), where a soldier suffering from an amnesia brought on by shell shock believes himself back in a youthful love affair that took place fifteen years earlier. Despite the fact that both he and the woman he loved are now middle-aged and married, the soldier, Chris, treats Margaret as if she had not aged or changed. West draws on the connection between English identity and the metaphor of the island, by locating the love affair in a pastoral location on a Thames island near Bray, "where the green grass seemed like a precious fluid poured out on the earth and dripping over to the river, and the chestnut candles were no longer proud flowers, but just wet white lights in the humid mass of the tree, when the brown earth seemed just a little denser than the water."[28] This fantasy of a prewar idyll at the heart of England is marked by West as precisely that—a national fantasy about the war's significance as the herald of a fallen modern era and the gulf between this era and an older, happier England. West's clarity in the story about the class relations that conditioned the original love affair make it impossible to accept the imaginary idyll of English life before the war at face value. The link in *Return of the Soldier* between the rich possibilities of the island for representing England as a utopia and the war's relationship to nostalgia is very relevant to Hall's writing.

At the time of writing *The Forgotten Island*, Hall hadn't needed to confront the potential bifurcation of her lost paradise motif. But by the time of her 1920s short story about the war, "Miss Ogilvy Finds Herself," Hall makes explicit the different meanings of the island, as English Eden and sapphic paradise, and attempts to define their relationship.[29] The forgotten island, this time, is a little island off the south coast of England, where the heroine rediscovers her inverted sexuality. After her return to civilian life at the end of the war, Miss Ogilvy finds herself trapped between a new consciousness of desires and capacities that her war service as an ambulance driver fostered, and the intensely dull and restricted life she must lead as a spinster in provincial England. She flees to the island unconscious of the fact that she has lived there in an earlier incarnation. In an episode defined somewhere between dream and memory, Miss Ogilvy relives her previous life and rediscovers her true self.

In this story, the island is now explicitly related to England, but split off from the mainland, as a kind of disavowed fragment. Chronologically, because Miss Ogilvy discovers a past of which she in 1918 is only a late reincarnation, the island stands also for England's prehistory. In the flashback to a prehistoric past, the island is not yet separated from the mainland and provides the pastoral setting for a love affair in which Miss Ogilvy's former self achieves sexual fulfilment.[30] But neither the island nor the female invert can be integrated with England in the present, where the island is the setting for Miss Ogilvy's death. The complicated spatial and temporal relationships of past and present in "Miss Ogilvy" show Hall wrestling with the lesbian's relationship to the present. The war is the only time in which Miss Ogilvy can live in the present as an invert, but the story actually begins with the end of both the war and that freedom. Moreover, the war has not allowed Miss Ogilvy her sexuality, only her mannishness. Before the war she does not understand her oddity, and after the war she finds herself a freak. When she does find herself, it is in prehistory and as a man.

The temporality of sapphic love is also a problem in *The Forgotten Island*, where that love is also relegated to a mythic past. This is not in itself surprising, especially in light of later reaction to *The Well*, but the issue of the representability of explicit sexual love between women masks another concern. The features of Hall's poetry that were able to capture a wartime audience, such as the potent mix of loss, nostalgia, and pastoralism in "The Blind Ploughman," bind her poetry to a very specific story of the war's effects, concerning an idyllic England destroyed forever by the war. This assimilation of nostalgic pastoralism to a backward-looking English nationalism is arguably the general fate of both the prewar ballad and the Georgian lyric. In other words, the dominant modes of modern English poetry, both during the war and in the immediate prewar period, come to look outmoded not simply because modernist poetics won out, but because the claim to be modern was difficult to make for a poetry that had become absolutely the register of the myth of prewar Englishness. As Kathryn Ledbetter says of Osbert Sitwell, who helped steer English culture toward modernism in the 1920s, "He never forgave the home front poets of *Georgian Poetry* for ennobling the war effort with sentimental poetry that clung to Victorian ideals."[31] For this reason, Hall's sapphic verse moves rapidly at the onset of the war from a poetry "that has a great future" to one that strands the lesbian in a premodern moment, beached on the forgotten island by the collection's dominant register of nostalgic loss.

Radclyffe Hall's own self-representation in what Laura Doan has described as the "exquisitely ultra-modern look" of cropped hair, cravat, and suit jacket signals her assumption of modern sexuality. Doan has shown that the task of reading the sexuality of that image is complicated.[32] Like sapphism, Hall's image was open to more than one reading, and could connote new womanhood rather than lesbian sexuality. Nonetheless, the image aligns both Hall and the invert with an idea of modern femininity that cannot coexist with the sapphic poetic discourse of *The Forgotten Island*. For Hall, after 1914, fiction seems to offer the possibility of linking the lesbian to the modern through the sexological discourse of inversion rather than Victorian sapphism.

If we turn now to H.D. we can see a parallel picture of the war impacting on a sexual, poetic discourse derived from Victorian Hellenism, but this time in the work of a modernist. The authenticity of H.D.'s Hellenism was the subject of heated debate from 1912 onward, with Robert Graves and Laura Riding among the most scathing on the subject.[33] Both Cassandra Laity and Diana Collecott have demonstrated convincingly that H.D.'s classicism has its origins in Victorian Hellenism. According to Laity, "H.D. and others used the Decadents to fashion a modernist poetic of female desire" that ran counter to the poetics of impersonality central to a male high modernism.[34] Swinburne, in particular, offers H.D. a model of a poetics that "explores alternate forms of desire," and in her prose fiction H.D. interweaves quotations from his poetry to invoke a perverse or decadent eroticism that links to lesbian sexuality.

More recently, in *H.D. and Sapphic Modernism*, Diana Collecott has supplemented Laity with an account of Ezra Pound's attack on Victorian Hellenism in the pages of *The Egoist* in 1914. Collecott analyses the rhetoric of this attack, making explicit Pound's definition of a hard-edged classical modernism against a soft, effeminate Hellenism associated with both women and male homosexuality. The qualities that he discredits in Hellenism, such as "caressability" and sentimentality, are not only sexualized; they are also defined as old-fashioned. For example, he accuses Richard Aldington of "Paterine sentimen-talesque Hellenism."[35] H.D. remained outside the public exchanges in the *Egoist* between Pound and Aldington. She makes her contribution to the debate in her poetry and in editorial decisions about what the journal should publish during her brief period as editor. Her skepticism, however, about Pound's demand that the imagist poets represent their modernity by rejecting Hellenism and Decadence is crystallized in a handful of reviews written between 1914 and 1916.

In an unpublished review of W. B. Yeats's *Responsibilities* from 1914, H.D. makes explicit her understanding of what Gary Burnett calls the "irreducible conjunction" between a machine-based aesthetics (futurism or vorticism, for example) and militarism.[36] H.D. writes, in the review, that the enemy of beauty "is the great overwhelming mechanical daemon, the devil of machinery, of which we can hardly repeat too often, the war is the hideous offspring."[37] And in a 1916 review on Marianne Moore, she reiterates that "Beauty is destined to endure longer, far longer than the toppling sky-scrapers, and the world of shrapnel and machine-guns in which we live."[38] The violence of modern warfare and the aesthetics of the modern city are again opposed to the Paterian term "beauty." Burnett, Collecott, and Susan Stanford Friedman have used these reviews to establish H.D.'s early consciousness of the connections between militarism and a modernist aesthetics associated with heterosexual masculinity.[39] But I want to focus less on H.D.'s critique of militarism than on the way that the war itself offered H.D. an unassailable justification for her repudiation of the modern.

Whereas, for Hall, the war rendered her elegiac version of sapphism old-fashioned by assimilating it to a pastoral rhetoric of Englishness, H.D. was able to turn the war to her own uses, even to the point of borrowing the resources of English patriotism. "[I]n reading Miss Moore's poems," H.D. writes:

we in England should be strengthened. We are torn in our ambitions, our desires are crushed, we hear from all sides that art is destined to a long period of abeyance, and that the reconstruction of Europe must take all the genius of the race. I do not believe that. There are others here in England who do not for one moment believe that beauty will be one whit bruised by all this turmoil and distress.

Miss Moore helps us. She is fighting in her country the same battle. And we must strengthen each other in this one absolute bond—our devotion to the English language.[40]

Here H.D. uses both the rhetoric of wartime England and that of Victorian Hellenism to depict an aesthetic war that places the true artist against modernity depicted as urban, mechanized, commodified, and violent, the antithesis, that is, of beauty. She uses the authority of nationalism and patriotism—for example, "we in England should be strengthened" and "we are fighting the same battle"—to articulate the responsibilities of the artist and establish her oppositional and nonutilitarian aesthetic. Moreover, her imagined community of the avant-garde is rendered a community through the rhetoric of the beleaguered nation, England, against the Kaiser. In "Responsibilities," H.D. likewise constructs a community of true artists whose unity depends on her use of war imagery. She writes: "crouched as in a third line of battered trenches, are the few of us who are left, hanging on against all odds, in the wavering belief that we are the link, the torch-bearers. And upon us, almost with us, is the enemy."

The artist is both literally the remnant of the war-ravaged generation and metaphorically still in the trenches defending England and Beauty. These two categories become inseparable in the Marianne Moore review, because H.D. grounds aesthetic endeavor in "one absolute bond—our devotion to the beautiful English language." For H.D., these are not dissonant categories, since it is from Victorian English poetics that she derives the Hellenism that defines her break with both the modern world of "shrapnel and machine guns" and the machine-based aesthetics of vorticism and futurism. The relationship between England and Beauty is central, however, to Victorian Hellenism as a double-voiced homoerotic discourse. As Linda Dowling has argued, "the study of Greek culture" can represent "nothing less than a surety for England's future life as a nation" at the same time that it invokes homosexuality.[41] And here we see the context of the Great War foregrounding that nationalist agenda even within a manifesto against the conjunction of militarism and modernist aesthetics. Paradoxically, the war not only fosters H.D.'s criticisms of the destructiveness she sees as inherent in high modernist aesthetics, it also revises the terms of Hellenism's homoeroticism in problematic ways.

In *Sea Garden*, the impact of the war on her Hellenism turns not on its Englishness but on the link between violence and the erotic. Victorian Hellenism is most evident in H.D.'s persistent articulation of a desire for beauty. This desire provides a central dynamic of the collection, particularly in the repeated motif of an opulent "beauty without strength/[that] chokes out life." This beauty is rejected in the quest "to find a new beauty/in some terrible/wind-tortured place." The two kinds of beauty correlate, as Laity argues, with a sexualized opposition between a "decadent overflowered Venusberg" and the androgynous male ideal of Greek statuary which is to be found in the work of Decadent poets.[42] The antithesis is primarily represented through the landscape in which the stultifying claustrophobia of sheltered, inland gardens contrasts with wild, exposed headlands that confront a fierce and violent ocean. The sea flower "lies fronting all the wind/among the torn shells/on the sandbank," like Swinburne's "foam flowers," able to "endure when the rose-blossoms wither."[43]

Where the human body is represented in these poems it is almost always a nude male body described in terms associated with the Greek statue, and therefore associated with a Victorian discourse of aesthetic appreciation and male homoeroticism. In "The Contest," for example, H.D. writes: "The ridge of your breast is taut,/and under each the shadow is sharp,/and between the clenched muscles/of your slender hips." The contestant is posed as a statue with light and shadow defining each sexualized detail. This mode of detailed physical description of the male body is more fully eroticized in the poem "Loss," where the speaker's desire is made explicit; addressing his "beloved" and "wondering" "at the strength of your wrist/. . . and the lift of your shorn locks,/and the bronze/ of your sun-burnt neck," the speaker's gaze lingers over the body, in a piling on of paratactic phrases that mimic breathless desire.[44]

H.D.'s borrowings from a homoerotic Hellenism make ambiguous the sexuality that the poems articulate. Through the rest of the volume, a more diffuse Decadent rhetoric makes it difficult to define desire according to a particular sexuality. Thanks to the complex weaving of Decadent motifs, desire loses its moorings in heterosexuality. This is the argument, made most compelling by Laity with regard to the impact of Victorian Decadence on H.D.'s work, but which is also central to feminist rereadings of modernism in which H.D.'s writing plays a large part. Laity's particular contribution has been to show, through her exploration of H.D.'s debt to a discourse of male homosexuality, that we can't hold female modernism to an idea of female gender and sexuality that can be identified separately from the diverse sexualities and genders that emerge as a result of the several discourses operating at the period. Neither, I want to argue, can we isolate sex and gender from the effects of the Great War and its particular configuration of sexuality, gender, and English patriotism.

Although not explicitly about the war, H.D.'s 1916 collection registers these effects very strongly as both Friedman and Collecott have noted. "Loss," for example, its title marking the death toll of the war, is one of a handful of poems about battles. More important, H.D. registers the war in the treatment of the male body. The loss that the poem represents is not simply for the dead lover, but also for the unmarked body: "I am glad the tide swept you out,/O beloved,/you of all this ghastly host/alone untouched,/your white flesh covered with salt/as with myrrh and burnt iris." Repeatedly, through the poems of this collection, the body is torn or wounded: " I was splintered and torn," "pierced in the flank," "you dragged a bruised thigh." Even in poems about landscape, there is a pervasive rhetoric of destruction: H.D.'s flowers are "slashed and torn," "marred," and "broken," like the war-torn bodies.[45] As Laity argues, the "thematic of disruption and displacement" is linked to the eroticism of her verse, and to a Decadent poetics.[46] Paul Fussell notes, for example, that the homoerotic elegy on a dead boy was stylish well before the war in Uranian publications like *The Artist* and *Journal of Home Culture*, and *The Quorum: A Magazine of Friendship*.[47] In 1891,

Frederick Rolfe describes St. Sebastian as "bound to a tree,/His strong arms lifted up for sacrifice,/His gracious form all stripped of earthly guise,/Naked, but brave as a young lion can be,/Transfixed by arrows he gains the victory."[48] This sadomasochistic eroticism of the wounded male body in the verse of the 1890s has to contend by 1916 with traumatic imaginings of a kind reported by May Sinclair shortly before leaving for Belgium with an ambulance unit: "Every night before I went to sleep I saw an interminable spectacle of horrors: trunks without heads, heads without trunks, limbs tangled in intestines."[49] By looking at *Sea Garden* in this context, we can see that it is suspended between two impulses: the dismemberment of the perfect male body in the interests of an eroticism detached from heterosexuality, and the preservation of that body intact. *Sea Garden* is uncomfortably caught up with a perverse eroticisation of violence that is central to H.D.'s rejection of heterosexual norms, yet is also at odds with her critique of militarism and masculinity.[50]

We can see then that, like Hall, H.D.'s rendering of both sexual desire and aesthetic commitment through the poetics of Victorian Hellenism are complicated by the effects of the Great War. And, as with Hall, the impact of the war on her writing is linked for H.D. to a question of her modernity. Hall, I have suggested, abandons her attempt to write same-sex desire in the sapphic verse tradition when the war assimilates her use of a lost Eden, the island of Lesbos, to a discourse of English nationalism. Although she was intensely patriotic, the nostalgic structure present in both her verse and the trope of an English Eden destroyed by the war threatened to relegate the lesbian to the premodern, so that when Hall turns to fiction, we can see her struggling to align the lesbian with the modern images of the new woman and the invert. H.D.'s relationship to an idea of the modern is almost exactly opposite.

Whereas Hall needs the aura of the modern, H.D. struggles to escape it. As Laity has demonstrated, H.D. turns to Swinburne and the Decadents for a language that will resist and restructure the alignment of aesthetics and masculine heterosexuality that high modernism legislates. In doing so, H.D. looks back to a moment in the past that her fellow modernists Pound, Eliot, and Lewis are defining as most retrograde. Thus, it is not H.D.'s interest in the past per se that counts as a refusal of the modern; Pound, for example, praised her for being "as straight as the Greek."[51] Rather, H.D. breaks with high modernism when she aligns her work with the past that defined the modernist break, Victorian aestheticism. Her strategy allowed her, as we have seen, to open a space for the representation of perverse desire. But, as with Hall, the Great War interferes with H.D.'s turn to the past, complicating her sexual dissidence by making Beauty a term in her allegiance to an English patriotism that was a support for the war, as well as naming her reinscription of homoerotic Hellenism.

H.D. is a key figure in the feminist rewriting of modernism's history. Critics such as Laity, Rachel Blau Duplessis, Friedman, and many others analyze H.D's sexual and textual experimentation as part of the prehistory of contemporary feminism. For this reason, it is important that we also analyze the connections between her radical experimentation with poetics and sexuality and the rhetoric of English nationalism. Without such an analysis, the history of gender and sexuality remains sealed off from the history of nationalism so that we can continue to tell the same story of sexual and textual experimentation as inevitably and unchangingly progressive. Moreover, it is only by complicating this feminist version of the modernist equation between formal innovation and political progressiveness that we can move beyond an oversimplified picture of Radclyffe Hall's place in literary history, in which Hall's failure to be modernist becomes a failure to be modern. My somewhat perverse yoking of H.D. and Hall reverses the usual association of Hall with the old-fashioned and H.D. with the new as a function of their relationship to modernist aesthetics. I have argued instead that Hall's search for the proper form for the representation of early twentieth-century modes of sexuality is shaped more by the effects of the war than by modernism. The modernity of her forms in the years before and during the war is not yet necessarily defined by modernism, although it does involve a desire to be modern. H.D.'s version of the modern is specific to the configuration of aesthetics, sexuality, and gender in high modernism. The modern is thus not a fixed category to which these writers have a stable relationship. As a result, it is no longer useful to assess the relative merits of their sexual or formal dissidence. Instead, we need to understand both writers' engagement in the difficult negotiations between rhetorics of sexuality and rhetorics of the modern in the early twentieth century.

NOTES

1. Lovatt Dickson, *Radclyffe Hall at the Well of Loneliness: A Sapphic Chronicle* (New York: Scribner, 1975), 45.

2. Radclyffe Hall, *Songs of Three Counties & Other Poems*, with an introduction by R. B. Cunninghame-Graham (London: Chapman & Hall, 1913), 32.

3. Review of *Songs of Three Counties & Other Poems*, by Radclyffe Hall, *Times*, February 27, 1913.

4. Radclyffe Hall, *The Forgotten Island* (London: Chapman & Hall, 1915).

5. See Diana Souhami, *The Trials of Radclyffe Hall* (London: Virago, 1999), 60.

6. Michael Baker, *Our Three Selves: The Life of Radclyffe Hall* (New York: Morrow, 1985), 57; Dickson, *Radclyffe Hall at the Well of Loneliness*, 44–45.

7. Osbert Sitwell, *Who Killed Cockrobin?* quoted in Kathryn Ledbetter, "Battles for Modernism and Wheels," *Journal of Modern Literature*, 19, 2 (Fall 1995): 324.

8. Radclyffe Hall, *A Sheaf of Verses: Poems* (London: John & Edward Bumpus, 1908), 36–38.

9. Baker, *Our Three Selves*, 57–58.

10. The Georgians reacted against the poetics of the 1890s, for example, the decadents, emphasizing clear diction and the experience behind the poem, rather than an aesthetic of "art for art's sake." Between 1912 and 1922, they published five anthologies under the editorship first of Edward Marsh and then of J. C. Squire. In the immediate prewar period, their work represented the most modern developments in poetry for the majority of their English contemporaries.

11. Harold Monroe, *Some Contemporary Poets*, quoted in Robert H. Ross, *The Georgian Revolt, 1910–1922* (Carbondale: Southern Illinois University Press, 1965), 14.

12. Review of *Poems of the Past and Present*, by Radclyffe Hall, *Scotsman*, October 13, 1910.

13. H.D., *Sea Garden* (London: Constable, 1916). All quotations derive from the 1984 edition of *The Collected Poems, 1912–1944* (New York: New Directions, 1984).

14. Hall, *Forgotten Island*, 9.

15. Review of *A Sheaf of Verses*, by Marguerite Radclyffe Hall, extracted in Hall, *Songs*, 1913, 56.

16. Yopie Prins, *Victorian Sappho* (Princeton: Princeton University Press, 1999), 14.

17. Thaïs E. Morgan, "Reimagining Masculinity in Victorian Criticism: Swinburne and Pater," in *Sexualities in Victorian Britain*, ed. Andrew H. Miller and James Eli Adams (Bloomington: Indiana University Press, 1996), 141.

18. Souhami, *Trials of Radclyffe Hall*, 60. Subsequent citations of Souhami are given parenthetically in the text.

19. By contrast with Hall's sapphic poetry, the first edition of Hall's *The Well of Loneliness* was contextualized via Havelock Ellis's prefatory comments. Sexology rather than literary sapphism provided it with a frame.

20. Hall, *Forgotten Island*, 7.

21. Ibid., 31, 59, 65.

22. Gillian Beer, "The Island and the Aeroplane: The Case of Virginia Woolf," in *Nation and Narration*, ed. Homi K. Bhabha (New York: Routledge, 1990), 270.

23. Richard II, 2.1.40–42, in *The Riverside Shakespeare* (Boston: Houghton Mifflin, 1974).

24. Beer, "*The Island and the Aeroplane*," 266.

25. H. E. Marshall, *Our Island Story: A Child's History of England*, with pictures by A. S. Forrest (London: T. C. & E. C. Jack, 1905).

26. See, e.g., Ford Madox Ford [Hueffer, pseud.], *Between St. Dennis and St. George: A Sketch of Three Civilisations* (London: Hodder & Stoughton, 1915), 60; Quidnunc, "The New Elements of Sea Power," *English Review* 25 (July 1917) 47; "Europe in Arms," *Times*, August 1, 1914, 9.

27. Quidnunc, *"New Elements of Sea Power,"* 46, 49.

28. Rebecca West, *Return of the Soldier* (London: Virago, 1984), 77.

29. Radclyffe Hall, "Miss Ogilvy Finds Herself" (1934), in *The Norton Anthology of Literature by Women*, ed. Sandra M. Gilbert and Susan Gubar, 2d ed. (New York: Norton, 1996), 1395–1407.

30. I have argued in Claire Buck "Some Obstinate Emotion," in *Women's Fiction and the Great War*, ed. Suzanne Raitt and Trudi Taitt (Oxford: Clarendon Press, 1997) 174–196, that the complicated temporalities of Hall's short story are a response to the bitter experience of patriotism's hierarchies.

31. Ledbetter, "Battles for Modernism and Wheels," 324.

32. Laura Doan, "The Lesbian in Modernity" (paper presented at the New Modernisms Conference, Penn State., October 9, 1999).

33. Robert Graves and Laura Jackson Riding, *A Pamphlet Against Anthologies* (Garden City, N.Y: Doubleday, Doran, 1928).

34. Cassandra Laity, *H.D. and the Victorian Fin de Siècle: Gender, Modernism, Decadence* (Cambridge: Cambridge University Press, 1996), xi. See also Diana Collecott, *H.D. and Sapphic Modernism* (Cambridge: Cambridge University Press, 2000).

35. Ezra Pound, "The Caressability of the Greeks," letter to the editor, *Egoist* 1, 6 (March 16, 1914): 117.

36. Gary Burnett, "H.D.'s Responses to the First World War," *Agenda* 25, 3–4 (1987–88): 54–63.

37. H.D., "Responsibilities" (Review of W. B. Yeats's *Responsibilities*, ca.1914), *Agenda* 25, 3–4 (1987–88): 51–53. Reprinted in *The Gender of Modernism: A Critical Anthology*, ed. Bonnie Kime Scott (Bloomington: Indiana University Press, 1990), 127–29.

38. H.D., "Marianne Moore," *Egoist* 3, 8 (August 1916): 118.

39. Susan Stanford Friedman, *Penelope's Web: Gender, Modernity, H.D.'s Fiction* (New York: Cambridge University Press, 1990).

40. H.D., "Marianne Moore," 119.

41. See Linda Dowling, *Hellenism and Homosexuality in Victorian Oxford* (Ithaca, N.Y.: Cornell University Press, 1994), xv.

42. Laity, *H.D. and the Victorian Fin de Siècle*, 42.

43. H.D., *Collected Poems, 1912–1944* (New York: New Directions, 1984), 20, 21, 25; Algernon Charles Swinburne, *Poems and Ballads. Second Series* (London: Chatto & Windus, 1882), 29.

44. H.D., *Collected Poems*, 13, 23.

45. Ibid., 22, 27, 22, 12, 14, 5, 36.

46. Laity, *H.D. and the Victorian Fin de Siècle*, 44.

47. Paul Fussell, *The Great War and Modern Memory* (Oxford: Oxford University Press, 1977), 283.

48. Ibid., 285.

49. May Sinclair, *A Journal of Impressions in Belgium* (London: Hutchinson; New York: Macmillan, 1915), 8.

50. The homoerotic and the martial are already connected in Victorian Hellenism. See, Dowling, *Hellenism and Homosexuality in Victorian Oxford*, 32–66.

51. Ezra Pound, *The Letters of Ezra Pound*, 1907–1941, ed. D. D. Paige (New York: Harcourt Brace & World, 1950), 11.

The Heir Unapparent

Opal Whiteley and the Female as Child in America

The child study movement, that peculiarly American endeavor flourishing around 1900 and committed to the "science of the child,"[1] treated
its young specimens as objects whose bodies and minds, play and
pathologies, were under so exhaustive a surveillance that the movement made
Bronson Alcott's probing of his daughters' journals seem genially unobtrusive.
The new paedology, with its charts and graphs on male and female characteristics, remained as preoccupied with the distinction between men and women
as with that between boys and girls. Taking their cue from Franz Boas, Cesare
Lombroso, and Havelock Ellis, paedologists like A. F. Chamberlain in his important work *The Child* (1900) and G. Stanley Hall in his two-volume *Adolescence* (1904) constructed the woman as perennially "childlike." Such studies
mapped the woman's anatomy as a constellation of childish parts and expressions, from her "scattered" exercise of "abstract thought" to her gift for "ruse."[2]
According to the logic of the prevailing "recapitulation theory," which detected
in the stages of individual human development the more spacious epochs of
the race, the female became the modern version of the primitive, a repository
of "affectability" on the one hand and tribal "conservatism" on the other.[3]

Because the female was for sexology a diathesis, enfolding the child in the
adult, and the ancient in the modern, she was perceived more and more as
an alluring surface upon which others could discern both their individual
and their cultural beginnings. Along with Lombroso and Paul Topinard, Ellis
went so far as to connect female identity with that of the male genius, who
was considered similarly "child-like" in his physiology and psychology.[4] And
Chamberlain even mused that the female might serve a special function in her

capacity to mirror back to men in particular the prodigiousness of a vanished childhood: "Nature in fact seems to have made woman somewhat like the child in order that, in growing up, man might not depart too far from the original model."[5] Femininity was fast being implicated in the shift in the adult's perception of the child which occurred around 1900, when, as Gary Cross explains, "American children were beginning to serve more the psychological than the economic needs of adults."[6] As nature's contribution to national primordial therapy, the woman's story became a form of bioevolutionary nostalgia. Hall·likened it to the "embryology of the soul."[7] In linking the woman to the vitality of origins, the child study movement began to reconcile the atavistic character of the female with her role in the future. She remained a generic everychild who, spanning continents, races, and time, possessed the "power of strengthening manhood."[8]

Yet the woman's role as "the racial type" permitted her spectators to rush not only backward into the mists of memory, but also forward toward a more nuanced modernity. While child study discerned a certain stability in the role of woman as supreme child, that belief coexisted with an equal investment in woman as the avatar of evolution. Ellis, especially, exploited the association of woman, child, and the future of the race. Because, he reasoned, the genius represented the "highest human types," and woman resembled the genius in her facial expression and temperament, she thus typified civilized advancement as much as she did the lure of origins. If the female "represents the human type to which man is approximating," and if, as Herbert Spencer argued, woman was "undeveloped man," then certainly men were also "undeveloped women," Ellis concluded.[9] In his interpretation of Ellis, Chamberlain envisioned "feminization" as "'one of the marked tendencies of our modern, complex civilization.'" As the "race type" of the future, not just the past, woman was "already shaping man in her image."[10]

What was routinely diagnosed as the female's "precocious" development, then, became humanity's precocious destiny. Yet that precocity, albeit a type of the race's betterment, also carried the taint of a physiological and psychological instability. Perhaps the clues to the ambivalence toward female modernity lay coiled up in Lombroso's treatment of the woman as genius, for in his hands, the identification became only an apparent compliment. To Lombroso, the female and genius were equally open to suspicions of degeneracy, to an apprehension that such idiosyncratic types might dispel the promise of American exceptionalism.[11] At the same time that "feminization" signaled civilization, its complexity also denied the female's role as an unswerving icon of American destiny. Hall wrote that the woman was "a half way between" whose desire never anchored in its object. Too often, her subjectivity expressed itself as a seismic split "between the life preferred and . . . the race."[12] She became the exemplar, not just of the "highest" humanity, but of the looming dangers of modernity, of that "caprice" in which analysts still imagined the girl, genius, and child convened. The romantic American narrative of the child was thus ironically haunted by modern anxieties about the "New Woman," a figure who threatened to derail national expectations with an unreadable ambiguity,[13] and functioned as an opaque sign against which the transparency of capitalist manhood defined itself.

Even after the blight of World War I, the hopeful gusto of centennialist rhetoric in child study hardly dissipated into its more aloof scientizing impulses. In fact, the insistence on the female's proximity to the child got plaintively amplified into a democratic salvo. In the March 1922 issue of the *Pedagogical Seminary*, child study's major magazine, Raymond Fuller asserted that "'the child and the woman are the . . . representations of what is best in the race.'" When Fuller endorsed those who called the twentieth century the "'Century of the Child,'" and America the "'Nation of the Child,'"[14] he placed both century and nation under a female aegis. Even as postwar paedologists reeled off the manifestations of hysteria in schoolgirls, their heuristic inquiry still served the ache of romantic yearning.

Opal Whiteley and the Primordial Sophisticate

In light of her resistance to a steadfast allegory of American progress, what was a girl to do? Was there a version of the female that might resolve, if only temporarily, the contradictory articulations of child study? The answer, though hardly simple, lies partially in one of the most overlooked bestsellers of the American twentieth century. In 1920, while the nation was purchasing diminished expectations in Sinclair Lewis's wildly popular *Main Street*, it also savored the twenty-two-year-old Opal Whiteley's publication of her childhood diary, *The Story of Opal: The Journal of an Understanding Heart*, a supposed six- to seven-year-old's idyll of rapt communion with animals and plants in the woods outside a logging camp in Cottage Grove, Oregon. In one year, the book, selling 15,000 copies, surged through three editions, though its editor Ellery Sedgwick discontinued its publication the next year when rumors spread that it might be a hoax.

Traveling to Boston at the age of twenty-two in 1919, Opal Whiteley had first appeared in the office of the *Atlantic Monthly* with a book called *The Fairyland Around Us*, self-published in 1918.[15] Sedgwick rejected this work because he claimed that it was an amateurish conglomeration of pictures and words too childish for publication. And yet, though the book's pictures were indeed cut-outs from other works, the writing was clearly that of an educated adult who had created a biological fantasy suspended between scientific classification and the memories of a girlishly mystified Oregon nature. For the market-wise Sedgwick, however, it was not really the unversed girl who compromised the adult's refinement, but the adult who somehow diluted the child's appeal. He appeared to want a girl's perspective that had not been refracted through adult consciousness at all, for it was not the girl in the woman that was fetching English and American audiences, but the girl herself, some marketable distillation of the adult female into her childlike quiddity. Sedgwick had witnessed the un-paralleled success of the "Young Visiters" series of books written by a coterie of child prodigies after World War I, the most prominent of whom were the British writer Daisy Ashford, who published an eccentric narrative called *The Young Visiters* (1920) about social rituals among the nobility she claimed to have written as a nine-year-old, and the American girl-poet Hilda Conkling, who in *Poems by a Little Girl* (1920) described nature in order to beat a moody retreat to primeval origins. Although the series included some boys, it gener-ally precipitated a girl prodigy craze by keeping the muddled desires of wom-anhood at bay and offering a notion of female genius untainted by modern "degeneracy." Sedgwick preferred a diary Opal tearfully claimed she had writ-ten between the ages of six and twelve and that a sister had ripped apart.[16] Sending for the box of fragments in Opal's residence in Los Angeles, he dis-covered not only that the handwriting and spelling looked like that of a young girl, but also that its very language displayed a paradoxical genius that made its author both a primitive seer and high culture's protector. After Opal arduously pasted the pieces together in the *Atlantic*'s office for a secretary to type, Sedg-wick might have thought he had witnessed the merger of Daisy Ashford's cul-tural and Hilda Conkling's primitivist precocity.[17] The poor logging girl had written the text in block letters with crayons on the backs of butcher-bags, bark, and envelopes, its words unseparated from one another. Yet the crudity of the scrawl housed a variety of languages—which included American dialect, French, English fractured by French idioms, King James archaisms, and Latin liturgy—that oddly gentrified her. In her "Introduction," the adult author gave such erudition a false genealogy by claiming that she had once been "la petite Françoise," daughter of a royal French couple whom she called her "Angel parents"—the real-life Bourbon, Henri Philippe Marie, prince d'Orléans (1867-1901), a famous French naturalist, and his wife[18]—but was kidnapped at the age of five after their deaths and transplanted to the Pacific Northwest, where the American Whiteleys renamed her Opal and consigned her to labor.[19]

The diary's extraordinary accomplishment resides in its presentation of the female as child-primitive and civilized prototype while also healing any apprehensions growing out of this paradox. Indeed, it seemed to coax into synthesis the optimal attributes of child study's "diathesis" while keeping the threats of both a dangerous primitivism and an untoward modernity firmly at bay. In one sense, Opal was certainly the archaic child-mirror held up for regenerative viewing. Because the diary was ostensibly written by a rural villager, it was spatially sequestered from the urban market, where too many girls had materialized into women, "New" or otherwise, and it was temporally removed from its readership because it was purportedly written by a girl. Opal fulfilled the role of child as a tool for adult maintenance because she represented the "as yet unexplained mystery of part of the child's early life."[20] As if in a countermove against the oppression of American time, the book shattered the traditional temporal organization of the diary by refusing to date its entries. Instead, it presented an inventory of chores only so that they might be redeemed from the context of labor into the imperium of the child's "explores." Constructing herself as an original speaker who coined neologisms, held sway over reproduction, understood plants and animals in a way that predated formal scientific education, and talked to the shadows and winds in their own language, Opal easily converged with the male genius who was the woman's alter ego. Even the photographs of Opal were ones in which she assumed what others invariably called a "fluttering" childlike expression and the demeanor of a nature prodigy on whose fingers butterflies alit.[21] Those readers sighting femininity in the diary as the gifted locus of childhood included not just women but the very class of men who, as Chamberlain theorized, longed to see their early genius grinning back at them. Opal's audience included, among so many others, the British foreign secretary, Lord Edward Grey; Lords Raleigh and Curzon; and the U.S. attorney general.

This frontier *savante*, however, had a decidedly sophisticated bent; and the familiar formulation of a primitive genius spontaneously shaping her utterances into a unique vocabulary got radically redefined. Though the diary followed the primitive's belief in the word's "real existence,"[22] Opal's literalism, more a feat of recovery than discovery, was not entirely grounded in the organic discourse imagined by Rousseau as the child uttering nature as it utters itself.[23] When Opal corrects her teacher, her linguistic innocence is bound up with the very erudition from which the untutored yearling is traditionally exiled: "She did ask me what is a pig and a mouse and a baby deer and a duck. . . . And I did say in a real quick way, 'A pig is a *cochon* and a mouse is a *mulot* and a baby deer is a *daine* and a duck is a *canard*.' . . . [The] teacher did shake her head and say, '*It is not*,' and I did say, '*It is*.'"[24] Opal paradoxically elaborates her primitive literalism through a French lexicon that seems to arrive fully formed and self-explanatory. Repeated in her usual trinitarian litany, and omitting, after the first series, the italics for the French, the response makes her tongue the universal language, and American English the fallen anomaly. Because her Angel Father's French is "what things are" (114), it expresses the submerged continuum between saying and being.

In capacious French inventories of birds, flowers, and rivers, the diary compounds its biological wisdom. Through an ur-language richly packed with cultural signification, Opal suggests that at the word's beginnings is civilization, a compendium of classical, religious, and transglobal luminati. She calls her pet crow "Lars Porsena of Clusium"; a fir tree, "Michael Angelo Sanzio Raphael"; a calf, "Mathilde Plantagenet"; a mouse, "Nannerl Mozart" (87–91). She chants the Angelus and Ave Maria in triplicate to beribboned animals in her hospital's nursery at "Saint-Germaine-en-Laye"; sings them French lullabies; and arranges crops to memorialize the "borning days" and "dying days" of luminaries like "Saint François of Assisi," whose "years were near unto forty-four" (122). When Opal names her dirty woodrat "Thomas Chatterton Jupiter Zeus" (120), she suggests that, at its source, nature and the diverse spectrum of accumulated knowledge are bizarrely reconciled, that mythology can open itself to English plagiarism. In 1918 she had surreally pictorialized this apparent oxymoron of primordial sophisticate on the frontispiece of *The Fairyland*, in which a teenaged Opal, roughly clad, barefoot, covered by long ringlets of hair, plays the violin as she stands in a circle of leaves (fig. 5.1). Opal's diary unraveled the masculine democratic liberalism behind the boys' books written since the 1870s; while deeply invested in Huck Finn's affinity with nature, for example, the diary perpetuated the very European heresy that Twain's novels contemptuously satirized. Its defiance lay in nothing less than the colonization of America for France, that European context from which logging girls seemed hopelessly

FIG. 5.1. Opal Whiteley playing the violin. Frontispiece to *The Fairy-land Around Us* (self-published by Opal Whiteley, 1918). Oregon Historical Society #OrHi 102314. Courtesy Oregon Historical Society.

banished. As Opal's account of her clandestine smuggling out of France suggests, to be an American girl entailed a kidnapping from the home of culture.

Who Has Begot Your Tongue? The Defense of Genteel Childhood

If the diary somehow managed to portray its author's heroism as the san-
guine meeting of natural and cultural genius, it fetched its readers' admiration
all the more because of its romantic narrative about her struggle to maintain
that primordial sophistication in a hostile America. Opal claimed that her illiterate foster parents Lizzie and Ed Whiteley tried to repress her genius. She
distinguishes between her French "Angel parents" and the Oregon clan, whom
she reduces to "the mamma," "the papa," the "other girl" (her sister), and "the
baby." Their two-room shack in the logging camp is the "house we do live in"
(93), a reifying epithet that refuses the sentimental transubstantiation of heavenly home and suggests her alienation from Oregon through a foreign syntax.
By divesting the Whiteleys of the possessive, she ensures that they, and not the
indentured girl, take their impersonal place among household objects.

The diary's family romance does not just split the parental presence into
Angelic and coldly inanimate; it expresses the relation between these two families as a break between language and body. The "mamma," circumscribed in
the unrelieved domesticity of washing, sewing, and agricultural production, is
the American marker of labor who dispenses Opal's chores and beats her when
she departs from her literal instructions. Her personality is largely felt through
its effects, the "aches" and "sore feels" on Opal's body. The Angel Mother, on
the other hand, merges maternity and knowledge. Opal claims that the Angel
Mother once engaged her daughter through an ideal pedagogical discipline of
reading, writing, and recitation, which exists outside the fierce exertions or
punishments of a laboring body. Though the Angel parents resist a loving corporeality, their very abstractness now allows their daughter to keep their presence intact, making of them an endless, if deferred, site for her desire and enabling her to engage them just by reading or spelling out the discourse they
wrote for her before they died.

From the diary's beginning, the distinction between the two families is made
manifest in diametrically opposed relations to language. In a protracted strategy of word-rescue, Opal defends the priority of Angel-speak against American
usurpers. The diary readily translates even moral distinctions between good

and evil, secular and saintly, into terms of literacy and illiteracy. In their library's rows of books, the Bourbons possessed language as the Whiteleys, ignorant laborers shoving their besmirched practical books to the top of the cupboard, do not. The Bourbon language entails a complex dual legacy. The Angel parents disseminate a lush high culture, a heterodox vocabulary of classical mythology, Catholicism, and pan-aestheticism that nods to figures as diverse as Aphrodite, Savonarola, "Geoffroi Chaucer," and Elizabeth Barrett Browning; yet it also contains a dense vocabulary of rivers, flora, and fauna. Theirs is a cosmological literacy through which they decipher the natural elements' voices and understand the language of the "shadows" to which the Whiteleys are deaf. They teach Opal both to name her menagerie after cultural celebrities and to litanize it into Catholic ritual, thereby healing the breach between nature and civilization that America represents. In designating as her real father Henri d'Orléans, an actual natural historian who explored India and Indonesia, she ensures that the wilderness and civilization are held in regal equipoise and enshrined in a historical referent.

In the "Introduction," Opal images the private event of her French family's writing as a verbal mutuality that enacts the give-and-take of nurture itself. As the older author recasts such moments, the knit between the Parents' and child's words begins to resemble a morphic bonding. After her Parents write lessons for her in several notebooks, Opal copies those inscriptions word for word and utters them back to them. Maternal attentiveness, especially, is configured not through caresses but along verbal lines, for Opal and her mother once "listened together" (37) as a single ear to nature's dialect. The lexical stroll begun in the French countryside comes full circle in the diary itself, as Opal now assumes the maternal role in the primal pedagogical moments with her infantilized Oregon "folk," who are acculturated into Angel discourse. Like her first Parents, Opal preaches her text but listens, ear firmly to the ground, to the utterances of crops, animals, and insects about their genealogy in the soil.

In the diary, Opal projects her Angel parents into the verbal traces of two notebooks, which she conceals from her Oregon elders in a sliding box-drawer, her own covenantal ark. The reduction of the original notebooks at their estate to *two* in America enhances the notion that the pair of remaining books stands as a Parental dyad, though each journal is not exclusively the gendered province of either mother or father. With these books kept cautiously in her possession, her Angel Parents' traces sealed in words—recited to others, obsessively rewritten in the diary—Opal makes French America's Parent tongue. Other exercises, buried within several sections of the book, hint that the Angel parents not only prescribe the verbal logic that pulls nature and civilization into unison, but are themselves prescribed by it. As attentive readers discerned, the repetition of certain names in various lists formed acrostical patterns. In one the first letters of rivers roughly spell out HENRI D'ORLEANS, and other songs about birds and flowers carry the names and birthdays of his relations, as if the diary bore a linguistic unconscious that Opal inscribes while least suspecting it.

Lizzie Whiteley's sinister function in this allegedly autobiographical narrative is to block the transmission of Angel language and to reconnect it, as if it were sin, to postlapsarian physical toil. Opal must awkwardly scribble her diary in secret at home, hunched over her desk at school, or in the secrecy of the woods. Yet Opal's heroic retrieval of a privileged language from the onus of labor is no blushing rite of female self-abnegation. Overcoming the friction between two parental regimes, she stands up Lizzie's kitchen woodsticks as trees and names them the "foret[s] de Chantilly" and "Ermenonville" and floods the floor of this diorama with dipper water to form the "Nonette," "Lounette," and "Aunette" rivers (136). This gestalt of conversion and conquest informs the entire diary. "Today. . . . [t]he mamma dyed," Opal sinisterly comments (242), after watching Lizzie dye her domestic implements, and she commemorates the "borning days" of notebook figures like "Saint Louis II" and Torquato Tasso. She thereby not only consigns Lizzie to an early figurative death; she kills off American drudgery with Angel ceremony, reclaiming nature for the estate of culture.

The Confidence Author as Girl

Although Opal delights in her dependence on the Muses of Europe, she chooses a family whose identity rests so abstractly in the names of French cartography, ancestry, and natural data that her alternative history becomes but the dream of nominology, the preference of utterance over experience. To consider Opal's girlish *Walden* history articulated but unlived, however, is to undermine the success with which she converted the hybrid role of wilderness naïf and cultural defender into that of professional author. By envisioning, within the diary's pages, a future career in natural history, and by carrying that design out in its publication, Opal assured her girl's play an urban truck in London, Boston, and New York. Even her mongrel Opalese was quoted in newspapers here and abroad—mystical proof that the Angel parents survived in the will to reinscribe them. First appearing in installments in the *Atlantic Monthly*, whose subscription list multiplied vastly, the narrative of lost gentility had ironically restored it, lifting its author close to the enclaves of privilege she claimed had always been her rightful home.[25] Having falsely advertised *The Fairyland* with blurbs from Teddy Roosevelt and Elizabeth of Austria, Opal now had actual celebrities in her thrall.

Yet the story of Opal's diary is also about its failure to sustain the myth of female authorial entitlement. Both the writing and marketing of the diary turned on the spectacle of prodigious innocence. The discovery that Opal's parents were probably not the Bourbons rankled the public; still more threatening to the book's longevity was the skepticism over whether its author was an ingenious *child*. The prospect of a yearling hoax, the impersonation of a natural innocent, seemed a heretical contradiction in terms. The reviews after the doubts emerged reflect the outrage of a public that felt it had glimpsed the nature child of Jewett's "The White Heron" winking knowingly at them. The audience returned the book in droves. This furor of abandonment suggests how entrenched the female remained in child study's contradictory narrative: once the woman as primordial child, Opal was now Hall's volatile adult modern. In terms of the debate over the female as "genius," she was no longer the primitive mirroring back to enervated Americans their prodigious origins, but Lombroso's "degenerate," bridling against stable femininity and the race's "aims." Yet there were no other categories that could encompass the woman whose genius lay precisely in the authoring of genius itself.

Skeptical journalists like Ellery Bede and intrepid supporters followed the assumption that it was child authorship that preserved the book's authenticity.[26] Angrily contradicting Bede decades later, Benjamin Hoff, in his 1986 and 1994 editions of the diary, vigorously argued that Opal was six when she wrote the diary and was thus a "real" author. Hoff cited several species of evidence to show that the diary was written by a girl around 1905. But supporter and avenger unconsciously collaborated in the same literalism. For Hoff, as for the unvenerable Bede, Opal's authenticity was commensurate with childhood giftedness. Despite his valid criticism of Bede for not perusing original documents, Hoff tended to divert the reader's attention from Opal's swerves from literal fact in order to keep his prodigy from becoming prodigal.

Dr. Françoise, I Presume? Opal Claims Her Inheritance

It is in the author's post-publication experience that we most closely glimpse the remarkable extent to which Opal's Angelic fantasy seems to effect its own partial realization. Opal's self-imposed exile to Britain in 1923 literalized the diary's fetish for what she called her "explores" in the Oregon woods. Because of the book's fame, Henri d'Orléans's real mother Marguerite took Opal to her own English estate and seemed to toy with the possibility that this *faux* transmitter of Henri's majesty still possessed some ineffable claim to him. She financed Opal's trip to India in order to determine how her son had died. Opal's adventures there seemed progressively (or regressively) to follow the paternal footsteps. Reconstituting Henri through an emulation of his dual status as learned royal and pathfinder of nature, she traveled 9,000 miles by train, camel, and elephant and was welcomed by Udaipur's maharana as "Françoise d'Orle" and feted by the Bengal Lancers.[27] She both embarked on tiger hunts, which Henri had famously enjoyed, and planned her own book on nature. Opal's Udaipur here somewhat resembled that in Henri d'Orléans's *From Tonkin to India* (1898),[28] as if she wrote in filial paraphrase. Sending accounts to England's *The Queen*, she invariably compels us to inquire whether her supposed gentility spawned her representations, or vice versa.[29] By the time she returned to England, she had advertised herself as the love child of Henri and an Indian and now emerged as "The Princess of India." The flutter of ancestral fantasy was pinned down in exotic history.

With Princess Marguerite d'Orléans's death in 1925, Opal's rejection by the remaining members of the house of Bourbon-Orléans led to a desperate search for the mere material rudiments of printed identity she thought would verify her heritage. Observers spotted her in a basement flat in London with over 15,000 books, and later, in World War II, foraging among the blasted ruins for others. The lexical intimacy with Angel parents was now reduced to the bibliophile's stacks and piles. Opal was incarcerated in England's Napsbury Hospital for schizophrenia from 1948 until her death in 1992 at the age of ninety-four. In that ultimate "house we do live in," she achieved the "second childhood" that mocked her prodigious girlhood.

NOTES

1. A. D. Cromwell, *Practical Child Study* (Chicago: W. M. Welch, 1895), 7.

2. See Alexander F. Chamberlain, *The Child: Study in the Evolution of Man* (New York: Scribner, 1900), 418–23; and G. Stanley Hall, *Adolescence: Its Psychology and Its Relations to Physiology, Anthropology, Sociology, Sex, Crime, Religion, and Education*, 2 vols. (New York: D. Appleton, 1904).

3. Havelock Ellis, *Man and Woman: A Study of Human Secondary Sexual Characteristics* (London: Walter Scott, 1904), 297–315.

4. Ibid., 392.

5. Chamberlain, *Child*, 445.

6. Gary Cross, *Kid's Stuff: Toys and the Changing World of American Childhood* (Cambridge, Mass.: Harvard University Press, 1997), 85.

7. G. Stanley Hall, "Life and Confessions of a Psychologist," as quoted in John Cleverly and D. C. Phillips, *Visions of Childhood: Influential Models from Locke to Spock* (New York: Teachers College Press, 1986, 1976), 50.

8. Child study advocates concluded that the average woman was the transracial and transhistorical model. See Chamberlain, *Child*, 445.

9. Ellis, *Man and Woman*, 390–92.

10. Chamberlain, *Child*, 417.

11. See Bill Brown's important work on boy's play, *The Material Unconscious: American Amusement, Stephen Crane and the Economics of Play* (Cambridge, Mass.: Harvard University Press, 1996), 175–77.

12. Hall, *Adolescence*, 392.

13. See Brown, *Material Unconscious*, 175–77.

14. Raymond G. Fuller, "Child Labor and Child Nature," *Pedagogical Seminary* 29 (March 1922): 64–71.

15. Opal Stanley Whiteley, *The Fairyland Around Us*, Pr. Opal Stanley Whiteley (Los Angeles: Sunset Bindery, 1918).

16. Opal later said that it was not her sister Pearl who tore the diary apart, but a friend. For information about the controversy surrounding the diary, see especially Elmore Bede, *The Fabulous Opal Whitely: From Oregon Logging Camp to Princess in India* (Portland: Binsfords & Mort, 1954), 15–160, and *The Singing Creek Where the Willows Grow: The Rediscovered Diary of Opal Whiteley*, ed. Benjamin Hoff (New York: Ticknor & Fields, 1986), *foreword*, 6–18.

17. See, among these authors' many other works, Ashford's *Daisy Ashford: Her Book* (New York: George H. Doran, 1920) and Conkling's *Poems by a Little Girl* (New York: Frederick A. Stokes, 1920).

18. Henri was not known to have married, and Opal's accounts about the identity of her mother vary.

19. Opal was born in Colton, Washington State, December 11, 1897.

20. See *Outlook* 126 (September 29, 1920): 201.

21. See the photograph of Opal advertising her Oregon Nature Lecture, *Singing Creek*, ed. Hoff, 24.

22. Chamberlain, *Child*, 30.

23. Jean-Jacques Rousseau, *Discours sur l'origine et les fondements de l'inégalité parmi les hommes* in *Oeuvres complètes*, vol. 3 (Paris: Gallimard, 1966), 149–50.

24. Benjamin Hoff, ed., *The Singing Creek Where the Willows Grow: The Mystical Nature Diary of Opal Whitely* (New York: Penguin Books, 1995), 113. Subsequent citations of this source are given parenthetically in the text.

25. See "A Child of Seven is Hailed as a Great Writer" in *Current Opinion* 69 (November 1920): 692, and "The Quarrel over Opal," *Literary Digest* 67 (October 30, 1920): 34–35.

26. Ellery Bede's book on Opal is a protracted argument against Opal's child-authorship, yet even Bede, despite his fairly convincing proof that Opal did not write the book at six or seven, entertains the possibility that she wrote sections of it as an adolescent and in a series of notebooks while she was a freshman at University of Oregon. He also grants the book its romantic authenticity. See Ellery Bede, *Fabulous Opal Whiteley: From Oregon Lumbering Camp to Princess in India* (Portland: Binsford & Mort, 1954). For Benjamin Hoff's arguments against Bede, see *Singing Creek*, ed. Hoff, 47–61.

27. For the New York musicals, books, and parks based on the diary, see Jane Boulton, *Opal: The Journal of an Understanding Heart* (New York: Crown, 1984), 186.

28. *Prince Henri d'Orléans, From Tonkin to India by the Sources of the Irawadi, January '95–January '96*, trans. Hamley Bent (London : Methuen, 1898).

29. In 1929, a book Opal had written about the maharana began serialization in *The Queen* under the title *The Story of Unknown India*. See *Singing Creek*, ed. Hoff, 64–65.

Part II ∾ *Outside the Metropolis*

In-Between Modernity

Toru Dutt (1856–1877) from a Postcolonial Perspective

This chapter begins with an elaboration of Homi Bhabha's concept of "time-lag" in order to develop a postcolonial perspective on modernity, specifically, its "occurrence" in the colonies (in this case, India) in the body of work produced by the poet and translator Toru Dutt.[1] In his influential essay " 'Race,' Time and the Revision of Modernity" (the concluding chapter to his book *The Location of Culture*), Bhabha inflects modern and postmodern thought postcolonially, clearing the way for a better account of subaltern agencies within modernity, those who are "overlooked" in both senses of the word, policed yet disavowed: "women, the colonized, minority groups, the bearers of policed sexualities."[2] He takes as his starting point the poignant essay "The Fact of Blackness" by Frantz Fanon, the psychiatrist and revolutionary from Martinique, and, within it, those lines in which Fanon assumes the alienating tone of a white man: "*You come too late, much too late, there will always be a world—a white world between you and us*" (237; Bhabha's emphasis). In such a way is the temporality of modernity signified by the *belatedness* of the black man, Bhabha suggests, that Man emerges as not a universal but a *historical* entity. What is enacted between *you and us* is an enunciative space that is beyond the past (of the black man with the white man as his future), beyond the minor term of an oppositional dialectic.

This space signifies a pause, what Bhabha calls a "temporal caesura," a "time-lag" (237). Bhabha has already alluded to such liminal, in-between moments—within time but beyond time—in, for instance, his introduction to *The Location of Culture*. Discussing the African American artist Renée Green's use of museum architecture to break down binaries of black and white, to de-essentialize ethnic identity, he writes: "Social differences are not simply given to experience through an already authenticated cultural tradition; they are the signs of the emergence of community envisaged as a project—that takes you 'beyond' yourself in order to return, in a spirit of revision and reconstruction, to the political *conditions* of the present" (3; emphasis in original). In her work *Sites of Genealogy* (Out of Site, Institute of Contemporary Art, Long Island City, N.Y.), Green uses the physical architecture of the museum to suggest metaphors of cultural difference. In particular, she uses the stairwell as a liminal, in-between space, of which Bhabha comments: "The hither and thither of the stairwell, the *temporal* movement and passage that it allows, prevents identities at either end of it from settling into primordial polarities. This interstitial passage between fixed identifications opens up the possibility of a cultural hybridity that entertains difference without an assumed or imposed hierarchy" (4; my emphasis). It is this *temporality* implicit in the workings of modernity that Bhabha feels is so missing in the *spatial* Eurocentric accounts of modernity provided by Michel Foucault and Benedict Anderson. Turning again to his introductory essay:

"Beyond" signifies spatial distance, marks progress, promises the future; but our intimations of exceeding the barrier or boundary—the very act of going *beyond*—are unknowable, unrepresentable, without a return to the "present" which, in the process of repetition, becomes disjunct and displaced. . . . The present can no longer be simply envisaged as a break or a bonding with the past and the future, no longer a synchronic presence: our proximate self-presence, our public image, comes to be revealed for its discontinuities, its inequalities, its minorities. (4)

What makes articulations of modernity (not to mention postmodernity) so problematic for Bhabha is that, for the most part, they deploy spatial metaphors for this act of going beyond, neglecting the temporally conceived pauses or time-lags that fall between modernity as an epochal event/symbol and modernity as a reiterative, circulating sign/meaning in the everyday. Indeed, for modernity to even emerge as a sign of the present, the lag is necessary: "*The new or the contemporary* appear through the splitting of modernity as event and enunciation, the epochal and the everyday. Modernity as a *sign* of the present emerges in that process of splitting, that *lag*, that gives the practice of everyday life its consistency as *being contemporary*" (242).

Where else but in the colonies, those places "where progress is only heard (of) and not 'seen'" (244), are we afforded a chance to witness the time-lag between modernity as epochal event and modernity as enunciation, as everyday utterances and practice? If articulations of modernity imagine a reinvention of self that is synchronous and spatial, what of situations in which the self *cannot* be reinvented? If modernity is linked to notions of freedom, what is to be made of colonized subjects in the context of *unfreedom*? Thus, Bhabha develops a concept of "contramodernity" in the colonies, using as his template the tragic figure of François-Dominique Toussaint Louverture, ex-slave liberator of Saint-Domingue who ultimately died at the hands of the very French whose revolutionary ideas of liberty, equality, and fraternity helped fuel his revolt against the Spanish. I conclude this elaboration of Bhabha's concept of the time-lag by emphasizing the lesson learned there: the colonized subject as witness of the "time-lag" of modernity is privileged to speak supplementarily, *beside* the "Great Event" that then gets estranged and reinscribed differently. Such a renaming of modernity, such a transformation of the "site of enunciation," is essential for authority to be challenged, for real change to occur (242).

Taking my cue from Bhabha, I place the subject of this essay, Toru Dutt and her work, within the time-lag, in-between, in conditions of contramodernity. By doing so, I add a further destabilizing category to Bhabha's race-inflected intervention in the universalizing of "our" moment as *the* modern moment, whose best articulation is modernism: that of gender. I believe that what needs refusing the most in a feminist postcolonial analysis of culture and literature is the invitation to occupy simply anti-oppositional positions; these invariably leave the basic structure of authority unquestioned and undisturbed by assuming—wrongly—that the reinstantiation of the minor term as major (i.e., female instead of male) has amounted to a serious revolution. Doing away with oppositional and anti-oppositional positions means acknowledging that the ground is always already hybrid and that hybridity—emerging from those liminal, in-between spaces Bhabha discusses—may in itself offer a powerful critique. For the rest of this essay, I focus on the late nineteenth-century writing of the Indian poet and translator Toru Dutt (1856–77). With the help of this "time-lagged" example, I intend to show that late nineteenth-century Indian women's writing in English traversed a risk-ridden, in-between, yet productive space in the newly emerging international arena of modern textual production and reception.

∾

I BEGIN BY OFFERING a historical account of the political, social, and cultural pressures operating upon Indian women writers from the late nineteenth to the early twentieth century. This was a period of volatile changes brought about by the interface of nascent nationalist awareness and imperialist policy. Significantly, it is in this period that women's concerns and ameliorative campaigns to redress women's wrongs—sati, purdah, child marriage, women's literacy and education, and widow remarriage—gained importance. Yet the route that these campaigns for social reforms took was a peculiarly circuitous one. The postcolonial historian Partha Chatterjee has argued that in nineteenth-century India, even as the outer or material sphere of Indian culture conceded to the modernizing impulse, the inner or spiritual sphere insisted on its inviolability and resistance to British influence.[3] The custodians of this essential inner core of the nation were women, whose potential Westernization/modernization and formal education thus entailed a complicated maneuver: women's progress had to be charted in such a way that women's traditional identity would not be sacrificed for the superficiality of Western "trends." Ultimately, however, by the early twentieth century, campaigns for social reform lost their urgency and the "women's question," according to Chatterjee, was resolved by its disappearance from the public sphere of nationalist debate.

The editors of the two-volume anthology *Women Writing in India: 600 B.C. to the Present*, Susie Tharu and K. Lalita, concur with Chatterjee's argument, but they usefully shift attention from Chatterjee's emphasis on resolution to, instead, women's *creation* of a "new resilient self, one that is not easily understood or explained, but is, all the same, a power to be reckoned with."[4] In the nineteenth-century texts excerpted by Tharu and Lalita, we see strikingly subversive and overtly feminist articulations, which, while they contrast visibly with the muted tones of the early twentieth-century texts, still share with this later material a common goal to locate "dignity and personhood *outside* the double-edged promises of the Enlightenment and the social reform movement" (186; my emphasis).

Tharu and Lalita include some wonderfully aggressive and articulate female authors in their first volume. For instance, one writer, Mokshodayani Mukhopadhyay (ca. 1848–?), an advocate of women's education and independence, when provoked by a leading male poet's depiction of Bengali women as vain and frivolous, responded with a satirical poem of her own, "The Bengali Babu" (1882). The poem portrays men as puffed up, self-important hypocrites who drink pegs of whiskey, spit tobacco, and espouse nationalist views at night but who, in the sober light of the morning, all hatted, booted, suited, with cheroot and cane in hand, go tremblingly to work for the same English they had trashed the night before. For her deflating depiction of cultured and educated

Bengali men, this writer received much censure from her male reviewers. Another writer, Tarabai Shinde (ca. 1850–ca. 1910), wrote a bitter feminist essay in response to a weekly magazine article which attacked the apparent loose morals of a woman who aborted her baby and received a death sentence from the court as a result. In her 1882 essay "A Comparison of Men and Women," Shinde isolates each of the charges leveled against women—suspicion, impudence, adultery, transgression, deceit, and so on—and redirects them at men. In her down-to-earth, idiomatic language, a deliberate departure from the "standard" diction of normative patriarchy, Shinde reveals a withering contempt for men, including her husband, for whom she had lost regard very early in their marriage. For her lively riposte, she was attacked by men who did not even read her essay carefully. Finally, there were writers who, like the novelist Indira Sahasrabuddhe (ca. 1890–?), tackled the key reformist issues of the day—child marriage and widow remarriage—head-on, risking the charge of Westernized feminism as they did so. That Sahasrabuddhe's feminism cannot simply be dismissed on the grounds of Westernization is tellingly asserted by one of her prefaces, in which Sahasrabuddhe states: "Significantly even the Western-educated characters in the novel cannot appreciate that women may want more than home, marriage, and motherhood" (Tharu and Lalita, 385).

Bold articulations such as Mukhopadhyay's, Shinde's, and Sahasrabuddhe's are the more valuable for their explicit willingness to explode the constricted social and religious walls that sought to imprison these women. In contrast to their lives of public protest stands the sheltered life of young Toru Dutt. Toru was one of three children born to an upper-class Bengali couple (the oldest, a son by the name of Abju, died in 1865 at the age of fourteen). Her father, Govin Chunder Dutt, worked for the colonial government but soon resigned due to the lack of promotion opportunity for Indians in government jobs; later, in his autumn years, he was to become honorary magistrate, justice of the peace, and a fellow of the University in Calcutta. Govin Chunder Dutt was a convert to Christianity along with his brothers, following the oldest brother's mystical vision of the other world while on his deathbed; the remaining brothers and their families were all baptized in 1862. Toru doted on her father, who whiled away his time writing poetry fashioned after his favorite poet, William Wordsworth. At age twelve, she went with her family to Europe; she learned French in Nice, music in London, and, in 1871, attended the Higher Lectures for Women in Cambridge. The family returned to Calcutta in 1873, and within a year the older sister, Aru, died of tuberculosis.

Toru, who was to outlive her sister by only three years, began to publish her writing at this time: essays on Leconte de Lisle and Henry Derozio for the *Bengal Magazine* and translations of French verse into English, compiled in *A Sheaf Gleaned in French Fields* (1876). She took up the study of Sanskrit in 1875 and was preparing a collection of translated verse from Sanskrit to English at the time of her death in 1877; the collection appeared posthumously in 1882 under the title *Ancient Ballads and Legends of Hindustan*, with an introduction by Edmund Gosse. Two novels were also published posthumously: *Bianca, or the Young Spanish Maiden* (1878) and *Le Journal de Mlle. d'Arvers* (1879). She died a painful death at the age of twenty one, leaving behind a prodigious amount of writing, feverishly produced in a mere three years.

Given the different trajectory of her life and her prolific literary output, it is remarkable that there is very little written on Toru Dutt. What little there is tends either to glorify her as one of India's "true daughters" or to dismiss her as imitative of Western poetic trends (noteworthy exceptions are Alexander and Tharu, each of whom has written a useful, albeit brief, feminist analysis of her work).[5] Certainly no critic has credited Toru with a full-blown ability to address the major issues of her day and to nuance her poetry accordingly. For many Indian critics in particular, Toru's work merely represents a precedent—and a rather isolated one at that—to Indian literature in English, which they perceive as coming into its own only in the early to mid twentieth century with the novels of R. K. Narayan, Mulk Raj Anand, and Raja Rao. Her own biographer, Harihar Das, often resorts to an apologetic tone when analyzing perceived weaknesses in her writing.[6] Nor is Toru's work read by Western feminists or anthologized in Western publications; it is even absent in Tharu and Lalita's anthology of women's writing in India.

However, I would argue that what makes Toru's case distinctive and worthy of critical attention is that, despite her extensive nontraditional education and middle-class Christian identity, both of which spared her the tricky maneuverings Chatterjee describes as the common denominator of educated Indian women in the nineteenth century, Dutt achieved neither literary success in England nor freedom and mobility in India. Excluded by orthodox Hindu society on account of her family's conversion, yet not wholly included in the British social order on account of her Indian/"native" origin, Toru traversed the improvisational space in between these two positions. European reviewers of her French translations were more astounded at than accepting of her polished literary skills; they neutralized their astonishment with a patronizing stance toward the imagined oddity of the exotic colonial creature they were dealing with. Indian readers, on the other hand, felt that Toru's Sanskrit translations redeemed and corrected her prior Westernization, making her a genuine "daughter of India"; still others regarded her Sanskrit translations as naive and amateurish forays into a world about which she knew very little. Thus, Toru's life and work constitute an overdetermined site upon which both colonial and anti-colonial imperatives competed to weave a complicated pattern indeed. When read against the grain of these overdeterminations, her poetry demonstrates that it is produced, not from the site of a monolithic "truth" and "native" authenticity, but from the infinitely more fascinating site (in Bhabha's time-lagged language, an "interstitial passage between fixed identifications") of reinvention and improvisation (4). Such a reading, in turn, may make possible a subversive reading of both the European colonial and Indian patriarchal systems prevalent in Toru's time.

The critical reception of Toru Dutt's Indian publication of *A Sheaf Gleaned in French Fields*, a translation project she undertook with her sister Aru (who died two years before it appeared in print), occurred accidentally and abroad. Edmund Gosse happened to visit the office of the *Examiner*, stumbled upon *A Sheaf*, and subsequently reviewed it for the newspaper in August 1876. Very put off by the book's appearance ("a most unattractive orange pamphlet of verse . . . destined by its particular providence to find its way hastily into the wastepaper basket"; a "shabby little book . . . without preface or introduction"; a "hopeless volume . . . with its queer type"),[7] Gosse nevertheless steels himself to read the verse, only to be shocked out of his complacency by a great surprise, "almost rapture," for he reads:

> Still barred thy doors! the far East glows
> The morning wind blows fresh and free.
> Should not the hour that wakes the rose
> Awaken also thee?
>
> All look for thee, Love, Light, and Song,
> Light, in the sky deep red above,
> Song, in the lark of pinions strong,
> And in my heart true love.[8]

Gosse appears to resolve his unexpected surprise at this lyrical verse by assuming a benevolent and paternalistic attitude toward the Dutt sisters. According to him, Toru achieved brilliance not because of, but *in spite of*, her

Indian identity; it is as if she had to surmount the greatest odds to produce such accomplished verse in English. In his introductory memoir to *Ancient Ballads and Legends of Hindustan*, he says: "[*A Sheaf*] is a wonderful mixture of strength and weakness, of genius overriding great obstacles and of talent succumbing to ignorance and brilliance. That it should have been performed at all is so extraordinary that we forget to be surprised at its inequality." And again: "Toru's command of English is wonderful, and it is difficult to realize that the book is not the work of an English writer." Gosse's fluctuating between praise and criticism reveals a measure of baffled colonialist outrage that an Indian, a "native," could write sophisticated English verse (translations, no less, from French to English). How interesting, then, that he refers to her as "Hindu": "The English verse is sometimes exquisite; at other times the rules of our prosody are absolutely ignored, and it is obvious that *the Hindu poetess was chanting to herself a music that is discord in an English ear*" (my emphasis).[9] Thus Orientalized, even though she wrote as a Christian, Toru's case demonstrates that an Indian writing fluently in English was still, in imperialist eyes, only second-best, a shadow, a mere copy whose chief merit was to accentuate the power and authority of the original "English book." It is telling to add, in this regard, that Toru Dutt is markedly absent in Gosse's editorship of Heinemann's new series of international "classics," launched in 1895.[10]

But herein also lie the theoretical conditions for a subversive reading of Toru's verse. Although her poetry takes the power and authority of the original—the great Western male tradition—for granted, it is not located at the source of that "original truth" and "authenticity" but finds its articulation elsewhere, in another place where textual play and improvisation replace cultural pieties and fixed literary standards. The rules of Toru's poetic translation are best described as arbitrary. If a word or idea sounded good and looked good, it went in. This is not to say that her verse was sloppy or haphazard. But, cloistered at home and accessing European literature through her father's library, English newspapers, and articles of random interest to her in the *Revue des Deux Mondes*, she subjected her verse to her own rigorous standards and the influence of her own personal favorites in the canon. Gosse points out some of her subsequent (mis)readings : "She eschewed the Classicist writers as though they had never existed. . . . She was ready to pronounce an opinion on Napol le Pyrénéen or to detect a plagiarism in Baudelaire. But she thought that Alexander Smith [a Scottish poet and novelist, who died in 1867] was still alive, and she was curiously vague about the career of Sainte-Beuve." But what constitutes an "inequality of equipment" for Gosse is, for those perhaps somewhat removed from the "Great Event" of modernity, an enunciatory site of unexpected revision and translation. For instance, Toru rendered Victor Hugo's dislike of Emperor Louis-Napoléon Bonaparte: "Toi, tu te noyeras dans la fange, / Petit, petit!" thus: "Thou too shalt drown, but drown in slime, / Tom Thumb, Tom Thumb!"[11] Worth noting here is the free translation of "Petit" as "Tom Thumb," which rather irreverently and delightfully transfers Louis-Napoléon from Hugo's literary France to the annals of British nursery rhyme.

Toru's translations from French to English did not, of course, make her an "Indian poet" in the eyes of Indians. It took her translations from the Sanskritic texts of the *Mahabharata, Ramayana, Vishnu Puranas*, and *Bhagavata Gita*, compiled in *Ancient Ballads and Legends of Hindustan*, to make this poet "the genuine daughter of Hinduism."[12] These translations were inspired by the Hindu hymns young Toru's mother often sang at dusk, which moved the daughter almost always to tears; she discusses this deep emotional response to her mother's songs both in her letters and in her poetry. This has led critics to read her translations from the Sanskrit as evidence of her great need to connect with her quintessentially Indian past. Symptomatically, the mother-figure (in nationalist thought always standing for the nation) constitutes the locus for a feminized nationalism. Says the Indian critic K. R. Srinivasa Iyengar:

She was an Indian poet writing in English,—she was "autochthonous" [*sic*], she was one with India's women singers. . . . No room now for artificiality or stimulated hot-house efflorescence: now Toru has roots in her own land, and she agreeably responds to the heart-beats of the antique racial tradition. As children, she and her brother and sister had heard stories of the Hindu epics and Puranas, stories of mystery, miracle and local tradition from the lips of her own mother. . . . They really seemed to answer to a profound inner need for links with the living past of India, and she cared not if Christian or sceptic cavilled at her.[13]

The mother's oral narration of religious Hindu stories to the Dutt children, the young Toru's "profound inner need" to connect with an ancient racial memory: these combine, according to Iyengar, to create an "Indian poet" who has cast out all jarring, foreign, artificially induced tones. In short, the "real," the "Indian" Toru Dutt has emerged with *Ancient Ballads*. Similarly, according to Amaranatha Jha, who wrote the introduction to the 1941 edition of *Ancient Ballads and Legends of Hindustan*, the translations show that "[f]or all her

Western training and the faith under the influence of which she had been brought up, she never ceased to be Indian."[14]

The impulse to reclaim Toru on these nationalist grounds is hardly reprehensible. But, as with her Western readers like Edmund Gosse, it is her ambivalence that opens the door to the other side and accommodates nationalist interpretations such as Iyengar's and Jha's. Here too, "foreign" notes are struck, for Toru was not very conversant with Sanskrit in the short time that she devoted to its study (one year). If Toru's French-to-English poetry did not find altogether safe harbor on English soil (deemed not English enough), her Sanskrit-to-English verses did not meet with unanimous success in India either (they were not Indian enough). Thus, some felt that the "plaintive cadence" and "natural charm" of the original Sanskrit was lost in English.[15]

A reading of what is perhaps the most well-known poem in *Ancient Ballads*, "Savitri," shows that Toru's poetry traversed the risky in-between position that was neither purely English nor solely Indian. Viewed in connection with her letters to a friend in England, her poetry may offer us an alternative, interstitial locus from which to articulate Third World feminist politics. A free translation of a legend from the *Mahabharata* that produced the myth of the archetypal self-sacrificing wife so central to Hindu thought, the poem details the heroic and ultimately successful efforts a wife, Savitri, makes to bring her husband, Satyavan, back from the realm of the dead. While Hindu tradition emphasizes in this legend the wifely qualities of self-sacrifice and devotion—an emphasis greatly complicated by the fact that the texts of Hinduism were themselves largely shaped by the colonial encounter in the nineteenth century— it is interesting to note that Toru emphasizes other neglected aspects of the myth: Savitri's freedom, mobility, individuality, and right to self-determination. Unlike the women of Toru's time, who are "pent/In closed zenanas," her Savitri comes and goes as she pleases;[16] she chooses her own husband; and even when she obeys the rigors of tradition, she does so of her own volition. On the face of it, it would appear that Toru uncritically embraced and deposited in her Savitri post-Enlightenment Western values. For instance, in a letter to her English friend Mary Martin, she takes on a rather perky and audacious approach toward the sacred topic of Hindu marriage. However, her acutely felt cultural difference from her Hindu relatives is greatly complicated by Toru's nascent awareness of India, not England, as her "homeland." An earlier letter to Mary, written when the Dutt family had newly arrived back in Calcutta, made mention of Indians as "natives." Upon Mary's surprise and chastisement at Toru's use of this alienating word, Toru expresses shame and begins to practice a rather moving and rigorous self-censorship: "Thank you very much for what you say about calling my countrymen 'natives'; the reproof is just, and I stand corrected. I shall take care and not call them natives again. It is indeed a term only used by prejudiced Anglo-Indians, and I am really ashamed to have used it."[17]

Later letters show her growing political consciousness about imperialism in India; many of these angrily describe the one-sided workings of colonial law in events involving injustice, brutality, and wanton murders of Indians at the hands of British judges and officers. In a letter dated June 26, 1876, Toru writes: "You are indignant at the way some Anglo-Indians speak of India and her inhabitants. What would you think if you read some of the Police reports which appear in the Indian daily papers?" She proceeds to tell of some British soldiers who began shooting at peacocks on the property of a farmer. The farmer protested, was cursed, and soon, a fight broke out, in which the farmer's neighbors participated: "[O]ne soldier was severely beaten; the others decamped, leaving *nine* Bengalis *dead* and some seven Bengalis wounded. The case was brought before the magistrate; and what do you think his judgement was? The villagers were fined each and all; the soldiers acquitted: 'natives should know how precious is the life of one British soldier in the Eyes of the British Government.'"[18]

Toru returns to the subject of brutal and random violence exerted against Indians by the British again and again in her letters to Mary. Verging on an anti-colonial attitude toward the country in which she had spent some of her most formative years, these letters radically complicate any simple attribution of "Westernization" to her work. Indeed, according to Alexander, some of her translations from the Sanskrit (the poem "Prahlad," for instance) show Toru using Hindu mythology to *confront* British imperialism.[19] And if the poem errs on the other extreme—that of mythologizing a perfect distant past—this was a strategy used often by nineteenth-century Indian writers to counteract British stereotypes of Indians. Susie Tharu's essay "Tracing Savitri's Pedigree: Victorian Racism and the Image of Women in Indo-Anglian Literature" discusses the psychosocial anxieties underpinning Indo-Anglian women's literature at a time when educated Indians confronted their image in British eyes. Anxious, overwrought, and defensive, their reaction to British stereotyping was to try to prove that they were not inferior but equal to the British in intellect and character. Toru's competence in English *and* French proves, according to Tharu, that "[b]eing both Indian and female, she has not just to match, but to *outdo*, the British who found French notoriously difficult."[20] This sense of having to exceed expectations because she was writing against enormous odds and the psychosocial contortions produced as a result are throughout prevalent in Toru's writing, about which she herself was very modest and diffident. Hence, it is quite likely that Toru's Savitri, who goes wherever she wishes in "boyish freedom,"[21] whose mate will be chosen not by her parents in an arranged marriage but by her, has an individuality that has less to do with the idyllic mythic past the poem conjures up than with the defensiveness with which many elite Indians countered negative British stereotypes of Indians.

My own analysis adds two elements missing in Tharu and Alexander's. First, Toru's writings dislodge fixed binaries of sedimented thought and force us into a place where we may consider the productive politics of a time-lagged, in-between position. Not quite Indian yet not English either; well versed in European literature yet not writing from the "original" place of that literature's imagined "truth" and "value"; female and cloistered yet (relatively) liberated; young yet mature beyond her years; subject yet also object: it is conflicting positions such as these that make Toru's phrase, "[s]harp contrasts of all colours," in "Sonnet-Baugmaree," so descriptive of her own life and work, imparting to it a degree of latitude that allows her to seriously play with and unsettle aspects of the social and imperialist patriarchy of her time.[22] The implications of such a nonbinary, serious playing bring me to the second aspect perhaps missing in Tharu and Alexander's analyses, namely, the way in which Toru's case establishes a useful precedent for postcolonial women's writing in the modern and so-called postmodern eras. To make this point means articulating those interventionist aspects that appear to be only partially thought out by Toru Dutt herself. I conclude the essay by elaborating upon one of these.

While the disjunctive character of our current transnational era does not allow us to draw a direct continuum from the past to the present, discourses of modernity and imperialism continue to shape and inform the current moment. What, taking Toru's case as exemplary, may be the productive aspects of foregrounding a gendered postcolonial reading of such a complicated moment? One that I have attempted to outline is the power of an interstitial position that enabled Toru to seriously play with the patriarchal norms of her time. In particular, I would emphasize her inability and, to some extent, refusal to settle neatly into only one side of any number of binary relations: female/male, colonized/colonizer, Indian/Western, original/imitative, young/old, sheltered/ "free," and so on. Fixed binaries such as these would arrest the dynamic nature of her resistance to both the colonial *and* Indian patriarchy. Translated into current discourse, this is a way of saying that postcolonial feminists should not find it necessary to consolidate their politics in binary, simply oppositional and anti-oppositional, terms. Instead, authority—in this case, the modern neo-colonial nation-state, as true successor of colonialism—may be challenged without subscribing to an essentialized notion of national identity on one hand or falling prey to the charge of Westernization on the other.[23] If we are to read Bhabha seriously, the postcolonial translation of modernity makes possible not another totality but another time, within whose pauses a certain interrogation is rewriting the universalism of modernity and Man.

NOTES

1. An earlier version of this chapter appeared in *Going Global: The Transnational Reception of Third World Women Writers*, ed. Amal Amireh and Lisa Suhair Majaj (New York: Garland, 2000) under the title " 'Sharp contrasts of all colours': The Legacy of Toru Dutt" (209–28) and the author name Alpana Sharma Knippling. The earlier essay drew a continuum, however discontinuous, from Toru Dutt to contemporary Indian women writers (specifically, the short story writers anthologized in *Truth Tales: Contemporary Stories by Women Writers of India*, ed. Meena Alexander, and Alexander's own fine critical introduction to the anthology; and the short story writers anthologized in *The Slate of Life: More Contemporary Stories by Women Writers of India*, ed. Chandra Mohanty and Satya Mohanty, and their own equally fine critical introduction to their anthology). That essay looked especially at the politics of reception defining Indian women writers, whereas this chapter pays attention to a resistant reading of modernity and gender in the colonies.

2. Homi Bhabha, *The Location of Culture* (New York: Routledge, 1994), 5. Subsequent citations of this source are given parenthetically in the text.

3. See Partha Chatterjee, "The Nationalist Resolution of the Women's Question," in *Recasting Women: Essays in Colonial History*, ed. Kumkum Sangari and Sudesh Vaid (New Delhi: Kali for Women, 1989), 233–53.

4. *Women Writing in India: 600 B.C. to the Early Twentieth Century*, ed. Susie Tharu and K. Lalita, vol. 1 (New York: Feminist Press, 1991), 185. Subsequent citations of this source are given parenthetically in the text.

5. Meena Alexander, "Outcaste Power: Ritual Displacement and Virile Maternity in Indian Women Writers," *Journal of Commonwealth Literature* 24, 1 (August 1989): 12–29; and Tharu, "Tracing Savitri's Pedigree: Victorian Racism and the Image of Women in Indo-Anglian Literature," in *Recasting Women: Essays in Colonial History*, 254–68.

6. Harihar Das, *The Life and Letters of Toru Dutt* (London: Oxford University Press, 1921).

7. As quoted in ibid., 291.

8. As quoted in ibid.

9. As quoted in ibid., 300, 301, 300.

10. For a relevant interpretation of this series, see Ann Ardis's "'Shakespeare and Mrs. Grundy," in *Transforming Genres: New Approaches to British Fiction of the 1890s*, ed. Nikki Lee Manos and Meri-Jane Rochelson (New York: St. Martin's Press, 1994), 11–15, where she makes the point that Heinemann's active marketing of literary, as opposed to "scientific," values in relation to this series may have had much to do with Heinemann's disassociation from the controversial Oscar Wilde trials of 1895. Given Gosse's championship of Toru Dutt, it is certainly curious that Indian literature is absent from the listing of national traditions to be featured in this series, which was to include "French, Ancient Greek, English, Italian, Modern Scandinavian, and Japanese" "classics" (*Athenaeum*, July 27, 1895, 117).

11. As quoted in Das, *Life and Letters of Toru Dutt*, 300, 307.

12. Padmini Sen Gupta, *Toru Dutt* (New Delhi: Sahitya Academi, 1968), 83.

13. K. R. Srinivasa Iyengar, "Toru Dutt," in id., *Indian Writing in English* (1962; 4th ed., New Delhi: Sterling Publishers, 1984), 63–64.

14. Amaranatha Jha, "Introductory Memoir," in Toru Dutt, *Ancient Ballads and Legends of Hindustan* (1882; Allahabad, India: Kitabistan, 1941, 1969), 33.

15. Sen Gupta, *Toru Dutt*, 83. "[Some Indian readers] will remember the nectarean Sanskrit originals, and feel disappointed at the inadequacy of the English versions" (Srinivasa Iyengar, "Toru Dutt," 65).

16. Dutt, *Ancient Ballads*, 38.

17. Dutt to Mary Martin, May 3, 1876, quoted in Das, *Life and Letters of Toru Dutt*, 152, 131–32.

18. Dutt as quoted in Das, 169; emphasis in the original.

19. Alexander, "Outcaste Power: Ritual Displacement and Virile Maternity in Indian Women Writers," 14.

20. Tharu, "Tracing Savitri's Pedigree," 258; her emphasis.

21. Dutt, *Ancient Ballads*, 39.

22. Ibid., 171.

23. It is, I believe, precisely such in-between positions that are intimated in the work of the feminist critics Meena Alexander and Chandra Mohanty, among others. See, for instance, their critical introductions to the short story collections *Truth Tales* and *The Slate of Life*, respectively. See also Mohanty's useful pluralization of the category "Third World women" in essays such as "Under Western Eyes: Feminist Scholarship and Colonial Discourses," *Feminist Review* 30 (1988): 65–88; and Alexander's liminal ruminations in her memoir *Fault Lines* (New York: Feminist Press, 1993) and novel *Nampally Road* (San Francisco: Mercury House, 1991).

New Negro Modernity

Worldliness and Interiority in the Novels of
Emma Dunham Kelley-Hawkins

Historians of African American history often refer to the post-Reconstruction era as the nadir—the low point of black experience in the United States. Literary historians, however, have not yet devised a terminology that adequately describes African American literary production of this period. If black texts of the mid nineteenth century have readily been subsumed under the rubric of sentimentality and those of the later Harlem Renaissance period designated as modernist, the categories of realism, naturalism, or regionalism simply do not apply to black writing at the nadir. Any current attempt at naming would, I think, be premature; we need further engagement with both texts and their cultural context before proceeding to broader generalizations. In this vein, I propose to analyze Emma Dunham Kelley-Hawkins's *Megda* (1891) and *Four Girls at Cottage City* (1898), which to date have been defined as Christian conversion novels. Although their ethos of Christian regeneration seems to align them with traditions of nineteenth-century sentimentality, I want to argue that they also situate African Americans within the context of modern American culture and engage with crucial issues of modernity.

Kelley-Hawkins herself provides us with few clues as to how to read her novels, since as yet we know little about her life and literary career. She appears to have been a devout member of Boston's black Baptist community at a time when its churches were flourishing in the Greater Boston area and black Baptists equaled the combined total membership of all other denominations;[1] her novels were published by James H. Earle and Company, a religious publishing house especially interested in promoting Baptist causes.

In turning to literary composition, Kelley-Hawkins was following the lead of black Baptist ministers like the Reverend Joseph A. Booker, who maintained in a July 1896 article of the *National Baptist Magazine* that "if we want to persuade the present age and convince the future, *we must produce a literature*."[2] Writing was undoubtedly all the more important to black women Baptists in the 1890s as they struggled to make their voices heard beyond the denomination's male-dominated institutional structures; novel-writing in particular would have been an especially effective means of reaching a female audience. The plots of Kelley-Hawkins's novels are remarkable in their simplicity, because very little actually happens; they are complex, however, in that they are part courtship-marriage plots, part Christian conversion stories. Both texts center on a group of elite young women and their male friends as they struggle to achieve self-identity, and both trace their gradual steps toward Christian conversion. In the first novel, the pleasure-loving protagonist, Megda Randal, falls in love with the minister Mr. Stanley who, however, prefers the saintly Ethel; it is only Ethel's death that prevents their marriage from taking place, and it is only years later, when Meg has achieved true conversion, that Mr. Stanley asks her to marry him. *Megda*, then, is rooted in sentimental traditions in which fulfillment of romantic desire is the heroine's reward for the abandonment of selfish individualism and submission to patriarchal religious authority. In particular, critics have suggested that the novel echoes aspects of Louisa May Alcott's *Little Women* and most especially Jo March's marriage to Professor Bhaer.[3]

Four Girls at Cottage City marks a rupture with sentimental tradition, however, because the romance plot is displaced in favor of a portrayal of the four girls as a community of women who treat their two male acquaintances at best as mere friends, at worst as nuisances; the marriages of Vera Earle and Jessie Dare that conclude the novel are a self-conscious concession to the courtship-marriage plot. The novel focuses instead on the poor laundress Charlotte Hood, who, in relating the story of her life and that of her crippled son Robin, displaces male authority to become the agent of the young people's spiritual transformation and engagement with benevolence. It is quite possible that Kelley-Hawkins was inspired here by Elizabeth Stuart Phelps's novel, *The Silent Partner* (1871), in which a well-to-do young woman precipitously breaks off her engagement and abandons all worldly pursuits; she befriends a poor working-class girl, who cares for her sick sister and becomes an itinerant preacher after the latter's death.

I want to suggest, however, that the ethos of Christian regeneration that permeates Kelley-Hawkins's novels is embedded in a context of modernity. The elite communities that inhabit the novels partake in both the material advantages and cosmopolitan high culture offered by modern society. Hence, the novels emphasize the characters' enjoyment of worldliness just as they insist on an exploration of inner life through the spiritual experiences of repentance and conversion. From this perspective, they raise the question of whether the modern subject may enjoy the outward forms of worldliness and at the same time attend to the spirit that saves, whether or not it is possible to reconcile these two modes of being. These questions are posed within a broader modernist dilemma: how does one interpret exteriority? How may one read beyond the outward forms of self to apprehend interiority? What is the relationship between exteriority and interiority?

The problem of reading exteriority and its relationship to interiority is first raised in Kelley-Hawkins's novels in relation to race. The novels posit a raceless world of characters who are not racially marked, in which the category of whiteness refers most immediately to skin tone; narrator and characters alike repeatedly remark upon the white skin of the elite female protagonists, which is contrasted to the brownness of the male characters and the more working-class women. Whiteness here is ambiguous; are the characters racially white, or are they light-skinned blacks—white mulattos? If the latter, is their mulatticity, which links lightness of color to social status, so evident that it needs no comment, or are they passing for white in the readers' eyes? Such racial ambiguity reminds us that exteriority does not always reveal racial identity, that visible signs cannot always serve as an epistemological guarantee. Kelley-Hawkins creates a dilemma of reading here that forces her readers to define the "codes of intelligibility" at work that enable a proper reading of the visible signs of the characters' whiteness.[4]

No such dilemma exists in a reading of the photograph in the frontispiece of *Megda*. The visible signs of the photographed figure (fig. 7.1) announce the author as black and the text as black-authored. I want to suggest, then, that we need to adopt Kelley-Hawkins's own subject position and ask how she, as a black writer, wanted her readers to read her novels. I want to posit that she sought to offer her readers—particularly African Americans—a vision of what it would be like to live in a modern world in which racial difference no longer existed. In such a world, characters are no longer the objects of racial discrimination, nor do they suffer from the trauma of double consciousness, nor are

FIG. 7.1. Emma Dunham Kelley-Hawkins. Frontispiece to *Megda*
(1891). Courtesy Moorland-Spingarn Research Center, Howard
University.

they burdened by the obligations of racial uplift. Instead, they are freed to pursue other goals—namely, the twin exploration of modern worldly pleasures
and of an inner self divorced at last from an inauthentic racialized outer self.

In the 1890s, African American intellectuals collaborated in discourses of
modernity to insist on their participation in the broader American culture.
These discourses grounded American progress both in an adherence to Christianity as a marker of civilization that distinguishes the modern subject from
the heathen and in material advances brought about by industrialization, commerce, mechanical inventions, and scientific research. In line with the Protes-
tant ethic, such economic gains were seen to coincide with Christian values.

Yet, in a radically modern twist, these discourses insisted that prosperity must now encourage leisure time and the development of a high culture, resulting in turn in what Thorsten Veblen called "conspicuous consumption," whereby the elite class indistinguishably consumes both material objects (luxury items) and immaterial goods (culture).[5]

Inevitably, such concepts of civilization were both racialized and gendered: it is the white race alone that has attained the civilized stage; only white men, as embodiments of true manliness, can function as agents of civilization; only white women, in their purity and delicacy, can be construed as civilized. Yet, articles such as the Reverend William D. Woods's "The Thought of the Age," published in the July 1899 issue of the *National Baptist Magazine*, underscored the degree to which elite blacks also celebrated the nation's progress despite the severe deterioration of their political and social status.[6] Black leaders sought to counter these losses not only through political and economic struggle but also through culture. Hence, they turned to representation to craft an image of the modern African American as a "New Negro" who negates the image of the "Old Negro" marked by the "primitiveness" of slave culture. According to Henry Louis Gates, the New Negro is above all a "Public Negro Self" identified by the acquisition of "education, refinement, and money."[7] Self-definition shifts from race to culture; what becomes important is one's inner capacity to achieve bourgeois respectability and propriety.

The social worlds of Kelley-Hawkins's novels are sites of modernity that remove characters from the primitive and place them squarely within American culture at large. The characters of *Megda* live in a town near B—, which we may take to refer to Boston, and their life of ease accords with contemporaneous autobiographical accounts that detail the lifestyle of an exclusive social circle of African Americans who associated with white neighbors, hired white servants, frequented Boston's cultural affairs, and summered in white resorts.[8] The depiction of Cottage City on Martha's Vineyard in *Four Girls* takes a closer look at this latter activity. The town was originally known for its Methodist camp meetings held every August; Baptists were welcomed from the 1870s on, and there is evidence showing that African Americans did attend meetings. Significantly, in the 1870s Cottage City also became a summer resort for middle-class Americans, so that religious practice and leisure activities came to complement one another. Well-to-do blacks visited Cottage City as well, although Oak Bluffs did not become a specifically African American resort until the early twentieth century. Newspaper accounts indicate that racial discrimination in home ownership

F I G . 7 . 2 . African Americans in Edgartown or Cottage City, Martha's Vineyard, late nineteenth century. Courtesy Martha's Vineyard Historical Society.

did exist but also suggest that African American vacationers were able to lease and board in homes; photographic evidence clearly reveals their presence (fig. 7.2).[9] It is both plausible and fitting, then, that the final spiritual transformations of both novels' protagonists should take place in Cottage City.

Within Kelley-Hawkins's social world, the characters' whiteness constitutes it own norm. In the late nineteenth century, whiteness was a notoriously unstable signifier, referring variably to color, the Caucasian race, or a person's European origins; but in all instances it connoted civilization—participation in Western culture, including Christianity, and adherence to Western standards of beauty—as opposed to savagery. I suggest that the code of intelligibility operative in the novels asks us to read beyond whiteness as a sign of either Anglo-Saxon heritage or mulatticity to whiteness as a set of cultural and behavioral norms. The girls' whiteness represents, then, the high cultural and Christian values of Western civilization as well as social success and refinement. More specifically, the girls can be read as representing different types of American womanhood—the American Girl as Charmer (Meg) or as Outdoors Girl (Jessie), the New England Woman (Vera), the Invalid (Ethel)—untainted by racial or ethnic lineage.[10]

I want to suggest, however, that the New Negro also possessed a "Private Self" that sought recognition and representation. Intellectual historians have long argued that issues of subjectivity, of consciousness and self-consciousness, are equally important features of modernity; they have termed this turn-of-the-century moment the "golden age of the subconscious" inhabited by "psychological man."[11] This fascination with interiority manifested itself in movements as diverse as the popular New Thought movement and the more academic discipline of New Psychology, both of which owed a debt to earlier mesmerism, which itself was considered a form of mental *and* religious healing. Significantly, these two movements flourished in the Boston area—the former in Boston's Metaphysical Club, the latter at Harvard University. As a Boston intellectual, Kelley-Hawkins was undoubtedly aware of these newly developing ideas. In *Megda*, Meg and her sister quote from a poem by Ella Wheeler Wilcox, a popular New Thought poetess; and we know that the work of William James, a chief proponent of New Psychology, was well known to Boston writers like W. E. B. Du Bois and Pauline Hopkins.

Like mesmerism, New Thought and New Psychology were convinced of their effective mediation between psychology and religion. New Thought posited that "the truth regarding life and its laws is to be found in man's inner consciousness rather than in the study of phenomena," and that it is God, who is present everywhere in the universe, including our consciousness, who directs our thoughts and actions.[12] In his early work, James was interested in the ways in which both the "waking self" and the "secondary self" interacted with the social world through the operation of the will. Later on, however, he became increasingly concerned with the "subconscious self" or "consciousness beyond the margin" as the locus of all religious experience—experience that includes conversion, which James conceived to be a surrender of the will, "a willingness to close our mouths and be as nothing in the floods and waterspouts of God."[13]

This growing interest in the problem of consciousness inevitably raised the important question of the relationship of interiority to exteriority. In midcentury, both sentimental and scientific discourse had posited a perfect congruence between the exteriority of the body and its interiorized essence: one's character or soul is reflected in one's outer appearance. These theories too were gendered and racialized: the transparency of the (white) woman's body is indicative of the purity of her soul; the Negroid features of the black were obvious signs of his/her inferiority. But modernist philosophers, many of whom were Harvard professors, came to reject any easy reading of exteriority as a sign of inner meaning and insisted that the interpretation of the relationship between exteriority and interiority is a subjective act, dependent on the interpreter's past experience and prior acquaintance with the subjects under observation. This recognition of the complex relationship between exteriority and interiority lies at the core of Kelley-Hawkins's novels.

In both *Megda* and *Four Girls at Cottage City*, this tension between inner spirit and outward form is represented as a seemingly irreconcilable conflict between sacred religion and profane theater. This position seems especially clear in *Megda*. In the early chapters, we are told that Ethel Lawton, the text's spiritual female center, has recently risen for prayers at a Church meeting and refused to participate in the young people's society until it banishes "such dissipations as whist, dancing and theatricals."[14] When Meg substitutes for Ethel in the society's planned theatrical evening, Mr. Stanley's reaction is one of displeasure. Similarly, in *Four Girls*, one of the heroines, Vera Earle, wonders "whether it is wicked to go to the theatre."[15] In this novel, however, arguments are made that trouble the seemingly clear-cut opposition between religion and the theater. One of the girls' friends, Erfort Richards, reads from an article, "The Common Sense View of the Theatre," written by the Reverend Madison C. Peters. The essay pointedly deconstructs the religion-theater dichotomy, arguing that in all ancient world cultures, drama was originally religious in nature. It is only over time that the theater has lost its religious sensibility to become art, and religion its dramatic power and hence its popular appeal. Peters's solution is twofold: accept the theater as a fact of worldly modern life but reform it by ridding it of its immoral aspects; reintroduce drama into a modernized church by encouraging preachers to be " 'as natural and impressive, as audible and interesting as the actor' " (101). Vera and Erfort continue to worry about the value of theatrical performance, however, until the last pages, when Charlotte Hood, this novel's spiritual savior, asserts that although she herself does not care for dancing and theatergoing, such choices are a matter of individual conscience.

The plots of Kelley-Hawkins's novels seek to resolve this debate over the incompatibility between religion and the theater by suggesting that the female protagonists may become modern by pursuing a self-development that is both worldly *and* Christian, that reconciles outward form and inner spirit. Thus, on the one hand, the girls' theatergoing underscores Kelley-Hawkins's conviction that familiarity with the theater, in particular that of Shakespeare, is a claim to participation in U.S. fin de siècle high culture and hence to membership in modern civilization. Yet it urges further questions: what kinds of performances are acceptable? What are appropriate ways of "reading" performance? On the other hand, the girls' Christian conversions attest to Kelley-Hawkins's deep commitment to the Baptist faith. The novels suggest that if Christianity continues to teach the important doctrinal lessons of the Christ story, it also encourages forms of dramatic performance that lead toward interiority and promotes a "theater of interiority" that encourages the expansion of the modern subject's inner self.

Both *Megda* and *Four Girls* are regulated by an economy of pleasure that marks their world as peculiarly modern. The characters take full advantage of the advances made by modern technology and a modern economic system that promotes consumerism and the enjoyment of leisure time. In Cottage City, for example, the four girls ride bicycles, take trips to the department store, and eagerly anticipate the turning on of electric lights that illuminate the resort at night. The characters are also modern in their conspicuous consumption of material goods. The girls and their families do not belong to a leisure class in Veblen's sense, given that the fathers must engage in productive labor to earn a livelihood and provide for those under their protection. Yet theirs is not the manual labor identified with the "Old Negro"; it is the professional labor of the modern judge, lawyer, or doctor. Hence, in the novels, the men work outside the home to accumulate capital, while the wives and girls, who inhabit the domestic interior, spend it. The households become the site of "the consumption of food, clothing, dwelling, and furniture by the lady and the rest of the domestic establishment" (111); the girls enjoy, for example, a variety of foods, particularly sweets, dress with lavish care in the latest styles, and surround themselves with elegant furnishings.

The exteriority of conspicuous consumption is of course never entirely divorced from interiority. Claudia Tate, for example, has argued that in the romance plot of *Megda* dress and interior space function as "a repository for displaced eroticism," in particularly for the intense sexual feelings of Mr. Stanley, Ethel, and Meg that cannot otherwise be expressed.[16] Veblen himself argued that "the need of dress," or fashion, "is eminently a 'higher' or spiritual need." Beyond highlighting elevated social status, disdain for productive labor, and a level of financial success that readily accommodates wasteful expenditure, fashionable dress points to the wearers' "restless search for something which shall commend itself to our aesthetic sense"; unlike the Christian quest, however, this search can never be satisfied, since that would then spell the end of fashion.[17] As we shall see, it is the girls' religious aspirations that rescue them from restlessness and prevent them from being consumed by their acquisition of material goods.

Nowhere is the girls' enjoyment of the worldliness of modern life more evident than in their consumption of the immaterial goods of high culture, emblematized by book reading and most especially the theater. Even Ethel's rooms contain material icons—"white marble busts of Shakespeare, Dickens, Hawthorne and Irving"—that glorify high culture (271–72). In *Highbrow/Lowbrow*, Lawrence Levine offers a compelling narrative of how the postbellum elite created a distinct realm of high culture that it came to think of as sacred, as a religion unto itself. This high cultural domain functioned to underscore the elite's exclusive class standing and to separate it from the masses, most especially the illiterate and non-English-speaking population. Given the rise in ethnic prejudice created by the increase in immigration from southern and eastern Europe in the 1890s, the elite asserted high culture to be specifically Germanic or Anglo-Saxon in origin. Its chief figure was William Shakespeare, whose plays were no longer considered popular entertainment, as in the antebellum period, but were now viewed as serious, elevating, imbued with transcendent value.[18]

Not surprisingly, Shakespeare is the central cultural icon of Kelley-Hawkins's fictional world, underscoring the characters' participation in Anglo-Saxon high culture. African Americans' eagerness to belong to that culture and their anxiety about achieving that goal are betrayed in the one explicitly racial comment made by a character in the novels: theatergoing remains pleasurable, remarks Jessie Dare in *Four Girls*, even "if we do have to get seats in 'nigger heaven'" (81; the upper galleries reserved for African Americans and the lower classes). When *Megda*'s young people decide to put on an evening of entertainment, they choose a Shakespearian play as the centerpiece of their program. Beyond signaling their familiarity with high culture, their choice of plays is instructive. When Ethel, who had agreed to play the part of Ophelia, withdraws from the planned theatrics, Meg substitutes *Macbeth*, gives herself the role of Lady Macbeth, and selects scenes that highlight fearless ambition and scorn for male weakness. Lady Macbeth's ambition is doubled here by Meg's own worldly vanity. As one of the girls, May, remarks: "'What a grand thing it must be to have the world at your feet. Just think! your simple appearance on the stage to be the signal for a mighty burst of applause'" (176). In this novel, moreover, theatricality spills over the boundaries of the stage to permeate the lives of the girls themselves. From the first pages, the narrator composes many of their interactions as scenes created for the readers' spectatorship. In addition, the girls frequently view each other pictorially. Such self-conscious theatricality reaches its height with Meg herself who repeatedly transforms events in her own life into a form of theater which then allow her to indulge in "private theatricals" (80).

Megda's narrator suggests, however, that such theatricality must be viewed with suspicion. Stage and private theatricals alike all too often encourage in both actor/performer and viewer/reader an appreciation of exteriority alone. Meg, we remember, enjoys displaying herself on stage, and May believes an actor's mere appearance to be enough to merit the audience's applause. It is this unseemly self-display and desire for the world's homage that incur Mr. Stanley's displeasure; hence, if Lady Macbeth is punished for her ambition, so must Meg be. Just as significantly, when Mr. Stanley preaches from the pulpit one Sunday, Meg adopts the position of theatergoer and misinterprets his sermonizing as pure theatrical performance rather than as the dissemination of religious values. Paying attention only to his "remarkably fine appearance" (129) and "rare elocutionary powers" that would make him a "grand Macbeth" (112), Meg remains oblivious to the meaning of his words.

Meg's mode of performance and spectatorship here is linked to the broader developments in theories of the self referred to earlier, specifically to new concepts of personality. Warren Sussman has persuasively described how the late nineteenth century witnessed a shift from notions of "character," whereby the individual matures through mastery of self and a strict obedience to law, morality, and social values, to those of "personality" in which the individual seeks self-fulfillment by presenting him/herself as unique, as different from and even superior to those in the crowd.[19] In the world of the theater this shift was reflected in the emergence of the personality school of acting, which came to rival the older classical school. While adherents to this traditional method of acting did idealize the behavior of the tragic figures they portrayed on stage, they nonetheless sought to project the illusion of separate dramatic characters; in contrast, the personality school glorified the actor's own personality and substituted it for the dramatic character.[20] The many appreciative comments made by the girls about the acting style of the great classical players Edwin Booth, Lawrence Barrett, Miles Levick, Mary Anderson, and Margaret Mather clearly indicate Kelley-Hawkins's valuation of character over personality; her condemnation of Meg's theatricality suggests that Meg is in danger of doing just the opposite, of valuing personality over character.

Such a promotion of personality over character has potentially dangerous consequences for Reverend Peters's conception of preaching as acting. Given congregants like Meg, performance may all too readily elicit modes of interpretation based on self-aggrandizement that are distinctly at odds with Christian notions of worship and community: religious ceremony may become desacralized, divorced from spirituality, and transformed into merely another good available for the elite's conspicuous consumption; additionally, it may facilitate highly individualized reactions on the part of audience members instead of the collective response expected of congregants during religious service.

The novels, then, alert us to the dangers of both overvaluing and misreading exteriority, and insist that protagonists and readers alike consider what constitutes appropriate performance and spectatorship. In sum, Kelley-Hawkins confronts us with the modernist dilemma of how to read from the outside in and work out the proper relationship of exteriority to interiority. Kelley-Hawkins had already acknowledged this problem in her handling of her characters' race. Her task now becomes one of persuading her girls to temper their fascination with the exteriority of theatrical performance to attend to the interior life. In *Megda* and most especially in *Four Girls*, this project is first carried out through characters' attempts to read the inner traits of others from the outside in. They do so by means of the "false religions" of palm reading, clair-

voyance, mesmerism, and phrenology. These latter two were modern techniques brought from Europe to the United States during the nineteenth century; highly popular, they coincided with the religious revivalist movements
that punctuated the century. They promised to reconcile religion and science
and thus answer heretofore unanswerable questions concerning the inner self.
Yet in Kelley-Hawkins's novels, they too are ultimately deemed to be inadequate.

In both novels, palm reading and clairvoyance are readily dismissed as
"primitive" practices that ill befit modern subjects. Even though it is Ethel,
Megda's spiritual touchstone, who reads Meg's palm, rightly identifying "a vein
of deep, earnest feeling" beneath her friend's merry exterior (13), the legitimacy
of this practice is undercut by Meg's association of it with heathenism: "'Quite
a palmist, Ethel, you ought to make a profession of your talent, and send all the
money it brings you out to the poor heathen'" (15). In *Four Girls*, the medium
Madam Hazel is even more closely associated with the "primitive": she maintains that the spirit with whom she communicates is that of an old Indian
squaw and hence falls into broken English once in her trance. More important,
however, clairvoyance is rendered suspect given the primacy it gives to the will.
Once Vera decides that clairvoyance is a form of mind reading, she easily asserts her own superior will power to block Madam Hazel's access to her inner
thoughts; this exertion of the will runs counter to James's religious ideal of passive surrender to a larger force outside the self.

A similar misuse of Vera's will occurs in her battle with Professor Wild, a
practitioner of mesmerism and phrenology, whose authoritative title of professor is undercut by the "wildness" of his surname. Mesmerism purported to
be compatible with both religion and science: it held that its belief in a universal fluid permeating all living organisms accorded with Christian notions of a
preestablished universal harmony.[21] Its materialist basis betrayed itself, however, in its contention that certain individuals hold within them greater con-
centrations of fluid and are thus able to mesmerize their patients, exercising
total control over their will; Professor Wild is one such person. Here again, Vera
reveals the theory's fraud by exerting her own willpower and denying Wild any
control over her mind. Wild himself subsequently admits "spiritualism, mesmerism, and palmistry" to be "nonsense," but insists that phrenology—the
physiological explanation of moral character on the basis of topographical observation—is no "sham" (336, 334). In the culture at large, phrenology had
racist overtones, finding signs of "primitiveness" in the distinctive features of

the Negro, for example; Wild's phrenological examination of the girls' heads rebuts the possibility of such racial interpretations, however, because it fully corroborates our knowledge of their moral and civilized character. Nonetheless, given its materialist methodology, phrenology is of limited value; in suggesting that personality is physiologically determined, it offers no outlet for moral improvement or spiritual elevation. Such inner transformations are of course what Christian conversion makes possible. Hence, it is no accident that Wild's phrenological examinations take place within the narrative context of Charlotte Hood's conversion story, which in turn converts the four girls and their male acquaintances.

In her novels, then, Kelley-Hawkins suggests that it is Christianity alone that allows both a proper reading of exteriority *and* exploration of interiority. In *Megda*, only Mr. Stanley can adequately read Meg (180–83), and it is his sermons as well as her friends' warning that "'trouble . . . must come some day as it comes to all, and then you will need the Father'" (142) that gradually make possible Meg's spiritual regeneration. As Claudia Tate has noted, Meg's trouble manifests itself first in her growing awareness of Mr. Stanley's preference for Ethel; Meg's "romantic distress" aligns itself with feelings of "spiritual disquiet," and it is the suffering of unrequited love that prepares the way for her salvation.[22]

Not simply content with bringing about Meg's conversion in accordance with sentimental conventions, however, Kelley-Hawkins seeks to find ways for Christianity to provide a forum for performance as pleasurable to her characters as the worldly plays of Shakespeare, to transform Christian life into theater and ultimately reconcile worldly and Christian values. Nowhere is this better shown than in the narrator's description of Meg's baptism in the river which takes place in "the most beautiful spot in that section of the country" and in which there was not one thing to mar the beauty of the scene (321–22). Meg's baptism is a public testimony to her spiritual regeneration in the bosom of her community. Fictional characters and readers alike cannot help but be captivated by the intense beauty of this scene that appeals so powerfully to the visual imagination. But the scene remains a static spectacle of exteriority, incapable of providing a full narrative of Meg's inner transformation. Its limitations as Christian theater become fully evident in light of Charlotte Hood's dream in *Four Girls*, in which Christ asserts that baptism by water is but an "'outward form but that is all. It is not the *form* that saves; it is the *spirit*'" (309–10).

How then can the Christian enjoy both outward form and inner spirit, while in the process reconciling worldly and Christian values? The Christian life invites dramatic narrative because, as Mr. Stanley proclaimed in his first sermon, prayer is often not answered immediately but requires the "exercise of faith"; unfolding over time, the work of faith perforce takes narrative form. In both novels, the girls come to seek modes of performance that allow an exploration of interiority. Initially, this search takes the form of the novels' main protagonists' desire to become "first class elocutionist[s]" (179). During the young people's theatrical evening in *Megda*, for example, Meg not only plays the part of Lady Macbeth but also recites several sentimental poems, among them Marianne Farningham's "The Widow's Light" and Ann Stephens's "The Polish Boy," poems that tell stories of suffering and redemption brought on by the loss of loved ones. Elocutionism places Meg squarely within middle-class American culture and is deemed socially acceptable even by Mr. Stanley, who praises her performance and encourages her ambitions (179).

In the late nineteenth century, elocutionism found increasing acceptance as a female profession; it became a middle-class ideal for white, and a growing number of black, women—Hallie Quinn Brown, Henrietta Vinton Davis, Ednorah Nahar, Alice Franklin, and Frances Harper's daughter, Mary E. Harper, to name a few—who were widely praised in both the black and the mainstream press. Boston was the center of the elocutionary movement and home to many of its schools, teachers, and practitioners; but elocutionists also found a wide arena in the increasingly popular chautauquas and lyceums that combined religious services with the reading of literary texts. In this mass culture movement, the female elocutionist was acceptable to churchgoers because she was perceived as a reciter rather than a creator, a reader rather than an actress, and hence the display of her body was not scandalous. Moreover, many elocution teachers of the time promoted theories that emphasized the ways in which elocution allowed for the proper expression of inner feeling and thus harmonized exteriority and interiority. In particular, the French theorist René Delsarte shifted elocutionism's focus from the physiology to the psychology of speech: in the elocutionary act, the inner self (the mind and soul) finds direct expression in the outer body by means of voice, word, and gesture. Finally, the female elocutionist's recitations reflected the literary tastes of the nation; in particular, the frequent selection of sentimental pieces fully accorded with prevailing notions of femininity. In this way, elocutionism became a culturally acceptable performative mode for women, including Kelley-Hawkins's girls.[23]

As they move toward conversion, the girls choose more immediate perfor-
mances of interiority in music, specifically in the singing of hymns. Both novels
contain references to many different hymns, but three stand out: Charles Wesley's
"Jesus, Lover of My Soul," and two nineteenth-century hymns, "Just as I Am" by
Charlotte Elliott and "Nearer, My God, to Thee" by Sarah Flower Adams. "Jesus,
Lover of My Soul" narrates a movement from exterior to interior as the singer,
frightened by a storm, begs Jesus for the refuge that is "Grace to cover all my sins."
As women-authored texts, the other two hymns allow the female preacher to
come to voice; both lead to meditations on interiority. Meg is identified in par-
ticular with "Just as I Am"; in contrast to the spectacle of her baptism, this hymn
asserts a total disregard of exteriority in the promise to come to God "just as I am."
Finally, "Nearer, My God to Thee" is the central hymn of *Four Girls*; it calls attention to itself as song, in particular as song that mediates between worshipper and
God: "Still all my song shall be,/Nearer, my God, to Thee,/Nearer to Thee!"[24]

It is in Charlotte Hood's narrative of her life in *Four Girls*, however, that Christianity as a theater of interiority is most fully explored. From the outset, Charlotte makes it clear that it is God himself who is the source of her narrative
power. Her story follows the pattern of Christian allegory, and her telling of it
transforms her into a female preacher whose narrative authority exceeds that of
both the elocutionist and the hymnist. Charlotte begins with an acknowledge-
ment of her early sinful nature and desire for rebirth, proceeds to an account of
a narrowly missed opportunity for conversion, and continues with a harrowing
tale of a life of trouble; the burning of a beloved younger brother; storms that, as
literal analogues of the tempest of "Jesus, Lover of My Soul," kill father, uncle,
brother, and husband; an epidemic of scarlet fever that takes both her sister and
children from her; and the despair that leads her into "the gay life" (297). She
concludes, finally, with the retelling of a "dream that saved my life from everlast-
ing death" (299). In this dream—by her own account "somewhat similar to those
described by Elizabeth Stuart Phelps in 'Beyond the Gates'" (299)—Charlotte
finds herself on a road accompanied by "fellow-travellers," many of whom are
denied entrance to heaven for, despite their external show of godliness, they have
lived a life of deceit; their exteriority has belied their interiority. Like Meg before
her then, Charlotte must learn to read beyond the outward form of others to
attend to their spirit; in so doing, she discovers her own inner self. Here again,
music mediates between spectacle and inner transformation: Charlotte hears
"heavenly music" and the Christ of the Crucifixion appears before her to teach
her the ultimate values of suffering and submission to his will (320).

Charlotte's parable might strike us as highly conventional given its traditional lesson of Christian submission. I would argue, however, that its appropriation of the rhetoric of allegory intimates more complex concerns. As a genre, allegory demands both an intensive and extensive engagement with the narrative mode. Allegorical narrative itself unfolds on two levels of meaning—surface and depth; outer forms are meant to represent inner states of being. It is the responsibility of the reader—the girls, Kelly-Hawkins's contemporaneous readers, and today's readers as well—to read from outer to inner meaning just as Charlotte did in reading the fellow-travelers of her dream. Yet it is important to recognize that in allegory, inner meaning cannot substitute for outer, just as outer meaning never substitutes for inner; the two co-exist, indeed collaborate, inviting the reader to take pleasure in exteriority while at the same time exploring interiority. If allegory, then, allows Charlotte the privilege of an intense focus on her self, it also permits her to particularize, materialize, and embody this self, as well as the selves of others who figure prominently in her pilgrimage toward self-understanding. The result is the creation of a dynamic theatrical narrative in which visual imagery—that of the burning of her brother, of the storms that kill the men in her family, of the disease that robs her of her children, of the suffering of her fellow-travelers—offers the reader a pleasure that is both spiritual and sensuous.

Such a valuation of the materiality of the body carries over into the novel's conclusion. Charlotte's narrative converts the girls and their friends and leads to both their spiritual rebirth and their commitment to benevolence. Significantly, however, the last chapters of the novel emphasize not so much the necessity of Christian obligation and submission as their rewards: the enjoyment of worldly material life. Thus, the marriages that end the novel affirm the young people's engagement in the pleasures of this world. Even more significantly, their benevolent provision for a surgical operation that cures the crippled Robin and paves the way for his eventual entry into the medical profession signals the narrative's commitment to bodily health, scientific achievement, and socioeconomic advancement offered by the modern world.

As readers, we might well feel critical discomfort with the partiality of Kelley-Hawkins's social and political perspective, her portrayal of an exclusive elite, and her seeming lack of racial consciousness. But I believe that we need to pay greater attention to the enormous complexity of African American post-Reconstruction society, in which blacks of all classes struggled to redefine themselves and find a place for themselves in the nation's culture. From this perspective, Kelley-Hawkins offers us a compelling vision of new possibilities for African Americans at the close of the nineteenth century. In her novels, she imagines a set of characters who fully share the cultural vision of the dominant society and enjoy the pleasures of the modern world. At the same time, she insists that they must attend to the inner life of the mind and spirit, and illustrates how they may reconcile Christian values with worldliness, thereby opening the way for African American representations of interiority in later modern fiction.

NOTES

1. See John Daniels, *In Freedom's Birthplace* (Boston: Houghton Mifflin, 1914), 242.

2. Joseph A. Booker, "National Federation of Negro Baptists," *National Baptist Magazine*, July 1896, 157.

3. See Claudia Tate, *Psychoanalysis and Black Novels: Desire and the Protocols of Race* (New York: Oxford University Press, 1998), 29.

4. Amy Robinson, "It Takes One to Know One: Passing and Communities of Common Interest," *Critical Inquiry* 20 (Summer 1994): 715–36.

5. See Thorsten Veblen, *The Theory of the Leisure Class* (1899), in *The Portable Veblen*, ed. Max Lerner (New York: Viking Press, 1948), 196.

6. William D. Woods, "The Thought of the Age," *National Baptist Magazine*, July 1899, 5–9.

7. Henry Louis Gates Jr., "The Trope of a New Negro and the Reconstruction of the Image of the Black," *Representations* 24 (Fall 1988): 129–51.

8. Adelaide M. Cromwell, *The Other Brahmins: Boston's Black Upper Class, 1750–1950* (Fayetteville: University of Arkansas Press, 1994), 55–56.

9. See Henry Beetle Hough, *Martha's Vineyard, Summer Resort, 1835–1835* (Rutland, Vt.: Tuttle, 1936), 146; Adelaide M. Cromwell, "The History of Oak Bluffs as a Popular Resort for Blacks," in *African Americans on Martha's Vineyard*, ed. Arthur Railton (Oak Bluffs: Dukes County Intelligencer, 1997): 52; and *Martha's Vineyard Herald*, July 13, 1889.

10. See Kathy Peiss, "Making Faces: The Cosmetics Industry and the Cultural Construction of Gender, 1890–1910," in *Unequal Sisters: A Multicultural Reader in U.S. Women's History*, ed. Ellen DuBois and Vicki L. Ruiz (New York: Routledge, 1990), 386; and Martha Banta, *Imaging American Women: Idea and Ideals in Cultural History* (New York: Columbia University Press, 1987), 53–58.

11. Alan Gauld, *A History of Hypnotism* (New York: Cambridge University Press, 1992), 412, as quoted in Ann Taves, *Fits, Trances and Visions: Experiencing Religion and*

Explaining Experience from Wesley to James (Princeton: Princeton University Press, 1999), 253.

12. Charles S. Braden, *Spirits in Rebellion: The Rise and Development of New Thought* (Dallas: Southern Methodist University Press, 1963), 11.

13. William James, *Varieties of Religious Experience* (1902; Cambridge, Mass.: Harvard University Press, 1985), 46.

14. Emma Dunham Kelley, *Megda* (New York: Oxford University Press, 1988), 37. Subsequent page citations of this novel are given parenthetically in the text.

15. Emma Dunham Kelley-Hawkins, *Four Girls at Cottage City* (New York: Oxford University Press, 1988), 83. Subsequent page citations of this novel are given parenthetically within the text.

16. Tate, *Psychoanalysis and Black Novels*, 38.

17. Veblen, *Theory of the Leisure Class*, 197, 202.

18. See, in particular, chapters 2 and 3 of Lawrence Levine, *Highbrow/Lowbrow: The Emergence of Cultural Hierarchy in America* (Cambridge, Mass.: Harvard University Press, 1988).

19. Warren Sussman, "'Personality' and the Making of Twentieth-Century Culture," in *New Directions in American Intellectual History*, ed. John Higham and Paul K. Conkin (Baltimore: Johns Hopkins University Press, 1979), 214–20.

20. See Benjamin McArthur, *Actors and American Culture, 1880–1920* (Philadelphia: Temple University Press, 1984), 183–87.

21. See Robert C. Fuller, *Mesmerism and the American Cure of Souls* (Philadelphia: University of Pennsylvania Press, 1982).

22. Tate, *Psychoanalysis and Black Novels*, 33.

23. See Mary Margaret Robb, *Oral Interpretation of Literature in American Colleges and Universities* (New York: H. W. Wilson, 1941), 144–54; and Elizabeth Bell, "Performance Studies as Women's Work: Historical Sights/Sites/Citations from the Margin," *Text and Performance Quarterly* 13 (1993): 353–62.

24. Amos R. Wells, *A Treasury of Hymn Stories* (Grand Rapids, Mich.: Baker Book House, 1945), 49–62.

Olive Schreiner, South Africa, and the Costs of Modernity

In 1883, a novel was published that caused a considerable stir, especially among London's literary intelligentsia. It was called *The Story of an African Farm*, and a good deal of its appeal lay in its impassioned call for women's emancipation. Its author was Olive Schreiner, who had arrived in England two years earlier from her country of birth, South Africa. Unlike her elder brother, who was sent by their missionary parents to England and a Cambridge education, Schreiner was largely self-taught. Oppressed by the evangelical and Calvinist doctrines of her family, and stifled by the intellectual narrowness of colonial culture, Schreiner found solace in reading, which helped her to imagine a changing world. In the works of Charles Darwin, Herbert Spencer, and John Stuart Mill, she encountered a vision of progress with which she could combat the dogmatic Christianity dominating her colonial home.[1] Thus, despite the apparently gloomy ending of *The Story of an African Farm*, in which its feminist heroine dies, many readers discerned in its pages a passionate conviction that progress was under way, and that in a modern world, the lives of both women and men would be transformed.

Schreiner first traveled to England full of hope that in the metropolis her ideals of progress might be realized; almost a decade later, she returned to South Africa no longer so optimistic. During the extraordinarily turbulent decade that followed, Schreiner began to question the moral health of England and the image of modernity with which it was associated. As she witnessed the devastating effects of imperialism and capitalist modernization in the colony, which reached a crisis at the end of the century when Britain went to war with the Boer republics, Schreiner wrote almost exclusively about South Africa.

Nevertheless, the vision of women's emancipation that had animated her throughout the 1880s remained a crucial point of reference. More and more strongly, Schreiner came to see the issue of women's emancipation as inseparable from that of colonization as she began to contend with the ways in which "progress" calculates and levies costs in very different ways, for different places and peoples. This essay examines two of Schreiner's fictional responses to the crises of the 1890s: her 1897 allegorical novella *Trooper Peter Halket of Mashonaland* and a posthumously published war story, "Eighteen Ninety-Nine." It argues that both can be seen as part of Schreiner's ongoing, often difficult and conflicted, attempt to produce a convincing narrative of opposition to imperialism, one that would be capable of mobilizing those people—especially women—associated with progressive thinking in Britain.

Cecil Rhodes and Peter Halket

When she arrived back in Cape Town in 1889, Schreiner discovered that she was regarded as a celebrity. Among the many admirers of *The Story of an African Farm* was a man who, in the following year, took office as the Cape Colony's premier. He was Cecil Rhodes, and Schreiner quickly came to know him, not least because her Cambridge-educated brother Will was already active in Cape politics and was soon to join Rhodes's administration. Like so many of his contemporaries, Schreiner was overwhelmed by a sense of Rhodes's energy and vision, describing him as: "The only big man we have here . . . he seems to enlarge the horizon."[2] Rhodes had made his vast fortune, which fueled his political and empire-building ambition, in diamonds. Diamonds had been discovered in the 1860s and marked a newly distinctive phase in South Africa's colonial history, when mining capital and its consequent processes of industrialization began to transform the old colonial order in South Africa.[3]

Rhodes's wealth made him an important player in this changing South Africa. W. T. Stead, also an admirer of Rhodes, commented that there might have been richer men than Rhodes, but that none before him had "recognised the opportunities of ruling the world which wealth affords its possessor."[4] Rhodes was fired by the imperial ideal inculcated at Oxford University during the premiership of Benjamin Disraeli—he was deeply affected by John Ruskin's 1870 inaugural lecture, which called for the founding of British colonies across the globe.[5] He became convinced that the only means of securing British supremacy in an increasingly competitive economic world was through the colonization of vast portions of the globe. In 1889, Rhodes's British South Africa Company had a Royal Charter granted and its troops crossed the Limpopo river to begin the occupation of a large area of African land, which he named Rhodesia. Rhodes wanted limitless British expansion—a contemporary account tells of him, early in the 1880s, with his hand spread out across a map of Africa, saying, "That is my dream, all English"[6]—and imperial dominance across the globe.

In witnessing Rhodes's behavior—and especially his support for measures that shored up the right of white colonists to exploit black Africans, such as the infamous "Strop" Bill, which sanctioned physical punishment of farmworkers—Schreiner swiftly came to see that modernization in South Africa was not going to be the progressive force she had hoped it would. She quickly became openly antagonistic to Rhodes. In 1895, she published an attack on his "monopolistic" capitalism, and the politics that supported it, entitled *The Political Situation*. Shortly afterward, Rhodes's involvement in the infamous "Jameson Raid" (in which troops from the Chartered Company bungled an attempt to invade the gold-rich Boer Transvaal Republic) confirmed Schreiner's sense that South Africa was urgently imperiled by monopolist capitalism. Under such capitalism, human beings were reduced to calculable means to an end, and social powerlessness served only as a catalyst to increasingly brutal forms of exploitation. *The Political Situation* had made a central part of its argument the erosion of political and economic rights of Africans under Rhodes's administration—including, for example, restrictions on the Cape's color-blind franchise, and the development of labor legislation designed to produce and secure an African industrialized workforce.[7] By the mid 1890s, Schreiner was clear that the African population would pay the cost of capitalist modernization in South Africa.

Making an industrial workforce was only possible through a process of enforced proletarianization, which effectively severed portions of the African population from their lands. Schreiner thus saw, in the Chartered Company's appropriation of Matabeleland and Mashonaland (out of which "Rhodesia" was made), more evidence of Rhodes's ruthless drive to transform South Africa into an imperialist-capitalist machine for profit-making. The Chartered Company occupation was characterized by endemic tension between the colonizers and the Ndebele and Shona peoples, resulting in the *Chimurengas*, or uprisings, of 1893–4 and 1896–7. The latter conflict was prompted by the ongoing dispossession of land and cattle, and conditions made even more perilous by the severe rinderpest, or cattle plague, epidemic of 1896. Schreiner was horrified by the Company troops' brutal suppression of the resistance. In August of 1896 she wrote to a friend: "the other morning I woke, and as I opened my eyes there was an Allegory full fledged in my mind! A sort of allegory story about Matabeleland."[8] Published the following year as *Trooper Peter Halket of Mashonaland*, the story tells of a young Englishman, employed by the Chartered Company to put down the uprising in Matabeleland. In it, Schreiner sets out the grim consequences of economic greed for both the victims and perpetrators of colonization. In doing so, she explicitly evokes for an English audience the modern dream of female emancipation, which had dominated her thinking throughout the 1880s. The story works, through its web of literary images, to connect that modern dream with what, for the metropolis, seems the far-off and unutterably different world of Africa. The text overtly targets male aggression for critique, but it also implicitly addresses a female audience concerned with progress and emancipation for women in the West and challenges that audience with its own complicity in what happens, in the name of progress, elsewhere.

The young volunteer soldier Peter Halket has been separated from his troop whilst scouting and has to spend a night alone on a small hill, or "kopje," in the vast loneliness of the African veld. There, a phantasmagoria of memory and guilt and desire plays itself out in his mind. He remembers his English home and his beloved, poverty-stricken mother and wonders why he should not, like others, become wealthy beyond imagining in South Africa and thus release her from poverty. As he daydreams about making money through speculation, Peter's mind grows hazy, just as it did when he tried to do equations at school, for Peter cannot see the relation between things: "he could not see the relation between the first two terms and the third."[9] In her study of the imperial romance, Laura Chrisman argues that in Peter's inability to grasp the operations of the capitalist system, Schreiner signals an opposition to "instrumental" or calculating reason that reduces everything, including human beings, to a "means."[10] Where later critics have seen Schreiner's project limited by her adherence to paternalist liberalism, Chrisman rightly points out that by the mid-1890s, liberal ideology was itself internally divided and disintegrating, and that *Trooper Peter* contributes to that process by way of its insistent materialist perspective.[11]

Peter's hazy daydream about his past then becomes confused with remembered fragments of the violence of his life as a mercenary in Matabeleland. Peter has shot people and destroyed their homes and the food on which they depend. One particular image brings his disordered thoughts to a stop. It is of a young black woman, found alone in the bush by Peter and a companion, "her baby on her back, but young and pretty." The unspoken fact of the woman's rape by the two white men means that Peter's narrative fails, as he suddenly thinks of his mother again. He does not yet know that he suffers from unacknowledged guilt, but he does know that he cannot think of his mother and of what he and his companion did to the young black woman at the same time (36–37). Schreiner thus signals the coincidence of imperial and sexual violence, made known in Peter's silence by the mediating presence of his mother back in England.

Peter's lonely hillside vigil is interrupted by the appearance of a stranger whom we as readers, although not yet Peter, recognize as Christ. Much of the rest of the book is made up of the stranger's stories, which tell of colonial conflict in South Africa and elsewhere, of greed and cruelty, of the overreaching ambition of Cecil Rhodes, and of the persistence throughout history of a humanist ethic that is clearly aligned in the narrative with a radicalized Christianity. The stranger's stories last throughout the night, and they transform Peter. They force him to realise that his own affective life and identity is echoed in the equally feelingful lives of the anonymous "niggers" he has been allowed to despise as less than fully human and is employed to uproot, dispossess, and kill.

The key to Peter's epiphanal recognition of Africa as something other than a chance to get rich quickly (he says to the stranger: "'If you don't want to make money, what did you come to this land for? No one comes here for anything else'" [60]), is the one story *he* tells. It concerns the two African women he buys while working for a prospector at the mines. The eldest is a woman of at least thirty, although Peter is not yet twenty-one, whom he knows to have been taken from her own husband and children. The woman works for him and makes him a garden. Hearing about the Matabele uprising, Peter volunteers. He leaves the women to tend his place, knowing that the elder is pregnant with his child. The point of Peter's story is his hurt and outrage on discovering that, immediately he had departed, the women also left, taking only a gun and the ammunition the older woman had tricked him into giving her. His repeated claim that the women's actions bewildered him, because he had treated them well and never beat them, serves ironically to underscore the violence of his enforced family-making.

Peter is most indignant about the fact that, after their escape, the women met an African man some miles off. Peter is certain that this man was the woman's African husband, and that the woman had been plotting to leave all the time she had been with him. After his night on the veld, when Peter rejoins his troop, he discovers that an African man has been captured by some members of the troop. He pleads with his captain for the prisoner's life, repeating over and over again that he thinks he knows the man, for he thinks the prisoner is the woman's husband. The irate captain ordains that the prisoner be executed the following morning and orders Peter to carry out the task. Instead, Peter frees the man and is himself shot by the captain. What he has really discovered, of course, is the fellowship of man, symbolized by "the red sand . . . in which a black man and a white man's blood were mingled" (120). But the identification that takes place between these two men at the end of the book is the consequence of a humanity gained in the context of sexual violence and forced family relations.

In making Peter's African story a story of double sexual standards and the abuse of women, Schreiner makes it impossible to avoid the question of *sexual* morality, which was so central to the arguments about women's emancipation in the metropolis. It is, of course, a commonplace of colonial discourse to deny African psychological interiority. The dominant discourses of social Darwinism and anthropology described Africans as collective rather than individual, and akin to immature "children" (this was a claim frequently made by Rhodes). In restoring an assumed interiority to the nameless African woman of Peter's story, Schreiner could be accused of a form of projection or appropriation, issuing the African woman with a European or Western subjectivity. But the gesture is surely strategic. Those central demands being made in metropolitan feminist debates for women's self-determination, the right to bodily integrity, and freedom from sexual coercion, are starkly brought into play in the colony. The African woman—silent, unnamed, and "other" though she may be—is subjected to sexual oppression and she too has the capacity to resist and to act for herself.

Even more tellingly, perhaps, is the fact that Peter's brittle machismo— usually he tells the story to men around the campfire, boasting of how he would like to put a bullet through the African husband—cannot disguise the psychic complexities Schreiner imports to her allegory of capitalist-imperialist greed and destruction. These are complexities expected, and demanded, in metropolitan gender debates. What is clear from the story is that Peter loves the African woman; she provides for him and she makes him a garden in the desert. He has an intimation of what this means for him—it means a home, and a family—but absolutely no sense at all of what it might mean for her. Peter's psychic defamation, in a colonial context, which allows the white man to value African life so cheaply that humanity is imperiled, echoes and mimics the actual violation of the African woman; just as his death at the end of the book "stands in," literally and symbolically, for that of the African man. But Peter's death is not a redemptive martyrdom: it is witnessed only by two men, who confirm that it will have no effect. Neither a Christian faith in the actions of the good man nor a liberal belief in the political potency of the individual can simply prevail. Schreiner's ironic manipulation of a Christian ethic that had long supported the extension of empire is explicitly and continually juxtaposed with the political and economic realities of modernizing South Africa.

Peter's story of "his" African women serves to push home Schreiner's point that Peter's actions as a wealth-seeking adventurer are not fundamentally different from his behavior as a mercenary soldier. As Laura Chrisman argues, "Schreiner denies a distinction between the categories of war and colonial economic settlement. The non-militarized operations of individual settlers, like those of Rhodes's Chartered Company, are necessarily a form of war."[12] Peter's woeful description of the loss of his nascent family (one woman pregnant, and the other probably so) cannot disguise the fact that his sexual and domestic use of the women is little different from the rapes conducted under "war" conditions in Matabeleland, raping done by Peter himself and others like him.

The sexual abuse and violation of family portrayed in *Trooper Peter* serves to heighten the contradictions set up in Schreiner's evocation of a radical Christian ethic. In 1895, she wrote to her friend W. T. Stead that "We want an 'If Christ Came to South Africa' from your pen."[13] The reference is to Stead's *If Christ Came to Chicago*, a set of essays that charted Chicago's social problems and incited its readership to moral reflection by asking: "If Christ came to Chicago what would he wish me to do?"[14] Schreiner's own version of Christ's coming to South Africa, by contrast, depends for its moral message on its literary form. As the critic Stephen Gray comments, Schreiner's techniques in *Trooper Peter* are "abundantly and importantly those of the fiction-writer."[15] If *Trooper Peter* does not quite work as realist fiction, despite the fact that its symbolical-allegorical proliferations are firmly anchored in a realist schema, Gray argues, it is because Schreiner "*rejects the morality which the realist novel encodes*" (emphasis in original) at the same time as she mocks the adventure and romantic quest novels popularized by writers such as Rider Haggard.[16] Over ten years earlier, in *The Story of an African Farm*'s famous preface, Schreiner

mockingly and ironically mourned her inability to write "a history of wild adventures," "'of encounters with lions and hair-breadth escapes'"—precisely
the adventure fiction that, via the pen of Rider Haggard and others, provided
the metropolis with its images of Africa. Schreiner concludes that such stories
are best written by metropolitans whose stake in other lands is not the same as
one "who sits down to paint the scenes among which he has grown."[17] The
often strange and discontinuous narrative method of *African Farm* is pushed
even further in *Trooper Peter Halket*. In particular, Schreiner puts into the most
uncomfortable formal juxtaposition a biblically inspired allegoric narrative
and the documentary-like details of South African politics, in order to indicate
that something has gone very wrong in English Christian culture.

War and "Eighteen Ninety-Nine"

After the Jameson Raid, Schreiner began to see the Boers—especially in the
republics—as the only force in South Africa capable of opposing the aggressive
aims of capital. In doing so, she was all too aware of Boer racism. Writing to the
liberal Cape politician John X. Merriman in 1896, she noted that "on the native
question we have to fight the main body of [the Boers] to the death for the next
20 years."[18] She saw Boer racism, however, as part of an old world: a result of
prejudices long held but potentially transformable. Afrikaners could, Schreiner
believed, eventually be educated in tolerance and were therefore simply not so
dangerous and divisive as the development of monopolistic and speculative
capitalism in South Africa. She concluded that racism would flourish most
tenaciously under a capitalist economic system. Refusing to describe black
Africans in the language of social Darwinism so dominant by the end of the
century (which put black Africans on an evolutionary "lower" scale than white
Europeans), she consistently constructed them in terms of political economy.[19]
The class divide created by capitalist modernity was "complicated by a difference of race and colour between the employing and propertied, and the employed and poorer classes," she argued.[20] Racial differences can cut across class
identifications and were used in South Africa to undermine class solidarity and
therefore allow an unfettered "propertied" power to reign.

In the run-up to the war, and for its duration, Schreiner thus became an
outspoken supporter of the Boer cause. She believed that resistance to capitalism could not—at that historical moment—decisively come from Africa's black
population. If the violence of capitalism could only be answered by violence

(a position Schreiner later came to reject), a hundred years of South Africa's history had demonstrated all too physically that black-white military conflict resolved itself, in the end, at the cost of African lives and lands. What industrial and commercial modernity had brought were increasingly efficient means of killing. This was the lesson Schreiner learnt in witnessing the making of Rhodesia; the Boers were, potentially at least, a force capable of staying capitalism. Her support for the republican cause was thus explicitly tactical, as she explained in 1899 to Jan Smuts, when she described the republics as "the two last little sluice-gates we have left keeping out the flood of capitalism which would otherwise sweep in and overwhelm South Africa."[21]

Schreiner wrote only one piece of fiction about the war, a story published posthumously in *Stories, Dreams and Allegories* (1923). Although a far more conventional format than *Trooper Peter*, like the latter "Eighteen-Ninety-Nine" insists that "back home" cannot remain untouched by, or innocent of, what happens at the colonial margins. Written after the end of the war, "Eighteen Ninety-Nine" reads, on the face of it, as a version of Afrikaner nationalist myth. It incorporates in its narrative elements that were to become central to the emergence of a full-fledged nationalist ideology: the Great Trek and the massacre by Zulus at Weenen, "Slachters Nek," Piet Retief, and Dingaan's Day.[22] I argue, though, that embedded in Schreiner's retelling of the story of Afrikaner nation-making is a moral appeal to recognizably *English* traditions, particularly by way of mobilizing the powerful anti-war sentiments provoked by the concentration camp controversies—controversies in which women and children, and the idea of family, were central.

The major military offensives of the South African war were all but over by the end of 1900; what continued was effectively a guerrilla war fought by a small number of Boer commandos. The British response to their successes was to initiate a program of farm-burning, designed to break the commandos' informal support systems across the veld. Thousands of Afrikaner and African refugees were, as a result, the first victims of concentration camps. Set up to control the displaced refugees, the camps' poor diet and sanitation resulted in widespread and endemic disease and death. Probably more than 50,000 Africans and Afrikaners died, the vast majority of whom were women and children. In Britain there was public outrage, led by Emily Hobhouse, secretary of the women's branch of the South African Conciliation Committee, who investigated and reported on conditions in the camps.[23] "When is a war not a war?" Sir Henry Campbell-Bannerman, the Liberal leader, famously asked, in response to the scandals exposed by Hobhouse: "When it is carried on by methods of barbarism in South Africa."[24] It is this history—and particularly the mobilization in England of women's support for other suffering women and children—that Schreiner exploits in her story. She implicitly addresses a central argument of metropolitan feminism: namely, the claim to universality. "Eighteen Ninety-Nine" makes the briefest of references to the camps (in a "postscript" to the main story): as Schreiner well knew, however, it would evoke a major emotional and political response from her women readers in Britain.

The story begins in the early 1880s. A Boer woman of about fifty and a younger woman, her daughter-in-law, are working a farm in the northern Transvaal. The narrative tells of the older woman's life: her parents' exodus from the Cape in the Great Trek of the 1830s, their deaths at Weenen when the *voortrekkers* were attacked by Zulu warriors, and her own escape, with a child companion. Married eventually to her companion, the young couple stake out land to farm and the woman gives birth to three sons, two of whom, along with the husband, die untimely deaths as victims of the harsh, perilous settler life. The youngest son marries and, when he dies from fever contracted while fighting the British at the battle of Majuba, his wife is carrying his unborn child.[25] The child's birth returns us to the story's beginning. It is essential to Schreiner's message that, after the death of their menfolk, the women farm the land without the aid of white men, and with only their black servants. I shall come back to this point, the importance of which emerges from the literal and the ideological battles being fought on the veld during the war years.

The narrative moves to the present and the boy child's growing up. His grandmother tells him stories of the Boers' past, especially of the Great Trek from the Cape Colony in the 1830s which culminated in the formation of the two Boer republics. This, in Afrikaner nationalism, is the first great manifestation of Boer determination to find freedom from British rule." 'Grandmother,'" the child asks, " 'do the English want *all* the lands of *all* the people?' "[26] The women plan to send the boy to school, at the Cape and then to Europe; they save all that they earn for this. When he is just turned eighteen, though, war is declared and, like his father, the boy goes to fight the "khakies" and is killed. The main part of the story ends with the two women rising in their grief to plant seeds for the next harvest. The story has two postscripts: the first, "Nineteen Hundred and One," briefly records that the two women died in a concentration camp and lie in unmarked graves; the second, "In the Year Nineteen Hundred and Four," explains that the farmhouse no longer stands, having been burned down by English soldiers. Some of the familiar objects with which the story begins—a polished gun kept on the wall and a small Boer stool, objects of pastoral and domestic life—are now to be found as mementos in English homes, as the farm had been looted before it was destroyed.

The story's ending is perhaps the obvious place to begin. The old flintlock gun that, in 1904, adorns the wall of a country house in the north of England, had been taken by an Englishman from the wall of the Boer farm before the farm was torched. The gun had belonged to the grandmother's husband and, with it, he had shot the lion that maimed him so badly he died of his wounds. After his death, the widowed woman hung the gun on the wall, taking it down every day to polish it. The Englishman tells his friends that "it must be at least eighty years old and is very valuable . . . it must have been kept in such perfect repair by continual polishing for the steel shines as if it were silver" (57). The silver is surely meant to remind Schreiner's readers of that other precious metal, gold. The idea that the war had been fought because of South Africa's gold had been popularized by J. A. Hobson. His classic critique of imperialism appeared in 1902; in it, Hobson argued that imperialism had to be understood as structurally related to a developing, internationalized capitalism, which, unchecked, would produce incessant military conflict and gross human exploitation. His test-case for this new theory of "economic imperialism" was South Africa. The 1899–1902 war was, he argued, fought for gold and was orchestrated behind the scenes by representatives of "international capital" who had extensive financial interests in the Transvaal's mines.[27]

The value of the silver gun for the Englishman who looted it thus evokes the exchange of the capitalist market, at the same time as it registers an extra (although bogus) value of imperial and masculine pride. As the man proudly shows it off, "he does not tell that he took it from the wall of the little mud house before he burnt it down" (57). The silvered steel, produced through love and labor and loss, commemorates a different order of value for the Boer women. Before it becomes mourning-work, the gun signifies use-value (the grandmother's husband used it to hunt for food) and symbolizes the "fair, free fight" with nature and environment so central to Afrikaner pastoral mythology (the flintlock kills a lioness, but the lioness kills the hunter).

The deaths that structure the first part of the story—the woman's husband and her three sons—are human notes in the temporality of the pastoral. Seasons unfold, the maize and the pumpkins are planted, husbanded, and har-

vested. Most important, the land is enriched with the blood of Boer manhood. The story is, in other words, saturated in pastoral motifs. J. M. Coetzee
argues that the pastoral became crucial to Afrikaner culture when the "unset-
tled settler" of South Africa, moving increasingly in the first half of the twentieth century to towns and cities, sought security in a nostalgia for the calm
and stability of the farm. Laboring on the land is the key to the metonymic relation between land and people that the pastoral evokes. Thus the Boer pastoral must represent Boer labor and, at the same time, occlude that of the
black Africans who, in fact, carried its burden: "As its central issue the genre
prefers to identify the preservation of a (Dutch) peasant rural order, *or at least
the preservation of the values of that order*. In (British) capitalism it identifies
the principal enemy of the old ways. Locating the historically significant conflict as between Boer and Briton, it shifts black-white conflict out of sight into
a forgotten past or an obscure future."[28] Schreiner's story plays with, and sub-
verts, the conventions of the pastoral genre in various subtle but telling ways.
Although the depiction of African servants on the farm is marginal to the
main narrative, it is made absolutely explicit that the women, first the older
and then the younger, refuse the advances of neighboring Boer men who visit
as potential suitors. They depend entirely upon their own labor, and upon the
labor of their African servants. When the grandmother's husband dies, she
buries him with the help of the African servants; and afterward the servants
plough the land, while she plants and waters it. All through the story there are
reminders of the Africans who work the farm, including the woman who,
after the death of the last living son and grandson, witnesses the Boer
women's grief. It is she who notices work not done: the milk unstrained, the
fire allowed to die out, and the window shutters still unopened, and it is she
who undertakes these tasks (51–52).

Certainly, the economic and social exploitation endemic to black and white
relations on the Boer farm is muted, rather than highlighted, by Schreiner. As I
have argued, her express motive for supporting the Boer cause in the war
stemmed from a conviction that the latter constituted a historic opportunity to
stay the advance of capitalism in South Africa. Thus "Eighteen Ninety-Nine"
works, on one level, simply as a sentimental portrayal of Boer resistance to
British capitalist-imperial aggression. Looked at contextually, however, the story
reveals a more complicated picture. The importance of the muted, but nevertheless insistently represented, relations between the farm women and their

African servants only becomes clear in relation to the farm burnings and estab-lishment of concentration camps, which seem to be so fleetingly mentioned in the story's postscript. For Schreiner, though, and for her potential audience, the farm burnings and the camps were absolutely central to the propaganda battle accompanying the military one.

One of the most important and ideologically charged propaganda defenses of British farm burning and the establishment of camps turned on the ques-tion of Boer women's safety. Pro-imperial commentators, most notably Arthur Conan Doyle in his *The War in South Africa: Its Cause and Conduct*, argued that Boer women made homeless by farm-burnings would be at the mercy of black men; their incarceration was, therefore, for their own safety: "It was not merely that burned-out families must be given a shelter, but it was that no woman on a lonely farm was safe amid a black population, even if she had the means of procuring food."[29] Conan Doyle makes it clear that Boer women are *sexually* imperiled. In part, this is because his book is an extended critique of a pam-phlet by W. T. Stead that accused British soldiers of raping Boer women. De-liberately evoking Campbell-Bannerman's condemnation of "methods of bar-barism" in his title, Stead shocked many people by arguing what Schreiner had suggested in *Trooper Peter Halket*—that, away from home, English boys are prepared to behave very badly indeed. In an earlier pamphlet, Stead had him-self used the image of black men raping white women, arguing that the farm-burning policy left Boer women terribly exposed, and only abandoning this ar-gument when he discovered its efficacy in justifying the camps.[30] Despite their very different propaganda aims, however, Conan Doyle and Stead both based their position on particular images of women and of Africa. For both, the rep-resentation of masculinity and its relation to national identity depends on a vision of women as either passive victims of sexual aggression or the moral regulators of a truly civilized society. Nowhere in their writing is African fem-ininity evoked, despite the death rates of African women in the camps. For both, "Africa" signifies a primitive and violent masculine sexuality; or, later for Stead, a sign of atavism and barbarism by which working-class British youth would become infected. These are all images Schreiner attempts to dispute.

In making her story about white women who do "procure food" *and* remain safe (until the English arrive), Schreiner thus registers three points of resistance: first, to the erasure of black Africans performed by the pastoral genre to which her story apparently conforms; second, to the displacing of "methods of barbarism" from the British to the African, exemplified in Conan Doyle's argument; and, third, to the implication that, without their men, women are unable to survive. By the time Schreiner finished "Eighteen Ninety-Nine" (around 1905), she must have been aware that its publication could no longer influence an audience. She was, indeed, increasingly aware that white hegemony was going to prevail at the cost of South Africa's majority population, and her support for the Boers stopped. But in the moment of its writing, the story is implicitly addressed to women in Britain who Schreiner believed might yet be able to influence the course of imperial policy. Thus it is crucial that things on the Boer farm do not add up in terms of gender. The only white male presence there, the adored son and grandson, is feminized (contrary to the maculinist emphasis of the Afrikaner pastoral). In addition, the women aspire for the boy to leave "pre-modernity," as represented by the Boer farm, and go to Europe to be educated. Their ambition, in other words—and it is crucial that they *have* ambition—is not so different from that of any English son's aspiring mother.

For it is this ambition that sets the women at odds with the portrait of Boer life Schreiner so painstakingly constructs, most notably in her collection of essays on Boer life, *Thoughts on South Africa*.[31] So too does their refusal to remarry: Tant' Sannie, in *The Story of an African Farm*, tells her stepdaughter Em that "'marriage is the finest thing in the world. I've been at it three times, and if it pleased God to take this husband from me I should have another.'"[32] This is Schreiner's exposition of the gulf between such "pre-modern" sensibilities and modern ones, in *Thoughts on South Africa*: "That essentially modern condition of mind, in which an individual remains sexually solitary and unmated because no other is found who satisfies the complex intellectual and emotional needs of a nature in which these needs are as imperative as the physical, and in which union with an individual not singled out by an almost immeasurable sympathy from the rest of their sex would be morally abhorrent . . . this is a condition of mind unintelligible to the primitive Boer."[33] By giving to her Boer woman protagonist precisely this "essentially modern condition of mind," Schreiner places her metropolitan women readers in a position where they are unable to avoid identification with the aspirations, and the plight, of the Boer women. Modern metropolitan desires and needs are, after all, to be found in a story about the "backward" Boer enemy and such feminist desires and needs should not, and could not, be kept separate from the politics of nation and empire.

144 ° CAROLYN BURDETT

NOTES

Some of the material here appears, in a slightly different form, in Carolyn Burdett, *Olive Schreiner and the Progress of Feminism: Evolution, Gender, Empire* (London: Palgrave, 2000)

1. For Schreiner's biography, see Ruth First and Ann Scott, *Olive Schreiner: A Biography* (London: André Deutsch, 1980). On Schreiner and the idea of progress, see Burdett, *Olive Schreiner.*

2. Olive Schreiner, *Letters*, ed. Richard Rive, vol. 1: *1871–1899* (Oxford: Oxford University Press, 1988), 175, 189.

3. The "old" colonial order began with Dutch, German, and Huguenot settlers who followed the route of the Dutch East India Company in the latter half of the seventeenth century. These Boer (or Afrikaner) colonists were largely farmers and this first phase of South Africa's colonization was marked by bitter and bloody conflict with indigenous Africans and the expropriation of African land and labor. British colonization came later, at the end of the eighteenth century, motivated by the desire to secure trade routes for the empire. The two Boer republics, which were the product of further colonial expansion in the 1830s, are seen in Afrikaner accounts as a response to British oppression in the Cape Colony. For an account of this history, see Timothy Keegan, *Colonial South Africa and the Origins of the Racial Order* (London: Leicester University Press; Charlottesville: University Press of Virginia, 1996).

4. *The Last Will and Testament of Cecil John Rhodes*, ed. W. T. Stead (London: Review of Reviews, 1902), 55.

5. Denis Judd, *Empire: The British Imperial Experience from 1765 to the Present* (London: Fontana, 1997), 121.

6. As quoted in Mordechai Tamarkin, *Cecil Rhodes and the Cape Afrikaners: The Imperial Colossus and the Colonial Parish Pump* (London: Frank Cass, 1996), 8.

7. Olive Schreiner and C. S. [*sic*] Cronwright-Schreiner, *The Political Situation*, (London: T. Fisher Unwin, 1896).

8. Schreiner, *Letters*, ed. Rive, 1: 288.

9. Olive Schreiner, *Trooper Peter Halket of Mashonaland* (1897; Parklands, South Africa: A. D. Donker, 1992), 33. Subsequent citations are given in the text.

10. Laura Chrisman, *Rereading the Imperial Romance: British Imperialism and South African Resistance in Haggard, Schreiner, and Plaatje* (Oxford: Clarendon Press, 2000), 128.

11. Ibid., 124, 129.

12. Ibid., 141.

13. Schreiner, *Letters*, ed. Rive, 1: 256.

14. W. T. Stead, *If Christ Came to Chicago: A Plea for the Union of All Who Love in the Service of All Who Suffer* (London: Review of Reviews, 1894), 432.

15. Stephen Gray, "The Trooper at the Hanging Tree," in *Olive Schreiner*, ed. Cherry Clayton (Johannesburg: McGraw-Hill, 1983), 200.

16. Gray, 200, 207.

17. Olive Schreiner, *The Story of an African Farm* (1883; Harmondsworth, U.K.: Penguin Books, 1971), 27–28.

18. Schreiner, *Letters*, ed. Rive, 1: 278.

19. See Paula Krebs, *Gender, Race, and the Writing of Empire* (Cambridge: Cambridge University Press, 1999), 109–142.

20. Schreiner, *Political Situation*, 14.

21. Schreiner, *Letters*, ed. Rive, 1: 344.

22. All key episodes in the establishing of a Boer "homeland." For a sympathetic portrait of this Afrikaner history, see Johannes Meintjes, *The Voortrekkers* (London: Corgi, 1975); for a more critical analysis, see Leonard Thompson, *The Political Mythology of Apartheid* (New Haven: Yale University Press, 1985). In relation to "Eighteen Ninety-Nine," Carol Barash provides a brief but helpful guide to reading the story as a sympathetic reworking of Afrikaner political mythology in *An Olive Schreiner Reader: Writings on Women and South Africa*, ed. Carol Barash (London: Pandora, 1987), 155.

23. See Hope Hay Hewison, *Hedge of Wild Almonds: South Africa, the "Pro-Boers" and the Quaker Conscience* (London: James Currey, 1989), 187–224; Krebs, *Writing of Empire*.

24. Quoted in Hewison, *Hedge of Wild Almonds*, 192.

25. The British empire, under the colonial secretary, Lord Carnarvon, annexed the Transvaal republic in 1877. This led to armed conflict with the Boers in 1880–81 and the defeat of British forces at Majuba Hill. Gladstone's Liberal government decided to back down, and independence was restored to the Transvaal.

26. Olive Schreiner, "Eighteen Ninety-Nine," in *Stories, Dreams and Allegories* (London: T. Fisher Unwin, 1923), 33–34.

27. J. A. Hobson, *Imperialism: A Study* (1902; London: Unwin Hyman, 1988).

28. J. M. Coetzee, *White Writing: On the Culture of Letters in South Africa* (New Haven: Yale University Press, 1988), 5–6.

29. Arthur Conan Doyle, *The War in South Africa: Its Cause and Conduct* (London: Smith, Elder, 1902), 81–82.

30. W. T. Stead, *How Not to Make Peace: Evidence as to Homestead Burning Collected and Examined* (London: Review of Reviews, 1900); id., *Methods of Barbarism: "War is War" and "War is Hell": The Case for Intervention* (London: Review of Reviews, 1901).

31. Olive Schreiner, *Thoughts on South Africa* (1923; Parklands, South Africa: A. D. Donker, 1992).

32. Schreiner, *Story of an African Farm*, 293.

33. Schreiner, *Thoughts on South Africa*, 170.

"Tropical Ovaries"

Gynecological Degeneration and Lady Arabella's "Female Difficulties" in Bram Stoker's The Lair of the White Worm

As the British empire reached its zenith in the 1870s, the clinical gaze of tropical medicine became increasingly centered on the management of the Englishwoman's reproductive capacities. Although the effects of tropical climates on European constitutions had been investigated in earlier medical texts, toward the fin-de-siècle, anxieties about gynecological decay in the "torrid zones" easily lent themselves to mainstream discourses of racial degeneration.[1] In his treatise *Health in India for British Women* (1875), Edward Tilt, one of the most prominent gynecological experts of the day, argued that the "morbid womb" was a major threat to the imperial vision and that Englishwomen returned "home" from the colonies with their "tropical" ovaries in dangerous states of debility and decay: "For it must be borne in mind, that whether in India or in our other tropical possessions, European women are generally young. They leave Great Britain at about twenty, and seldom remain in India after forty."[2]

Tilt repeatedly invokes the views of other important practitioners of tropical medicine such as Sir James Ranald Martin, presidency surgeon of Bengal, and Sir Joseph Fayrer, president of the India Office medical board, to support his thesis. He foregrounds the alarming statistics provided by his friend and colleague Duncan Stewart, professor of midwifery in the Medical College of Calcutta and physician to the Hospital for Native Women: "eight out of ten of the European female residents are habitually subject to deranged menstruation, leucorrhea, or to cervical inflammation" (Tilt, *Health in India*, 55). With her defective and monstrous womb harboring its "hideous progeny"[3]—the potential failure of empire—the memsahib returns home to England, in an effort to recuperate and re-anglicize her "orientalized" body. As Dane Kennedy has compellingly argued, the links between climate, racial decline, and reproductive chaos became a significant feature of debates within tropical medicine at this time because the proper functioning of the reproductive organs was central to the preservation of the Raj.[4]

Recent studies of feminism and early modernism have reconstructed the "New Woman" as a complex social and political being. According to Ann Ardis, for example, the New Woman's revolutionary sexuality, together with her ideological distances from various other feminist and socialist reformers, hybridized her political presence, allowing her to resist/evade categorization to a certain extent.[5] Sally Ledger and Lisa Hamilton have also explored the deployment of this figure in conservative as well as radical discourses of sexuality, while Nancy Paxton's work on Anglo-Indian rape narratives calls attention to the ways in which the New Woman's disruptive erotic potential inhabits and reconfigures colonial spaces.[6] I would like to extend these discussions by suggesting that the often overlooked "contact zone"[7] between the discourses of ethnology, empire, and gynecology is of crucial importance to our readings of the phenomenon of the monstrous New Woman in British fiction and culture at the turn of the twentieth century. Tilt's work provides fresh points of entry into the ways in which popular literary representations of the vampiric female body appropriate his notion of the "tropicalized uterus" and are themselves situated within the intersections of colonial gynecology and ethnographic discourses of racial hybridity. Focusing specifically on Bram Stoker's nightmare of the morbid womb, *The Lair of the White Worm* (1911), I shall argue that the serpentine Lady Arabella March dismantles biological and colonial imperatives by aggressively pursuing the pleasures of uterine devolution.[8]

Stoker's last novel presents us with his most sustained and compelling images of the terrifying spaces opened up within the female body when the reproductive process has gone awry. Critics have tended to dismiss this work as a product of psychosis brought on by tertiary syphilis, and in doing so have encouraged rather narrow readings of the text's horrific representations of female genitalia.[9] In fact, however, there is considerable doubt as to whether Stoker was actually suffering from syphilis toward the end of his life. In her recent biography of Stoker, Barbara Belford suggests, for example, that there is simply not enough evidence to prove this diagnosis conclusively, indicating that he may, rather, have died of a stroke.[10] I would go still further: resisting reading *The Lair of the White Worm* as a syphilitic/psychotic text allows for a more complex interpretation of the novel's racialized sexual dynamics. Far more fascinating than the purely autobiographical resonances of this text are the cultural ones, which reveal the connections between fictional treatments of the female body and gynecological "science" at the end of the nineteenth century. Stoker's narrative in *Lair* obsessively probes the relation between the deformed womb and questions of racial survival through miscegenation, a concern that resonates not only through Tilt's work but also through the leading ethnological debates of his time.[11]

In his recent study of Stoker's fiction, David Glover argues that "the forays into cultural criticism or the conjectures on history or religion in Stoker's novels frequently draw upon medicine or science," and he documents Stoker's preoccupation with ethnology, criminal anthropology, phrenology, mesmerism and psychiatry—concerns evident in *Dracula* (1897). Glover also points out that two of Stoker's brothers were part of the medical establishment: his elder brother William was appointed president of Ireland's Royal College of Surgeons and of the Royal Academy of Medicine, while George Stoker worked as a surgeon in South Africa.[12] Given Tilt's prominence, it is highly probable that they would both have been acquainted with his work. Stoker's library, auctioned off after his death, reveals his considerable interest in both ethnography and tropical medicine.[13]

Although Stoker's novel was published more than thirty years after *Health in India*, the debate over the effects of tropical "exhaustion" was at its height shortly before and after the publication of *Lair*. Addresses by prominent medical men on this subject appeared frequently in the *Transactions of the Royal Society of Tropical Medicine* between 1907 and 1913.[14] Tilt's *Health in India* was one of the texts that expanded the terms of this debate through his explanation of the probable causes of uterine degeneration. From the beginning, he reveals his preoccupation with ethnological categories; "amongst races little restrained by social position or the dictates of morality," uterine diseases in native women can be linked to their excessive sexuality, whether sanctioned by religion, poor hygiene, or the "first impulse of passion" (Tilt, *Health in India*, 53). This insidious contagion, which marks the body of the other woman, assaults the young memsahib, who arriving in India, is attracted to excessive behaviors—which ultimately results in a "morbid" and diseased uterus (Tilt, *Health in India*, 57). Tilt finds the permeability of European women's bodies particularly disquieting. As their boundaries are gradually loosened by contact with the tropical climate and with native women, these bodies endlessly "reproduce" uterine monstrosities instead of good imperialists.

The Lair of the White Worm opens with the budding imperialist Adam Salton's return home from the colonies to confront the horror of tropical ovaries at home. Stephen Arata, in a recent reading of *Dracula* as a reverse colonization narrative, sees Dracula as possessing a "vampiric fecundity . . . that threatens to overwhelm the far less prolific British men," paralyzed by "fears of degeneration."[15] In *Lair*, however, it is the monstrous Englishwoman's *lack of fecundity* that transforms *her* body into a site of fear and resistance. The deepest threat does not arise here primarily from either reverse colonization by the racial other (though the novel does agonize over the problem of miscegenation as a solution to degeneration) or from fears of male sexual impotence. Rather, it arises from within Englishness or "whiteness" itself—an Englishness transformed and depleted through its imperial activities, fascinated by its own "original" hybridity and lack of internal coherence.[16]

In search of the origins of British civilization, Salton returns from Australia to claim his inheritance in Mercia, the heart of "Roman Britain," which is also the subject of his anthropological research. On his arrival, he is greeted by his grand-uncle, who informs him that he is the last of his race and that by returning home, he is about to penetrate the "real heart of the old Kingdom of Mercia, where there are traces of all the various nationalities which made up the conglomerate which became Britain."[17] In a journey that formulates itself as the reverse of Marlowe's in Conrad's *Heart of Darkness*, Adam moves toward the racial chaos and mongrelization at the heart of "whiteness." His uncle narrates the history of Castra Regis, the great estate that dominates the landscape and is the family seat of the aristocratic but degenerate Caswall family. They are described as a "strange race" (17) characterized by certain stigmata: mesmeric and demoniac powers, which are "partly racial and partly individual," and "thick black hair growing low down on the neck" signifying "vast physical strength and endurance" (16–17).[18]

Arriving in Mercia, Adam encounters three women: the enigmatic Lady Arabella March, the Eurasian (half-Burmese) Mimi Watford, and her anemic half sister, the dove-like Lilla. Stoker presents us initially with an entire spectrum of racial types. On one end stands Edgar Caswall, the last scion of the Caswall family: the tropicalized European, a "cultured savage" whose physiognomy displays "traces of the softening civilization of ages" (27), and who returns from Africa, accompanied by Oolanga, his African servant, a "pure, pristine, unreformed, unsoftened savage" (28). On the other end is Lady Arabella, who is classified as belonging to "the Caucasian type, beautiful, Saxon blonde, with a complexion of milk and roses, high-bred, clever, serene of nature" (28). Yet, interestingly, the text proceeds to interrupt and dislocate these ethnological categories as it begins to articulate its anxieties: Arabella's perfect Caucasian physiognomy conceals her monstrously "deranged" womb.

Adam first sees Arabella "glide" into a mound of black snakes, "clad in some kind of soft white stuff, which clung close to her form, showing to the full every movement of her sinuous figure" (25). Georges Clairin's 1876 painting of the actress Sarah Bernhardt's serpentine body, wrapped in white satin, closely resembles Stoker's visualization of Arabella; both articulate anxieties about the public woman's body. Indeed, as Patrick Bade notes, Bernhardt, with her "satin-lined coffin, menagerie of wild beasts, interest in executions and necklace of petrified human eyes" deliberately manipulated these anxieties in order to cultivate her public image.[19] Racialized images of snake-women proliferated in late nineteenth-century European culture.[20] Perhaps the most notorious conflation of the exotic and the serpentine occurs in Flaubert's *Salammbô* (1862), where the Carthaginian Salammbô's rituals of goddess-worship involve a seductive encounter with a python.[21]

In 1892, Sir Joseph Fayrer (also an expert on serpent poison) read a paper to the Victoria Institute in London on ophiolatry (serpent worship) in India, referring to a tribe called the Nagas who take "the serpent as their emblem or cognizance." In the process, he simplified the implications of serpent iconography in the Hindu religion, using it as an example of the "primitive" customs and superstitions of the colonized and stating categorically: "As regards Europe, there are next to no traces of its prevalence among the Germans . . . nor among the Gauls nor Britons." Contradicting Fayrer, others in the audience pointed out the prevalence of serpent mounds and worship in Europe's past: "in the British Isles, in America, Spain, France" lurking under sites that had been "Christianised" with a church or a cross.[22]

Stoker's novel seeks to uncover such sites in its search for Britain's "perverse" and racially tainted history. Adam takes to keeping pet mongooses, which attack Arabella viciously and are torn to pieces by her as a result. She inhabits "Diana's Grove," which, as Adam is informed by his archaeologist friend and mentor Nathaniel Salis (a Van-Helsing like figure), in the native Mercian language originally meant "the lair of the white worm." The actual lair, as Adam discovers later, is a well in Arabella's house, which is, of course, a striking enactment and figuration of Tilt's discourse of gynecological abjection. "The open well hole was almost under his nose, sending up such a stench as almost made Adam sick, though Lady Arabella seemed not to mind it at all. It was like nothing Adam had ever met with. He compared it with all the noxious experiences he had ever had—the drainage of war hospitals, of slaughter-houses, the refuse of dissecting rooms" (172). As Belford puts it: "The hole is repeatedly described in vaginal terms . . . Salton delubricates it and destroys it with dynamite."[23]

Here Stoker's language mirrors Tilt's invocation of the acute inflammation of the womb in the tropics, the change in the cervix: "the mucous membrane covering it is red, and the mouth of the womb is more or less ulcerated and patulous. Generally the lining membrane of the cervix is in a similar state, and from it there flows a yellow discharge" (Tilt, *Health in India*, 62). In the "second and most frequent variety of uterine disease," the diseased cervix is enlarged (which he also refers to as defective involution), characterized by: "the softness of the uterine walls," "the watery or bloody uterine discharges" (ibid., 63). Julia Kristeva's work on abjection is relevant here; in *Powers of Horror*, she meditates that "a wound with blood and pus, or the sickly acrid smell of sweat, of decay does not *signify* death" but instead represents the "border" between life and death, from which the body has to "extricate" itself in order to live—"something rejected from which one does not part," and which "beckons to us and ends up engulfing us."[24] The fear of degeneration then, could also be read as the fear of encroaching abjection, in the Kristevan sense. A more compelling case for a connection can be made if we consider the classification of the physical stigmata thought to be symptoms of the degenerative process, which often included the production of an excess of bodily fluids.

In *A Handbook of Uterine Therapeutics* (1863) Tilt recommends ways in which women could prevent their wombs from becoming abject, stressing "a right understanding and performances of the duties of married life," and the "careful management" of pregnancy, menstruation and lactation. Women are accustomed to commit "imprudences" during menstruation, which results in uterine disease. Though Tilt admits, unlike his contemporary William Acton, that women are capable of "strong passions," which need to be satisfied, the only legitimate means of satisfying these desires is through marriage. However, doctors should regulate women's desire to marry, since it is undesirable in some cases. For a menopausal woman, it is "imprudent" to marry "without the sanction of a medical opinion." Marriage is, however, the perfect solution for young widows with a tendency towards "ovarian congestion" and "uterine ulceration."[25]

In *Health in India*, Tilt refers to lactation as an important means of preventing female diseases. "The greater inability to nurse in India than in England" owing to the "debility" caused by the heat and other tropical diseases "helps to explain the frequency of uterine disease in India." He believes that "the act of suckling promotes the return of the womb to its proper size . . . except in some cases of extensive cervical ulceration" (Tilt, *Health in India*, 61). This fear supports Nupur Chaudhuri's contention that colonial women rarely breast-fed their infants, employing native wet nurses in many cases—a practice charged with ambivalence and the threat of contamination.[26] Lactation, both biologically and in terms of its iconic significance, was an important strategic device for maintaining the purity of the race and bolstering the memsahib's reproductive functions. The native wet nurse was yet another contagious body on whom both the mother and child might develop a dangerous dependency. The actions of sucking/giving suck are, of course, also a sign of vampiric propensities—a nexus Stoker had already explored in the famous "breast-feeding" scene in *Dracula*, in which Mina Harker is "suckled" by the Count.[27] Colonial narratives sometimes constructed the wet nurse, or *ayah*, as a vampiric figure. In Alice Perrin's short story "The Centipede," an ayah accidentally releases a centipede into a white child's bed while trying to cure the "babba" of an earache. The memsahib awakes screaming to see the centipede fasten "its poison feet" into the child's neck.[28] Therefore, for the colonial Englishwoman, both pregnancy and breast-feeding not only had curative influences, but were desirable for a variety of ideological reasons. In order to maintain their reproductive potential, women were continually encouraged to reproduce *themselves* as mothers.

Lady Arabella's vampiric project is, of course, predicated on a rejection of this imperative. In a later revised and truncated version of the novel, by sucking and contaminating the blood of young children, she "decolonizes the breast," unraveling the iconography of lactation, which from the late eighteenth century onward occupied a preeminent position in the European cultural imaginary, Ruth Perry theorizes, and served not only to dichotomize the maternal and the sexual but also to highlight the importance of women's reproductive role in nationalistic enterprises.[29] In *Lair*, Adam comes across the body of a female child with teeth marks on her neck; this prompts Sir Nathaniel to reveal something of Lady Arabella's history. As a child, she had "wandered into a small wood near her home," where she was found "unconscious and in a high fever," having "received a poisonous bite." From that moment, she had developed a "terrible craving for cruelty" (61), an appetite that resulted in the presumed killing of her husband, Captain March, years later. As Sir Nathaniel surmises, Lady Arabella has been both raped *and* suckled by the White Worm: "God alone knows what poor Captain March discovered— it must have been too ghastly for human endurance, if my theory is correct that the once beautiful human body of Lady Arabella is under the control of this ghastly White Worm" (62). Both versions of the novel compare her to a "co-cotte" or a courtesan. Adam reflects: "I never thought this fighting an ante-diluvian monster was such a complicated job. This one is a woman, with all a woman's wisdom and wit, combined with the heartlessness of a *cocotte* and the want of principle of a suffragette" (140).

In the nineteenth-century cultural imagination, whether at home or abroad, the most elusive, threatening, and fascinating public female body to consistently resist domestication was that of the courtesan. It is important, for the purposes of my argument, to understand the distinction between courte-sans, "clandestine" prostitutes, and street prostitutes. The courtesan's power to undermine and unsettle social hierarchies lay in her insidiousness and her adeptness at camouflaging her body (a characteristic shared by Lady Arabella), which could erupt at any moment into excessive exhibitionism, infecting re-spectable women. These women undermined the doctrine of the separation of spheres by eroticizing and feminizing public spaces. Experts at manipulating their visibility *and* invisibility, wealthy courtesans and clandestine prostitutes claimed public space cleverly and boldly, in contradistinction to the street prostitute, who was easily identifiable. Alexandre Parent-Duchâtelet, author of a monumental study on French prostitutes entitled *De la prostitution dans la ville de Paris* (1836), which provided the framework for analyses of prostitution for the rest of the century, divided kept women into several categories, includ-ing *femmes galantes, femmes à parties*, and *femmes de spectacles et de théâtres*. Women in the first category "are indistinguishable from respectable women ... but allow themselves to be accosted, pursued and escorted." To this chameleon-like quality, women in the second category bring "the grace and charms of a cultivated intelligence," presiding over private circles and salons, where they drain men of their "fortune and their health."[30]

Parent-Duchâtelet's fairly loose definition of women in the second and third groups would have included female writers, artists, actresses, dancers, opera singers, and revolutionaries who displayed their intellectual and erotic excesses outside the domestic sphere, and who seized the unique opportunities that the growth of urban centers offered them to be public women—among them Cora Pearl, Sarah Bernhardt, George Sand, Maria Malibran, Lola Montez, Rachel Felix, and Louise Colet.[31] The courtesan La Païva, for instance, not only filled a lavish house with ostentatious furniture, including a Moorish-style bathroom, but also presided over salons frequented by leading intellectuals. On seeing her with one of her lovers, a contemporary male poet described her as a vampire.[32] In his *Studies in the Psychology of Sex* (1899-1910), Havelock Ellis called for the recognition of the prostitute/courtesan as an independent woman and a professional who deserved respect.[33]

Sander Gilman's groundbreaking work on Manet's *Olympia* (1864) establishes the reciprocity that existed between cultural constructions of the courtesan and the exotic woman.[34] Like Tilt's "native women," the European courtesan's body was also ultimately a diseased one, as she succumbed to the "hectic pleasures" of her lifestyle—Dumas's consumptive Marguerite Gautier being the most famous example. In Verdi's opera *La Traviata* (1853), based on the Dumas novel, the courtesan Violetta attempts to keep her disease at bay by hurrying from "pleasure to pleasure," perishing in the "vortex of desire." The 1856 premiere of the opera in London aroused considerable controversy and anxiety because of its valorization of the courtesan.[35] Signifying both the French courtesan and the Italian opera singer, the spectacle of Violetta's body threatened to contaminate conservative British national and sexual agendas. Toward the end of the century, the demimondaine's frenetic exhibitionism and self-indulgence became yet another symptom of degeneration. For Max Nordau, writing in *Degeneration* in 1895, the wealthy woman's propensity for extravagant and luxurious clothing was a symptom of her devolution, and he excoriated the "oblique lines, incomprehensible swellings . . . expansions and contractions, folds with irrational beginning and aimless ending, in which all the outlines of the human figure are lost, and which cause women's bodies to resemble . . . a beast of the Apocalypse."[36] In 1893, the Italian ethno-criminologists Cesare Lombroso and Guglielmo Ferrero published *La donna delinquente: La prostituta e la donna normale* (translated as *The Female Offender*), in which they classified female criminals according to their facial and physiological stigmata. A considerable section of this work was devoted to prostitution. In contrast to Nordau, Lombroso and Ferrero commented on the prostitute's ability to disguise her atavistic stigmata (shared with other criminals and "primitives") through the cosmetic arts. Listing off famous historical/mythical courtesans such as Ninon de Lenclos, Phryne, and Thaïs, they marveled at the ability of these women to maintain their beauty and seductive power well into their seventies and eighties.[37]

We know from *Dracula* that Stoker was familiar with both Nordau and Lombroso.[38] My contextualization of *Lair* through reference to artistic as well as "scientific" representations of female sexual and social deviancy at the end of the century is designed to foreground the following: Lady Arabella's vampiric/serpentine body simultaneously recapitulates and aligns a range of fin-de-siècle anxieties: she is the native wet nurse, who, by suckling colonial children, contaminates their blood; she is the wife-turned-courtesan who, as depicted in a series of contemporary etchings by the French artist Albert Besnard entitled *La Femme*, degenerates from experiencing the bliss of "properly managed" lactation into a vampire bending over the emaciated corpse of her illegitimate infant;[39] and she is the colonial Englishwoman with an enlarged, deranged uterus "of abnormal growth," which, in its most terrifying incarnation, ultimately threatens to become phallic. As Adam and Sir Nathaniel pursue Lady Arabella after her metamorphosis into the worm, they see "a tall white shaft . . . an immense towering mass . . . tall and wonderfully thin" (151). This transformation embodies Lombroso and Ferrero's prognosis regarding the inevitable exposure of the cocotte's innate "masculinity" through aging, a process that would make her stigmata more visible: "when youth vanishes, the face grows virile . . . and exhibits the full degenerate type which early grace had concealed."[40]

Arabella is also the menopausal woman, who, according to Tilt, became capable of succumbing to demonomania or "belief in Satanic influence" upon losing her reproductive viability. *The Change of Life in Health and Disease* lists "demonomania," "erotomania," and "homicidal mania" as possible consequences of menopause.[41] Above all, though, she is dangerous because she possesses qualities associated with both the "cocotte" and the "suffragette." As is richly evidenced in Lisa Tickner's survey of the visual iconography of the suffrage movement, the suffragette's body was pathologized and racialized in the British press.[42] Antisuffragists compared the danger of women's entry into the political sphere to that of miscegenation, while a popular gynecological textbook published as late as 1917 speculated that suffragism arose from sexual frustration.[43]

At the same time, however, suffragists such as Christabel Pankhurst denounced the double standard of sexual morality by distancing themselves both from the prostitute and the racial other. In *The Great Scourge and How to End It* (1913), an exposé of venereal disease, Pankhurst condemned prostitution as a moral and sexual disease, the cause of "physical, mental and moral degeneracy and race suicide."[44] Here Pankhurst parallels Tilt closely through her repeated invocation of anxieties about racial survival and constant references to the falling birth rate, the primary reason for which, she argues, is the sterility of married women infected by their husbands with gonorrhea (Pankhurst, 17). The system of licensed prostitution in India contaminates the sexual innocence of white women: "Many soldiers return from India diseased, and they infect their unhappy wife and offspring" (Pankhurst, 150). By encompassing both the courtesan and the suffragette, therefore, Arabella mutates into that which is truly baffling, monstrous, and unclassifiable.

The worm's "whiteness" eventually comes up for discussion: "why white?" asks Sir Nathaniel, before proceeding to give a geological explanation (171-72). Aside from its anxieties about degeneration, the novel also envisions "whiteness" and "Englishness" as a problematic and deeply fissured ethnological category, rather than merely a mask or "veneer" that slips off to reveal the essential blackness beneath, as Jennifer DeVere Brody has recently suggested.[45] Lady Arabella never leaves England; her "tropical ovaries" are insidiously domestic, not foreign. Although *The Lair of the White Worm* may appear to valorize the late nineteenth-century imposition of racial hierarchies, particularly in its representation of Caswall's African valet, it repeatedly equivocates on the issue of their stability, coherence, and logic. While Arabella repels the sexual advances of Oolanga, on the grounds of his racial inferiority, she later "sucks" him into her well hole in a ferocious encounter, with Adam as a traumatized, voyeuristic witness. The transformation of the perfect Caucasian beauty into a white worm, which manifests its physical presence through images of uterine devolution, provides an important point of intersection between Tilt's medical discourse on the memsahib's lack of fertility and Nordau's definition of degeneration. In a chapter entitled "Diagnosis," Nordau defines degeneration as "a morbid deviation from an original type." He goes on to describe the actual process: "When under any kind of noxious influences an organism becomes debilitated, its successors will not resemble the healthy, normal type of the species, but will form a new sub-species; which like all others possesses the capacity of transmitting to its offspring in a continuously increasing degree, its peculiarities (Nordau, 16). In *Lair*, with the white woman's body under threat, mutating into another "species," the only solution (threatening in itself) seems to be miscegenation.

The covert desire for miscegenation, and the proposition of racial mixing as a way to diffuse the threat of the degenerate womb, is articulated through the figure of the half-Burmese Mimi Watford. Mimi is "almost as dark as the darkest of her mother's race," but she is repeatedly described as stronger and healthier than her white half-sister, Lilla, "sprung from old Saxon stock," who suffers from physical weakness as well as nervous disorders (33). The mere touch of Mimi's hand can momentarily infuse Lilla, "dead to sensibility and intention," with "youth and strength" (69). Significantly, Stoker pits Mimi's hybridity against the "monstrous whiteness" of Edgar Caswall and Lady Arabella; she continually battles them down with the power of her gaze in mesmeric struggles over Lilla. The latter eventually succumbs and dies after Mimi leaves her to marry Adam Salton. By co-opting and regulating Mimi's hybridity through marriage, Adam can experiment with racial regeneration. The marriage effectively separates Mimi from Lilla and Arabella, the "degenerate" white women in the narrative. In order for Adam (and Stoker) to reinscribe Mimi's hybridity for their own purposes, the "contagion" passing between black and white female bodies must be arrested. When Arabella invites Mimi to a tea party, she is narrowly prevented from slipping into the "black orifice," well lubricated by her hostess (157). At the same time, Mimi's body, being both "black" and "white," renders these categories profoundly unstable.

Fin de siècle orientalist paintings of harem women continually depicted dark and white women's bodies engaged in seductive encounters. The overwhelming sexual overtones of representations such as Jean-Léon Gérôme's *The Great Bath at Bursa* (1885), in which a white bather's body is intertwined with that of her black female slave, and Fernand Cormon's *Jalousie au Sérail* (1874), where a darker, serpentine rival leans over a murdered white woman's body with an attitude suggestive of rape, point to moments of lesbian desire/miscegenation, charged with considerable disruptive potential.[46] These juxtapositions also surface in British paintings of exotic women, especially with regard to classical subjects such as Alma-Tadema's well known *Antony and Cleopatra* (1883), in which Cleopatra glances obliquely at the viewer with a black female slave whispering in her ear. As Alison Smith has demonstrated, late Victorian art critics were troubled by Frederic Leighton's 1882 painting of the sun-tanned Greek courtesan Phryne: "Sir Frederic Leighton's " 'Phryne' " is a brown woman,—a colour for which we do not understand the reason, as Phryne was a Greek, and therefore a white woman."[47] The fantasy of collapsing the two bodies into one co-exists with the nightmare of a degenerative contagion which threatens to erode the reproductive base of the imperial fabric.

Health in India turns to miscegenation as a solution to the problem of reproductive failure and continued colonization. From recommending "a dash of

Hindoo blood" in colonial wives, Tilt moves on to considering "colonization by intermarriage" (Tilt, *Health in India*, 99). "The Company's servants frequently had matrimonial relations with Hindoo women of a better caste . . . if we find that we cross badly with the mild and inoffensive Hindoo, why not go northward for strength and stamina, why not seek more efficient mates in the Punjab?" (Tilt, *Health in India*, 108-10). This was consistent with ongoing speculations in Victorian race theory concerning the viability of different degrees of racial intermixture. Ethnologists such as Paul Broca, secretary-general of the Anthropological Society of Paris and honorary fellow of its counterpart in London, advocated the view that sexual relations between "proximate" or related races produced "eugenesic" hybridity measured by prolific fertility, while miscegenation with "distant" races resulted in infertility and degeneration. Broca suggested that the racial composition of the French nation had evolved out of eugenesic hybridity: "The population of France . . . presents everywhere the character of mixed races . . . nevertheless, this hybrid nation, so far from decaying . . . far from presenting a decreasing fecundity . . . grows every day in intelligence, prosperity and numbers."[48] Since hybridity, racial survival, and fertility were inextricably linked, the female body occupied center stage in theories of racial regeneration.

Even earlier in the century, the American ethnologists Josiah Nott and George Gliddon had promoted their theory of "plurality of origin" or polygenesis, "together with the recognition that there exist *remote, allied,* and *proximate* 'species,' as well of mankind as of lower animals."[49] Nott and Gliddon maintained that the crossing of remote species produced hybrids often doomed to extinction, whereas that between proximate species reproduced not mixtures, but "pure" or "primitive" types (*Types of Mankind*, 94-95). At the same time, they admitted that "every race, at the present time, is more or less mixed" (95) and therefore, distinct racial origins even among the Caucasian group had to be recognized/differentiated in order to anatomize the purity and vigor of the "blond" race (105-9). The original "commingling" between the "blond" and "brown" European races in Spain and Britain, for instance, had not produced a "complete fusion"—instead, "the types of each" remained "clearly traceable" particularly in the "dark-haired, dark-eyed and dark-skinned Irish" (109). At the heart of this ethnological dilemma was the slippery nature of "whiteness" itself—a racial category that, despite efforts, continued to resist clear delineation and definition.

Stoker agonizes over this issue through the figure of the half-Burmese Mimi Watford. The union of Mimi Watford's parents is clearly a coupling between races that would not have been regarded as "proximate," since her father is

British and her mother Burmese. (According to a chart provided in Nott and Gliddon's *Types of Mankind*, Mimi's mother would have belonged to the Malay group, the midpoint on the racial hierarchy between Caucasian and Negro).[50] Yet Mimi is presented as someone who clearly possesses intelligence, health, and stamina. If Adam's sexual pursuit of the Eurasian woman can be read as a desperate attempt to regenerate a national/imperial identity faced with the threat of decay through its overproduction of morbid wombs, Mimi neverthe-less, has, through her Burmese mother, inherited her "tropical ovaries." Despite Adam's attempts to co-opt her hybridity, she is always on the verge of slipping into Arabella's "lair," which, in true vampiric fashion, if not capable of repro-ducing the colonizing race, is always capable of reproducing *itself* as other: after being blown up with dynamite, the worm's dismembered fragments attract "every natural organism which was in itself obnoxious" (219).

Arabella's whiteness undermines and assaults notions of racial "proximity" and "distance." The destruction of her body reveals "a shining mass of white"— "the vast bed of china clay through which the Worm originally found its way down to its lair" (220). In the heart of the English countryside, the cradle of English civilization, that which is most "proximate" becomes the most mon-strously alien. As I have shown, the articulation (and control) of the contagion flowing between dark and white female bodies is shared by several discourses that seek to organize relations between European and native women, including those of medical ethnography, orientalist art, and the women's suffrage move-ment. By expressing hesitation or doubt as to whether this contagion arises from within, or from the other, and embodying it through the specter of gyne-cological insurrection/degeneration, *The Lair of the White Worm* constructs the female body as the site of the most powerful resistance to any coherent sense of racial identity, uneasily acknowledging its capacity to lay bare the incoherence and inherent contradictions within the discourses of empire and ethnology.

NOTES

1. See Dane Kennedy, *The Magic Mountains: Hill Stations and the British Raj* (Berkeley: University of California Press, 1996), 19–38.
2. Edward Tilt, *Health in India for British Women and on the Prevention of Diseases in Tropical Climates*, 4th ed. (London: Churchill, 1875), 55. Subsequent citations of this source are given parenthetically in the text. Besides being the author of numerous

books on gynecology that went into several editions, including *On Diseases of Menstruation and Ovarian Inflammation* (1850), *A Handbook of Uterine Therapeutics* (1863), and *Health in India for British Women* (1875), Tilt was one of the original fellows of the Obstetrical Society of London, eventually became its president, and held various important appointments throughout his medical career, which ended in 1893. While pushing the innovative use of the speculum and challenging certain contemporary gynecological practices, such as the excessive use of surgery, he also clung to others, including recommending clitoridectomy as a cure for masturbation and the application of leeches to the vagina.

3. See *Frankenstein: The Original 1818 Text*, ed. D. L. Macdonald and Kathleen Scherf (Ontario, Canada: Broadview Press, 1999), 358.

4. Kennedy, *Magic Mountains*, 19–38.

5. Ann Ardis, *New Women, New Novels: Feminism and Early Modernism* (New Brunswick, N.J.: Rutgers University Press, 1990), 12–28.

6. Sally Ledger, "The New Woman and the Crisis of Victorianism," in *Cultural Politics at the Fin-de-Siècle*, ed. id. and Scott McCracken (New York: Cambridge University Press, 1995), 22–44; Lisa Hamilton, "New Women and Old Men: Gendering Degeneration," in *Women and British Aestheticism*, ed. Talia Schaffer and Kathy Alexis Psomiades (Charlottesville: University of Virginia Press, 1999), 62–80; and Nancy Paxton, *Writing under the Raj* (New Brunswick, N.J.: Rutgers University Press, 1999), 196–99.

7. Mary Louise Pratt, *Imperial Eyes: Travel Writing and Transculturation* (New York: Routledge, 1992), 6–7.

8. For recent readings of *Lair*, see Jeffrey Richards, "Gender, Race and Sexuality in Bram Stoker's Other Novels," in *Gender Roles and Sexuality in Victorian Literature*, ed. Christopher Parker (Aldershot, Hants.: Scolar Press, 1995), 143–71; *Bram Stoker: History, Psychoanalysis and the Gothic*, ed. William Hughes and Andrew Smith (New York: St. Martin's Press, 1998); and Jennifer DeVere Brody, *Impossible Purities: Blackness, Femininity, and Victorian Culture* (Durham, N.C.: Duke University Press, 1998), 170–76.

9. See *The Critical Response to Bram Stoker*, ed. Carol Senf (Westport, Conn.: Greenwood Press, 1993), 173–83; and David Seed, "Eruptions of the Primitive into the Present," in *Bram Stoker*, ed. Hughes and Smith, 201.

10. Barbara Belford, *Bram Stoker: A Biography of the Author of Dracula* (New York: Knopf, 1996), 319–21. The suggestion of syphilis comes from Daniel Farson, who allows this conviction to color his interpretation of *Lair*; see his *The Man Who Wrote Dracula: A Biography of Bram Stoker* (London: Michael Joseph, 1975), 223.

11. Nancy Stepan, "Biology and Degeneration: Races and Proper Places," in *Degeneration: The Dark Side of Progress*, ed. J. Edward Chamberlin and Sander Gilman (New York: Columbia University Press, 1985), 97–120.

12. David Glover, *Vampires, Mummies and Liberals: Bram Stoker and the Politics of Popular Fiction* (Durham, N.C.: Duke University Press, 1996) 10–11.

13. See Leslie Shepard, "The Library of Bram Stoker," in *Bram Stoker's Dracula: Sucking Through the Century, 1897–1997*, ed. Carol Margaret Davison (Toronto: Dundurn Press, 1997), 413.

14. See Havelock R. Charles, "Neurasthenia and Its Bearing on the Decay of Northern Peoples of India," *Transactions of the Society of Tropical Medicine and Hygiene* 7 (1913): 2–31.

15. Stephen Arata, *Fictions of Loss in the Victorian Fin-de-Siècle* (Cambridge: Cambridge University Press, 1996), 117. For other recent discussions of Stoker and race, see Cannon Schmitt, *Alien Nation: Nineteenth-Century Gothic Fictions and English Nationality* (Philadelphia: University of Pennsylvania Press, 1997); H. P. Malchow, *Gothic Images of Race* (Stanford: Stanford University Press, 1996); Glover, *Vampires, Mummies and Liberals*; and Rebecca Stott, *The Fabrication of the Late Victorian Femme Fatale: The Kiss of Death* (Houndmills, Basingstoke, Hants.: Macmillan, 1992). Most of these (except for Glover and Stott) focus on *Dracula*.

16. For the construction of whiteness as an ongoing process prior to, during and after colonial encounters, see Robert Young's rereading of Victorian ethnological texts in his *Colonial Desire: Hybridity in Theory, Culture and Race* (New York: Routledge, 1995).

17. All textual references are to the American reprint of the original 1911 version of *The Lair of the White Worm*, which was published in the United States under the title *The Garden of Evil* (New York: Paperback Library, 1966), 11. Subsequent citations of this source are given parenthetically in the text.

18. For a discussion of stigmata in degeneration theory, see Eric Carlson, "Medicine and Degeneration: Theory and Praxis," in *Degeneration*, ed. Chamberlin and Gilman, 127–36.

19. Patrick Bade, *Femme Fatale: Images of Evil and Fascinating Women* (London: Ash & Grant, 1979), 36.

20. See Bram Dijkstra, *Idols of Perversity: Fantasies of Feminine Evil in Fin-de-Siècle Culture* (New York: Oxford University Press, 1986).

21. Gustave Flaubert, *Salammbô* (1862; Harmondsworth, U.K.: Penguin Books, 1977), 174.

22. Joseph Fayrer, "On Serpent Worship and on the Venomous Snakes of India," *Journal of the Transactions of the Victoria Institute* 26 (1892): 88, 86, 107.

23. Belford, *Bram Stoker*, 318.

24. Julia Kristeva, *Powers of Horror: An Essay on Abjection* (New York: Columbia University Press, 1982), 3–4.

25. Edward Tilt, *A Handbook of Uterine Therapeutics* (New York: William Wood, 1881), 289, 292–93, 293.

26. Nupur Chaudhuri, "Memsahibs and Motherhood in Nineteenth Century Colonial India," *Victorian Studies* 31, 4 (Summer 1988): 517–35.

27. Bram Stoker, *Dracula*, ed. Nina Auerbach (New York: Norton, 1997), 247. See also Joan Copjec, "Vampires, Breast Feeding and Anxiety," *October* 58 (Fall 1991): 25–43.

28. Alice Perrin, "The Centipede," in *Stories From the Raj: From Kipling to Independence*, ed. Saros Cowasjee (New Delhi: Harper Collins, 1992), 124–25.

29. Ruth Perry, "Colonizing the Breast: Sexuality and Maternity in Eighteenth Century England," *Eighteenth Century Life* 16, 1 (February 1992): 185–213. See also *The Lair of the White Worm* (London: W. Foulsham, 1925).

30. A.-J.-B. Parent-Duchâtelet, *De la prostitution dans la ville de Paris considérée sous le rapport de l'hygiène publique, de la morale et de l'administration* (Paris: J.-B. Baillière, 1836), excerpted in *Violetta and Her Sisters: The Lady of the Camellias: Responses to the Myth*, ed. Nicholas John (London: Faber and Faber, 1994), 44–48. For Parent-Duchâtelet's influence, see Alain Corbin, *Women For Hire: Prostitution and Sexuality in France after 1850* (Cambridge, Mass.: Harvard University Press, 1990), 3–4.

31. See Elizabeth Wilson, "Bohemians, Grisettes and Demi-Mondaines," in *Violetta and Her Sisters*, ed. John, 24.

32. Emile Bergerat writes: "You either believe in vampires or you don't, I believed in them at that concert" (as quoted by Bade, *Femme Fatale*, 9).

33. Havelock Ellis, *Studies in the Psychology of Sex*, vol. 2 (New York: Random House, 1936), 305–11.

34. Sander Gilman, "Black Bodies, White Bodies: Towards an Iconography of Female Sexuality in Late Nineteenth Century Art, Medicine and Literature," *Critical Inquiry* 12, 1 (Autumn 1985): 204–42.

35. Giuseppe Verdi, *La Traviata* (New York: Sony Music Entertainment, 1993), 68. For *Traviata's* reception in London, see *Violetta and Her Sisters*, ed. John, 249.

36. Max Nordau, *Degeneration* (London: William Heinemann, 1895), 8. Subsequent citations are given parenthetically in the text.

37. Cesare Lombroso and Guglielmo Ferrero, *La donna delinquente: La prostituta e la donna normale* (Turin: Roux, 1893), trans. as *The Female Offender* (London: T. Fisher Unwin, 1895), 101, 128–29.

38. See *Dracula*, 295–96. Salli Kline comments on Nordau's favorable reception and popularity in Britain in *The Degeneration of Women: Bram Stoker's Dracula as Allegorical Criticism of the Fin de Siècle* (Rheinbach-Merzbach: CMZ Verlag, 1992), 160–61.

39. See Jean Adhémar, *Albert Besnard: L'Oeuvre gravé* (Paris: Bibliotheque nationale, 1949).

40. Lombroso and Ferrero, *Female Offender*, 102.

41. Edward Tilt, *The Change of Life in Health and Disease: A Clinical Treatise on the Diseases of the Ganglionic Nervous System Incidental to Women at the Decline of Life* (New York: Bermingham, 1882) 167–69.

42. Lisa Tickner, *The Spectacle of Women: Imagery of the Suffrage Campaign, 1907–14* (Chicago: University of Chicago Press, 1988).

43. "Women's Suffrage and National Danger," in *The Opponents: The Anti-Suffragists*, ed. Marie Mulvey Roberts (London: Thoemmes, 1995), 71–72; see also *The New System of Gynecology*, ed. Thomas Watts Eden and Cuthbert Lockyer (London: Macmillan, 1917), 402.

44. Christabel Pankhurst, *The Great Scourge and How to End It* (London: E. Pankhurst, 1913), 17.

45. Brody, *Impossible Purities*, 172.

46. See Emily Apter, "Female Trouble in the Colonial Harem," *Differences: A Journal of Feminist Cultural Studies* 4, 1 (Spring 1992): 203–24.

47. Quoted in Alison Smith, *The Victorian Nude: Sexuality, Morality and Art* (Manchester: Manchester University Press, 1996), 168.

48. Paul Broca, *On the Phenomena of Hybridity in the Genus Homo* (London: Longman, Green, Longman and Roberts, 1864), 22.

49. J. C. Nott and George Gliddon, *Types of Mankind* (Philadelphia: Lippincott, 1854), 409. Subsequent citations of this source are given parenthetically in the text. For an exploration of the ethnological term "Caucasian," see ibid., 88–110.

50. Ibid., 450.

Two Talks with Khun Fa

The lack of information about each other and the
strong, newly established information borders prevent
us from organizing ourselves across class, race, and culture, thus keeping women in their specific places . . .
Knowledge about each other requires a strong information wave in both directions—to the East and West.
                    —Valentina Stoeva, "Women against the
                                    Information Borders"

In July of 1998, I went to see Khun Fa, the mother of Chinese-Thai
friends of mine in Bangkok. At the time she was eighty-seven and had
lived in Thailand for sixty-seven years. She was born in Fujian Province
in China in the year of the Chinese revolution and embarked from the port of
Soochow (Swatow) for Thailand in 1931. In July 1998, our group consisted of
Khun Fa, her daughter, our translator, my husband, and myself, who taped her
story.[1]

Story it was: like her daughter and son whom we had known for several
years, Khun Fa was a raconteuse. Little prompting was necessary; her daughter
had arranged the first meeting and told her that we wanted to hear about her
experiences, and mother and daughter had thoroughly prepared to retell the
highlights. In September, we went back and listened to her without taping, now
conversing more freely, going back to earlier topics, and chuckling over familiar incidents.

I approached Khun Fa for this piece in order to begin an archive of life histories by women in Asia who had experienced modern "development," a term
for a process that has brought not only economic change but also regression in
some aspects of women's lives. Khun Fa could tell me about modernity from
the point of view of one who had lived through its most difficult passages. She

was not simply the product of a modern consciousness, being neither a writer nor a reader. Rather, in a more complex way, she was both a target and a producer of modernity, thanks to, among other things, her minority status within China, her migration from China to Thailand, her decades of labor, and the education her labor provided for her eight children.

Secondly, Khun Fa had created success out of extraordinary hardship. Like many others, she migrated from China to join her husband in rural Thailand, bringing virtually nothing with her and scratching for a living, learning to farm, speak Thai, and assimilate to her husband's siblings while doing so. Unlike some, however, she experienced more extraordinary difficulties than these. Her husband died when her youngest child was two. A short time later her oldest son, then the main wage earner, also died quite suddenly. Keeping house for and rearing seven children, working by day in the fields, cooking at the local mill in the evening for the workers, and going back to work the fields at night, Khun Fa, widowed in a foreign country, had recourse to unstinting physical labor as a means to live through the worst of this period and go beyond it. By her own admission, the thought of trying to go on was almost too daunting to entertain. Yet by the time I met her family, they were successful in the professions, and Khun Fa was living in a spacious family compound. This "uneducated" woman had managed to educate her children in parochial schools and had sent three of them to universities in the United States. As an older woman, she had traveled much of the world, but by that time, she was mainly interested to see, as she said, how they farmed there. This was no ordinary success story, but the story of a woman's single-handed success against all odds, told in a manner neither pathetic nor heroic.

Khun Fa is Hakka, a member of the 37-million-strong Han-related Chinese minority who speak a separate dialect and have lived chiefly in the provinces of Fujian, Guangdong, and Jiangxi.[2] The Hakka are apt to identify themselves with certain characteristics differentiating them from the majority Cantonese among whom they traditionally lived. The Hakka diaspora spreads throughout South and Southeast Asia and North America and is diverse both from other overseas Chinese and within itself in terms of occupation and class. Many Hakka are known only as Chinese, and they may make no effort to bring up their minority status. Khun Fa, however, does not speak Mandarin or Cantonese and the first portion of her remarks was in Hakka. When we began to speak directly with her, she then switched to Thai. In her life in Thailand, however, beyond continuing to speak Hakka, she did not appear to convey to others a particularly regional or minority image of her youth in China, and her children and grandchildren have assimilated her image of China as "China," not as her Hakka background. They do, however, subscribe to tenets of Hakka identity, although without necessarily calling it such: hard work, strength in women, thrift, seemly or virtuous behavior, and prudence.[3] Her life story included vignettes to illustrate her adherence to these principles as she crossed from her native Fujian to the Thai province of Kanchanaburi.

To record Khun Fa's story meant an opportunity to cross certain scholarly borders as well: borders among the disciplines of women's studies, gender studies, literary criticism, anthropology, and discourse theory; borders between Asian and Western scholarship; borders between the human being and scholarly material; and, finally, the older and less yielding boundary between the written and the unwritten. Furthermore, as the epigraph to this chapter quotes an Eastern European feminist saying, the advance of information technology has also meant "newly established information borders" that keep women's knowledge from being reciprocally exchanged across national or other boundaries. This is not a new problem. Any information border, whether conventional or newly technologized, can reinforce preconceptions about women by pathologizing their presumed "difference" and by hampering efforts to cross the boundary it establishes. It is continually necessary, then, to evaluate the position and function of such difference and the way it structures certain kinds of information that claim to represent others. Representations create ideal images, and idealizations objectify those whom they determine by gender and nationality. Chandra Mohanty critically examines one such gender representation by asking us what happens when an assumption that "'women [are] an oppressed group' is situated in the context of Western feminist writing about third world women? . . . Third world women . . . never rise above the debilitating generality of their 'object' status."[4] To meet such challenges, efforts to understand not only textual, but human, visual and audial sources become crucial: Penny van Esterik points out that "our reliance on vision and text still dominates ethnographic writing. We should not privilege text over senses as the only legitimate way of knowing about gender."[5] The first border to cross here, then, should be the border between the female human subject and the text that objectifies her.

Khun Fa does not present herself as an other or an object in her own view. She is someone who wanted to fit in and did, even helping to define fitting in and success in her own generation. She did not see her being Chinese as meaning a life of either poverty, of luxury, or of some other sort of determination by birth.[6] She did not enter the world as a peasant but made herself one: she did not know how to farm until she lived in Thailand. She did not survive or escape a miserable, or confining and elite, existence: she was the only child of an educated man in a family she called happy. In reading her story, then, which objectifies her to the extent that it is a textual rendering, one way to de-objectify the Khun Fa of the text is to consider her changing circumstances, her choices, and her work as existing beyond the conceptual meanings implied in these terms. If we look at Khun Fa as a working and acting subject, she gives us a description of how she and her work evolved from day to day. This description of her practical circumstances gives significance to the ways she and they changed in confrontation with one another.

Khun Fa also followed a plan she had made on the basis of available alternatives. Her choice was to join her husband in Thailand, where there was freedom—in contrast to other countries in Southeast Asia, Thailand was never colonized—and where there was more land available. This kind of choice as existing within a limited range of available alternatives is one that she would share with many other women. She rose in social status much later, again not through an entirely free choice but also through the unmerciful mechanisms of shock and loss. In neither country was she colonized either politically or intellectually, yet in neither country is she envied for her intellectual accomplishments, though they emerge from her narrative below. Her lack of an education did nothing to stop her using her mind to get out of difficult situations. Finally, Khun Fa was not only an experiencer of and respondent to modernization: she, like other laboring women, was also one of its producers.

Modernization, Modernity, and Gender

Khun Fa's lifetime spans much of the modernization period in China, her country of origin, and in Thailand, her adopted country. Her life is representative of some of the transitions and difficulties that modernization imposes on ordinary citizens, especially women,[7] and of the modernization that women also produce through their labor. I define the term "modernization," in its relation to women, as modernity in its physical, material form, including the social and economic transitions from noncash work to labor for capital, from settled agriculture and trade to migration for income, and from traditional gender roles to the doubling of traditional roles with society's new

gender expectations. The bodily impact on women of modernization is sometimes easily, sometimes with difficulty equated with scholarship on modernity,
but the connection between the two is important. In many areas of the world,
women have both produced the modernity their national governments decided to pursue and also endured it. The transition to labor for capital brings
with it the wage discrimination that helps structure modern gender positions
within social and educational systems. The woman's need to generate cash income and modernization's demand for unskilled labor often make women the
majority of labor migrants, thus pushing the large-scale transmigrations typical of modernity. Laborious tasks within entrenched gender and family roles
are compounded by new economic and social expectations of women in
household and outside work.[8] Finally, for a woman who has not yet had access
to the education offered to males and middle-class females, these very experiences may be wiped away, never to be learned from, through the sheer facts of
her illiteracy and lack of time and space to communicate her knowledge. Her
life history either becomes an oral history or no history at all.

Khun Fa is a woman who not only survived these phenomena but went on
to a life that even she, with her hopes for the future, could not have imagined.
What I wanted to record was the way in which her knowledge helped her to do
this. The lack or loss of women's records has meant the devaluing and forgetting of women's knowledge and memory in many eras and places. According
to our own scholarly notions of memory, however, records, to be records, must
at some stage be written. Yet when the subjects of oral histories, life histories,
interviews, autobiographies, and memoirs are women, these genres place their
subjects in a dilemma with regard to text.[9] Entering their discourse into text
often means it will be undervalued, yet the exclusion of women from text has
also delegitimized their records. Khun Fa was a person who had things of value
to tell me yet could not write them down. The issue was, then, can an illiterate
woman have an autobiography? For Khun Fa is, as she will tell you right away,
illiterate.

Illiteracy is the feature she shares with millions of the world's women; it is
the feature that never changes in their lives, despite the coming and going
of modernity and postmodernity. Nonetheless, being illiterate has not kept
Khun Fa inexpressive or uninformed. Her own history and that of her extended
family—extended over time and space, from her parents, born in the nineteenth century in Fujian, to her nephew in northern China, to her grandchildren
and great-grandchildren throughout the Asia-Pacific region—reposes in her

memory. So do the calculations of the financial transactions they made as they went from being farmers to professionals. She knows the exact sums she has lent to any one grandchild, and she has thirty grandchildren. In her narrative, she detailed the amounts she had paid for her children's tuition and the amounts they earned at part-time jobs as students. To have something to say and to say it—Khun Fa is an honest, even blunt, speaker—is, however, with her as with other women, only the first step. The difficult part is getting someone to listen.

Literacy, Women's Oral Literacy, and Memory

The oral life and practice described below are a woman's, and they belong to an oral subculture within the literate cultures of China and Thailand. In addition to her own memory of her father as educated, Khun Fa's ability to do mental arithmetic and her familiarity with major literary figures demonstrate her origin within a literate context. She was not shut out from the effects of literacy or an understanding of its significance, but rather situated between oral and literate discourse.[10] There is an important distinction to be made here, however, between two kinds of oral transmission. Examples of primarily one-way oral transmission are found in classroom education, political speeches, or broadcasting. They differ from oral transmission that is based on an exchange. Khun Fa's oral records have always been exchanged among groups of people who also participate in their content.

One modernist notion of identity is that of the individual, internal quality of memory in the construction of personal identity. Collaborative oral records like Khun Fa's, however, are produced through the checking and cross-checking of memories among members of the same household or community each time the record is rearticulated. On a wider scale, the social history of a nation's people is similarly the record of such collaborative or multiple memories. What Khun Fa narrates about her past is not a reduction of national or modern history to the personal level. On the contrary, it is an irreducible part of the memory of the nation and its modernity, which are in turn part of the self.

Women and the Economy of Silence: Theories, Records, Gender

Women perform the lion's share of work in subsistence economies, toiling longer hours and contributing more to family income than their male relatives—but are viewed as "unproductive" in the eyes of government statisticians, economists, development experts, and even their husbands. A huge proportion of the world's real productivity therefore remains undervalued.[11]

"If you travel around the world, especially in rural regions," observes Marilyn French, "you will notice that everywhere . . . women are doing most of the work."[12] Like the development economist whose epigraph begins this section, French long ago noted that women's labor, both inside and outside of the home, was the bulk of the world's work but was not considered important—indeed, not even recognized, let alone theorized, in most countries. As Marilyn Waring has pointed out, "Theory is used, first of all, in order to decide what facts are relevant to an analysis. . . . only some everyday experiences are stated, recognized, and recorded by economic theory. Overwhelmingly, those experiences that are economically visible can be summarized as what men do."[13]

As these remarks illustrate, it is not only in the field of identity but also in the fields of labor and economy that what is recognized is what is recorded. Women in many parts of the world have little access to means of publicly communicating or recording their lives, including their labor. For Khun Fa, this is important because she conceives the significance of her life as lying in her work. For the Chinese and Southeast Asian woman, work, both intra- and extra-household, can be life itself. Many women grow up expecting to work full-time in addition to household and family duties. Though this double burden is both exhausting and undervalued, Khun Fa appropriates it as the means by which she now lives the life she wants. In her view of the past, she accepts the fact that as a Chinese girl in a poorer family, she was not expected to go to school but to work, and she sees her farm and mill labor as the means by which she took her own family from agricultural labor to educated professionalism, thereby also gaining for herself a more comfortable existence. Until quite recently, she rejected such material comforts as full-time help, air conditioning, and leisure time. She instead cultivated her vegetable patch every day, seeing work as her means to health and self-esteem.[14] In one of her few bursts of ethnic pride, she explicitly contrasts herself and her extra work for her children's education with her earlier rural Thai neighbors, saying that they did not see the value of sending children to school when they could help on the farms, whereas she saw education as the means to a different future. Thai scholars would say that she was prescient in this regard, as many rural Thai have come to agree with her, or have had the means to agree with her, in recent years.[15]

To record Khun Fa's life, then, is to record her work and its value in her own eyes, including its value to her broader context of family, community, and nation. As feminist economists have pointed out, traditional economies depend heavily on women's labor for development, and mainland Southeast Asia is no exception. In Thailand and Vietnam, for example, where the domestic and export economies depend largely on agriculture, more than half of agricultural production is done by female labor. While some of her children were finishing school, Khun Fa worked as a tenant farmer, raised domestic animals, supplemented her income by cooking for the local mill workers, and, with her children, saved enough money to invest in their own mills. Her older daughter also worked in the fields, because Khun Fa told her to cut cane and sell it before school every morning. Again, she is representing Han Chinese and Hakka values here as well as her personal goals. As Mohanty points out, "the sexual division of labor is more than just a descriptive category. It indicates the differential value placed on 'men's work' versus 'women's work.'"[16] The idea that girls (and some boys) of certain classes would work so as to allow others the time to gain an education prevailed in many societies, and in Khun Fa's China, it continued until the Mao era. What Khun Fa adds to this is her personal value— literally an economic as well as a sociocultural value—that women can be strong and hardworking in addition to other attainments such as scholastic ones. For her rural Thai neighbors in the early twentieth century, however, neither girls' nor boys' education was seen as particularly valuable, as it would take the children away from the necessary labor of the farms. This is where Khun Fa differentiates herself from their ideas and the outcomes of their lives.

Khun Fa's labor, like that of many women of her region and generation, can be seen as what actually builds the modern nation. Her labor sent children to schools whose diplomas would guarantee them positions from which they could modernize infrastructures as well as gain entrée to different classes of society. Her labor produced the agriculture that fed both her nation and ours; modern nations import much of their food from developing regions, including hers. Her child-rearing labor produced human resources who would continue to expand the economy and in turn train and pay other workers, some of whom, still without skills, needed to earn capital in an economy that modernization was rapidly making capital-dependent. Whether such Western-style modernization was worth the price is still being debated. Yet without her and women like her, there would be no current generation of educated employers, skilled workers, or engineers to do everything from establishing the manufacturing and trade to building the schools, roads, sewers, and hospitals that modernity demands. Nor, without women, would there be a Thai export trade worth approximately U.S. $45 billion that pays the expenses of such modernization.[17]

Women have more to bear in the transition to modernity because as a planning concept it is usually imposed on them from outside, either by the policy specialists of their own culture or by those of another. Second, modernity means, in practical terms, more women's work for less value. A woman in a modernizing society may do both physical labor outside and provide family care, may forego home, religious, or public schooling to work in the fields for her brothers' education because they will be the ones hired for the new "skilled" work, may absorb the full impact of environmental degradation because she is the one working with soil, water, and crops more of the time, and may witness the displacement of traditional health care, including midwifery and women's herbal medicine, while still not having access to modern or other gender-appropriate health care. Khun Fa gave birth to eight children without help, as she describes below. Her husband slowly died of a stroke while the family looked on, powerless to pay for medical care and powerless to travel to the city where such care might have been found. The result was that she supported nine people on the basis of her genuine skills: oral literacy, child rearing, farm experience, stamina, and a vision of the future. If the greatest burdens of modernization end up on the shoulders of women, its greatest unrecorded achievements come from women as well.

The Nation, the Literacy Commodity, and Modern "Identity"

Literacy in modern nations is seen as a necessary indicator of human development. During the process of modernization and nation-building, however, literacy also provides a means to construct the nation's image both within and without. Increasing the membership of the literate class means increasing the production and consumption of various media, a process that helps distribute the images and constructions of national identity. For a modernizing nation literacy means not only a basic education in standardized reading and writing, but literacy in the new social, political, and economic forms. As Partha Chatterjee has shown, the arbiters and makers of modern forms of organization of the self and society are those who have gained the new kind of education,[18] normally males of the middle or upper classes who enter public life. In this sense, as Sheryl Gowen points out, "what was defined as illiteracy was actually a symptom rather than a cause of women's marginalization" (448).[19]

Those who have the new social literacy then need others who do not have it as providers of the labor that will implement a new social order. In my reading of Khun Fa's life work, one function she performed was to work to meet the demands of a new social life based on the acquisition of land, the exchange of labor for income, and the production of a middle class that was literate, in both senses, as the next generation of professionals.

In this way, constructions of the modern nation also make of literacy a commodity, a salable item. It has value both for the individual and for the organizations responsible for economic and cultural production. As with the production and consumption of other goods in developing regions, the producer of goods is often not economically able to consume the commodities she produces or not offered them, as Maria Mies has pointed out.[20] Literacy can be seen in the same way. It contains value because it produces not subsistence but income and upward mobility, and can thus be commodified. Modern and modernizing polities, including advanced nations, can trade literacy on this basis. Some of their citizens have no access to literacy or once having had access, cannot, in Shirley Heath's terms, use literacy for their own work.[21] Such persons often work to make opportunities for literacy of both the textual and socioeconomic kinds available to others. Like Khun Fa, women who cannot avail themselves of the literacy commodity will work to "provide" literacy to others. Yet in working to provide others with access to the literacy she did not have, Khun Fa saw herself as enabling them to choose the aspects of modernization that would benefit them. She was also, through them, importing into her life the aspects of modernization she desired from the national sphere.

Readers of autobiographies and life histories may judge them on the basis of a literate, modernist equivocation between the personal and the social, privileging either a distinction or an equivalence between the two. Yet this kind of judgment is not always applicable to life histories of women. The private, personal, or individual aspects of life have for many women writers and speakers been bound up with their social and economic positions, the political situations of their countries, and their relations with others (and management of those relations as part of their unpaid labor) in ways that do not align themselves only along the axes of the personal or the social. This is especially true in the case of a producer of a life and its story who does not circumscribe herself only within the sphere of self-reflexive identity.

The interviews with Khun Fa, for example, were not private but took place with household members (of hers) and kin or acquaintances (of mine) present. During our interviews, several persons could and did interject, add, question, disagree with, and talk at the same time as Khun Fa, who nevertheless did not yield the floor. This sort of multiple vocality contributes to Khun Fa's "identity" as one that is constituted in part by her relationships and activities outside and inside her household and is not only a product of reflection and self-examination. Reflection and self-examination, however, were by no means absent from her narrative.

Postmodern readers and writers can use text as a form of self-reflection or self-projection if they desire. Others who have no access to text, or have not grown up with a textualized identity because their labor, as Jack Goody points out, was more urgently needed than their written articulations,[22] reflect on their lives and project themselves by other means. This is not a question of the absence of consciousness or of self on the part of women like Khun Fa. That question must be turned around: it is a challenge to us as to whether we, the textualized, have the ability or willingness to understand the actions and self-consciousness articulated by her. In his work on orality and literacy, Walter Ong proposed that in oral cultures "speech is . . . a way of doing something to someone,"[23] but with Khun Fa, speech is a way of doing something with someone. The speaking of her life to another person whom she can physically see and know seemed appropriate for one whose life and knowledge grew through speech and through working for and with others. Khun Fa spoke to me at first primarily because her daughter brought me. She was not necessarily expecting a certain kind of person; but as she would wryly admit, an outsider would not be likely to appear too busy, bored, or inattentive with her discourse, and she could thus have the refreshing opportunity to re-engage with her own story. Furthermore, by talking to a recording listener, she could provide knowledge beyond that listener to others, as she well understands the disseminative power of recording and publication.

The anthropologists L. L. Langness and Gelya Frank long ago pointed out that "a life history, unlike a biography or an autobiography, is always a delicate and complicated collaborative venture."[24] Khun Fa's illiteracy offered the potential for collaboration. It was not so much an inability of hers to produce a text, but a challenge to our ability to listen, record, or place appropriate value on her oral statements. My concern is that it is not only Khun Fa's background in a non-wealthy family in early twentieth-century China that disbarred her from reading and writing. It is that outsiders, through gaps in our knowledge that we do not even perceive, will silence her without knowing it. Reading her story challenges our own literacy to hear as well as read her. To succeed in understanding the life stories of non-writing women, we ourselves need literacy not only of a written but of an oral kind, one that requires the skills of collaboration.[25]

Migration and Modernity: Crossings in Time and Memory

Race, migration, and nation in the Western sense, as in Homi Bhabha's Western nation with its "forgetting" of its past and its "desolate silences of the wandering people,"[26] can be related to the devaluing of an oral culture that dominates the modern text-dependent society. As far back as the Platonic dialogue the *Phaedrus*, we find Socrates telling of an Egyptian king who rejects the gift of writing on the grounds that "it will implant forgetfulness in [men's] souls; they will cease to exercise memory because they rely on that which is written, calling things to remembrance no longer from within themselves, but by means of external marks."[27] In our textual modernity, we expect memory not only to rely on writing but in some ways to be identified with writing. Those who lose writing or the textual environment of their native language are seen as having lost some portion of memory and identity. For Bhabha, the migrant who tries to remember simply becomes silent, or is taken as silent, in his new country. Khun Fa, on the other hand, did not lose writing but never had it to rely on: she would have been illiterate in either of her countries, and thus she used other means to record and to bequeath her record. As Anne McLaren points out, for women born in pre-Mao China, illiteracy and expressiveness did not cancel each other out, and certainly there is no one in Khun Fa's family, young or old, who does not know the history of her journey, her hardships, and her achievements.[28]

Khun Fa, like many citizens in the construction of the modern nation-state of Thailand, came from elsewhere. Furthermore, in Thailand as elsewhere in Asia there had always been a culture of diversity, of varied ethnic groups, "hill tribes," and language minorities in the long history of Southeast Asian migrants and ethnic groups that predates Western theories of racial boundaries. In her own view, the most important border Khun Fa crossed was not necessarily that of nationality or ethnic origin but that of time, if modernity is seen as a point along a progression in time. She like others sailed from China to Thailand in order to cross from the past to what she hoped was the future, and that is how she articulates her journey. Her country is her memory, and memory, unlike nations and geopolitical borders, can be crossed and re-crossed at will. The boat that takes immigrants into new waters, the letters or characters that take the reader forward over the page, go in one direction only. Memory is not always bound by directionality, and though its content can be textualized, its action and its freedom of movement, like the action and movement that are the storyteller's identity here, are more vividly rendered in living speech and to the listening, not the reading, audience.[29]

If the movement of memory, national and personal, is better rendered through oral literacy, we need other skills to understand the texts generated from it. Some scholars assert that information technology will push us in the direction of re-valuing orality; Robin Lakoff suggests that we are tending toward a "merging of the oral and literate traditions."[30] Although Khun Fa does not depend on writing to remember and record the past, her textual silence is not the "desolate" one Bhabha described. If a silence exists it is likely to be, as Rey Chow says, the product of social and transnational constructions that do not listen to or simply pigeonhole certain women, effectively silencing them despite their written or unwritten articulations.[31]

Khun Fa's grandson, watching our video of her, remarked, "I guess back in those days they didn't give women names." He did not merely not know her name; he assumed it didn't exist. Khun Fa's son, told that there were substantial tomes on the Hakka, lamented, "We don't know our history," though presumably his mother would know some of it. The themes of migration and unwritten or unvalued memory underlie the fundamental questions of this chapter. As Sandra Gilbert and Susan Gubar point out, women's relation to language, including their own naming, is problematic enough. But women's relation to writing and recording itself—what Gilbert and Gubar call an "alphabet,"[32] though I extend it to mean all writing, characters included—can be an even harder choice between disenfranchisement or collusion. We can remain outside the text and thus outside recognition. Or we can learn to write and therefore forget, just as written cultures have forgotten women like Khun Fa. Women's illiteracy is usually described as a stage in the evolution of a culture, a stage that is overcome by "modernity." But what of the tens of millions of women who will still not read, write, or be read, within or without modernity? Hearing and reading them, can we educate ourselves, confined in literacy, to recuperate and recognize the value of the names, labors, and histories that they possess?

∾

Two Talks by Khun Fa

Day 1: July 22, 1998, 2:00 P.M.   Rainy season, sunny day
Day 2: September 30, 1998, 9:00 A.M.   Rainy season, rainy day

I left China when I was twenty. Left from Soochow [Swatow] port to go to Thailand and find a better life. It took the boat nearly a month to get to Bangkok. I've never been so sick in my life. Couldn't eat; just threw up all the time. That was bad.

I was born in the year of the Pig [1911]. I had married my husband back in China. He was from a different village. He went to Thailand with his one older brother and one younger brother and started up on a plot of land in Kanchanaburi. Sad to say, the oldest brother thought it was his due to keep the money we earned together. I never got over my indignation at that. His wife, though, was perfectly nice. She's over ninety now, still up there in Kanchanaburi, not doing all that well we hear; can't walk.

When I first got to Bangkok I stayed with some distant relatives for a little while. I had been awfully sick on the boat. In those days, quite a few people from our area of China went to Thailand to start up their own enterprises. We had the idea of going to Thailand to get rich. My uncle and some others we knew, including my own stepfather, had done so and had come back to China. Why Thailand and not Annam [Vietnam] or Burma or Cambodia? Maybe because those other countries were under foreign rule, but Thailand was free.

The first thing I noticed when I got to my husband's and his brothers' place was the sun. It was much stronger than in China. I never knew it could be so hot. We started farming although we had practically nothing. But the other thing that impressed me about Thailand then was that the people were so good and kind. They would smile, they would help, they would be neighborly. They shared what goods they had with us. And in my area of China, the land was divided up into small pieces. But in Thailand, the available plots of land were much bigger.

At first I decided to start selling eggs to make a little money. But, as I said, we had nothing—not even a chicken. So I asked my neighbor if I could borrow a hen. She was kind enough to lend me one of her brooders. That day I went to the market in the early morning, bought a dozen eggs for a satang[33] each and rushed home with them. I set the hen on the eggs right away, and eventually they hatched. That was the beginning of my egg-selling.

Hearing the thunderclaps outside today reminds me. One of the businesses I tried to start was growing and selling tobacco. Of course, you have to dry the leaves somehow. That year we had a heavier rainy season than usual and flooding. I could have cried with frustration. My beautiful tobacco leaves never dried.

I was from a happy family in China, and I knew nothing about farming. I learned about it from watching my Thai neighbors and with their help. That's how I started learning to speak Thai, too. Many daughters of my generation were never sent to school. I don't read or write to this day and I'm eighty-eight. So when I came to Thailand, I just had to pick up Thai as I went along.

I bore eight children, all of them by myself. No, not even a midwife. I mean it, all by myself. I asked some people who knew about it what to do. Yes, my sister-in-law, the nice one, was there with me, but she had no idea what to do. How did I avoid infection afterwards? I had some Chinese medicine. And I took ginger.

The most important thing for the children, it seemed to me, was to get them through school. Right down the line, they worked and studied. My neighbors thought I was foolish. Here I was with eight children and I was sending them to school rather than having them help me out on the farm. Well, that was their way of thinking, not mine. They had always been farmers, and they didn't see the need for education. In fact, they thought that sending kids to school all that time would just make them lazy.

I thought differently. I didn't see any future for my kids in small-time farming. After the oldest boys got to working, we got ahead a little bit. The income was enough to send the younger ones to a Catholic school, and eventually we got shares in a mill or two. We started with the rice mills in the area. From the third oldest down to the youngest, they all finished school, and you know that three of them went to university in America. My younger daughter who just left the room, she is smart. She won a scholarship and got to go to medical school in America.

❧

WHEN I WAS FORTY-FIVE and my youngest was only two, my husband died. That was the worst time of my whole life. He had been unwell for about a month I suppose. He complained of severe headaches and had to lie down all the time. Of course, we had no hospital thereabouts in those days, and even if we'd had one, we couldn't have afforded it. He just tried to treat himself with the local medicines like Tamjai when his bad headache came on.

The two littlest boys were just seven and two when he went. The two oldest boys were already over twenty and were working. I told all the children, "You can't compare us with other families. They have a father and a mother and you only have a mother." But there was worse to come. Soon after that my oldest son, the one who was earning good money, suddenly died as well. He must have had a heart attack. Now I was going to have to do everything all on my own to keep the family going.

At that point I really thought I couldn't go on. My husband had unexpectedly gone, leaving me with small children, and then my oldest son went. I really didn't want to go on living. In fact, when the children didn't behave, I sometimes told them that I would go to join their father. The older children remember that I even collapsed a couple of times. But whenever I looked at the two youngest boys, who were completely dependent on me, I had to go on somehow.

Now I have my five sons, two daughters, and quite a few grandchildren, both boys and girls. I have over thirty grandchildren. I have great-grandchildren too.

∿

WHEN MY HUSBAND DIED we moved out of his older brother's house. Not only us, but all our children had worked for him and ended up with practically nothing. He was cheating them, I felt. My daughter here worked for him during her lunch break from school. When I was left with the children, I was farming during the day and working other jobs at night. I got up at five in the morning, made breakfast for the family and cleaned up the house, and then finished my own breakfast. After that I could go out to the fields. Every single day was like that. Then from five in the afternoon, I would go to the mill and be the cook for the workers. I cooked for about twenty of them. The baby was strapped to my back. If he cried, I just had to go on working so I strapped him to my back to stop him crying and worked standing over the big pots.

The sun was so hot in Thailand that I got the idea of farming at night. After the sun went down I used to tell the family and neighbors that we should go back out to the fields. That's really what you might call moonlighting. I actually did work in the fields at night because it was so much cooler.

My kids had to work hard in order to stay in school. I sent some of them away to the Catholic school. At that time we had a little money, because my husband was still alive, [and] we were both working and selling some. At the Catholic school in Ban Pong, my son and younger daughter had to help clean—

scrub the toilets and the floors and wash the school car—and help cook the food in order to earn their board and keep. In that way, they could earn two or three hundred baht a month to pay for their own meals.

In my day, girls didn't go to school, they worked. Both my daughters went to school as well as working. But mornings, my older daughter cut sugarcane and sold it on her way to school in order to contribute her part to the family income. When my older sons could earn enough money for the family, that meant all the younger ones could stay in school. But it still cost a lot of money to send them all to school, and I still worked day and night. My neighbors called me silly for not taking it easier when my children could have worked with me. But if you can't finish school, it's really not good.

~

I TOLD MY CHILDREN: keep working and don't stop. I haven't stopped; I still work in the vegetable garden every day. I pushed them. I told them that if you're lazy or you take it easy like other children, you'll never get anywhere; you don't have two parents to rely on. I was determined. When one of the boys wanted to play football [soccer] after school, I went there with a stick to remind him that he had to study and work at home; like I said, other children had both father and mother, but mine had only a mother. We had to try harder. If they slept late, they found me with my stick at their bedside, even when they were already university students. My children make fun of it now: "What a way to take care of children!" and so on. It's not for the new generation.

When two of my sons went to school in America, that was very expensive, and they had to work over there. One of them was tall and made a good impression, so he was able to get a nice job—custodian at the university who would lock up all the buildings at night. The other one was short, and he ended up washing dishes in the back of a Chinese restaurant. He went to live in the same city as my daughter, who was in medical school there. One day, when she was eating at that restaurant with her friends, the busboy came out to clear their dishes and it was her brother. She started crying and had to explain to them why.

Speaking of short, you know about my oldest son who died. Like a peanut— he was full of brains, even though he was small. Didn't get the chance to go to university, but was he smart. We used to call him "Kon Beng."[34] He had a good business head, and he was doing so well before we lost him, I'm sure he would have succeeded at anything.

And he was very much like his father. My husband was very nice and very polite and never said a harsh word to anybody. That's why it made me so angry that his brother kept the money we earned. My husband never complained about it. That brother of his was a mean one. Even when we, the parents, had nothing, we always gave the children something to eat first, and I would take their rice to them before school started. Their uncle couldn't understand that.

So you see it paid off. My children are all educated and as a result have done well. When I got older, my children started taking me places. I've been to Hawaii and seen how they farm there. I've been to [the mainland of] America more than once, to Japan, to Europe, and back to China. But my area of China had changed so much that I couldn't recognize it. I was the only child of my parents. My mother remarried after my father died, and when my third son was ten years old, she died. My one remaining close relative back in China was my step-brother. He was only two when I left China. He went up into the northern part of China when the Communist era started. His son, my nephew, became a doctor. Through a letter from our family, he was able to trace me here. He came here a few years ago to visit me.

I don't really need a house like this, but my children want me to have it. I've gotten used to it. What I really like is to work in the garden. When we bought this parcel of land, it seemed large, but when we divided it up so that five families could live here, it didn't seem so big anymore. The air conditioner, the pool, I don't need these things. In the past, I did farming. We moved here because there's no flooding here.

I can't read, but I keep everything in my head. My sons and daughters consult me about their plans and business, and I tell them my ideas. I never forget anything. I keep track of how much money I've lent to my children—and how much interest they should be paying me on it . . . if only!

Young people today are lazy. They don't even cook for themselves anymore; eat out or take out. Please have some of this corn; I grew it myself. It's very delicious. Fresh. These bananas aren't big enough yet. I've seen farming in lots of countries: Japan, France, Hawaii, Australia, everywhere. How did we manage during wartime? During the war, we moved our farm from Kanchanaburi to Rajburi, about four or five kilometers away. At night there was a blackout. Some of us dug holes and went to hide in them.

∾

WHEREVER, WHENEVER I GO, when any of my sons or daughters go anywhere by plane, I go to the temple to pray for safety. I go often to Wat Rai King in Nakhon Pratom to pray for things, for health. If something goes well I bring a gift to the temple, a chicken or something. When the family moved their mill to Kalasin, I went to the temple. If everything goes all right, I always go back to the temple.

∾

WOULD I SAY my life was really happier now than before? Well, my husband died, and I had to stay here. Here's a family picture from just before my husband died. I'm holding the baby; he's two. There's my sister-in-law, the nice one. Standing in the back is my second oldest son, the one whose house we're in right now. My daughter says the house and yard in the picture look like hill tribe people's. Back then everybody lived like that. Here's my photo portrait from the time I received the Mother of the Year award just a few years ago. That was quite an honor because the award comes from the queen.

You'd like to see the vegetable garden? I work in it every day. I'll show you.

These beans I started myself, and now they fill two rows. This I transplanted myself, and see how big it's gotten? You have to take care of a garden every day. That way it produces and you'll always have something. Yes, my back hurts, but I feel I've got to do it. It's what I enjoy.

Epilogue

We thought about what to give Khun Fa, the woman who now can have everything but doesn't want it. What we did want her to have was her name in the original Chinese characters, which are beautiful whether one can read them or not. We gave her her name drawn in calligraphy on rice paper and framed.

Khun Fa's website is at *http://www.sfc.keio.ac.jp/~thiesmey/khunfa1.html*.

NOTES

Epigraph: Valentina Stoeva, "Women against the Information Borders," in *Women, Information and the Future: Collecting and Sharing Information Worldwide,* ed. Eva Steiner Moseley (Fort Atkinson, Wis.: Highsmith Press, 1995), 12–13.

"Khun" is the contemporary Thai form of address used regardless of gender; it is polite without being overly formal. Fâ (華), meaning "flower(s)," is her first name. For the sake of privacy I have used only first names or nicknames throughout. I thank Khun Jaew, Khun Giaw, and Pa Mor for their assistance in and additions to the interpreting in both senses of the term.

1. I had already heard the outlines of Khun Fa's life from her younger daughter. Michio Umegaki took the video of her.

2. Mary S. Erbaugh, "The Hakka Paradox in the People's Republic of China," in *Guest People: Hakka Identity in China and Abroad*, ed. Nicole Constable (Seattle: University of Washington Press, 1996), 196–231.

3. Nicole Constable investigates a Hakka migrant community's construction of identity out of these characteristics in her first book, *Christian Souls and Chinese Spirits: A Hakka Community in Hong Kong* (Berkeley: University of California Press, 1994).

4. Chandra Talpade Mohanty, "Under Western Eyes: Feminist Scholarship and Colonial Discourses," in *Third World Women and the Politics of Feminism*, ed. Chandra Talpade Mohanty, Ann Russo, and Lourdes Torres (Bloomington: Indiana University Press, 1991), 71. Others point to similar issues in Thai gender studies as "the frameworks, myths, and fantasies . . . of Thai gender and sexuality" (Nerida M. Cook and Peter A. Jackson, "Desiring Constructs: Transforming Sex/Gender Orders in Twentieth-Century Thailand," in *Genders and Sexualities in Modern Thailand*, ed. Peter A. Jackson and Nerida M. Cook [Chiang Mai: Silkworm Books, 1999], 2).

5. Penny van Esterik, "Repositioning Gender, Sexuality and Power in Thai Studies," in *Genders and Sexualities*, ed. Jackson and Cook, 286.

6. Rey Chow, "Violence in the Other Country: China as Crisis, Spectacle, and Woman," in *Third World Women*, ed. Mohanty et al., 93.

7. Barbara Ramusack and Sharon Sievers, *Women in Asia: Restoring Women to History* (Bloomington: Indiana University Press, 1999), 105–6.

8. Patrick Bell writes on these issues and recent scholarship on them in "Thailand's Economic Miracle: Built on the Backs of Women," in *Women, Gender Relations and Development in Thai Society*, ed. Virada Somswadi and Sally Theobald (Chiang Mai: Chiang Mai University Women's Studies Center, 1997), 1: 55–82.

9. Sandra Gilbert and Susan Gubar, "Ceremonies of the Alphabet: Female Grandmatologies and the Female Autograph," in *The Female Autograph: Theory and Practice of Autobiography from the Tenth to the Twentieth Century*, ed. Domna C. Stanton (Chicago: University of Chicago Press, 1987), 21–48. Works on women's autobiographies have tended to focus on written autobiographies. See also *Women's Autobiography: Essays in Criticism*, ed. Estelle C. Jelinek (Bloomington: Indiana University Press, 1980), and id., *The Tradition of Women's Autobiography from Antiquity to the Present* (Boston: Twayne Publishers, 1986).

10. Deborah Tannen, "The Oral/Literate Continuum in Discourse," in *Spoken and Written Language: Exploring Orality and Literacy*, ed. Deborah Tannen (Norwood, N.J.: Ablex Publishing, 1982), 82.

11. Jodi L. Jacobson, "Gender Bias: Roadblock to Sustainable Development," Worldwatch Paper 110 (Washington, D.C.: Worldwatch Institute, 1992), 6.

12. Marilyn French, *The War against Women* (New York: Penguin Books, 1992), 23.

13. Marilyn Waring, *If Women Counted: A New Feminist Economics* (New York: HarperCollins, 1988), 17.

14. Again, even given the fact that most rural Chinese women worked in the fields, this is one of the areas in which many Hakka women take particular pride. See Constable, *Christian Souls and Chinese Spirits.*

15. "[I]n contemporary times, parental roles and duties have altered primarily in response to the increased importance of education. . . . Parents now want their children to obtain a secure, usually non-agriculturally-based, job," Bencha Yoddumnern-Attig et al. note in *Changing Roles and Statuses of Women in Thailand: A Documentary Assessment* (Nakhon Pathom, Thailand: Mahidol University Institute for Population and Social Research, 1992), 34.

16. Mohanty, "*Under Western Eyes,*" 68.

17. Alpha Research Co., Ltd., and Manager Information Services Co., Ltd., *Thailand: Export Focus 1995* (Bangkok: Alpha Research Co., Ltd., and Manager Information Services Co., Ltd., 1995), 16.

18. Partha Chatterjee, *The Nation and Its Fragments: Colonial and Postcolonial Histories* (Princeton: Princeton University Press), 145.

19. Sheryl Greenwood Gowen, "Beliefs about Literacy: Measuring Women into Silence/Hearing Women into Speech," *Discourse and Society* 2, 4 (1991): 448.

20. Maria Mies, *Patriarchy and Accumulation on a World Scale* (London: Zed Books, 1998), 112–20.

21. Shirley Brice Heath, "Protean Shapes in Literacy Events: Ever-Shifting Oral and Literate Traditions," in *Spoken and Written Language*, ed. Tannen, 92–93.

22. Jack Goody, "Alternative Paths to Knowledge in Oral and Literate Cultures," in *Spoken and Written Language*, ed. Tannen, 201–2, 212–14.

23. Walter Ong, *Orality and Literacy: The Technologizing of the Word* (London: Routledge, 1988), 177.

24. L. L. Langness and Gelya Frank, *Lives: An Anthropological Approach to Biography* (Novato, Calif.: Chandler & Sharp, 1981), 61.

25. The main way I chose to represent Khun Fa (to present her back to herself) was online. The online presentation allows her and her audience to see and hear her as she represents herself. In a pleasing irony, a woman who might have been silenced by illiteracy can use the Internet to gain recognition and response.

26. Homi Bhabha, *The Location of Culture* (London: Routledge, 1994), 160, 165.

27. *The Collected Dialogues of Plato*, ed. Edith Hamilton and Huntington Cairns (Princeton: Princeton University Press, 1961), 520.

28. Anne E. McLaren, "Chinese Cultural Revivalism: Changing Gender Constructions in the Yangtze River Delta," in *Gender and Power in Affluent Asia*, ed. Krishna Sen and Maila Stevens (London: Routledge, 1998), 212.

29. "It appears that readers and listeners do adopt somewhat different strategies in comprehending narrative discourse. The listeners pay primary attention to the theme of the story, building a coherent representation of what was meant," Angela Hildyard

and David R. Olson note in "On the Comprehension and Memory of Oral vs. Written Discourse," 31–32, in *Spoken and Written Language*, ed. Tannen, 19–33.

30. Robin Tolmach Lakoff, "Some of my Favorite Writers are Literate: The Mingling of Oral and Literate Strategies in Written Communication," in *Spoken and Written Language*, ed. Tannen, 259–60.

31. Rey Chow, *Writing Diaspora: Tactics of Intervention in Contemporary Cultural Studies* (Bloomington: Indiana University Press, 1993), 32–36.

32. Gilbert and Gubar, "*Ceremonies of the Alphabet*," 21–23.

33. 1 satang = one-hundredth of a baht; the denomination was more frequently used in Khun Fa's youth than it is now.

34. Kon Beng (孔明) is a figure in the Ming Dynasty epic *San guo yan yi* [*Three Kingdoms*] known for his wisdom and strategy.

Part II ∿ *The Shifting Terrain of Public Life*

"Stage Business" as Citizenship

Ida B. Wells at the World's Columbian Exposition

℘ The 1893 World's Columbian Exposition commemorated (a year behind schedule) the four-hundredth anniversary of Columbus's arrival
in America. At the behest of several of Chicago's well-heeled industrial
entrepreneurs, and flush with congressional appropriations, the architect
Daniel Burnham and the urban planner Frederick L. Olmsted collaborated to
produce The White City, a dreamlike vision on the banks of Lake Michigan,
composed of neoclassical buildings whose alabaster façades gleamed off of reflecting pools, and an adjoining Midway Plaisance, where the pseudoscience of
ethnology merged with Barnumesque display in a panoply of spectacles. The
Fair was not only an unprecedented achievement in architecture, education,
and entertainment, it was also, many scholars have argued, a reflection of and
catalyst for the public sphere's transformation. "Above all," Miriam Hansen
writes on this transformation, "alliances between industrial-commercial publicity and the disintegrating bourgeois public sphere work to simulate the fictive coherence and transparency of a public sphere that is not one," and nowhere is the fictive coherence and transparency to which Hansen refers better
exemplified than in the 1893 Fair.[1] Its administration imitated parliamentary
procedures, appointing representatives and soliciting displays from every state,
the federal government's endorsement provided further legitimacy, and the
astonishing array of secondary publicity the Fair generated—from continuous
press coverage to countless authorized and unauthorized guidebooks—
established it as a site of national and international fascination. Hosting an es-
timated twenty-seven million guests, the Fair served as a cultural "pedagogy,"
Alan Trachtenberg writes, "a model and a lesson not only of what the future

might look like but, just as important, how it might be brought about."[2] A site for producing an imagined community of national citizens, it cast commodity consumption as citizenship's primary modality, showcasing "progress" not in the form of "simple matter and things, but matter and things as commercial products."[3] It also reproduced the founding contradictions of bourgeois publicity, obscuring the roles of women, nonwhites, and labor in the development of American industry and culture, while offering an iconic spectacle of democratic inclusiveness.

If the Fair embodied the success of white America, its exclusion of African Americans "embodied the definitive failure of the hopes of emancipation and reconstruction," Hazel Carby writes, "and inaugurated an age that was to be dominated by 'the problem of the color line.'"[4] To criticize and compensate for the Fair's racial exclusivity, the journalist and anti-lynching activist Ida B. Wells solicited contributions from other black public intellectuals for a pamphlet. The resulting eighty-one pages of "The Reason Why the Colored American is Not in the World's Columbian Exposition" exposed the systemic racism behind the Fair's refusals to permit African American contributions and, highlighting black culture and accomplishment since emancipation, served as a kind of exhibit itself. "The pamphlet is intended as a calm, dignified statement of the Afro-American's side of the story, from the beginning to the present day," Wells writes in the preface, "a recital of the obstacles which have hampered him; a sketch of what he has done in twenty-five years with all his persecution, and a statement of the fruitless efforts he made for representation at the world's fair."[5] The pamphlet opens with Frederick Douglass's discussion of slavery, discriminatory laws, and the convict lease system. Wells then analyzes lynch law, offering a statistical and descriptive account of lynching, the rates of which were near their peak in the early 1890s. I. Garland Penn documents the "progress of the race" since Emancipation, demonstrating population increases, improved literacy rates, the establishment of schools and churches, and gains made in the arts, labor, and many professions. Finally, the attorney and editor Ferdinand Barnett recounts the frustration with which African Americans met the Fair's persistent refusals of their petitions for inclusion. In short, as the United States put itself on display in Chicago for a multinational audience, the pamphlet meant to clarify that the absence of African Americans was a result not of their shortcomings but of the legacy of slavery and a set of deliberate local exclusions.

"The Reason Why" exposes what its authors call a duplicity on the part of

Fair officials that constituted an international outrage, impoverishing the Fair as a whole. By failing to appoint a single African American to the 208-member National Board of Commissioners, President Benjamin Harrison established "a precedent which remained inviolate throughout the entire term of Exposition work."[6] Barnett's chapter thoroughly documents the many levels at which efforts by African Americans to secure representation were thwarted. Initially, the Fair's director general denied a petition for a black voice in the direct management of the Fair and the National Directors rejected a suggestion for a Department of Colored Exhibits.[7] Since several members of the Board of Lady Managers had been active abolitionists, they were thought to be a more sympathetic audience than the central administration had been. Two African American women's organizations were formed to encourage alliances with this board, which was chaired by the wife of one of the Fair's leading organizers. However, the two associations failed to agree on which African American woman could best "represent the race" on the board and on whether white and black women's work should be exhibited separately. By amplifying the discrepancy between the two associations' agendas, the Lady Managers cast the groups as rivals and cited their fear of internal divisions among the African Americans as a justification for turning them away. It would be impolitic, they claimed, to recognize either "faction." "The promptness which marked [the Lady Managers'] assumption of this position," Barnett wrote, "is fairly indicative of the hypocrisy and duplicity which the colored people met in every effort made."[8]

Even on this most promising of avenues, then, white administrators devised an excuse for excluding African Americans, all the while maintaining a pretense of liberality. Though a black woman eventually was appointed to the New York State Board of Lady Managers, the National Board effectively absolved themselves of responsibility for African Americans' inclusion in the Fair administration. Last-ditch requests for a "separate Negro exhibit" were denied. Barnett notes that even the doctors hired by the Fair administration to perform physical exams on applicants for jobs as Columbian Guards fabricated physical inadequacies to disqualify African American men. A tacit but deliberate policy of exclusion made itself felt at every turn.[9]

Thus, while there are empirical reasons for the whiteness of the White City (a mere 1.3 percent of Chicago was black in 1890), its racial makeup was no demographic accident but the result of a systematic effort. The authors of "The Reason Why" sought to make this absence conspicuous to white fairgoers.

Indeed, we might understand it not simply as a conspicuous absence but as industrial-commercial publicity's reproduction of the classical public sphere's founding logic of exclusion, that is, as a constitutive absence. More than a mere effect of the biases and practices that preceded it, the absence of African Americans from the Fair served, in turn, to facilitate the retrenchment of imperialist social relations in the emerging forms of publicity. Regardless of what may have been a diversity of opinions among various white Fair officials regarding African American participation, the absence of African Americans became more than incidental to the Fair's function as a public sphere. The resolve with which this exclusion was pursued turned dark skin into a particular that could not be abstracted into the general category "American." To put a finer point on it, we need only recognize that nonwhite people were prevented from participating in the Fair only if they were from the United States.

As instructive as the pamphlet's arguments are about the reproduction of racism and white privilege, the circumstances of its publication may be more instructive still. They illuminate the contradictions of the contemporary public sphere and the strategies that were available to African American women to negotiate them. Frederick Douglass had been the U.S. ambassador to Haiti from 1889 to 1891, and Fair officials asked him to oversee the Haiti building. A paltry gesture of recognition for the venerable abolitionist, to be sure, but the building became "one of the gems of the World's Fair," Wells wrote, "and in it Mr. Douglass held high court."[10] Douglass gave Wells space in the Haiti building to distribute her pamphlet to fairgoers. Though she had long been vocal in print, Wells was new to public speaking. "The first time I had ever been called on to deliver an honest-to-goodness address" was the previous year, she writes in her autobiography; "I had no knowledge of stage business."[11] Nevertheless, unbidden and officially unwelcome, she took this stage daily in the summer and fall of 1893.

Two instances of African American women's participation in the Fair provide a generative context for discussing Wells's intervention. Not far from her desk, in the Food Building, a fifty-nine-year-old Chicago south-sider named Nancy Green brought the pancake trademark Aunt Jemima to life, emerging periodically from the giant flour barrel that the Quaker Oats corporation had built for her, singing songs, and telling tales—some drawn from the vaudeville Aunt Jemima song and others from her "memories" of plantation days. A living advertisement for one of the many new "convenience foods" the Fair showcased, Green's performance celebrated the "progressive emancipation" of the modern housewife from "the drudgery of virtual slavery in her kitchen."[12] Having been born into actual slavery herself in Montgomery County, Kentucky, Green performed the soothing stereotype of the southern mammy so convincingly that fairgoers jammed the aisles of the display, bought lapel buttons emblazoned with her likeness, and turned her signature cry, "I'se in town, honey!" into "the catchline of the Fair."[13] Also appearing at the Fair were six African American contributors to the week-long Congress of Representative Women. Among the roughly three hundred women who participated, Frances E. W. Harper spoke on "Woman's Political Future," Hallie Q. Brown and Sarah Early on "The Organized Efforts of Colored Women of the South to Improve their Condition," and Fannie Barrier Williams, Anna Julia Cooper and Fannie J. Coppin on "The Intellectual Progress of the Colored Women of the U.S. since the Emancipation Proclamation."[14] These two "official" versions of black women as public subjects—the Women's Congress speakers and Nancy Green's Aunt Jemima—form a backdrop against which Wells's act of counterpublicity comes into focus. I want to suggest that her decision to produce not just a pamphlet but also her body on the fairgrounds was particularly responsive to the racialized, commercialized public sphere of the Fair, and that the minoritized body she produced was neither depoliticized for consumption nor assimilable to a white political agenda.

Since the conventions and boundaries of the official political public sphere are never static, it is worth noting the forces that shaped the political public sphere to which Wells sought access. Late-nineteenth-century public life was marked by the juridical and demographic legacies of Reconstruction, by a tremendous influx of immigrants, and by the emerging women's and labor movements. Such a shifting terrain makes speaking of a unified, national public sphere problematic, and these social changes were linked inextricably to economic changes. Often characterized in shorthand as a shift from entrepreneurial to monopoly capitalism, the rise of corporations and trusts was enabled by new technologies of communication and transportation and fostered by a deregulated banking system. Moreover, economic change was accelerated by the compliance, indeed the encouragement, of the state. Progressive-era government took aim at corporate excesses through antitrust laws, protective labor legislation, and banking regulations, but it was also lax in the enforcement of these laws and lenient toward managerial efforts to quell labor movements. Its usual methods for helping business—whether through land subsidies, tariff protections, or funds for World's Fairs—proliferated during the 1890s.

On the one hand, then, corporations gained the authority to influence discourse in the public sphere and to shape public spaces. On the other hand, the state began to administer a wider range of services than had previously fallen to the public. These conditions helped produce what many have called a culture of consumption, in which the economic imperative to cultivate demand for an abundance of material goods had implications that were not merely economic but also broadly social and ideological. Participation in consumer culture became a modality of national citizenship, and although the channels through which Americans went public proliferated, the very function of publicity was itself transformed from a means for citizens to check power, in the form of the state, into a means for the exercise of power, in the form of capital. In order to account for these factors, questions about who was included in or excluded from the public sphere might be better cast as questions about what versions of inclusion were being produced. What were the terms in which inclusion was offered? How did the stakes of exclusion from the public sphere vary among subjects who were constructed differently both socially and juridically?

The utopian promise of bourgeois publicity was that particular people could stand in for people in general, mere citizens. But this ideal of abstract citizenship rested on a contradiction: its privileges and protections were acquired in exchange for bracketing the socially legible particulars of the person whose body would enjoy those privileges and protections.[15] Minoritized subjects (including women, those who did not own property, and bondsmen) were prevented from experiencing themselves as universal, while privileged subjects performed the ideological gesture of mistaking their own particular attributes for universals. This contradiction was reproduced as the public sphere became both more inclusive and more commercial. A rhetoric of self-abstraction was offered to a broader portion of the population, but it required in exchange capitulation to the terms of industrial-commercial publicity. In other words, along with the democratization of the privilege to abstract oneself as a public citizen came a shift in the terms of that abstraction. For later publicity required not only discursive participation, but also physical participation, spectacle, and display, the use of new urban spaces that were neither strictly public nor strictly private. If the bodies of people in public had impeded their citizenship claims under the discursive conventions of bourgeois publicity, industrial-commercial publicity made available versions of citizenship that depended precisely on rendering bodies visible. World's Fairs played a major part in this "exhibitionary complex," as Tony Bennett calls it, for they hypostasized a public by rendering the crowd visible to itself. "Please remember when you get inside the gates you are part of the show," enjoined the 1901 Pan-American Expo, and however paradoxical, it was through such iconic forms of embodiment that one achieved a version of the self-abstraction of public subjects.[16]

We can best read Wells's response to the Fair's exclusivity with these changes in the terms of participation in mind. By the spring of 1893, her prominence buoyed by a speaking tour in Great Britain on the atrocities of lynch law in the South, Wells had collected chapters for "The Reason Why." But the project foundered when many black papers refused to endorse it publicly or to back it financially. She was compelled to solicit popular support and money by publishing letters to editors, from whom she "beg[ged] space to say in a few words what we are trying to do."[17] Her contributions to black papers during the Fair show her discomfort with the possible antagonism between public political discourse and corporeality. She bristled at the comparison some editors made between her pamphlet and the highly publicized "Colored Jubilee Day," the Fair administration's own proposal for including African Americans. Her chief antagonist was George Knox, editor of the conservative *Indianapolis Freeman*. Conflating the two projects in an editorial titled "No 'Nigger Day,' No 'Nigger Pamphlet,'" he opposed both for the same reason: "Both designs, if carried out, while they may add to the evanescent notoriety of certain individuals who may be active participants, and who thrive and grow robust on such things, and are charmed to see their names in print, will only serve to attract invidious and patronizing attention to the race, unattended with practical recompense or reward."[18]

In fact, Wells too objected to "Negro Day," calling it "a sop to our pride in [a] belated way" whose tacit goal was to fill the Fair's anemic coffers.[19] Mindful of the corporate interests backing the Fair, she warned *Cleveland Gazette* readers that "Negro Day" was a "scheme to put thousands of dollars in the pockets of the railroad corporations and the world's fair folks who thought no Negro good enough for an official position among them."[20] Even more disturbing to Wells than this bald profiteering, however, was the prospect of a physical display of aimless black bodies gathered to consume:

The horticultural department has already pledged itself to put plenty of watermelons around on the grounds with permission to the brother in black to "appropriate" them. . . . The self-respect of the race is sold for a mess of pottage and the spectacle of the class of our people which will come on that excursion roaming around the grounds munching watermelons, will do more to lower the race in the estimation of the world than anything else. The sight of the horde that would be attracted there by the dazzling prospect of plenty of free watermelons to eat, will give our enemies all the illustration they wish as excuse for not treating the Afro-American with the equality of other citizens.[21]

A "calm, dignified statement of the Afro-American's side of the story," the pamphlet was to be the antithesis of "Negro Day."[22] Despite journalists' efforts to yoke the two projects, then, Wells characterized her pamphlet as a more cerebral, and therefore more politically promising, alternative for African American participation in the Fair. It would signal African Americans' fitness for inclusion in the political public sphere because it would observe the bourgeois norm of suppressing the body to approximate an ideal of critical-rational discourse.

Why did Wells not simply publish "The Reason Why" and leave its distribution to someone else? That is, why risk the humiliation of minoritized public embodiment—the humiliation that she identified in the "Negro Day" proposal and that is borne out in accounts of other appearances of nonwhite people on the fairgrounds—by putting herself "on display"? After all, there were alternatives that avoided this risk. Her remarks in an April 1893 article in the Baltimore *Afro-American* illuminate her decision. Aware that African Americans' presence at the Fair might confirm racist stereotypes, Wells nevertheless maintained that it was their *absence* that posed the more pressing danger. "The absence of colored citizens from participation in the Fair," she wrote, "will be construed to their disadvantage by representatives of the civilized world." Or as Charles Morris, the African American editor of the Washington, D.C., paper the *Pilot* put it: "The World's Fair could do more to raise the negro in the estimation of people at home and abroad as a valuable industrial agent in the future development of this country than anything I know of. . . . No class of Americans need[s] the World's Fair as badly as the negro, for the ability of no class has been so universally denied."[23] Morris clarifies the premise on which Wells's response was based: however inaccurate the representations of America offered up by commercial publicity were, their role as a cultural pedagogy should not be underestimated. In other words, "sham" public spheres like the 1893 Fair were not simply a "sham," for they served to enact and naturalize a mode of social segregation and economic and political subordination as much as to reflect an existing one.

Wells's effort to occupy the fairgrounds flouted the widespread opinion among her colleagues that African Americans should abandon the Fair that had abandoned them. Charles Morris reported the "wide circulation" being given "to a series of whereases and resolutions of an organization of colored men in this city declaring a boycott against the World's Fair."[24] "We object!" cried the editors of the *New York Age* when they learned of the Fair's refusal to appoint an African American woman to the Board of Lady Managers. "We carry our objection so far that if the matter was left to our determination we would advise the race to have nothing whatever to do with the Columbian Exposition or the management of it."[25] Clearly, Wells would not have stood alone had she merely published the pamphlet and boycotted the Fair. Since African Americans were denied a part in *producing* the Fair, a boycott would, in turn, withhold from the Fair the benefits of their *consuming* it. However, it was the Fair that was boycotting African Americans, and in her determination not only to publish the pamphlet but also to place herself within the Fair's circuits of publicity, Wells insisted on the priority of this point.

Some African American journalists cast Wells and Douglass as self-aggrandizing, impractical, and out of touch with plain black folks. It was suggested that they express their grievances in a letter to the president or the people of the United States, which the Associated Press would gladly carry.[26] Wells was compelled to raise most of the publication funds in Chicago's black churches. It was not until August, therefore, with the Fair already "in full blast," that she began to distribute ten thousand copies of the "creditable little book" from her propitious post: "The peculiar thing about it was that nearly all day long it was crowded with American white people who came to pay their respects to this black man whom his own country had refused to honor. Needless to say, the Haitian building was the chosen spot, for representative Negroes of the country who visited the Fair were to be found along with the Haitians and citizens of other foreign countries."[27] Though a boycott was symbolic, it meant capitulating more broadly to the Fair's effort to discipline African Americans.

In an important sense, Wells's physical presence posed a more vexing challenge to the Fair than did the arguments her pamphlet contained, for she was neither the kind of woman nor the kind of nonwhite that it was producing as a public subject. The fairgrounds were a well-orchestrated sign system and the fairgoing experience was highly managed; the size and arrangement of buildings suggested their relationships to one another and their relative importance. While the White City offered instruction and cultivation, the Fair's more frivolous and plainly commercial diversions were found on the Midway. The absence of African Americans from the White City belied (as Wells feared it would) their centrality to the material and intellectual progress it celebrated.

The corresponding presence of nonwhites on the Midway served further to establish and confirm white supremacist thinking, for there, under the direction of experts in the newly established discipline of anthropology, nonwhites were gathered into communities that ostensibly simulated real life but effectively exoticized their inhabitants, making them testaments to white superiority. From atop the Ferris wheel at its center one might see not only the German beer garden, the belly dancers in the "Streets of Cairo," and a simulated destruction of Pompeii, but also a Bedouin "encampment," a Javanese "village," and ensembles of scantily clad people from African Dahomey and the South Sea Islands. If the White City defined nonwhites as irrelevant to Western progress, the Midway located them centrally in a field of white fascination and amusement.

Frederick Douglass identifies the racism of "exhibit[ing] the Negro as a repulsive savage" in "The Reason Why," and recent historians have argued further that the racialization of the Fair's spaces served to confirm white supremacist thinking and to justify imperialism.[28] It invited whites to understand dark-skinned people as objects at which to gaze, marvel, and learn of their own superiority. Research into the Fair's secondary publicity suggests that the exhibition of Africans had disastrous implications for African Americans. It shows that white fairgoers readily mapped the racist logic of the Midway's international representations onto the domestic context of U.S. race relations. "Blacker than buried midnight and as degraded as the animals which prowl the jungle of their dark land," one popular magazine wrote about the Dahomeyans, "in these wild people we easily detect many characteristics of the American negro."[29]

For Wells, the racist assumptions that shaped her reception on the fairgrounds were inseparable from her gender. White women were well represented at the Fair, through the Women's Building, the Women's Congress, and the extensive displays of women's artistic productions. To be sure, in and of themselves they did little to mitigate the more general patronizing uses to which "woman" was put at the Fair, whether as the repository of ideals of domesticity and civic virtue or as bodies for display. Nevertheless, they were more than mere gestures, and they reflect the legitimacy white women had secured, however imperfectly, as public subjects, a legitimacy that black women were denied. As Ann Douglas writes, the prevailing assumptions about black women as public subjects derived from the structural relations of slavery. Since "most whites after the Civil War believed that black women were cut off from any type of moral elevation," those women who "wanted to market themselves as exemplars of uplift" commanded an audience that was "not only skeptical, but incredulous and hostile."[30]

We might consider, therefore, how the "exemplars of uplift" in the Women's Congress negotiated this potential incredulity and hostility. Hazel Carby argues that their participation was not entirely unproblematic. The larger discourse of black exoticism at the Fair placed these women in "a highly contradictory position." The Congress was an "international but overwhelmingly white women's forum," Carby writes, and the African American women were "at once part of and excluded from the dominant discourse of white women's politics."[31] The white framework within which they operated helped to validate their presence as public subjects, as representative women. Their tone was evidently crucial for shoring up this status: the president of the National Council of Women said approvingly that they spoke "with temperance and without bitterness [on] the social, intellectual, and industrial status of [their] race."[32] Their publicity was purchased, then, at the price of a restrained mode of address and marked by a horizon of white women's interests. Moreover, even this dominant discourse of white women's politics itself functioned ambivalently in relation to the Fair. To be sure, the Women's Congress's ties to the Fair were unmistakable—it convened under the auspices of the Women's Branch of the Fair's World's Congress Auxiliary. Yet only a few of the meetings convened on the fairgrounds proper, and these were the "more informal" gatherings. The majority of the meetings took place downtown at the new Memorial Art Palace (now the Art Institute), and records of the Congress confirm that the African American women were among those annexed from the fairgrounds. Thus, while women's handiwork filled the Women's Building, and "woman" figured prominently as a symbol of domestic and civic virtue, the effect of the Congress's annexation must have been to bracket from the business of the fairgrounds the voices of women with extradomestic concerns. The presence of African Americans in the Congress constituted a risk on the part of Fair organizers, but one that was contained by the terms of their inclusion.[33]

The version of going public pursued by the representative women was incompatible with the demands of publicity on the fairgrounds proper, where instruction was made enjoyable as spectacular display. Nancy Green's Aunt Jemima fulfilled these demands all too well. Posing as an instructor of sorts—"three hundred pounds of affable kitchen wisdom"—Green was not herself at the Fair but a living advertisement for the nationally branded pancake batter.

By identifying her own body with a commercial trademark, Green accessed a new rhetoric of disembodiment, a kind of iconic national citizenship. But her access was predicated on performing a stereotype to soothe and delight white audiences. She served as "domestic consolation" that the "happy darkie" figure lived on despite the drastic changes of modernity.[34] In exchange for the sensations of public citizenship that her performance of a national brand afforded, however, Green relinquished the possibility that it would be her own body that experienced these sensations. The Quaker Oats history puts it literally: "The personality of Aunt Jemima completely absorbed the identity of Miss Green. She was Aunt Jemima for the remainder of her life."[35] Rather than occupy an always-already humiliated body whose particulars were unrecuperable in the official public sphere, Green identified herself with a public subject whom she could imagine as parallel to her private person. She exchanged her body for "a better model," one that the emerging industrial-commercial public sphere made available in the guise of inclusiveness.[36]

Green's version of going public is one Lauren Berlant names the "commercial hieroglyphic," "a body that condenses a narrative whose form seems to assure the impossibility of choosing otherwise, of being something other than a function in a system of conventions."[37] Her appearance both answers and recasts Marx's question about what commodities would say if they could speak. When commodities speak by inhabiting the bodies and voices of black women to whom alternate versions of public citizenship are unavailable, what might black women say and be in public without also signaling their availability to a regime of display and consumption? Wells faced this question implicitly by putting both her pamphlet and her self on the fairgrounds. Presenting not only a disembodied argument but also a black woman, she risked being conflated with the commercial hieroglyphics that shared her space and cried, "I'se in town honey!" But perhaps more pressing still was the risk of being drowned out by that cry. However precarious her reception, the Fair's successful posture as an ideal public sphere made it an even greater risk to fail to appear there at all. Wells's effort to produce herself publicly at the Fair can be understood as an alternative to these two official versions of public subjectivity. The Representative Women avoided the commercial hieroglyphic that absorbed Nancy Green's identity in exchange for its rhetoric of disembodiment. But they too paid for their publicness with their bodies, for the Fair partly immunized itself against the political risk that their embodiment signified. Wells appropriated space at the White

City to disarticulate publicity from commercial hieroglyphics, being public from being commodity.

Too tidy an opposition between mass culture and authentic citizenship has overorganized public sphere talk. Examining Wells's work at the Fair productively complicates this opposition. Far from treating the Fair's pseudopublic sphere as a foreclosure of citizenship, Wells took industrial-commercial publicity as the precondition for her intervention, turning it against its intended purpose. The Fair's project to bring the public sphere into a seamless alignment with consumption became an opportunity for Wells to mime the privileges of the national citizen, whose protections she had been denied. Going public with "The Reason Why," Wells staged what Ann Massa has called "a radical black symposium . . . not on official display."[38] The Fair aimed to reconstitute the nation on local grounds and to narrate this reconstituted nation's relationship to other nations and to its own citizens. Wells produced a counternarrative to this reconstituting process and produced a citizen where there should not have been one.

NOTES

1. Miriam Hansen, "Foreword," in Oscar Negt and Alexander Kluge, *Public Sphere and Experience: Toward an Analysis of the Bourgeois and Proletarian Public Sphere*, trans. Peter Labanyi, Jamie Owen Daniel, and Assenka Oksiloff (Minneapolis: University of Minnesota Press, 1993), xxx.

2. Alan Trachtenberg, *The Incorporation of America: Culture and Society in the Gilded Age* (New York: Hill & Wang, 1982), 209.

3. Ibid., 204; see also ibid., ch. 7; James Gilbert, *Perfect Cities: Chicago's Utopias of 1893* (Chicago: University of Chicago Press, 1991); and Robert Rydell, "The World's Columbian Exposition of 1893: Racist Underpinnings of a Utopian Artifact," *Journal of American Culture* 1 (1978): 253–75.

4. Hazel Carby, *Reconstructing Womanhood: The Emergence of the Afro-American Woman Novelist* (New York: Oxford University Press, 1987), 5.

5. "The Reason Why the Colored American is Not in the World's Columbian Exposition: The Afro-American's Contribution to Columbian Literature," ed. Ida B. Wells, in *Selected Works of Ida B. Wells-Barnett* (New York: Oxford University Press, 1991), 46–137.

6. Ibid., 119.

7. The advisability of segregating exhibits by race was debated strenuously among African Americans. In fact, internecine squabbling was cited by the directors to justify

their denial. "Dissension within the ranks" became a convenient excuse for the white directors to deny African Americans' proposals. The same rationalization would reemerge thereafter, as African Americans appealed to the less centralized officers in the Fair bureaucracy.

8. "Reason Why," ed. Wells, 122.

9. For a fully elaborated discussion of the women's negotiations, see Ann Massa, "Black Women in the 'White City,'" *Journal of American Studies* 8 (December 1974): 319–37. On the issue of federal appropriations, it is instructive to note that Congress refused to grant $2,000 for a "Negro Annex," a "Statistical Exhibit which would show the moral, educational, and financial growth of the American Negro since his emancipation" ("Reason Why," ed. Wells, 135). There were exceptions to the Fair's racist policies, but even taken together, the exceptions prove the rule; that they can be counted suggests their more general absence from the Fair. See "Reason Why," ed. Wells, 128–29, and Dreck Spurlock Wilson, "Black Involvement in Chicago's Previous World's Fairs" (MS, Library of the Chicago Historical Society, 1984), 6–11.

10. Ida B. Wells, *Crusade for Justice: The Autobiography of Ida B. Wells*, ed. Alfreda Duster (Chicago: University Chicago Press, 1970), 116.

11. Ibid., 79–80.

12. Arthur Marquette, *Brands, Trademarks, and Goodwill: The Story of the Quaker Oats Company* (New York: McGraw-Hill, 1967), 139. Critical accounts of Aunt Jemima's commercial deployment include M. M. Manring's *Slave in a Box: The Strange Career of Aunt Jemima* (Greenwood Publishing Group, 1994), and Marilyn Kern-Foxworth's *Aunt Jemima, Uncle Ben, and Rastus* (Charlottesville: University Press of Virginia, 1998).

13. Marquette, *Brands, Trademarks, and Goodwill*, 146.

14. *The World's Congress of Representative Women*, ed. May Wright Sewell (2 vols.; New York: Rand McNally, 1894), 433, 696–729.

15. On the institutionalization of this principle of self-abstraction, see Jürgen Habermas, *The Structural Transformation of the Public Sphere: An Inquiry into a Category of Bourgeois Society*, trans. Thomas Burger (Cambridge, Mass.: MIT Press, 1989), sec. 2, "Social Structures of the Public Sphere." On the ways this principle served not only as a utopian promise but also as an instrument of domination, see Michael Warner, "The Mass Public and the Mass Subject," and Nancy Fraser, "Rethinking the Public Sphere: A Contribution to the Critique of Actually Existing Democracy," both in *Habermas and the Public Sphere*, ed. Craig Calhoun (Cambridge, Mass.: MIT Press, 1992), 377–401, 109–41.

16. Tony Bennett, "The Exhibitionary Complex," *New Formations* 4 (1988): 81.

17. Ida B. Wells, letter to the editor, *Cleveland Gazette*, July 22, 1893, 1.

18. George Knox, "No 'Nigger Day,' No 'Nigger Pamphlet,'" *Indianapolis Freeman*, August 12, 1893, 4.

19. Wells, *Crusade for Justice*, 118.

20. Wells, letter to the editor, *Cleveland Gazette*, 1.

21. Ibid.

22. Ibid.

23. Charles Morris, *The Nation and the Negro* (Washington, D.C., 1891), 18.

24. Ibid., 17.

25. "The Women and the World's Fair," *New York Age*, October 24, 1891.

26. George Knox, "Douglass' Wasted Zeal," *Indianapolis Freeman*, August 5, 1893, 1.

27. Wells, *Crusade for Justice*, 117.

28. Wells, "Reason Why," 58. See Massa, "Black Women in the 'White City'"; Elliott Rudwick and August Meier, "Black Man in the 'White City,'" *Phylon* 26 (Winter 1965): 354–61; Robert Rydell, "The World's Columbian Exposition of 1893: Racist Underpinnings of a Utopian Artifact," *Journal of American Culture* 1 (1978): 253–75; James Gilbert, *Perfect Cities: Chicago's Utopias of 1893* (Chicago: University of Chicago Press, 1991); and Trachtenberg, *Incorporation of America*. Gilbert and Rydell both make this argument based on their interpretations of the Midway in particular. "The habits of these people are repulsive," one guidebook observed of the Dahomey villagers. "They eat like animals and have all the characteristics of the lowest order of the human family" (Gilbert, *Perfect Cities*, 116). Another 1893 guidebook, *The Best Things to be Seen at the Fair*, notes a "barbaric savagery" in the African sentinels perched upon the village's gates "in full war regalia." It goes on to confirm their abnormality by depicting a perversion of gender roles, calling the women "savage-looking, masculine in appearance, and not particularly attractive," and the men "small and rather effeminate in appearance" (John J. Flinn, *The Best Things to Be Seen at the World's Fair* [Chicago: Columbian Guide Co., 1893], 168–69).

29. Quoted in Rydell, "World's Columbian Exposition," 271. *Harper's Weekly* carried this equation to an extreme in a series of cartoons that caricatured an African American family's visit to the Fair. When the fictional Ezwell Johnson pauses to greet a Dahomey villager, his wife scolds him: "Stop shakin' hands wid dat heathen!" she shouts, "You want de hull fair ter t'ink you's found a poo' relation!" (quoted in Rydell, "World's Columbian Exposition," 256).

30. Ann Douglas, *Terrible Honesty: Mongrel Manhattan in the 1920s* (New York: Farrar, Straus & Giroux, 1995), 264.

31. Carby, *Reconstructing Womanhood*, 3, 6.

32. *World's Congress of Representative Women*, ed. Sewell, 633.

33. See Mary Oldham Eagle, *The Congress of Women, Held in the Women's Building* (New York: Wilson Publishers, 1894). Further illustrations of the ambivalence of the Fair's endorsement of politicized women abound. The Midway's parodic "World's Congress of Beauty" was an ensemble of belly dancers and "Forty Ladies from Forty Countries," mimicking the internationalism of the Women's Congress yet reinscribing the pleasure of the male gaze that the politicized version of women's publicness subordinated. Moreover, discussions at the Women's Congress were "widely known, influential, and provocative," as one contemporary put it, but studies also note tellingly that its best-attended session was "Women's Place in Drama." See *A History of the World's Columbian Exposition*, ed. Rossiter Johnson (4 vols.; New York: D. Appleton, 1898), 6; and Stanley Appelbaum, *The Chicago World's Fair of 1893: A Photographic Record* (New York: Dover Publications, 1980), 106.

34. "National Brands," 177.

35. Marquette, *Brands, Trademarks, and Goodwill*, 147.

36. "National Brands," 177.

37. Lauren Berlant, *The Queen of America Goes to Washington City: Essays on Sex and Citizenship* (Durham, N.C.: Duke University Press, 1997), 92.

38. Massa, "Black Women in the 'White City,'" 335.

Phenomena in Flux

The Aesthetics and Politics of Traveling in Modernity

In July 1929, the London *Observer* ran a series of articles celebrating George Shillibeer's opening of the first omnibus line in London exactly a hundred years earlier. In response to that series, Katie Salomon, Amy Levy's sister, wrote the following letter to the editor:

Dear Sir,

In connection with your article about the omnibus, your readers might be interested in the following verses. The writer was among the first women in London to show herself on the top of omnibuses. She excused herself to her shocked family circle by saying that she had committed the outrage in company with the daughter of a dean, who was also the granddaughter of an archbishop of Canterbury.[1]

Salomon enclosed in the letter Amy Levy's poem "Ballade of an Omnibus," the opening stanza of which launches a celebration of the "modern" woman poet's urban pleasures by contrasting her travel by omnibus with that of men who choose more expensive and prestigious modes of transportation such as the private carriage and the hansom cab. Levy was one of the most fascinating urban poets of the Victorian fin de siècle, and "Ballade of an Omnibus," as her sister well knew, epitomized Levy's greatest achievement: her figuration of the female mass-transportation passenger as an icon of modernity, and her conception of mass-transportation facilities in general, and the omnibus in particular, as vehicles which enabled late-Victorian middle-class women to defy patriarchal gender and aesthetic ideology. In this chapter, a brief history of mass transport in London and a discussion of its effect on the presence and visibility of women in the metropolis will set the stage for my main focus: consideration of Levy's characterization of urban mass transport as a vehicle of late Victorian women's political and poetic transgression.

A "Fast" History of Modern London

OMNIBUS—G. Shillibeer, induced by the universal admiration the above vehicle called forth at Paris, has commenced running one upon the Parisian mode from PADDINGTON to the BANK.

The superiority of this carriage over the ordinary stage coaches for comfort and safety must be obvious, all the passengers being inside and the fare charged from Paddington to the Bank being one shilling, and from Islington to the Bank or Paddington sixpence.

The proprietor begs to add that a person of great respectability attends his vehicle as conductor; and every possible attention will be paid to the accommodation of ladies and children.

Hours of starting:—From Paddington Green to the Bank at 9, 12, 3, 6 and 8 o'clock; from the Bank to Paddington at 10, 1, 4, 7 and 9 o'clock.[2]

George Shillibeer's first London omnibus line covered five miles in forty minutes. At the cost of one shilling for the entire journey, sixpence for half, it was an immediate success with the middle classes, to whom Shillibeer appealed by stressing its respectability, its safety and comfort, and of course, its Parisian cachet. As Roy Porter has argued, this transportation revolution started a "commuter revolution" as London started to grow outwards.[3] The omnibus was instrumental in bringing about a new sociospatial spectrum within the metropolis, as the middle classes, thanks to the gentility of the omnibus, were able to escape from London's congested city center to newly created suburbs. The working classes, however, either remained in the city center or moved into inner-city suburbs no more than three or four miles away from their place of work. The poorer classes were forced to remain in the congested slums of London, unable to pay for decent accommodation and for transport.[4] This division of the metropolis also engendered urban space in new ways, as middle-class women remained in suburbia while men came daily into the city to work.[5]

During the 1840s and 1850s, omnibus lines and omnibus traffic continued to grow, although fares remained much the same. The Great Exhibition of 1851 gave the omnibus a crucial boost, as Londoners queued up en masse to ride to the Crystal Palace.[6] This boost was followed by the creation of the London General Omnibus Company in 1855, which regularized services around all areas of London.[7] By the end of the 1850s, London's busiest streets were heavily congested because of the increasing volume of omnibus traffic. The situation was becoming critical, because London lacked a system of wide roads through which the increase in traffic could easily flow.[8]

In the 1860s, Charles Pearson envisaged a solution to London's congestion: going underground. He clearly saw that the working classes could not afford to travel daily to the metropolis and hence were "chained" to the place where they labored, living in appalling conditions in the slums of the city.[9] In 1863, his first underground line, the Metropolitan Line, opened, serving more than 30,000 passengers on its first day.[10] Connecting to the major train stations (King's Cross, Euston, and Paddington), the Metropolitan facilitated passengers' travel in and out of London; however, its main aim was to ease cross-city transit. The introduction of cheap rates—threepence return—allowed working-class travelers for the first time to move out of the slums, but the Metropolitan Board's contract with the government also created a transport system based on class divisions: the working classes traveled in the early hours of the day to go to work (in what was called the workingmen train) and the middle classes traveled later in the day at a greater cost, in trains that were divided into first- (sixpence single), second- (fourpence single) and third-class carriages (threepence single).[11]

With underground tickets as cheap as threepence return, the omnibus had to reduce its fares to compete, and the middle-class character of the omnibus disappeared as the working classes started to use it. T. C. Barker and Michael Robbins calculate that, through 1854, 200,000 people came into the city daily on foot, roughly 6,000 commuted daily by suburban railway, and omnibuses transported 20,000 people. By 1890, the Metropolitan Railway alone transported a total of 84 million people annually, the District Railway (another underground railway line) carried 35 million, the London General Omnibus Company transported a total of 112 million, and the Road Car Company (another omnibus company), 37 million people.[12] If the majority of the population came into the city on foot through the mid nineteenth century, by the end of the nineteenth century they came using mass-transportation facilities. London had become a city of passengers.

Arthur Symons's 1909 comments on this change are quite illuminating:

Does any one any longer walk? If I walk I meet no one walking, and I cannot wonder at it, for what I meet is an uproar, and a whiz, and a leap past me, and a blinding cloud of dust, and a machine on which scarecrows perch is disappearing at the end of the road.

The verbs to loll, to lounge, to dawdle, to loiter, the verbs precious to Walt Whitman, precious to every lover of men and of himself, are losing their currency; they will be marked "o" for obsolete in the dictionaries of the future. . . . It will live on for some time yet in the country where the railway has not yet smeared its poisonous trail over the soil, but in London there will soon be no need of men, there will be nothing but machines.[13]

Symons was quite right in perceiving a change in the peripatetic character of urban life. Walking, Symons feared, was to become obsolete as mass-transportation facilities took over the city. The growth of the metropolis made it impossible to walk everywhere, and as urban dwellers started to travel using omnibuses and tubes, it would become increasingly difficult for the *flâneur* to claim privilege as an observer.

Schooling Female Consumerism and Urban Spectatorship

There is yet another reason to challenge the male *flâneur's* privilege as an observer of "modern" urban life. As Elizabeth Wilson has noted, "with the coming of 'modernity' the cities of veiled women had ceded to cities of spectacle and voyeurism, in which women, while seeking and sometimes finding the freedom of anonymity, are often all too visible." Wilson has highlighted the difficult position of women in modernity: "Commerce, consumerism and pleasure seduce them into its thoroughfares, yet men and the state continue their attempts to confine them to the private sphere or to the safety of certain zones."[14] As recent feminist critiques of Georg Simmel's and Walter Benjamin's influential modeling of the *flâneur* as the archetypal figure of modernity would also suggest, women's relationships with the spaces of modernity are indeed complex, as their presence in the public sphere is mediated and moderated by both the economics of a buoyant empire and the scrutiny of the *flâneur*, who sexualizes their presence in public spaces and controls their representation.[15]

A study of women's use of mass transport in late Victorian London offers the opportunity to deepen the feminist analysis of women's experience of urban modernity through consideration of material changes in women's means of access to the public sphere. The question to ask is not simply how women entered the sphere of the public, but also in what way the appearance and expansion of mass transport affected the presence and visibility of women within the spaces of the modern metropolis. If, on the one hand, mass-transportation facilities were partly responsible for resegregating the metropolis and its new suburbs by class and gender, on the other, they facilitated middle-class women's participation in urban life. In fact, for women poets such as Amy Levy and Katharine Tynan, mass transportation was a crucial means of access to each other, as well as to the public spaces of the city; for them, mass transportation was synonymous with democracy, equality, and both poetic and social transgression.

Shillibeer's interest in attracting middle-class female passengers is worth revisiting briefly here. When he advertised the Paddington-Bank Line by emphasizing that "every possible attention will be paid to the accommodation of ladies and children," he was not just promoting the gentility of the vehicle; he was also selling a new fetish of the modern for the fashionable woman. This he did by associating the omnibus service quite distinctly with fashion, shopping, and everything bourgeois. Omnibus companies needed and encouraged this kind of traffic for obvious economic reasons: omnibuses (and later the underground for exactly the same reason) were eager to attract middle-class women who would fill buses and trains in the afternoon, when the flow of early-morning commuters had subsided.[16] Mass transport became an essential component of consumer culture, and certainly the development of the department store was directly linked with the expansion and growth of mass transport.[17] This did not change throughout the nineteenth century. Middle-class women were the major afternoon users of the omnibus (and later, underground trains) throughout the nineteenth century;[18] and women chose between the omnibus and the underground depending on the length of the journey (for short journeys, the omnibus, and for longer ones, the underground, because it was faster).[19]

For women writers and poets of the Victorian fin de siècle, mass-transportation facilities were more than instruments with which to enter and enjoy the "city of dreadful delight."[20] They were instruments with which to analyze and question the experience of modernity, as the following note from the diary of the poet "Michael Field" (Katharine Bradley and Edith Cooper) demonstrates: "In Curtain Road, Shoreditch, we ordered our canopied 'Cisy-corner' [*sic*]—then drove past the sad, mis-shaped, mis-featured work-people of the East, through the crowds of the mid-city where the fervour of business + [*sic*] professions gives something of the stir of happiness—on to the self-sufficient, yet dependent, West End with its clearer light, and streams of those who gaze + [*sic*] buy."[21] Although Bradley and Cooper travel to the city to shop, and participate uncritically in "modern" consumer culture, the omnibus serves them as more than simply a mode of transport. It functions also as an optical apparatus enabling them to transform their cross-town journeys into a visual study of the conditions of life and the stratification of the social classes in London.

In similar fashion, the poet Katharine Tynan's omnibus and underground journeys sparked ideas for articles on urban life in magazines such as the *Westminster Gazette*. She writes with amusement of her friends' response to this practice of traveling with pen in hand, ready to make note of any visual eventuality, in her autobiography *The Middle Years* (1916):

That Christmas night [1895] we dined with the Meynells; I remember only the homeward journey, when, in the carriage from Paddington, there was a party returning from a family party, the members of which discussed the entertainment and the relatives with the characteristic lack of reserve of the English people. . . . I gave a *verbatim* report of this Dickensian conversation in the *Westminster* a day or two later. Some of my friends were scandalised. One said that he could not think of it and my poetry without being hurt.[22]

What is it in her behavior that "scandalizes" her friends? They thought that Tynan had tainted her reputation as a poet by recounting her experiences in an underground train. Treating modern life and poetry as if they belonged to two different realms of experience, they believed that Tynan, who was mostly admired for her religious poetry, should not have mixed them in her public persona. Moreover, they seem to have been displeased that Tynan used mass transport as the panorama of her writings. Yet Tynan was not alone in this practice. As I have argued elsewhere, the poet Alice Meynell also published her notes of her visual experiences of modern life as a passenger in essays such as "The London Sunday" (inspired by a journey in an omnibus) and "The Smouldering City" (the result of one of her journeys in the underground).[23]

What Bradley and Cooper's, Tynan's, and Meynell's writings together begin to suggest is that mass transportation transformed the relationship of late Victorian women writers to the metropolis. If at the beginning of the transport revolution, omnibus companies were eager to attract middle-class women purely for economic reasons, by the end of the nineteenth century, women writers used mass transport to enter, enjoy, and critically observe the public sphere.

Katharine Tynan gives us the clearest idea of the impact that the transport system had for women poets:

Regularly I lunched at 21 Phillimore Place [where the Meynells lived], perhaps once a week. . . . I was staying in the North of London. Certain 'bus routes of that time are associated in my mind with happiness. One was the ugly stretch between Camden Road along the Caledonian Road to King's Cross Underground. London was still an adventure to me. I still thought how surprised some of my Dublin friends would be to see me plunging into these dark depths and springing on to the black trains that waited for no one. I used to crane my neck to catch sight of the engine with "Inner Circle" on it, for by that I travelled to Phillimore Place. I had great adventures in those days for a country-mouse, exciting adventures.[24]

Marshall Berman has claimed that "[t]o be modern is to find ourselves in an environment that promises us adventure, power, joy, growth, transformation of ourselves and the world."[25] This is exactly what Tynan feels as an omnibus and underground passenger. She is excited by these journeys and associates the bus routes with happiness—specifically, with the pleasures of female friendship and of association with a community of London-based women writers. These trips are delicious optical ventures. Moreover, the experience of the mass-transportation passenger is also strongly connected with democracy and transgression: with democracy because the "train waits for no one," man or woman, rich or poor, as it democratizes access to the public sector; with transgression because, for Tynan—always aware of her status as an Irish immigrant and of her gender—technology annihilates class and gender differences. Rosalind Williams has persuasively argued that "[f]or the people of the nineteenth century," the excavation of tunnels to build sewers, water mains, steam pipes, subways, telephone lines, electrical cables and the new transportation network of underground railroads "provided a visual image of social upheaval."[26] Tynan's writings confirm Williams's argument, although Williams does not associate the social revolution that mass transportation produced with the sort of gender revolution that Tynan seems to be arguing for. For Tynan, the evolution of mass-transportation facilities is ultimately to be equated not simply with the presence of women within the space of the city. Rather, omnibuses and trains become the female school of the visual in modernity: the place where women learned how to look.

Walter Benjamin has argued that the predominance of the visual in modernity had its roots in mass transportation. Quoting Georg Simmel at length in the following passage, he suggests that mass-transportation facilities forced new kinds of visual intimacy on urban travelers.

People had to adapt themselves to a new and rather strange situation, one that is peculiar to big cities. . . . "Interpersonal relationships in big cities are distinguished by a marked preponderance of the activity of the eye over the activity of the ear. The main reason for this is the public means of transportation. Before the development of buses, railroads, and trams in the nineteenth century, people had never been in a position of having to look at one another for long minutes or even hours without speaking to one another." This new situation was, as Simmel recognized, not a pleasant one.[27]

In the streets, the field of the visual was dominated by the gaze of the *flâneur*. But in mass-transportation vehicles, although women could still be the object of the male gaze, women were forced to learn how and when to look because of the spatial conditions of omnibuses and trains (two rows of seats facing each other). Passengers thus had to acquire a new code of the visual, one that regulated space and vision. In 1836, the London *Times* offered a number of instructions to make omnibus travel more agreeable. One of these related specifically to the question of the male gaze: "Behave respectfully to females and put not an unprotected lass to the blush, because she cannot escape from your brutality."[28] By the end of the century, however, instructions regarding the regulation of space and vision are being directed at female lookers as well. Contrast the *Times*'s 1836 reminder of the need for "gentlemanly" visual decorum with Henry Stacy Marks's advice to the ladies in 1894 about how to deal with "the starer" of both sexes, an increasingly common annoyance for women travelers:

The ignoble army of starers is of great and daily increasing magnitude. It includes members of both sexes and of every form of religious persuasion. . . . The male starer can be coped with by fixing your eyes firmly on his boots . . . and smiling never so faintly. This treatment utterly routs and demoralises him. Try it, ladies, the next time you are troubled with the bold gaze of an offensive male. It appals the stoutest stares. . . . With women-starers one has more mercy; you can't look at her feet unless you are an admirer of the enlarged toe-joints or bunions which they so carefully cultivate by wearing boots with toes like VV's.[29]

What Marks's closing reference to women starers' devastating visual critiques of other women indicates is that women have now mastered the gaze and are active lookers, wielding it against themselves and each other as well as against the male "starer" who has forgotten gentlemanly decorum. The spacing of the visual is now subject to compromise as men and women are redefining how, and how much, one is entitled to look. Although women are no more or less protected from the male gaze in buses or trains than in the streets, the omnibus and the train gave them a space in which to learn the trade of the visual.

The Poet as Passenger: Amy Levy

In her last collection of poems, *A London Plane-Tree and Other Verse* (1889), Amy Levy describes the modern woman poet's constrained spectatorship in the private sphere and contrasts this with the freedom represented by the figure of the mass-transportation passenger. Levy's figuration of the passenger works on two levels: it assumes women's freedom of access to the public sphere; and it celebrates the change in visual perspective that results from women's new freedom of movement around the city.

Levy's collection opens with a celebration of urban life—and a critique of the woman poet's limited access to the modern metropolis.

A London Plane-Tree

GREEN is the plane-tree in the square,
 The other trees are brown;
They droop and pine for country air;
 The plane-tree loves the town.

Here from my garret-pane, I mark
 The plane-tree bud and blow,
Shed her recuperative bark,
 And spread her shade below.

Among her branches, in and out,
 The city breezes play;
The dun fog wraps her round about;
 Above, the smoke curls grey.

Others the country take for choice,
 And hold the town in scorn;
But she has listened to the voice
 On city breezes borne.[30]

The remarkable regularity of these quatrains evokes both the urban space in which the plane-tree is located and the garret in which the woman poet is confined. In one sense, the speaker (the woman behind the window) and the object of the poem (the plane-tree) occupy the same structural position with respect to the city and to the square. In fact, the plane-tree and the woman poet seem to be mirror images of each other. They are both squarely constrained, and they both love the city. The poem thus seems to be an expression of the freedom that London offers to city dwellers and to urban women poets.

In another regard, however, although the tree and the woman poet are re-flections of each other, they are not in similar positions. The tree is free in the square; the woman poet is not. She is behind the windowpane watching the city. The contrast between the physical incarceration of the woman poet and her more free-ranging urban spectatorship is at the core of Levy's "A London Plane-Tree." Although the poem is clearly situated within a whole discourse of city lit-erature that deals with the dichotomy of the country and the city, it seems to me that what makes this poem so very crucial within Levy's aesthetics is the posi-tion of the woman behind the windowpane, both as prisoner and spectator.

On the one hand, the woman seems to be incarcerated in an almost trans-parent prison. Only one line in the poem is dedicated to her, "Here from my garret-pane, I mark," and the rest of the poem is devoted to the free play of the plane-tree in the metropolis. This transparency is symbolic. It seems to mock the illusion of the modern transparent, as Henri Lefebvre puts it, the illusion that the space that separates the woman from the plane-tree "appears as lumi-nous, as intelligible, as giving action free rein."[31] On the other hand, and para-doxically, it is because of this transparency that the woman poet can be a spec-tator of modern life (hence "I mark" accurately describes the woman poet as a spectator). If the windowpane is that which frames the woman poet and that which situates her as outside urban life, it also enables her spectatorship.

The questions this poem seeks to answer are thus: how does the speaker be-hind the windowpane manage to break through the barriers of the window? How does the urban woman poet cross the transparent border that divides the private realm, where she exists, from the public sphere where she wants to be? How can the woman poet enter the space of the city and still be a spectator of modern life? In "A London Plane-Tree," Levy achieves this transgression through both empathy and metaphor: the woman in the poem identifies so powerfully with the plane-tree that she seems to participate in its physical sen-sations. She is so absorbed in contemplating the plane-tree that she becomes what she contemplates—hence Levy's feminization of the plane-tree. Yet Levy's reference to the plane-tree suggests something else. Plane-trees are typically found in London, so what is interesting about Levy's use of the plane-tree is that it symbolically represents both London and the poet's love for London. In the poem, this love for the city metaphorically *takes* her to the square where the tree is situated, *merging* with the subject of her love. As Michel de Certeau has argued, metaphors are means of transport; they take us from one place to another, from one signification to another, creating a passage that links both. Metaphors "are spatial trajectories."[32] By merging with the plane-tree, the woman is metaphorically transported to the center of urban experience. The plane-tree and the woman become indistinguishable, and the title of the poem, "A London Plane-Tree," and by extension that of the collection, explicitly shows Levy's attempts to use transportation to materialize the presence of women in the modern metropolis.

Perhaps Levy's most nuanced discussion of transportation, gender, and class in modernity is her 1888 novel *The Romance of a Shop*, whose characters, four orphaned sisters, as photographers, epitomize the figure of the modern female spectator.

At Baker Street Station they parted; Phyllis disappearing to the underground railway; Gertrude mounting boldly to the top of an Atlas omnibus.

"Because one cannot afford a carriage or even a hansom cab," she argued to herself, "is one to be shut up away from the sunlight and the streets?"

Indeed, for Gertrude, the humors of the town had always possessed a curious fascination. She contemplated the familiar London pageant with an interest that had something of passion in it; and, for her part, was never inclined to quarrel with the fate which had transported her from the comparative tameness of Campden Hill to regions where the pulses of the great city could be felt distinctly as they beat and throbbed.[33]

Gertrude Lorimer, Levy's fictional self, sees in mass-transportation facilities the possibilities for transcending the incarcerating ideology of the separate spheres. The specific reference to the "Atlas Omnibus" (a green omnibus that ran from Camberwell to St. John's Wood) indicates Levy's knowledge of London's transportation network and her interest in exposing women's engagement with the city via its transport system.[34] It is by bus and underground that Gertrude travels to the British Museum to attend a course on photography. However, it is by reason of her economic and social decline (the result of her father's death and his debts) that she has been "transported," as Gertrude puts it, to the core of the city, and it is from this new social (albeit lower) status that she has begun to enjoy the pulses and rhythms of the metropolis. For indeed, "because one cannot afford a carriage or even a hansom cab . . . is one to be shut up away from the sunlight and the streets?" Like Beatrice Webb and later

Virginia Woolf, Levy had witnessed the relative freedom of working-class women from the physical restraints imposed on the middle-class Victorian lady by gender ideology.[35] By emphasizing Gertrude's newly found freedom in omnibus travel, Levy exposed the class barriers established by Victorian gender ideology, carefully presenting mass transport as both a tool for and a symbol of social as well as political transgression.

Mass transportation thus emerges in the work of Amy Levy as the key means of renegotiating the imbrications of class and gender identity in middle-class women's everyday experience of the city. It is in "Ballade of an Omnibus" where this reconfiguration appears most clearly:

Ballade of an Omnibus

SOME men to carriages aspire;
On some the costly hansoms wait;
Some seek a fly, on job or hire;
Some mount the trotting steed, elate.
I envy not the rich and great,
A wandering minstrel, poor and free,
I am contented with my fate—
An omnibus suffices me.

In winter days of rain and mire
I find within a corner strait;
The 'busmen know me and my lyre
From Brompton to the Bull-and-Gate.
When summer comes, I mount in state
The topmost summit, whence I see
Croesus look up, compassionate—
An omnibus suffices me.

I mark, untroubled by desire,
Lucullus' phaeton and its freight.
The scene whereof I cannot tire,
The human tale of love and hate,
The city pageant, early and late
Unfolds itself, rolls by, to be
A pleasure deep and delicate.
An omnibus suffices me.

Princess, your splendour you require,
I, my simplicity; agree
Neither to rate lower nor higher.
An omnibus suffices me.[36]

This woman poet is no longer incarcerated behind her garret-pane; she rides unencumbered through the metropolis. She has become one with the city and rides across the metropolis inside the omnibus in winter, and on the omnibus roof in summer. She is finally immersed in the metropolis as she glides across it. One must remember here that at the Victorian fin de siècle, the upper level of an omnibus had no windows or roof, which meant that passengers traveled in the open air. It is in this sense that, in the third stanza, she remarks that she is "untroubled by desire." As a passenger, the woman poet has freed herself from the burden of desire, because her desire to be engrossed in the materiality of the metropolis has finally been accomplished. It is not that the poet desires no more, it is that her desire does not trouble her. Desire has been transformed into something more enjoyable. It is not the constraining desire of the woman behind the garret-pane in "A London Plane-Tree" or the suffocating desire of Eleanor Lloyd in Amy Levy's short story "Eldorado at Islington," where Eleanor's craving for the city forced her to crane her neck out of the window to see the "ceaseless stream of trams and omnibuses."[37] In "Ballade of an Omnibus," her desire to see has been set free. In this bus journey, she finds the *jouissance* she has been searching for.[38] She cannot "tire" of the scenes that occur in the omnibus; "the tales of love and hate," the tale of the "city peasant," and the circularity of the scenes produce in the poet, a "deep," "delicate," "pleasure." In short, the omnibus "suffices" her.

Equally significantly, in "Ballade of an Omnibus" the woman poet is ultimately in control of her gaze. The poet-passenger uses the omnibus as an optical apparatus to "*see* Croesus look up, compassionate." From her seat she "mark[s] Lucullus' phaeton and its freight," "the human tale of love and hate," the "city pageant early and late." While Levy uses fairly neutral verbs such as "see" in the second stanza, in the third stanza, she uses a much stronger verb, "I mark," to emphasize the distinctive visual quality of the experience of the passenger and to further proclaim that, as a passenger, she is in control of the gaze.

By considering urban mass transport in the work of Levy and other fin de siècle London poets, I have sought not only to examine the impact of transport on the presence and visibility of women in the city, but also to suggest a different view of women and their changing position within urban culture and modernity. For Levy, as for many late-Victorian middle-class women writers, the figure of the mass-transportation passenger becomes the site of a social and aesthetic transformation because *going somewhere* was in itself an act of transgression and liberation. By aligning the figure of the passenger with the poet, Levy argues that the woman poet's experience of modernity is intrinsically linked to a new rendering of urban life and culture. Amy Levy, Alice Meynell, Katharine Tynan and "Michael Field" used omnibuses and trains to go shopping, to eat at restaurants, or just to go for a ride, but they also used them as devices with which to redefine women's experience of "modern" urban life.

NOTES

I am grateful to La Consejería de Educación y Juventud (to La Junta de Extremadura, Spain), and to the European Social Funds (FSE) for granting me a scholarship that has enabled me to undertake this research.

1. Katie Salomon, *Observer*, July 7, 1929, 10.

2. T. C. Barker and Michael Robbins, *A History of London Transport: Passenger Travel and the Development of the Metropolis* (London: George Allen, 1963), 1: 20.

3. Roy Porter, *London: A Social History* (London: Hamish Hamilton, 1994), 225.

4. Christopher Hibbert, *London: The Biography of a City* (London: Penguin Books, 1980), 183–84.

5. For a study of suburbia and gender, see Robert Fishman, *Bourgeois Utopia: The Rise and Fall of Suburbia* (New York: Basic Books, 1987), and Elizabeth Wilson, *Hallucinations: Life in the Post-Modern City* (London: Radius, 1988).

6. Barker and Robbins, *History of London Transport*, 1: 61.

7. L. C. B. Seaman, *Life in Victorian London* (London: B. T. Batsford, 1973), 58.

8. Hibbert, *London*, 184.

9. See R. Trench and E. Hillman, *London under London: A Subterranean Guide* (London: John Murray, 1993), 139.

10. "Opening of the Metropolitan Railway," *Illustrated London News*, January 17, 1863, 74.

11. Barker and Robbins, *History of London Transport*, 1: 122.

12. Barker and Robbins, *History of London Transport*, 1: 240, 57–58, 261, 253.

13. Arthur Symons, "London: A Book of Aspects," in *Cities and Sea-Coasts and Islands* (London: W. Collins, 1918), 173–74.

14. Elizabeth Wilson, *The Sphinx in the City: Urban Life, the Control of Disorder, and Women* (London: Virago, 1991), 16.

15. See Susan Buck-Morss, "The *Flâneur*, the Sandwichman and the Whore: The Politics of Loitering," *New German Critique* 39 (1986): 99–140; Rita Felski, *The Gender of Modernity* (Cambridge, Mass.: Harvard University Press, 1995); Deborah Epstein Nord, *Walking the Victorian Streets: Women, Representation and the City* (Ithaca, N.Y.: Cornell University Press, 1995); Elizabeth Wilson, "The Invisible *Flâneur*," *New Left Review* 191 (January-February 1992): 90–110; Janet Wolff, "The Invisible *Flâneuse*: Women and the Literature of Modernity," in *Feminine Sentences: Essays on Women and Culture* (Cambridge: Polity Press; Berkeley : University of California Press, 1990), 34–50; and Deborah Parsons, *Streetwalking the Metropolis: Women, the City and Modernity* (Oxford: Oxford University Press, 2000).

16. Barker and Robbins, *History of London Transport*, 1: 202.

17. Alison Adburgham, *Shops and Shopping, 1800–1914: Where, and in What Manner the Well-Dressed Englishwoman Bought Her Clothes* (London: George Allen, 1964), 149–50; Barker and Robbins, *History of London Transport*, 1: 202.

18. In this chapter, I focus on the middle-class female mass-transportation passenger. It is important, however, to note that the growth of urban transport and the appearance of two new forms of mass-transportation vehicles (the tram and the underground) slowly transformed the social patterns of traveling. By the end of the nineteenth century, trams were used by working-class men and women. Omnibuses were used in the early hours of the morning both by working-class men and women and by middle-class men. In the evening, omnibuses and underground trains were used by both middle- and working-class men and women for their homeward journey. See Henry Charles Moore "Tram, 'Bus and Cab London" in *Living London*, ed. George R. Sims, 3 vols. (London: Cassell & Col, 1903), 2: 94–99.

19. Barker and Robbins, *History of London Transport*, 1: 168.

20. Judith R. Walkowitz's phrasing, *City of Dreadful Delight: Narratives of Sexual Danger in Late-Victorian London* (London: Virago, 1992).

21. British Library, Add. MS. 46779.f.25.

22. Katharine Tynan, *The Middle Years* (London: Constable, 1916), 147–48.

23. Alice Meynell, *London Impressions* (London: Archibald Constable, 1898), 1–3, 29–31. See my "Poetics of the Inner-Circle: Alice Meynell and the Aesthetics of Travelling at the *Fin de Siècle,*" in *Nineteenth-Century Geographies: Anglo-American Tactics of Space*, ed. Helena Michie and Ronald Thomas (New Brunswick, N.J.: Rutgers University Press, forthcoming).

24. Katharine Tynan, *Memories* (London: Eveleigh Nash & Grayson, 1924), 24.

25. Marshall Berman, "The Experience of Modernity," in *Design after Modernism: Beyond the Object*, ed. John Thackara (London: Thames & Hudson, 1988), 36.

26. Rosalind Williams, *Notes on the Underground: An Essay on Technology, Society, and the Imagination* (Cambridge, Mass.: MIT Press, 1990), 53.

27. Walter Benjamin, *Charles Baudelaire: A Lyric Poet in the Era of High Capitalism*, trans. Harry Zohn (London: Verso, 1997), 37–38.

28. As quoted in Barker and Robbins, *History of London Transpor*, 1: 37.

29. Henry Stacy Marks, *Pen and Pencil Sketches*, 2 vols. (London: Chatto & Windus, 1894), 2: 97–98.

30. Amy Levy, *A London Plane-Tree and Other Verse* (London: T. Fisher Unwin, 1889), 17.

31. Henri Lefebvre, *The Production of Space*, trans. D. Nicholson-Smith (Oxford: Blackwell, 1991), 27.

32. Michel de Certeau, *The Practice of Everyday Life*, trans. Steven Rendall (Berkeley: University of California Press, 1998), 115.

33. Amy Levy, *The Romance of a Shop*, in *The Complete Novels and Selected Writings of Amy Levy, 1861–1889*, ed. Melvyn New (Gainesville: University Press of Florida, 1993), 86–87.

34. *ABC Omnibus Guide from Anywhere to Everywhere, Revised by the General Omnibus Road Car, and Various Railway Companies* (London: H. Vickers, 1888), 50.

35. After visiting a working-girls' club at Westminster, Levy wrote to Vernon Lee that working-class girls did not "excite" her "compassion half as much as small bourgeoisie shut up in stucco villas at Brundesbury or Islington." She found "[t]heir enforced 'respectability' . . . really tragic." This letter was probably written in 1887 and is in the Vernon Lee Collection at Colby College, Waterville, Maine. It is reprinted in Linda Hunt Beckman, *Amy Levy: Her Life and Letters* (Athens: Ohio University Press, 2000), 266–67. See also Beatrice Webb, *The Diary of Beatrice Webb*, vol. 1: *Glitter Around and Darkness Within*, ed. Norman MacKenzie and Jeanne MacKenzie (Cambridge, Mass.: Harvard University Press, Belknap Press, 1982) and Virginia Woolf, *The Pargiters: The Novel-Essay Portion of The Years*, ed. Mitchell A. Leaska (London: Hogarth Press, 1978).

36. Levy, *London*, 21–22.

37. Amy Levy, "Eldorado at Islington," *Woman's World* 2 (1889): 488.

38. The term *jouissance* is Hélène Cixous and Catherine Clément's, *The Newly Born Woman*, trans. Betsy Wing, foreword by Sandra M. Gilbert (Minneapolis: University of Minnesota Press, 1986). As Wing notes, "this word. . . [has] *simultaneously* sexual, political, and economic overtones" (165, emphasis in original), so its use here to describe Levy's narrator's liberation from Victorian gender and aesthetic ideology through her experience on the omnibus is particularly apt.

The New Woman's Appetite for "Riotous Living"

Rebecca West, Modernist Feminism, and the Everyday

Decidedly what we need is a militant movement for
more riotous living. Schoolmistresses must go to their
work wearing suffrage badges and waving the red
flag. . . . And we must make a fuss about our food. "The
milk pudding must go" shall be our party cry. I can see
in the future militant food raids of the most desperate
character. I see the inmates of the YWCA . . . pelting the
central offices with bread-and-butter and threatening a
general massacre of hens if the boiled egg persists in
prominence. Armies of nurses would visit the homes of
the hospital governors and forcibly feed them with that
horrid breakfast dish, porridge and treacle. And in
Simpson's some day the blenching stockbroker shall
look down the muzzle of the rifle and hand over his nice
red-and-black beefsteak to his pale typist. . . . Wages
would go up then.

—Rebecca West, 1912

It is hard to know how to characterize modernist feminist work—
literary, polemical, performative or strategic—when one relies upon the
oft-cited but now frequently troubled great divide between modernism
and mass culture. During the militant phase of the suffrage movement in England (roughly 1905–14), feminist discourse entered and often dominated the
public sphere in ways that are only now being fully understood. Not only did
suffragists and suffragettes command the streets in large open-air marches, but
feminists developed savvy poster campaigns that demanded public attention,

created brand-name identities for specific organizations through ownership of colors and other markers of group identity (most famously, the use of purple, green, and white to signal the Pankhurst's Women's Social and Political Union), and marketed tea sets, card games, and any other commodities that would hold still to bear the imprint "Votes for Women." Newspapers responded to the marketing sensation that was suffrage by devoting front pages and photographs to the images of women in the street that were bound to send papers off the stands and into customer's hands. The London *Times* went so far as to recognize the persistent appeal of these no longer irregular narratives of riot and revolt by devoting a regular "Women's Page" to coverage of the spectacular suffrage show. One of the effects of this constant and often sensational coverage was that a feminist discourse about all sorts of issues—not just citizenship and the vote, but employment, sexuality, art, and literature—not only became a central part of public debate in the mainstream press but in fact created what some critics have termed a feminist "counter-public sphere."[1] During the militant suffrage period and after, feminists developed and circulated gendered readings of modern everyday life in essays published in alternative publications, daily newspapers, and political pamphlets.

The young Rebecca West, as a socialist-feminist commentator on the Edwardian political and cultural scene, provides us with an excellent example for studying the formation of this emerging feminist periodical culture.[2] During the years 1912–13, at the height of militant suffrage activity in England, West honed her critical skills as an essayist, book reviewer, short story writer, and political commentator for two of the most interesting journals of Edwardian England, the individualist-feminist-anarchist journals the *Freewoman* and the *New Freewoman*, edited by Dora Marsden, and the collectivist-socialist journal the *Clarion*, edited by Robert Blatchford. West's writings blended two distinctly different notions of everyday life derived from these journals—one focused on sexual life, and the other focused on rational recreation—in order to formulate a radical and sexualized notion of feminist consumption. This endorsement of feminist consumption facilitates West's development of precise and rigorous forms of feminist cultural and literary criticism. Poised as she was between the *Freewoman* and the *Clarion* during the years 1912–13, West stood at the intersection of feminist movements, women's experiences of modernity, and socialist and feminist deliberations about the practices of everyday life. West's attempt to attach revolutionary significance to the rituals of feminist consumption, outlined in her essay "A New Woman's Movement: The Need for

Riotous Living," which was published in the *Clarion* on December 20, 1912, is especially useful in thinking through modernist feminism's responses to the everyday. Through her emphasis on what Michel de Certeau calls the "tactics" of consumption—reading, buying, eating—West developed feminist reading strategies that both rewrote Clarion Movement socialism for feminism by writing women's "appetite" into the picture and described new locations of modernist production in the daily activities of the *New Freewoman* and the spaces that belonged to her.[3]

Feminine Consumption and Feminist Reading Practices

In locating West between the two agendas of Marsden and Blatchford, I build upon Laurie Langbauer's insightful reading of the work of gender in theories of the everyday. Langbauer notices the ways in which women serve as a sign of the boring routines of everyday life for many theorists, but are considered to be incapable of criticizing it. Langbauer points to the example of Henri Lefevbre, who notes that the everyday, so difficult to define, "weighs heaviest on women. . . . They are the subjects of everyday life and its victims or objects and substitutes." But, Langbauer notes, Lefevbre also argues that "because of their ambiguous position in everyday life . . . they [women] are incapable of understanding it." Within this theory, Langbauer argues, "The feminine indoctrinates mankind into a dominant culture whose terms of everydayness it also teaches these subjects not to contest." Langbauer argues that in associating the everyday with a "smothering" "feminine" or feminized activity, most theorists leave unexplored those forms of feminist activism that contest dominant culture.[4]

Feminine consumption as a register of the linkages between the everyday and modernity has a long and much studied history. At the beginning of the century, feminist modernists as different from one another as Virginia Woolf, Teresa Billington-Greig, members of the Co-operative Women's Guild, and Rebecca West herself considered feminist consumption as a particularly salient, and potentially radical, aspect of women's experience of modernity. For these thinkers, feminine consumption brought together issues of economic activity (shopping), physical appetite (eating), and desire (sexual activity), thus highlighting the linkages between cultural fields usually considered distinct and separate.[5] It is precisely this set of linkages that West exposed and exploited in her essays published in the 1910s. In our own time, feminist critics involved in writing this history have used questions of consumption to explore the gendered discourses used to describe modern life while also drawing our attention to modern anxieties organized around and expressed through representations of the consuming woman. For example, Rita Felski has recently outlined the ways in which women's experience of modernity was shaped by consumer culture, the world of department stores and factories, popular romances and women's magazines. Attending to the "everyday and the mundane," Felski argues, gives us a "nuanced way of approaching the gender politics of cultural texts within the uneven histories of the modern."[6] She notes that the development of a feminine consumer culture in particular gave women access to the experience and vocabularies of modern fashions and lifestyles. Through consumer culture, women gained access to new forms of subjectivity; women's "intimate needs, desires, and perceptions of self" were formed in relation to "public representations of commodities and the gratifications that they promised" (62).

Felski also notes, however, that the consuming woman, even when absorbed in the seemingly decorous activity of reading, enjoyed at best an ambivalent status as a figure for the modern. Insofar as the consuming woman signaled the feminization of modernity, she also exemplified its "growth of irrationalism, the return of repressed nature in the form of . . . desire." Woman was portrayed as a "buying machine" subject to impulses "beyond her control" to "squander money on the accumulation of ever more possessions" (62). The terror expressed in modern representations of the consuming woman was accompanied by efforts to control, manage, and organize feminine consumption. Special efforts were made to control women's reading practices, for modernists such as Flaubert characterized reading women as engaged in rabid forms of consumption untouched by rational deliberation. Kate Flint has traced these dominant representations of the woman reader through newspaper editorials, medical textbooks, psychological discourse, advice manuals, pictorial representations, as well as commentary included within novels, to expose the central belief in the "affective power of print" that governed discussions of women's reading practices. Women were thought to be easily influenced by what they read—because women were sentimental and overly sensitive, subject to easy identifications with novelistic heroines, and even susceptible to a kind of hysteria that could be produced through improper reading. Women's capacity for maternity and "sympathetic identification into the lives of others" had distinct consequences for her status as a reader of texts: "women's susceptibility to identificatory modes of reading was perceived to be related to the inescapable facts about the way in which her biological makeup influenced the operations of her mind."[7]

It is within this context that Flint describes the feminist reading tactics (to borrow de Certeau's language again) that emerged from the Edwardian militant suffrage campaign during the first two decades of the twentieth century. During this period, feminist activists consciously and carefully created a culture for alternative reading practices: activists created a feminist press, opened women's bookstores, started reading groups, developed new feminist subgenres like the women's prison narrative, established women's history and women's literary history as foundations for forming new subjectivities and new collectivities, and generated new critical reading strategies that focused on women's issues in book reviews. Suffragists, in Flint's eyes, appropriated the central notion that books function through "influence," directing readers through identification to proper political action. In autobiographical writings, feminists remembered the central role that histories of women, narratives of women's exploitation, or texts by William Morris, Walt Whitman, and Edward Carpenter played in their lives. These books provided foundations for the formation of new political identities. Feminist periodicals such as the official organ of the Women's Social and Political Union, *Votes for Women,* urged such transformative reading by publishing reviews of biographies, histories, and polemical texts that prepared readers for future discussions and debates on women's issues (234-49). Central to this feminist project was a theory and practice of feminist critique focused on women's experiences of modern daily life and a rethinking of consumption as a potentially revolutionary gesture. It is the connection between feminine appetite and subversive consumption that West traced in her essays for the *Freewoman,* the *New Freewoman,* and the *Clarion,* linking Marsden's journals' interest in feminine desire with Blatchford's journal's interest in rational recreation.

The Freewoman, *the* New Freewoman, *and Sexuality*

In the official literature of most official suffrage organizations, suffragists focused on women's political culture while carefully avoiding the still thornier issues of women's sexual life—except in relation to discussions of women's rights to her own body, as in Christabel Pankhurst's unique campaign of "chastity for men and votes for women" outlined in *The Great Scourge and How to End It.* With humor and frank talk about sexuality, Rebecca West joined freethinkers such as Christabel Pankhurst who broke this general silence in the pages of the *Freewoman* and the *New Freewoman*. Dora Marsden's journal *The Freewoman* was published between November 1911 and May 1912; it was then renamed the *Free Woman: A Humanist Weekly* and ran until October 1912 when it was rejected by W. H. Smith and banned from its shops. The *Free Woman* then collapsed briefly due to lack of funds and was renamed and launched again as the *New Freewoman: An Individualist Review* in June 1913. The *Freewoman* had yet another incarnation when it was renamed the *Egoist* and published under the editorship of Ezra Pound in 1914. Unlike many feminists of early twentieth-century England working to secure votes for women, Dora Marsden insisted on stretching the purview of political activity beyond questions of citizenship and equal participation in the political sphere.[8] Marsden's journal, like the *Clarion*, drew attention to aspects of everyday life, such as reading habits, often excluded from political debate, but her interests lay with the less respectable topics of free love and the sexual life of unmarried women, reproductive rights and birth control, and Uranian and other emerging discourses of homosexuality. The *Freewoman* drew on a stable of freethinkers from diverse fields (H. G. Wells, Edward Carpenter, Havelock Ellis, Teresa Billington-Greig, and Ada Nield Chew, to name a few) and appealed to a rather small and highly selective readership. The radical politics of the journal, especially in the arena of gender relations and sexuality, gave the *Freewoman* a scandalous reputation far beyond its circle of readers and subjected Marsden and her journal to public scorn (Mrs. Humphrey Ward called the journal "the dark and dangerous side of the Women's Movement"), criticism from feminists (Millicent Fawcett, head of the National Union of Women's Suffrage Societies, thought the journal was "objectional and mischievous and tore it up into small pieces"), and a bookseller's boycott.[9] For Marsden, the focus on the sexual life of women was part of a larger critique of Edwardian social life in general and its feminist cultures in particular. As a former suffragette, Marsden leveled specific criticism at the militant feminist organization the Women's Social and Political Union, whose tactics she found both autocratic and insufficiently radical. She sought to expose the limitations of narrowly emphasizing the vote at the expense of larger questions of gender relations, sexual life, and more broadly, women's physical, spiritual, and intellectual experience of modernity.

Launching a new moment of feminist critique, Marsden argued in the first issue of the *Freewoman* that the publication of the paper "marks an epoch. It marks the point at which feminism in England ceases to be impulsive and un-

aware of its own features, and becomes definitely self conscious and intro-
spective. For the first time, Feminists themselves make the attempt to reflect
the Feminist movement in the mirror of thought."[10] Most of the journal's essayists agreed that modernity and everyday life were characterized by stifling
attitudes toward feminine sexuality, and that feminists could be distinguished
from suffragettes/suffragists through their efforts to redefine sexuality. In the
pages of this journal, articles sketched out a feminist psychology that would
blend the life of the sexual body with that of the intellect. A set of essays on the
sexual lives of unmarried women isolated the "Spinster" as a cultural type and
distinguished her from those other modern women of interest to Marsden,
"Bondswomen" and "Freewomen." One author challenged the "withered"
"bloodless and boneless" lives of spinsters and claimed that "if prurience has
slain its thousands, chastity has slain its tens of thousands."[11] Marsden wrote of
a new sexual morality of free unions and limited monogamy that would sub-
vert the doctrine of "indissoluble monogamy" that locked women into the
supporting roles of wife, prostitute, and spinster. Within Marsden's new
morality, women's pleasure, desire, and appetite were seen as transformative:
Marsden scorned readers who might "regard it as an indecent exhibition, if
they saw a woman looking as though she were very obviously enjoying food,
or obviously gratifying any of her senses."[12]

Despite her interest in sexual life and the body, Marsden insisted on a language of spiritual life that distinguished her methods from the materialist-
feminist approach of West or that of her socialist or Fabian contributors. Increasingly suspicious of mass political movements and collective identities
after her break with the WSPU, Marsden turned her attention to the individual freewoman. Freewomen, as individuals, were distinguished by genius from
ordinary "bondswomen." Their "spiritual distinction" lay in an "individual revelation of life-manifestation, made realizable to others in some outward form."[13]
Freewomen, unlike bondswomen and suffragists, felt the stirrings of "new
powers and of growing strength" and hoped to make "realisable to the world a
new revelation of spiritual consciousness." The journal devoted itself to the
freewoman "herself," "her psychology, philosophy, morality, and achievements,
and only in a secondary degree with her politics and economics."[14]

The discussions of free love and sexuality held in the pages of the *Free-*
woman occurred alongside these efforts to define the freewoman as a new evolutionary type and to describe her genius. To a certain extent, West's essays,
especially her book reviews, placed contemporary women's issues and repre-

sentations of women within the context of these efforts. D. H. Lawrence, August Strindberg, and, famously, H. G. Wells were read in terms of their inadequate efforts to come to terms with modern freewomen. Lawrence, despite his genius, is faulted for his depiction of the "spinster" who "looking out on the world through the drawn curtains of the boarding-school or the equally celibate boarding-house, sees men as trees walking—large, dignified, almost majestic."[15] Strindberg's "theoretical anti-feminism" exposes misogyny in its crudest form and thus must be required reading for women: "Since the publication of Sir Almroth Wright's letter, we have known that men were swine. Now we know that they are asses. Another anti-feminist publication, and no woman will ever think of loving a man again."[16] Yet, during the period that West brought feminist literary criticism to the pages of the *Freewoman*, she rejected Marsden's individualism by turning her attention to the plight of modern women who were not so free while she worked to define a collective feminist identity in the pages of the *Clarion*.

The Clarion *and Rational Recreation*

The *Clarion* was launched in 1891 to popularize socialist ideas in Lancashire and Yorkshire. Robert Blatchford created his journal and his movement (the journal launched clubs, organizations and campaigns) on the model of a religious crusade, drawing on and revising the sentiments and discourses developed in churches and chapels (though he himself remained suspicious of organized religion). Where other socialist organizations linked politics to a puritanical religious discourse, the *Clarion* took seriously the question of leisure and sought to develop a set of avenues for a vibrant intellectual and communal life. As part of his interest in "rational recreation," Blatchford emphasized reading as a progressive activity and likened it to the other healthy and transformative activities he promoted in his periodical, such as, for example, riding a bicycle in the Clarion Cycling Club.

West's essays in the *Freewoman* and the *New Freewoman*, particularly her reviews of Strindberg's *The Confessions of a Fool*, drew Blatchford's attention. In the pages of the *Clarion*, he praised West for revealing Strindberg's naïveté regarding gender, a naïveté "at which a sane man would shrug his shoulders and smile" but which made the freewoman "a little enraged." Despite his mocking tone, Blatchford was delighted by West, who "gave him the chuckles for a whole day," and he brought her onto the journal's staff later that month.[17] West wasn't the first feminist to hold a position of prominence in the pages of the *Clarion*, nor did she introduce feminist issues to the journal. Julia Dawson had long been a contributing editor, Blatchford himself had written on the topic of women's suffrage, and a number of suffragettes, General Drummond among them, debated specific aspects of the campaign in the pages of the journal. But from her first days on the staff of the *Clarion*, West's writings significantly revised Blatchford's philosophy of rational recreation and the editorial policy of assuming that women were "consumed by their 'trivial' domestic concerns."[18]

Blatchford's ruminations on the radical possibilities embedded in everyday leisure activities were symptomatic of cultural debates about rational recreation that took place in England at the turn of the century and responded directly to the double threats of mechanized labor and mass culture.[19] His best-selling *Merrie England* (1895) outlined the importance of fulfilling leisure activity and socialist philosophy in general for an imaginary working-class citizen, "John Smith." According to editorials published in the *Clarion*, *Merrie England* converted more Englishmen to Marxism than the works of Karl Marx. Since men "work to live" rather than "live to work," leisure held the key to a transformation of the social sphere. Leisure activity, when taking the form of "rational recreation"—particularly reading, participating in social organizations such as the Clarion Vocal Union or attending festivals such as the Merrie England fair—had the potential to uplift and elevate members of the working class and the lower middle classes: "the people need more than wages. They need *leisure*. They need culture. They need humane and rational amusement. They need the chance to exercise those 'splendid ambitions and aspirations' about which our critic is eloquent."[20] Just as *Merrie England* trained readers to appreciate respectable forms of leisure activity, Blatchford's tract on reading, *A Book About Books* (1903), provided key texts and reading strategies for the "John Smiths" in his readership: "[B]ooks about books are not written wholly for the inner brotherhood of the elect. Outside the shining circles are busy crowds of mere human beings who do not know everything, who have not read everything, who have not had time to make a special study of literature, and so are glad of a hint, and hold themselves favoured when they are given an introduction to some new and pleasant literary friend."[21]

In the pages of the *Clarion*, rational recreation often meant a kind of rational consumption; articles and advertisements for the proper sorts of bicycles (important for participating in the Clarion Cycling Club), household wares, and "turkish baths for winter health"—"particularly powerful for good in the winter time"—were scattered throughout.[22] A weekly column entitled "Book-sellers Row" recommended one or two new books and encouraged the reader to buy: "All lovers of beautiful literature should read Blackmore; and those of you who prefer your luxuries at an inexpensive tariff will do well to send to Messers. Dent and Son for a catalogue of the Everyman Library. Lorna Doone you will find there, and also Springhaven."[23] In *A Book about Books*, Blatchford firmly linked reading to other aspects of daily life: walking through the city forced one to recognize that "fiction and drama are, or should be, pictures of human life, and the streets of the world are full of men and women" (82). Read-ing was an activity meant to cheer, inspire, and please (49), and proper regula-tion was required if the consumer was to stop at cheer and avoid inebriation (76). Blatchford was especially fond of the trope of reading as eating, which stitched reading firmly into a network of pleasurable daily activities: "But let us try other dishes. Shall I help you to a slice of Lamb?" After quoting Lamb, he then asked his readers if this was not "good book talk" (27).

Rational consumption—described in weekly articles like the Booksellers Row, Home Notes, The Woman's Outlook, all (predictably) written by women—was posed as an alternative to the feminized, sexualized, and (therefore) threat-ening aspects of modern consumption. It was primarily through rational con-sumption for the home that women entered into the world of the *Clarion*, addressed in the pages of the periodical as mothers, cooks, and wives interested in creating a supportive environment for the cultivation of respectable activi-ties. West's relationship to the journal is most interesting on this point, for she recognized the unacknowledged linkages between women's exclusion from the masculine world of socialism and the association of sexuality, femininity, and unruly consumption embedded in the *Clarion's* rejection of mass culture. In a *Clarion* piece entitled "Christmas Shopping: The Psychology of Regent Street," West described the West End as a "hateful place" based on a "foundation of squeezed-out small tradesmen, unprosperous factory hands, sweated home-workers, and anaemic shop-assistants."[24] The consuming women of the West End exhibit the "predatory enthusiasm" of "a hen picking at random round a rubbish heap" (135). The rich woman, with her "devotion to self-adornment," be-comes an "amateur of provocation" as she gazes upon window displays of corsets and feminine underclothing without associating herself "with the pet-ticoats" and "facing the attitude of mind which this display provoked" (136). It is not consumption itself that West rejected, nor, following Blatchford's supremely rational recreation, an unruly and unregulated feminine appetite

that she wished to diagnose. Rather, West exposed the "sneakish" form of dis-
avowal exhibited by most middle- and upper-class consumers and by advocates of rational recreation that severed feminine consumption from both the
real exploitation of women and from dominant representations of sexuality.
Turning from the sneakish "passion for ornament" of the upper-class shopper,
West embraced two very different examples of bold feminine appetite: the per-
former Gaby Deslys, who "made a sensation by appearing in a sketch at the
Palace in not quite the customary amount of clothing," but who "took the full
responsibility of this exhibition" and an activist selling copies of the *Suffragette*,
who exhibited "the excellent thing about the suffrage movement," "its insa-
tiable appetite for life" (136–37). The careful regulation and dissection of leisure
activity that characterized the *Clarion* was disrupted by these essays that focused on the consuming woman and her cultural significance.

The New Woman's Riotous Appetite

West thus brought to the *Clarion* a discourse of feminine appetite and feminist sexuality that she took from the pages of Dora Marsden's journals the
Freewoman and the *New Freewoman*. As both a literary and a cultural critic,
West brought questions of women's desire (and representations of women's
desire) to an understanding of the politics of everyday life. While Marsden's
bondwomen were seen as "followers," "servants," "great numbers of individuals . . . born without creative power in regard to any sphere of life whatever,"
West associated "creative power" with a wide range of social practices, eating,
dressing, dancing among them: "It is amazing how angrily the well-to-do
speak of the poor girl's love of finery. Yet there is really something very hopeful about the pert face of a Cockney beauty, smiling at life from under a wide
and worthless hat tipped with nodding, spurious plumes. She is a better rebel
than the girl who accepts her poverty as a matter of fate and wears its more
durable badge of drab garments and sailor hats."[25]

West's essays, especially "A New Woman's Movement: The Need for Riotous
Living," insist on radicalized, sexualized, and feminist acts of consumption
rather than the respectable gestures favored by Blatchford. Her waitresses flirt
with customers, her schoolmistresses refuse their bread and milk (130–34), just
as her feminists in other essays reject the "sins of self-sacrifice" generally associated with the angel of the house.[26] "A New Woman's Movement" documents
West's long-standing curiosity about woman's pleasure in oppositional activism

and in everyday life. Unlike those reformers who sought to redirect workers away from commercial culture, West exposed the determination of employers to "buy their employee, body and soul, off duty as well as on" by overt regulation of leisure activity (131). Countering this misguided effort to "provoke piety in the poor" by seeing the mildest amusements of the rich as vices of the poor, West calls for "riotous living" that rejects "enforced asceticism" and embraces pleasure (133). "Leisure" met "sexuality" for West at the site of the consuming female body characterized by riotous appetite, rebellious ornamentation, and aggressive desire: "the repression of the animal in woman, with its desires for food and freedom and comfort, accounts for her greater liability to nervous irritability and hysteria" (134). The "feminine" diseases of modernity—hysteria and nervous disorders—become a direct result of the "unnatural lives of repression" women are forced to lead when feminine consumption is seen as unruly and disordered (134). When West concentrates upon eating, then, in her depiction of "riotous living"—"Armies of nurses would visit the homes of the hospital governors and forcibly feed them with that horrid breakfast dish, porridge and treacle. And in Simpson's some day the blenching stockbroker shall look down the muzzle of the rifle and hand over his nice red-and-black beefsteak to his pale typist"—she expands Blatchford's world of leisure to encompass women (134). At the same time, her efforts undermined the culture of regulation that worked to identify Blatchford's rational forms of recreation. In addition, she also reworked the discourses of feminism most available to modern women: those vocabularies of sacrifice, martyrdom, and transcendence of the body circulated by militant suffragettes and exemplified by the rituals of imprisonment, hunger-strikes, and forcible feeding. If West wished a "red-and-black beefsteak" for her "pale typist," what food might she have wished for Sylvia or Emmeline Pankhurst as they exited frail and emaciated from prison?

In essays such as "A New Woman's Movement," West brought her understanding of socialism to the pages of the *Freewoman*, a journal which self-consciously described its audience as a kind of "intellectual elite," a group of "geniuses."[27] She also brought her understanding of a feminist politics organized around issues of sexuality to the nearly gender-blind pages of the *Clarion*. The question of consumption remained a pressing one for West in the early decades of the century, even after she stopped publishing with Blatchford and Marsden. It is in this context, for example, that we should read the subversive body of West's Evadne, who appears in the short story "Indissoluble Matrimony," which was published originally in Wyndham Lewis's *Blast* in 1914 and is reprinted in *The Young Rebecca*. From the point of view of the anti-so-cialist, anti-feminist, frail modern man George Silverton, the consuming fem-inist body of his wife Evadne registers as a collection of disruptive feminine at-tributes. Reading and writing, speaking, eating, and sexuality are permeated by unruly feminine appetite, an appetite he regards as "primitive" and animalis-tic: Evadne "ate with an appalling catholicity of taste"; talked "like a woman off the streets"; read "enormously" of economics; and "infected" all with her "ori-ental crudities."[28] This work of fiction employs West's interest in the critique of sexism embodied in subversive feminine consumption and provides an alter-native to the spare rigor of Lewis's vorticist avant-garde.

Noticing such cross-fertilization between periodical culture and literary en-deavors certainly aids current efforts to read West as a modernist—and through such readings to continue the long project of revising dominant definitions of modernism. Yet there are additional benefits to carefully reading feminist pe-riodical culture. When one examines women's efforts to chronicle their expe-riences of popular culture, politics, and modern life in the essay form, one finds that the example of feminist periodical literature is unique in its ability to assist us in our efforts to rethink the connections between women's experi-ence of modernity and the definitions of "modern" everyday life that have come to characterize the period for us. One could argue, in fact, that feminist periodical culture was central to the modernist project of defining (a gendered) everyday life—if feminist periodical literature is broadly defined to include the specialized alternative feminist periodicals that characterized first-wave ac-tivism (from the *Freewoman* to the *Suffragette*) and the work of experimental women writers in little magazines (*Poetry, transition*), "slicks" (*Vanity Fair*), and weekly newspapers devoted to cultural politics (the *Clarion*). In the fierce journalism of the modernist feminist Rebecca West for the *Clarion*, the auto-biographical writings and feminist essays of Vera Brittain and Winifred Holtby (published by Margaret Haig's [Viscountess Rhondda's] *Time and Tide*), the *New Yorker* essays of Janet Flanner, the whimsical and sometimes dark pieces of Djuna Barnes for *Vanity Fair*, the travelogues and cultural criticism of Jessie Fauset in the *Crisis*, and Dora Marsden's discussions of a "new freewoman" in the pages of her journals the *Freewoman*, and the *New Freewoman*, a complex narrative of women's everyday life developed in relation to images and narra-tives about the modern woman in city-space, in relation to the emergence of explicit theories of female desire, and in relation to a feminist tradition of writ-ings about unpaid domestic labor and activist writings about working-class women's labor. These writings offer a feminist theory of the everyday that counters the image of a boring and repetitive modern daily life offered by everyday practice theorists such as Henri Lefevbre, Walter Benjamin, and Georg Simmel with an examination of feminism's disruption of sexism's monotony. Emphasizing feminist periodical culture thus allows us to continue the newer projects (begun by Rita Felski, Laurie Langbauer, and others, including the contributors to this volume) of charting women's experience of modernity and defining modernity in such a way that aspects of feminine culture such as fashion, consumerism, women's reading practices, and cooking are seen as central rather than beside the point. What is at stake, then, is not just an expanded definition of literary modernism, but an enhanced vision of "what modernity might mean for women and other subaltern groups."[29]

NOTES

Epigraph: Rebecca West, "A New Woman's Movement: The Need for Riotous Living," in *The Young Rebecca: Writings of Rebecca West, 1911–17*, ed. Jane Marcus (Bloomington: Indiana University Press, 1982), 134.

1. Wendy Mulford, "Socialist-Feminist Criticism: A Case Study, Women's Suffrage and Literature, 1906–14," in *Re-Reading English*, ed. Peter Widdowson (New York: Methuen, 1982), 179–92; Lisa Tickner, *The Spectacle of Women: Imagery of the Suffrage Campaign, 1907–1914* (Chicago: University of Chicago Press, 1988); Rita Felski, *Beyond Feminist Aesthetics: Feminist Literature and Social Change* (Cambridge, Mass.: Harvard University Press, 1989). See also Felski's reflections on this early work in her Afterword to this volume, pp. 290–99.

2. West's modernist feminism has until recently been largely overlooked by contemporary literary critics. For important new readings of West, see Bonnie Kime Scott's *Refiguring Modernism*, vols. 1 and 2 (Bloomington: Indiana University Press, 1995); Margaret Stetz, "Rebecca West's Criticism: Alliance, Tradition, and Modernism," in *Rereading Modernism: New Directions in Feminist Criticism*, ed. Lisa Rado (New York: Garland, 1994), 41–66; Sue Thomas, "Rebecca West's Second Thoughts on Feminism," *Genders* 13 (1992): 90–107; Lyn Pykett, "Writing Around Modernism: May Sinclair and Rebecca West," in *Outside Modernism: In Pursuit of the English Novel, 1900–30*, ed. Lynne Hapgood and Nancy L. Paxton (New York: St. Martin's Press, 2000), 103–22.

3. Michel de Certeau, *The Practice of Everyday Life*, trans. Steven Rendall (Berkeley: University of California Press), 1984.

4. Laurie Langbauer, *Novels of Everyday Life: The Series in English Fiction, 1850–1930* (Ithaca, N.Y.: Cornell University Press, 1999), 21.

5. See Virginia Woolf, "Street Haunting," in *The Essays of Virginia Woolf*, vol. 4, ed. Andrew McNeillie (London: Hogarth Press, 1994), 481–91; Women's Co-operative Guild, *Life As We Have Known It*, ed. Margaret Llewelyn Davis (London: Hogarth Press, 1931); Teresa Billington-Grieg, "The Consumer in Revolt," in *The Non-Violent Militant: Selected Writings of Teresa Billington-Grieg*, ed. Carol McPhee and Ann FitzGerald (New York: Routledge & Kegan Paul, 1987), 249–94.

6. Felski, *The Gender of Modernity* (Cambridge, Mass.: Harvard University Press, 1995), 28. Subsequent citations are given parenthetically in the text.

7. Kate Flint, *The Woman Reader*, 1837–1914 (New York: Oxford University Press, 1993), 14, 31. A subsequent citation is given parenthetically in the text.

8. See Lucy Bland, "The Shock of the *Freewoman* Journal: Feminists Speaking on Heterosexuality in Early Twentieth-Century England," in *Sexual Cultures: Communities, Values and Intimacy*, ed. Jeffrey Weeks and Janet Holland (New York: St. Martin's Press, 1996): 75–96; Bruce Clarke, *Dora Marsden and Early Modernism: Gender, Individualism, Science* (Ann Arbor: University of Michigan Press, 1996); Les Garner, *Stepping Stones to Women's Liberty: Feminist Ideas in the Women's Suffrage Movement, 1900–1918* (Rutherford, N.J.: Fairleigh Dickinson University Press, 1984); Robert Von Hallberg, "Libertarian Imagism," *Modernism/Modernity* 2, 2 (1995): 63–79.

9. For this, see Bland, "Shock of the *Freewoman*," 75; and Garner, *Stepping Stones*, 61, 69.

10. Marsden, "Notes of the Week," *Freewoman*, November 23, 1911, 7–8.

11. "The Spinster: By One," *Freewoman*, November 23, 1911, 7–8.

12. Marsden, "The New Morality-III," *Freewoman*, January 4, 1912, 121; Marsden, "The New Morality," *Freewoman*, December 14, 1911, 62.

13. Marsden, "Commentary on Bondwomen," *Freewoman*, November 30, 1911, 21–22.

14. Marsden, "Notes of the Week," *Freewoman*, November 23, 1911, 3.

15. Rebecca West, "Spinsters and Art," in *Young Rebecca*, ed. Marcus, 46.

16. Rebecca West, "Strindberg: The English Gentleman (1)," *Young Rebecca*, ed. Marcus, 56.

17. Robert Blatchford, "Of Confessions & Mixed Metaphors & Style and Other Vanities," *Clarion*, September 6, 1912, 1.

18. Chris Waters, *British Socialists and the Politics of Popular Culture, 1884–1914* (Stanford: Stanford University Press, 1990), 168.

19. "Finally, socialists argued that while the excitement found in music halls, at football matches and on Bank Holidays was not at all truly recreative, the proprietors of those amusements tried to claim that it was. Here socialists seemed to be disputing the very definition of leisure put forward by the new industry. . . . Socialists suggested that by claiming to offer rational recreation, the leisure industry was gradually coming to monopolize socially valid definitions of leisure" (ibid., 29).

20. Robert Blatchford, *Merrie England* (New York: Humboldt Publishing Co., 1895), 69.

21. Robert Blatchford, *A Book about Books* (London: Clarion Press, 1903), 19. Subsequent citations are given parenthetically in the text.

22. Advertisement, *Clarion*, January 5, 1912, 3.

23. Winifred Blatchford, "In the Library," *Clarion*, January 12, 1912, 2.

24. Rebecca West, "Christmas Shopping: The Psychology of Regent Street," in *Young Rebecca*, ed. Marcus, 135. Subsequent citations of this essay are given parenthetically in the text.

25. Rebecca West, "A New Woman's Movement: The Need for Riotous Living," in *Young Rebecca*, ed. Marcus, 132. Subsequent citations of this essay are given parenthetically in the text.

26. Rebecca West, "The Sin of Self-Sacrifice," in *Young Rebecca*, ed. Marcus, 235–38.

27. Dora Marsden writes: "To be a freewoman one must have the essential attribute of genius" ("Commentary on Bondwomen," *Freewoman*, November 30, 1911, 21).

28. Rebecca West, "Indissoluble Matrimony," in *Young Rebecca*, ed. Marcus, 268, 271, 272.

29. Rita Felski, "Modernism and Modernity," in *Rereading Modernism*, ed. Rado, 192.

Djuna Barnes Makes a Specialty of Crime

Violence and the Visual in Her Early Journalism

"You see," I continued, "I have a lot of friends . . . who
are either potential criminals or criminals in action; and
these somehow one likes—why?"
    "Why? Well, you see, we all love the specialist," he an-
swered and broke out into laughter.
                              —Djuna Barnes, "Commissioner Enright
                                        and M. Voltaire"

The expatriate modernist and literary provocateur Djuna Barnes began
her writing career at the age of twenty-one as a reporter and illustrator
for New York City's numerous daily newspapers. Between 1913, when
she began as a junior reporter for the *Brooklyn Daily Eagle,* and the end of
World War I, Barnes was to write for nearly every paper in the city.[1] Caught up
in the diversity of attempts made by the first "mass" circulation newspapers to
further expand their readership, she played a varied repertoire of roles for her
public in these years—from flamboyant female "stunt journalist" and investigative reporter in the tradition of Nellie Bly to straightforward chronicler of
local color and notable events around the city. In this, her early professional
work, Barnes tries out many themes that were later to make an appearance in
her experimental literary writing.[2] However, because they were produced in
the context of turn-of-the-century newspaper sensationalism, her articles are
of interest not only to collectors of Barnesian juvenilia but also to students of
American mass culture. For Barnes forges her distinct literary style in relation
to the cultural meaning of sensationalism and the dilemmas about the new
mass reader underwriting contemporary press debates. Making recourse to
what will become her signature literary preoccupations with dark jokes and

criminality, she echoes and exaggerates the claim that crime reporting and sensationalism were a threat to public welfare by figuring lurid journalistic writing as a kind of violence exercised on the impossible body of the reading masses. Her many portraits of public spectacles reveal not only that it was common in her day to understand sensational newspaper readers as a "crowd"—a fact also evident in press criticism of the time—but also that these understandings served as a signal component by which that very crowd came to constitute itself around scenes of public violence.

Police Commissioner Enright's rejoinder to Barnes—above, in a 1918 interview—exemplifies the ways in which her writing drew on the public debate that sutured her profession to criminality. As she is frequently wont to do in her other celebrity interviews, Barnes adopts an archly adversarial attitude toward her interlocutor. While waiting to see the police commissioner at the beginning of the interview, her speculations about Enright's "function" in society and the "mug" shots in his rogues' gallery give way to a decadent literary ramble that allows her to sympathize and implicitly to identify with Enright's enemy—the criminal:

As I sat there thinking of the Police Commissioner's functions and of the rogues' gallery and the whole dramatic side of life called crime, there came to mind a fable— the fable of the man who never knew when to end a thing while it still held a little something of beauty. When he reached the age of twenty, he discovered what was indeed the most beautiful thing: irrevocable finality . . . somehow I could not help thinking of this as I realized how many people die in a year because they do not know where to stop, because the murderer, for instance, does not know where to find his period.[3]

Murderers, journalists, and artists all have in common here a search for the beauty that inheres in the perfect ending. Barnes hence seems at first to figure an oppositional relation between writer and subject, female and male, criminality and the dispassionate rule of law. Yet when Enright arrives to argue with his fanciful interviewer about her overinvestment in murderers, the distinction between objectification and identification that underwrites each of these pairs becomes less easy to distinguish. Enright's explanation of criminality is even more romantic than the one Barnes offers; he tells Barnes that criminals are not "on an equal footing" with other people, and by implication herself, because they are born under a bad "star" and therefore fated to be what they are (301–2). The rogues' gallery, in the person of its most well-known representative, erroneously believes itself to be dispassionately enforcing the best of all possible worlds. Identifying criminals based on foreordained qualities such as physiognomy cannot be distinguished from a naive absorption in the question of fate—one that makes the very investigation itself, rather than the criminal, a meet subject for (Barnes's) bemused interest. By the article's end, Barnes has led Enright to acknowledge the underlying investments of his Panglossian belief. His answer to the question of what makes criminals and criminality attractive—"we all love the specialist"—acknowledges a hidden and perverse investment in disciplinarity for its own sake. The punch line is that not only the criminal act, the decadent artist, or the female interviewer may be an object of fascination and attraction, but also the male surveying eye.[4]

The revelation Barnes engineers for her readers about Police Commissioner Enright and his gallery of criminal photos takes its key terms from what was, by the time of her first writings, the relatively recent advent of mass sensationalism in her profession. For the kind of newspaper in which Barnes published interviews like this one had, itself, been reconceived *as* a rogues' gallery in the years following the adoption of high-speed printing techniques in the 1890s.[5] It had become not only possible but common by the end of the century for the papers to reproduce and widely circulate drawings and sometimes even photographs of criminals alongside stories about their crimes. Furthermore, there had been a general explosion in the sheer quantity of visual materials the reading public encountered daily. Up to the Civil War and just beyond, the penny press had been mainly characterized by small lines of print that ran in single columns, little differentiation in typeface, and only the occasional line drawing to serve as support for or further clarification of the text. By the turn of the century, it was not unusual to find text sometimes serving only as an adjunct to pictures, or perhaps no text at all. Cartoons, photographic portraits of celebrities and ordinary people on the street, pictures of wanted criminals, and illustrations of the latest society fashions became integral to a mass newspaper reading experience. Other chiefly visual innovations had also taken place within the format of the papers. First Pulitzer and then Hearst after him made widespread use of the varied typefaces that we now associate with sensational news stories or tabloids; headlines could became enlarged and darkened "screamers" if needed and subheadings frequently highlighted selective words and phrases to catch the reader's eye.[6]

With the massive growth in readership that accompanied the new production and distribution techniques, press commentators favorable to yellow journalism could indulge their wildest fantasies of a mass public surveillance through the increasingly visually oriented daily paper. The circulation of criminals' likenesses, it was frequently avowed by Joseph Pulitzer and others, had made it possible for the public to play the part of detectives and policemen.[7] Citing a case where a kidnapped child had been found through posters created by one of William Randolph Hearst's newspapers, Arthur Brisbane argued in 1904 that the press had "made evident to would-be kidnappers that they had something more than the police to deal with. They learned that a yellow newspaper could set to work a million amateur detectives among its readers, and that even amateur detectives are to be dreaded when they number a million."[8] Future criminal behavior might also be prevented by publicity given to crimes. Lurid coverage by the investigative dailies could convince a criminal that, in the words of one skeptical commentator, "*the eyes of the people are on him.*"[9] On the rare occasions when column-space given over to crime proved harmful (by biasing public opinion, for example), the dire necessity for a surveillance of the people, by the people, and for the people overrode all considerations. According to Charles E. Grinnell: "most persons need to be watched in some things, and the evils of the watching have to be endured for the sake of the good."[10] Necessary to a civil society, the "mass" public with the press as its tool could act, in Pulitzer's famous phrase, like "an Argus-eyed conscience."[11]

There was, however, another reason Pulitzer often put forth for using so many visual materials in *The World*.[12] He wanted to appeal to New York's rapidly expanding pool of non-English speaking immigrants, who might be better able to understand pictures than text. Despite his characterization of newspaper readers as detectives in full possession of the facts, therefore, Pulitzer also implied on occasion that most of his audience could police crime *only* by looking at pictures. "The majority of persons," he wrote in one of his daily front-page columns in the *World*, "require to be educated through the eye."[13] News of this apparent success with immigrants made common cause with widespread and unfavorable assertions that the thoughts of all sensational newspaper readers, even English-speaking ones, were less than cognitive. If images in the papers could serve to make readers into detectives, each one an individual surveying eye, it was—rather disturbingly—because newspaper readers were understood to think in images to begin with. In a widely reprinted study of yellow journalism published at Pulitzer's death in 1911, Will Irwin explains that the success of Pulitzer's strategy was due to the fact that the majority of lower-class readers were too tired to understand words:

Pictures first—for ten grasp with the eye to one with the mind. . . . Then reading matter so easy, with the startling points so often emphasized, that the weariest mechanic, sitting in his socks on Sunday morning, could not fail to get a thrill of interest. "Economy of attention"—that, unconsciously to [Pulitzer] probably, made up his whole formula. Nothing which called for any close attention; something which first caught the eye and then startled, tickled, and interested without wear on brain tissue.[14]

Irwin's notion of the image-oriented "popular mind" is likely to have drawn much of its inspiration from the widely influential theory of crowds propounded by the French sociologist Gustave Le Bon in 1895. When crowds read or listen to a speech, according to Le Bon, they are immediately galvanized into action as if representations could have the effect of physical force. The "image" is Le Bon's way of designating this process. The term floats free of actual photographs or drawings in his writing to indicate any form of simple communication, or "judicious employment of words and formulas" (102).[15] "Whatever be the ideas suggested to crowds," he notes, "they can only exercise effective influence on condition that they assume a very absolute, uncompromising, and simple shape. They present themselves then in the guise of images, and are only accessible to the masses under this form" (62). Such "accessibility" is, in fact, for Le Bon a direct unmediated impact on the body without the mediation of mind or consciousness. For the individual in the crowd, "the idea which has entered the brain tends to transform itself into an act" like "the button of an electric bell" (40, 70).

It is, therefore, as Police Commissioner Enright acknowledges: the keepers of the rogues' gallery harbor a potentially fatal propensity to themselves become a spectacle. Those readers who become all-seeing detectives fighting crime through the newspapers are, by the same token, also vulnerable to becoming the lurid object of attention. For visual materials in the paper could galvanize not just readers but, more specifically, the reading *body* into action.[16] Critics of sensationalism often argued in terms similar to Le Bon's that sensational newspapers manipulated readers in a particularly bodily way. In a 1914 *Atlantic Monthly* article, H. L. Mencken denounced the reading public as a mob liable to select "a deserving [political] victim, and then [put] him magnificently to the torture" when led by editorials that had aroused their "elemental feelings."[17] In order to contest the claims of editors such as Pulitzer and Brisbane that sensational newspaper readers can exercise a policing authority, Mencken continually stages the slippage between an abstract and a bodily economy of vision inherent in any understanding of readers as crowds. Once a newspaper has John Public "safely by the nose . . . he will be ready to believe anything, however absurd, so long as he is in his state of psychic tumescence" (291). Emotion, in addition to persuasion, accrues within a specific bodily location in Mencken's satire: "Such is the ebb and flow of emotion in the popular heart—or perhaps, if we would be more accurate, the popular liver" (294). Recalling Will Irwin's recourse to bodily fatigue, Mencken at another point locates the tiring effects of reading in the digestive system: "He [the newspaper reader] cannot read more than three columns of any one subject without tiring: 6,000 words, I should say, is the extreme limit of his appetite. And the nearer he is pushed to that limit, the greater the strain upon his psychic digestion" (292).

The newspaper's newly expansive reach and greater use of visual materials made it and its public over into a mode of display intended for, but often difficult to restrict to, the interests of the general good. But the graphic language of brain tissue and liver, rather than mind or heart, in the above accounts suggests further that to read in this economy makes one figuratively the object of violence. Not only the subject of sensational news stories—when "the victim" is put "magnificently to the torture," for example—violence is also the modus operandi of journalists. Although Mencken's language figures political scandal rather than stories about violent crime, his implication that editorials reduced readers to the contents of their insides was deployed by others as a particularly apt metaphor for the evils of gratuitous crime reporting. George Alger suggests that journalistic prose becomes stained with incriminating evidence when he denounces the "public demand" of papers "whose reporters are the sleuths." "Ghastly cartoons of the defendant, with murder drawn in every line of his face" are not demands for justice but "the headless Demos transformed into printers ink."[18] The connection between blood and ink, and the implication that journalists who "specialize in crime" have blood on their hands is made more strongly by Sydney Brooks. The yellow press, he complains, "explode[s] upon the city in a way there is no escaping," its pages "liberally bespattered with ink."[19]

This brief survey gives a taste of the way in which press commentators, in the decades before Barnes was to take up her illustrating and writing pen, often criticized the new visual appeal of the paper. The metaphorics of violence animating their prose came from a language of mass readership much like that used by sociologists such as Le Bon to describe easily persuaded crowds whose hunger for images dictated a violent collapse into the bodily. Barnes stood as a "specialist" in the glare of this public debate—one of the many newspaper men and women who now wielded the dangerously reflexive word-picture. It is therefore not surprising to find that her pieces not only focus on scenes of crowd spectatorship, but also take up the relationship between a violent reduction to the bodily and an undecidable distinction between words and images. Both were a part of the meaning that inhered in the relatively new look of the mass-circulated newspapers for which she wrote. Hence it was that in the years before she departed for Paris to begin her literary career, her aesthetic signature became irrevocably bound up with the paradoxical logic of the spectacle.[20]

Barnes's journalism could stand as representative of almost all that critics of sensationalism in her time most despised. The first and foremost indignity was that her pieces were designed to appeal to the eye. They were frequently accompanied by her own large pen-and-ink drawings and sometimes by photographs; on occasion, as in a few articles she wrote for the *New York World*, pictures of Barnes herself were included along with her text. To boot, her writing style was highly "imagistic," in Le Bon's sense. She wrote simple, snappy copy with titles that often took alliteration to an extreme, and her subject matter could barely qualify as weighty. Her assignments, which largely consisted of observing entertaining events and sights around New York, included several visits to Coney Island, a couple of tourist cruises around Manhattan, and many firsthand accounts of events at circuses, boxing rings, and fashion shows.

Nevertheless, charged as she was to write about public spectacles, Barnes's interpretative and descriptive energies were also inevitably attracted to at least one issue important to critics of sensationalism: what draws a crowd? Writing for the *Brooklyn Daily Eagle* early in 1913, Barnes provides an answer—bodily violence. "Twingeless Twitchell and His Tantalizing Tweezers" describes the public extraction of a man's tooth by a dentist eager to demonstrate his painless technique. Barnes, who gives the impression throughout that she witnessed the scene with a crowd of other fascinated onlookers on a street corner in Brooklyn Heights, paints a suspense-filled and humorous picture that focuses more on the crowd than on the dentist. When "Twingeless Twitchell," asks for a volunteer, "A thrill of anticipation ran through the crowd. People in the el trains twenty feet above leaned out of the windows, entranced at the sight. A taxi went chugging by and then suddenly stopped, and a fat man alighted and joined the throng. . . . A chic French maid came tumbling forth from a nearby millinery shop." The entranced crowd gathers not, it is clear, because of the promise of a painless extraction but rather for the thrill of it: "[O]n a sudden, a hush fell over the crowd. A man, collarless, red of beard and bald of hair, mounted the steps to the platform with his eyes fixed on the glaring lights, like a rabbit that has been charmed by the bead in the python's eye."[21]

Although the crowd is mesmerically drawn in by both "the judicious employment of words and formulas"[22] in Twingeless Twitchell's snappy speech— he tells his audience at one point, "I'm here to collar the dollars"—and the promised visual impression of the extraction, Barnes's humorous evocation of people's automatic responses to a public spectacle offers a challenge to crowd psychology. Her portrait is not of a mass, unidirectional mobilization of bodies, but rather of an exchange and substitution between viewers and viewed that blurs the lines of persuasive force. Within the text, the posture of the "fixed" and transfixed victim echoes the arrested crowd who stop to watch. The victim's body gapes open as the tooth is pulled, and the watchers gape at the sight. It is as if the crowd forms here because the victim represents the crowd to itself; what the red-bearded patient literalizes or "fixes" are the unstably figural characteristics of the "gaping" mob in the face of the spectacular.

One spectator offers an illuminating explanation of all this, challenging accounts such as Mencken's of newspaper reading crowds who select "a deserving victim, and then [put] him magnificently to the torture."[23] Barnes's Reginald Delancey, a fictional figure who disappears after a few early pieces, makes an aside to his girlfriend just before the victim takes center stage. He notes "learnedly" that "[i]t is the spirit of the arena . . . they all want to see a human being suffer," implying, like Mencken, a kind of public bloodlust. However, as he walks away in shock afterwards, Reginald offers a different analysis: "I say, . . . that's—that's not a bit nice. Just like washing one's linen in public and all that sort of thing" (24). Barnes implies through her character that the thrill is to be found in the obscene nature of the spectacle rather than in its ties to primitive or classical ritual.[24] The attraction of public dentistry lies in the way it troubles the boundary between public and private, just like the notion that the public might have a body or, in fact, be all body.[25] The crowd is drawn to watch by the lurid logic of its own constitution, as represented and literalized by the "unknown" individual in the dentist's chair.

This dynamic becomes clearer when taking full measure throughout Barnes's other pieces of the frequency of scenes of public watching and the constant recurrence in them of an often incongruous thematics of bodily fixity or suspension.[26] Assigned to cover a tourist cruise around Manhattan in the summer of 1917, Barnes joins a group of "stiff-backed, Middle West schoolteachers," for whom she displays a resident New Yorker's humorous contempt.[27]

The posture of the out-of-towners on the top deck is tied to their refusal to look at anything new; only a college on the Palisades bluffs stirs their interest. Although Barnes attempts to distance herself from such an attitude and to see her own home with new eyes, the thrust of the article soon becomes a very Barnesian paradox that anticipates *Nightwood*: "[Y]ou cannot reach into your home because it is from there you were found reaching out" (286). Watching the Manhattan skyline, she finds an instantiation of the fixity produced by this philosophical dilemma of spectatorship. The skyscrapers are "like a great wave that found it impossible to return again and so remained there in horror, peering out of a million windows men had caged it with" (289). A violent tension is also taken on by the city at the article's end through a play on the "hem" of the title. Absorbing and taking to another power the fixity and tension characteristic of everyone on deck, the city's buzz is like "a faint sound of fabric being rent: one half of the mass pulling one way and the other half in an opposing direction" (294).

The object, person, or even cityscape arrested in the public's view always suggests the possibility of a break or rupture in its precarious stillness. Hence, Barnes' s thematics of tension, suspension, and fixity allow her to incorporate intimations of violence into scenes of crowd spectatorship. At times, she makes this violent breaking or giving way explicit, often by means of a sudden release of laughter as in the Enright article above.[28] The police commissioner's laugh "breaks out" at the moment in which he acknowledges the blurring of distinction between the policing power of the rogues' gallery and its capacity to become the object of fascinated, perhaps erotic interest. Barnes's identifications in turn suggest a similar giving way of distinctions between fact-conveying words and entertaining pictures.

In another *Brooklyn Daily Eagle* assignment, Barnes suggests this idea by describing directly a form of writing whose violence might well figure her own. It is a story with the apotheosis of sensational appeal—a nighttime safari to Chinatown. Bemoaning, with tongue in cheek, the paucity of adventure she and her reporter colleagues actually found, Barnes nevertheless narrates the nonevent with gusto: "As from Park Row we picked our way toward Mott Street, did a hissing ball of fire shoot out? No! . . . Did the Chinese script suddenly break loose at us and impale our courage upon a sandalwood, scarlet-ink-dipped brush? No!"[29] The presence of Barnes's characteristic preoccupation with things that break violently loose, coupled with this invocation of writing that is also illustration, suggests that she subtly offers her own pen here as the only remaining source of sensational appeal for a Chinatown now "crumbled to dust" (123). It is perhaps not insignificant, too, that Chinese characters appear, like newsprint, in columns, and that Barnes often signed her portraits in a vertical script resembling them. Her rather primitivist vignette suggests that the violent hesitations and tensions to which she returns so often in so many different contexts may have their origins in her own "spiked language" (130), which, according to the logic of sensational writing and crowds, can only arrest and fix its audience somewhere between observer and reader. Herself a producer of the very spectacles intended to grab the newspaper reading "mob's" attention in the first place, she was to some extent always describing her own professional work when assigned to discover what it is that makes crowds look.

The self-referentiality of these figures for murdering journalism raises the question of Barnes's status as a female reporter in her imaginative negotiations of sensationalism during these years. The "joke" in "Commissioner Enright" that murderers may become specialists, and specialists, murderers, and that both—like sensational papers themselves—may thereby become an attraction, seems to be at Enright's expense, insofar as it displaces him from his position of all-seeing male authority. However, because "Twingeless Twitchell" and Barnes's numerous other articles involving crowds insistently situate the attractiveness of violence in the context of large numbers of viewers, the gendered dimensions of her early journalism should therefore be understood less as an opposition or antagonism between singular male and female figures than as a no less important one between female journalist and mass audience. As a means to figure, articulate, or justify her own journalistic work, she reveals not only that women but also that men, when part of a crowd, can be susceptible to spectacular events and the imagistic writing of the journalists who cover them.

A 1914 *New York World* piece in which Barnes is sent to a prizefight to discover why women watch boxing engages this gendered dynamic directly. The article's subheading notes that women are attending boxing matches in greater and greater numbers and suggests that Barnes's article will provide a firsthand account of what a woman feels like when she watches one: "Following the Example of Their French and English Cousins, New York Women Have Begun to Flock to the Ringside—Here Is an Impressionistic Picture of a Boxing Bout Before a Mixed Audience by a Woman Who Had Never Seen One."[30] Although the subheading solicits readers' attention by promising that an inexperienced and innocent female viewer will be the object of attention in the piece, Barnes's very first lines immediately reverse these terms. She situates herself instead as a reader lured by the spectacle of the female viewer offered within the supposedly objective and statistics-oriented sporting pages. Again, in relation to the question of female display, Barnes stages the giving way of a masculine objective gaze to an overwhelming absorption. Yet this time she plays the male reader whose solely knowledgeable interest in facts and statistics is humorously suspect:

"A large percentage of the spectators were women."

This bald statement of fact had repeatedly caught my eye and attention from the sporting pages of many newspapers.

Friends had several times asked me, "Have you noticed that, of late, women have taken to attending boxing matches?" I had not noticed it, but I wished to if it were fact.

Therefore, one night I found myself at Far Rockaway and in Brown's Athletic Club. (6)

Registering the compulsive power of her own interest, Barnes simply "finds herself" at the boxing match. She manages to suggest through this opening both the hidden and denied erotic lures of the sports pages for men and one possible answer to the ostensible question of her editors: what would draw a women such as Barnes to watch boxing? The answer: women are motivated to go to boxing matches by reading about the "fact" of their own interest in them. Drawn by a fascination for facts and knowledge about their own desire, women readers are cast in terms of the crowd. As in the "Twingeless Twitchell" piece, crowd-interest constitutes not a fascination for violence but a self-fascination.

Once inside the arena at Far Rockaway, Barnes does indeed discover a crowd of viewers, both male and female. However, after listening to the conversation around her, she discovers that the crowd's reactions to boxing fall along stereotypically gendered lines:

All the men are aware from the beginning that Bloom has the best of it; somehow they know the things that count in the game, and their interest is proportionate to their knowledge. But the woman's interest lies not in strength but in beauty. She is on the side of the boxer who has a certain trick of the head, a certain curve of the chin, a certain line from throat to brow. (6)

The male gaze is imagined as motivated only by knowledge; a man's interest in the boxers seems only to indicate perhaps a bet on the match's outcome.

By contrast, the woman's look is related to sexual desire and fixed on the image of the boxer's body. It bears no relation to statistics and the things that "count" in the game.

Yet it soon appears that Barnes has once again staged this familiar scene of gendered viewing only to knock it down. After the fight starts, she eventually turns to see for herself what her "sisters" are experiencing and finds that her initial impressions are not to be trusted. As with the dentistry scene, instead of concentrating on either the crowd she finds inside the arena or on the object of its interest, Barnes gives us an image of spectatorship as inextricable exchange or substitution—a kind of mutual miming between viewer and viewed. What Barnes sees instead of enthralled or terrified female boxing fans is women viewers who are themselves oddly, and bizarrely, violent:

After a sudden, uneasy stir, the crowd settles down to watch. Some lean forward with hands, palms outward, thrust between their knees. Others lean back, with arm extended over another's chair. But the women who dared the ringside and the girls further back sit rigidly upright, balanced between wonder and apprehension, their faces still set in a fixed smile, as of a man beheaded while a joke still hovered in his throat. (6)

Recalling the frozen wave of the Manhattan skyline and the "stiff-backed" schoolteachers who admire it or the transfixed dentistry patient and the el train riders who strain from their windows, the obscure Barnesian metaphor only becomes explained when she turns to describe the object of the crowd's attention, in this case the match itself, for the women resemble the bodies in the ring in their violently fixed positions. Barnes sees the boxers not as swinging freely at each other, but rather "coming to a lock, where head meets breast. They move stiffly, jerkily" (6). The ring is an enclosed, immobilizing space that places the bodies on display. Movement is seen in terms of its immediate constraint. "Each one of us . . . sits motionless, scarce permitting a breath to pass our lips. Then, like a bird thrown helpless against the bars of a cage one of them [the boxers] is hurled against the ropes" (6).

Barnes's observations lead her to a conclusion which serves as the punch for her final lines:

In the blank pause that followed the finish, a man suddenly struck a match. It illumined a face drawn, paler than it had been, with eyes more heavily lidded. The match went out, and I was left to puzzle and question.

Was it, after all, the men in the audience who had been careless and indifferent to pain? Was it the sound of a snapping fan that I had heard? Was it a woman's voice that had murmured, "He has fine eyes?" A woman's hand that had gripped my arm in the dark? A woman's breath that had ceased so suddenly?

And whose voice was it that had cried out just before the finish—"go to it, and show us that you're men"? (6)

Barnes's ultimately humorous conclusion that the women's mysterious smiles and violent fixity may come from their indifference to pain and their interest in the boxer's ability springs directly from her primary observation that men may in fact be the ones who admire the boxers' eyes and who become pale and drawn in the face of violence. What the crowd's behavior reveals, with women as its exemplary subjects, is an unexpected vulnerability for both men and women who watch boxing. Women may be knowledgeable, men may tremble, but the larger point of the article is that a knowledgeable and masculinized viewing position may not be an invulnerable one for either sex to assume.

While the direction of Barnes's irony in these articles appears to implicate both women and men in the violent exchange of spectatorship, one final piece suggests the extent of the pressure on her in the opposite direction—toward, that is, a feminized self-display for the male gaze in which she herself might be dangerously implicated. On another, earlier assignment for the *World* in 1914, Barnes underwent a mock rescue from a building by means of a rope and the assistance of a fireman. Most important for the theme of ambiguously violent tension and suspension that I have been tracing throughout this essay, the article features three photographs of Barnes herself literally suspended in midair outside a tenement building. A caption to one picture grants us, again, the characteristic moment of crowd-formation, this time from Barnes's perspective:

I reached across the crimson sill, and swung against the sky some hundred feet or so above the city pavement. Out on the other side of the wall the world had stopped to look on. An auto slowed down. A flock of school children and a couple of "white wings" all stood with heads upturned skyward. A man with a screaming white apron tied about a conscienceless girth, who had been cutting perishable merchandise, grinned in the glare of light shining and dancing upon his cleaver.[31]

The butcher's grin recalls the women's fixed smiles as they watch boxing-except that instead of an analogy that helps to explain women's viewing, and by extension the motivation of the crowd to stop to watch, the man with the knife here seems to portend violence for the dangling female reporter. Barnes's suspension in these pictures is therefore both real and metaphoric; she dangles halfway between being a newspaper reporter who gives readers the facts and a sensational woman who communicates with her simple and visual-minded audience only through pictures. The joke, this time, is on Barnes, for language that hesitates between visual immediacy and cognitive process needs a body, some body, to hang in the balance. We can wonder if the intervention of actual photographic reproduction in this piece tempted Barnes to allegorize her own possible scapegoating by the very dynamics of sensationalism from which she made her living. She leaves it finally up in the air whether the butcher is tempted to cut the rope and thereby establish once and for all that the female reporter will become the unambiguously graphic object for the crowd's enthralled gaze.

NOTES

Epigraph: Djuna Barnes, "Commissioner Enright and M. Voltaire," *New York Sun Magazine*, March 17, 1918, reprinted in id., *New York*, ed. Alyce Barry (Los Angeles: Sun & Moon Press, 1989), 296–97.

1. Phillip Herring, Introduction to Djuna Barnes, *Collected Stories* (Los Angeles: Sun & Moon Press, 1996), 7.

2. As Carl Herzig has noted, these include black humor, an interest in the "freak" or social outcast, and the tendency to view characters, such as Robin Vote in *Nightwood*, in terms of grim dualities ("Roots of Night: Emerging Style and Vision in the Early Journalism of Djuna Barnes," *Centennial Review* 31 [1987]: 255–69).

3. Djuna Barnes, "Commissioner Enright and M. Voltaire," in *New York*, ed. Barry, 296–97. Unless otherwise noted, all subsequent quotations from Barnes's journalism are taken from this reprinted collection. In cases where the layout and visuals of the article are important, a full reference is given to the original paper in which it first appeared. Privileging Barnes's work during these years as proto-literary or "juvenilia," the reprints do not include many original features of the articles, such as subheadings, captions, and some of the images—important details that can help to illuminate the cultural context of Barnes's work.

4. Barnes's strategy is evident also in her portrait of the commissioner, in which she turns her eye on him to slightly creepy effect: "As I have said before, the Commissioner has very nice white and curling hair; here he stroked it and smiled. 'Let us talk of less gloomy things,' he said" (301). For an analysis of Barnes's confrontational strategy in her interviews as an appropriation of "investigative desire" and the masculine gaze, see Barbara Green, *Spectacular Confessions: Autobiography, Performative Activism and the Sites of Suffrage* (New York: St. Martin's Press, 1997), 172–73.

5. The advent of the high-speed printing press meant that the last two decades of the nineteenth century alone witnessed an explosion in newspaper readership. The period was to become infamous in American journalism history. Joseph Pulitzer's pathbreaking *New York World*, in which, twenty years later, some of Barnes's most spectacular pieces were to appear, sold 15,000 copies daily in 1883; by 1898, after his notorious circulation battle with William Randolph Hearst during the Spanish-American War and the birth of photojournalism in that conflict, Pulitzer could claim to have increased his paper's circulation to almost 1,500,000 daily (George Juergens, *Joseph Pulitzer and the New York World* [Princeton: Princeton University Press, 1966], vii, and John Tebbel, *The Compact History of the American Newspaper* [New York: Hawthorn Books, 1969], 202–3). By the century's end, the high-speed printing press had enabled papers to be produced at greater speeds and lower cost. Technological innovations cut both production expenses and newsstand prices, swelling circulation; additional revenue was generated through advertising (Juergens, 347–49 and Richard Ohmann, *Selling Culture: Magazines, Markets, and Class at the Turn of the Century* [New York: Verso, 1996], 20–21).

6. For many media theorists and historians of journalism, technological innovations in newspaper production and distribution at the turn of the century transcend political and social meanings and limitations. As Michael Warner puts it in his critique of studies of print culture in the eighteenth century, print emerges in these accounts as "a mere technology, a medium itself unmediated" (*The Letters of the Republic: Publication and the Public Sphere in Eighteenth-Century America* [Cambridge, Mass.: Harvard University Press, 1990], 5). Instead, I try here to suggest a critical perspective on the ideological meaning granted to pictures in turn-of-the-century papers, one that situates print as a form of material reality that is irreducibly symbolic and cultural. In addition to Warner, my thinking on this point has been influenced by Neil Harris, who has argued that the newly visual mass circulation newspapers signaled a major "iconographical shift" in American culture that has largely been ignored by historians (*Cultural Excursions: Marketing Appetites and Cultural Tastes in Modern America* [Chicago: University of Chicago Press, 1990], 304–17). For a history of photojournalism, including a description of the halftone process that made it possible to print photographs on the same press as type, see Beaumont Newhall, *The History of Photography*, rev. ed. (New York: Museum of Modern Art, 1982), 249–66, and R. Smith Schuneman, "Art or Photography: A Question for Newspaper Editors of the 1890s," *Journalism Quarterly* (Winter 1965): 43–59. Histories of yellow journalism that discuss the importance of illustrations are offered by John D. Stevens, *Sensationalism and the New York Press* (New York: Columbia University Press, 1991), 87–88; Michael Schudson, *Discovering the News: A Social History of the American Newspapers* (New York: Basic Books, 1978), 95–98; and Juergens, *Joseph Pulitzer and the New York World*, 93–118.

7. Mark Essig has argued that reporters in this period also became redefined as detectives by advocates of sensational journalism, partly in response to a perceived "epidemic" of poisoning cases sweeping the city. In turn, critics worried that publicity given to poisoning crimes encouraged would-be poisoners to strike again ("Science and Sensation: Poison Murder and Forensic Medicine in Nineteenth-Century America" [Ph.D. diss., Cornell University, 2000], ch. 1).

8. "Yellow Journalism," *Bookman* 19 (1904), 402.

9. George W. Alger, "Sensational Journalism and the Law," *Atlantic Monthly* 91 (February 1903): 146.

10. "Modern Murder Trials and Newspapers," *Atlantic Monthly* 88 (November 1901): 672.

11. Quoted in Juergens, *Joseph Pulitzer and the New York World*, 72. The advent of mass reproducible illustrations, therefore, served to reconstitute the newspaper as a Foucauldian "panoptic" device. On panopticism, see Michel Foucault, *Discipline and Punish: The Birth of the Prison* (New York: Vintage Books, 1979), 195–231.

12. *The World* was the leader in illustration (Juergens, *Joseph Pulitzer and the New York World*, ii).

13. Quoted in ibid., 47.

14. "Yellow Journalism" (1911), in *Highlights in the History of the American Press*, ed. Edwin H. Ford and Edwin Emery (Minneapolis: University of Minnesota Press, 1954), 275.

15. All references are to Gustave Le Bon, *The Crowd: A Study of the Popular Mind* (London: T. F. Unwin, 1916). Subsequent citations are mostly given parenthetically in the text.

16. I am hence tracing here a discourse similar to that which surrounded sensational fiction reading. D.A. Miller has argued that the Victorian sensation novel was also understood to galvanize the body into action with little or no mediation from the mind (D. A. Miller, *The Novel and the Police* [Berkeley: University of California Press, 1988], 146).

17. H. L. Mencken, "Newspaper Morals," *Atlantic Monthly* 113 (March 1914): 289. Subsequent citations are mostly given parenthetically in the text.

18. Alger, "Sensational Journalism and the Law," 146.

19. "The Yellow Press: An English View," *Harper's Weekly*, December 23, 1911, 11.

20. In "Circuses and Spectacles: Public Culture in *Nightwood*," *Journal of Modern Literature* 21, 1 (Summer 1997): 7–28, Laura Winkiel argues that Barnes, in her journalism, contrasts modern spectacular entertainments unfavorably with the more interactive and transgressive pleasures of circus and vaudeville.

21. Djuna Barnes, "Twingeless Twitchell and His Tantalizing Tweezers," *Brooklyn Daily Eagle*, July 27, 1913, reprinted in *New York*, ed. Barry, 23–24. Subsequent citations are given parenthetically in the text.

22. Le Bon, *The Crowd*, 102.

23. Mencken, "Newspaper Morals," 289.

24. As such this may serve as one instance where Foucault's caution is appropriate: "At the moment of its full blossoming, the disciplinary society still assumes with the Emperor [Napoleon] the old aspect of the power of spectacle" (*Discipline and Punish*, 217).

25. I am influenced throughout this essay by Mark Seltzer's notion that fascinations with scenes of public violence serve as "a way of imagining the relations of private bodies and private persons to public spaces" (*Serial Killers: Death and Life in America's Wound Culture* [New York: Routledge, 1998], 21); Warner's understanding of the constitutively abstracted public that finds its bodily positivity through these same specta-

cles has also been formative ("The Mass Public and the Mass Subject," in *The Phantom Public Sphere*, ed. Bruce Robbins [Minneapolis: University of Minnesota Press, 1993], 377–401).

26. For an analysis of Barnes's thematics of arrest and their relationship to the image in Nightwood, see Louis Kannenstine, *The Art of Djuna Barnes: Duality and Damnation* (New York: New York University Press, 1977).

27. Djuna Barnes, "The Hem of Manhattan," in *New York*, ed. Barry, 288. Subsequent citations are given parenthetically in the text.

28. These moments are often oddly discontinuous or sudden themselves in the text, as when, with no warning, she injects a brief enigmatic and epigrammatic sentence into an account of backstage antics with Piccadilly chorus girls: "It is night which has been shattered into laughter; it is also laughter with the restraint of night" ("Futuristic Impressions of the Piccadilly Chorus Girls in 'To-Night's the Night,'" *New York Press*, January 31, 1915).

29. Djuna Barnes, "Chinatown's Old Glories Crumbled to Dust," in *New York*, ed. Barry, 124. Subsequent citations are given parenthetically in the text.

30. "My Sisters and I at a New York Prizefight," *New York World Magazine* (August 23, 1914), 6. Subsequent citations are given parenthetically in the text.

31. "My Adventures Being Rescued," *New York World Magazine*, November 15, 1914, 6.

In Pursuit of an Erogamic Life

Marie Stopes and the Culture of Married Love

Marie Carmichael Stopes's most famous work, *Married Love*, was first published in 1918 and listed in 1935 as "sixteenth out of the twenty-five most influential books of the previous fifty years."[1] The text was a best-seller by any standards. By the end of 1918, there had been five editions and seventeen thousand copies were in print. Over half a million copies had been sold by the mid 1920s.[2] *Married Love* continued to sell into the 1950s, although its style, language, and sensibility must have appeared increasingly outdated by this time, especially in the wake of the Kinsey Reports. At its height during the 1920s, Stopes also achieved significant personal fame (or notoriety), enjoying what Lesley Hall describes as a "flamboyant media presence."[3] In 1922, Noel Coward (with whom Stopes engaged in a brief correspondence) composed a song instructing the "panic-stricken," the deviant, the failed, and the hopeless to "fly," "apply," or "crawl" to Marie Stopes for some "normal soap to cleanse your soul."[4] Coward's song is testimony to Stopes's cultural status, a witty illustration of the extent to which her name operated as a "byword" for sex advice and birth control in the twenties.[5] It is also shrewd in its characterization of Stopes's intent to cleanse the sphere of sexuality with "normal soap." It is in part the constitution of norms and the social and aesthetic criteria underpinning the demarcation of cleanliness and dirt within Stopes's accounts of "married love" with which this chapter is concerned.

Samuel Hynes has argued that *Married Love* should be viewed alongside the gaining of the franchise as "a milestone in the history of women's rights," thus placing Stopes's text at the origin of women's apparent sexual liberation from the fetters of Victorianism in the interwar period.[6] Her work has not, however, met with such unqualified praise within feminist scholarship. Feminist evaluations of the historical significance of her writings for women vary considerably, reflecting debates around sexuality within contemporary feminism. Although it is generally acknowledged that texts such as *Married Love* provided women with a sexual role within marriage, the implications of her arguments for the legitimacy and importance of female (hetero-)sexual pleasure are subject to dispute.[7] Lesley Hall argues, for instance, that Stopes aimed to make "the marital relationship more pleasant for women and one in which they enjoyed greater power," but both Sheila Jeffreys and, more recently, Margaret Jackson view her writings on "married love" as profoundly disempowering for women primarily on the grounds of her appropriation of sexological models of human sexuality.[8] Thus for Jackson, Stopes's "initial commitment to female sexual autonomy" was "undermined by an essentially phallocentric model of sexuality in which sex was reduced to a coital imperative."[9]

While there's no getting away from the celebration of the delights of heterosexual intercourse in texts like *Married Love*, I would argue it is equally problematic to reduce Stopes's work to the sexological models upon which she drew in order to provide her vision of "sweet communion in the dusk" with the necessary scientific legitimation.[10] Such an approach diminishes those very aspects of her work that distinguish and differentiate it from the "scientific" texts of her male contemporaries. Although Stopes was trained as a scientist and well-respected in her field of paleobotany, as an advocate of sexual reform, she campaigned and wrote outside the institutions of the medical establishment, and in an area perceived to be a "male preserve."[11] Her transgression of the hallowed terrain of the medical establishment is evident in Dr Norman Haire's hardly veiled condemnation of her in an article in the *Practitioner* in July 1923, in which he castigated "non-medical doctors who write erotic treatises on birth control conveying misleading information in a highly stimulating form."[12]

Beyond the possibility that Haire, also a sex reformer, was not a little jealous of the success of his rival, at issue here is a distinction between the production of "primary" scientific research, and the transmission and dissemination of scientific discoveries in a popular form, a distinction that, as Barbara Gates has shown, has a long and gendered history.[13] In fact, contrary to Haire's suggestion, Stopes was extremely well-versed in contemporary theories of sexuality, having famously read "almost every learned treatise and medical account of sexual theory and practice in English, French and German" available in the British Library in her attempt to establish the cause of the miserable sexual relationship she experienced in her first marriage.[14] Many of her works also present so-called "original" research and findings; "I have some things to say about sex," she notes in the preface to Married Love, "which, so far as I am aware, have not yet been said."[15] However, despite these claims and her desire to be taken seriously as one involved in the "scientific" study of sexuality, medical professionals such as Haire persistently denied her writings scientific authority. This was not simply because she lacked medical credentials but also, one must conclude, because of the language and form in which she chose to write about sex, the related popularity of her texts, and, of course, her gender.

Most scholarly accounts of Stopes's work, particularly discussions of Married Love, note the poetic or literary qualities of her writing. Commenting on the lyrical nature of her descriptions of orgasm, Paul Ferris describes Stopes as an "imperious romantic" and associates the poetic tone of Married Love with its popular appeal.[16] Beyond acknowledging the literary tone and register of Stopes's writings, however, the significance of her engagement with literary discourses and aesthetics has not been adequately addressed. Hynes's comment that "for all its sentimental yearning and inexact science" Married Love should be viewed as "one of the documents that shaped post-war imaginations" misses the point somewhat, as if the form and tone of the text is somehow incidental to its cultural significance and popularity.[17] More recently, Hall's persuasive account of Stopes's attempts to "unite science and sensibility" begins to elaborate the conjunction of literary and scientific discourses in her writing but stops short of considering the wider implications of such a conjunction specifically in terms of the way in which Stopes's constructions of married love articulated and were shaped by prevailing notions of class and cultural distinction.[18]

Taking my cue from the excellent work produced by critics such as Barbara Gates and Ann Shteir on the role of women as "productive literary and artistic agents within science culture," this essay seeks to address the nature of Stopes's popular appeal to her audience.[19] Focusing upon a number of her works of sexual advice, chiefly Married Love (1918), Radiant Motherhood (1920), and Sex and the Young (1926), my aim is to explore the rhetoric of married love and the aesthetic and literary sensibility that pervades these writings. In doing so, I wish to consider the ways in which her works interpellate particular social constituencies and construct and evaluate heterosexual relations according to a range of interconnected social and aesthetic criteria. My argument is that the ideals of "married love" and "radiant motherhood" are constituted within these texts as middle-class cultural practices predicated upon their difference and distinction from the perceived sexual habits and behaviour of the working classes. In the context of her position as a middle-class woman working within a male domain, in addressing the intersection of literary, aesthetic, scientific, and class discourses in her writings, I wish to illuminate some of the ways in which she sought to define and legitimate her project to popularize sexual knowledge and also her right to speak about such a subject. For in exploring her discursive strategies, we can identify an attempt to "rescue" sex, not only from the vulgarity and "dirtiness" she associated with a working-class discourse of sexuality, but also from official, male-authored discourses on sexual science. Describing the experience of reading Havelock Ellis as "like breathing in a bag of soot," Stopes was at pains to emphasize her departure from the interest in the "perverse" and the "abnormal" she felt characterized psychoanalysis and sexology.[20] In this respect, her project to "cleanse" the sphere of sexuality with "normal soap," to propagate a vision of sex that was "safe" and socially acceptable for the respectable middle-classes, was also an assertion of her moral authority to write against the theoretical texts of male professionals in the field. Where they dwelt upon perversions and sexual neuroses, Stopes emphasized beauty, cleanliness, and spirituality, seeking to position herself as the proclaimer of a "new gospel" of sexuality that would revivify what she felt to be a degenerating culture.[21]

IN *SEX AND THE YOUNG* (1926), a book of advice to parents and teachers on the sexual education of children, Stopes argued that a significant barrier to progress in the fostering of a positive and healthy attitude towards (hetero)sexual relations was one of vocabulary, noting, "we must have words to use which enable those who consider sex a sacred, or at any rate serious, beautiful and dignified thing to express their meaning."[22] The neologism Stopes produced to fulfill this function was erogamic:

For the modern relation between man and woman mated or living in the innumerable interdependencies, the mutual obeisances, the mutual respects which are not paralleled at all in the sex relation of the primitive peoples or in the debased lives of the violently depraved, a clean, fresh, subtle word is wanted, and instead of the soiled and degraded word "sexual" life, for this new and elevated interplay between man and woman I propose the word erogamic life. . . . *For dictionary purposes the new word erogamic may be defined as: All that relation, in cultivated communities, between man and woman as mated pair which involves their mutual interplay and interdependencies in physical, mental and spiritual life.* (6–7; emphasis in original)

Stopes returned to the concept of erogamic life in *Enduring Passion* (1928), augmenting her initial definition:

Erogamic is a new word coined for the purpose of crystallising what I feel is a vital idea that is in our midst though yet scarcely recognised. The word is derived from the Greek: *eros*—love, and *gamos*—marriage or mating. I minted it with the intention that it shall designate that noble flower of the duality of human life, the mating and relation together of man and woman in all three planes—physical, mental and spiritual. The erogamic life is that which we who would elevate and enrich the relation between man and woman, hold up as standard. The physiological aspects of normal sex we all share with the animals as a physical basis in our lives; for the evolved interplay of man and woman we can speak of erogamic life and leave the ugly slimy sounding word "sexual" to those who still roll in the filth and who delight in the unclean echoes of the centuries.[23]

In coining "erogamic," Stopes forges a relationship between sexual and linguistic propriety, practicing what Deborah Cameron has termed "verbal hygiene." This term describes a process of critical reflection upon language "born out of an urge" to improve or to cleanse it. Cameron charts instances of verbal hygiene historically through the analysis of various projects ranging from debates around standard language and grammar to contemporary arguments about political correctness in written and spoken forms. This kind of work on language takes place on a decisively social terrain, for as Cameron puts it, "verbal hygiene and social or moral hygiene are interconnected; to argue about language is indirectly to argue about extra-linguistic values."[24] The connections between language, sexuality, and social and moral hygiene are explicitly asserted in Stopes's rationale for formulating a new vocabulary, although it is not entirely clear how these relationships are structured and mutually determined. She appears to link the social prohibitions that have historically surrounded the discussion of sexual matters to various sexual ills in the present, from the spread of venereal diseases to the sexual misery produced by the ignorance of both men and women; yet the rationale she provides for coining "erogamic" suggests that the term itself will play a constitutive role in fostering new and regenerated modes of sexual behaviour, moving beyond a sense of language as merely reflective of social and sexual behaviour to a sense of linguistic determinism.

The central issue for Stopes here is not the absence of a language of sexuality per se, but the absence of a socially legitimate language to express sexual matters. This legitimate language is repeatedly figured in her work in terms of hygiene; cleanliness and purity are set against filth, dirt, and contamination. As this indicates, it was not her intention to do away with the dirt but to redraw the boundaries between dirt and cleanliness and to elevate the erogamic practices of some against the slimy sexual filth of others. Of course, these oppositions are not socially neutral and she persistently locates the agents of contamination amongst the working classes, specifically those members of the working classes who came into daily and intimate contact with the middle classes (domestic servants, for example). A major area of anxiety in this respect is education and the dissemination of sexual information. As she argued in *Sex and the Young*, in the face of the linguistic prohibitions of polite society that restrict the flow of information, the curious middle-class child was often forced to turn from parents to servants to acquire knowledge of sex—and, hence, the vocabulary of—sex and sexuality: "Finding that it was socially taboo to speak of anything concerning sex among good class people the child listened eagerly in the servants' hall or the gutter and acquired a surprising amount of misinformation" (14). She reiterated the dangers of allowing a child to gain sexual information from an illicit source in her advice to parents that when teaching children about sex, they should impress upon them that they should never speak to anyone but their mother or father about the subject:

It is most important that the parents should take the greatest care to secure helps or nurses who will loyally adhere to such teaching and not interpolate anything of their own, and that the domestic staff, outdoor employees, retainers and any others with whom the child may come in frequent contact are instructed to reply to any such questions which may be asked them, "You must talk about that to your mamma." One nasty-minded maid-servant could do incalculable harm. (173-74)

As this suggests, there is more at stake than simply matters of vocabulary in the elevation of the concept of the "erogamic" and the devaluation of the language of the "sexual." As Pierre Bourdieu argues in another context, while this kind of evaluation may purport to describe a particular form of language, its premises are located, not "in the intrinsic properties of discourse itself, but rather in the social conditions of production and reproduction of the distribution between the classes of the knowledge and recognition of the legitimate language."[25] Stopes's engagement with language and sexuality is inextricably tied to questions of social authority and cultural power, middle-class parent versus maidservant, the language of the drawing room versus the language of the gutter, a socially legitimate discourse of sexuality versus an illicit, vulgar, and dangerous one.

In *Sex and the Young*, the putative correlation between sexual and physical dirtiness and the class discourse that underpins it is not limited to language alone, although the associations Stopes makes serve to legitimate her attempts to devalue and repudiate a working-class discourse of sexuality. She argues, for instance, that masturbation is far more common among the working classes:

One of the causes of undesirable local stimulus is irritation due to the lack of personal cleanliness. Coupled with the spontaneous feeling of developing sex, this local irritation induces fingering, leading to masturbation which otherwise might not have arisen. This is particularly likely to happen with lower class boys whose clothing is not so frequently washed and cleaned as is desirable and who are not accustomed in their poor hands to daily ablutions. (69)

In this passage, an explicit association is made between sexual behaviour and personal hygiene; dirty people, we are informed, engage in "dirty" sexual practices. In the context of her discussion of language, this correlation is extended to the realm of ideas and their dissemination, particularly regarding the language used to discuss sexual matters in the sense that "dirty" language is located as a key element in the production and reproduction of "dirty" sexual behavior. This associative chain is discernible, for instance, in her explanation of the genesis and spread of sexually transmitted diseases in an earlier work, *Truth About Venereal Disease* (1921):

The sex diseases would never have saddled themselves upon humanity had not all sex knowledge been befouled by prudery. For with a pure knowledge of sex no one could have endured foul unions, and no one could have tolerated an infectious disease as the associate of love. But through centuries children have learnt from dirty-minded servants, other children and school fellows, such filthy nonsense about sex.[26]

Here the "filthy nonsense" propagated by "dirty-minded servants" and other children is directly connected to the spread of sexual diseases, as if the infection and danger reside in the form of the discourse itself. Moreover, the passage identifies the dirty-minded servant as a key source of this "filthy" knowledge, thus establishing a causality that isolates the working classes as the agents of infection and threat. In *Sex and the Young*, Stopes almost obsessively returns to this perceived relationship between dirt, dirty speech, sexual danger, and the working classes:

The general lack of an honourable vocabulary is a very great national loss, and until a sound sex vocabulary can be incorporated into our national speech, vulgarity of language will be a sporadic offence. The vulgar terminology and the misapplication of ordinary words in vulgar senses which are characteristic of the gutter may issue from the lips of the most innocent and charming child. They may have been heard in the kitchen or on the streets. . . . Sheer dirtiness of mind will seldom be given much chance to be injurious in an ordinary class of nice-minded, healthy British children, whether boys or girls, but if as sometimes happens in large slums or city districts a considerable proportion of children have been nurtured in the gutter then vulgarity of diction may spread to all. (23–24)

Dirty language is viewed as a site of contamination, as Stopes figures the threat of a vulgar language through images of health and infection, going so far as to recommend the removal or segregation of the "foul mouthed child," arguing that the teacher has a duty "to try to have the child removed from a class that is suffering from its presence" (24). In locating the site of this linguistic contamination primarily within city slums, Stopes reproduces a dominant discourse of language that views urban space as the site of linguistic degradation.[27] There are certainly echoes here of the work of Margaret McMillan, the campaigner for nursery education, who wrote of the "defective" language of the slum-dwelling child with the same emphasis upon working-class language as "unhealthy" and degenerate, and of the educationalist George Sampson, who argued in 1925 that the "children of the poor" entered school with "their language in a state of disease."[28] Speaking to this anxiety about the relationship between the state of the language and cultural health, Stopes presents the problem in explicitly sexual terms, whereby the "vulgar language" of the slums is endowed with the menace and danger of a sexually transmitted disease. In a similar manner also to McMillan, who complained of the "rough, strained, ugly voices of the school," and Sampson, who characterized the language of working-class children as a "barely" recognizable "noise," Stopes's diagnosis of the dangers of dirty speech is derived not simply from the substance of such speech but from its perceived aesthetic qualities.[29] She writes of the "vulgarity of diction," thus moving from questions of vocabulary to questions of pronunciation, and thereby indicating a correlation between linguistic, sexual, and aesthetic proprieties, blurring the distinctions between the substance of spoken discourse and its form.

It is with a sense of the aesthetic criteria at stake in Stopes's evaluation of language and sexuality that I wish to return to the coining of erogamic. The neologism is offered on the basis that the language used to describe sexuality structures the mode of perception of sexuality. The term "sexual" is rejected both for its association with primitivism and purely animal passions and also because it sounds "ugly and slimy." She thus combines a moral evaluation of sexual behavior (the erogamic against the sexual) with an aesthetic judgement, indicating that both at the level of meaning and sound, "sexual" conveys a low, degraded, and regressive sexuality, while "erogamic" conveys a higher, exalted, and cultivated form of heterosexual union. In this sense, her explanation of the Greek roots of erogamic both signals and appeals to an educated sensibility. Using "erogamic" is not simply a sign of cultivation at the level of semantics; the constitution of the sign itself as a composite of two Greek terms expresses the higher values it conceptualizes, operating as a sign of education and learning, of symbolic capital.

In this respect, the legitimacy of "erogamic" as a sign of cultivated sexual relations is guaranteed by its distinctiveness and its departure from the ordinary and everyday usage of "sexual." Stopes's definitions are predicated upon the articulation of a number of oppositions: high/low, cleanliness/filth, cultivation/primitivism, and evolved interplay versus rolling in the mud. "Sexual" in this sense exhibits the looseness, lack of restraint, and disregard for boundaries and proprieties that Bourdieu, in his theorization of language and symbolic power, has pinpointed in relation to the representation of vulgar and commonplace language (Bourdieu, *Language*, 69). In contrast to this, "erogamic" is distinguished both semantically and in relation to its ascribed linguistic identity by its "cultivation" and control. This kind of evaluation is structured upon a social terrain, reproducing and asserting in the discursive hierarchies it evokes a hierarchy of social differences. When Stopes differentiates between the erogamic and the sexual, she differentiates between the sexual behaviour of different social groups.

However, Stopes's gloss on "sexual" is not altogether convincing, given the currency of the term not only within academic and medical discourses but also in her own writings. The sign "sexual" itself does not signal the filth and ugliness with which she associates it, although her emphasis upon how it sounds may point to a preoccupation with speech and to speakers, rather than simply the nature of the sign itself, again blurring the distinction between an attributed aesthetic quality and the social evaluation of speech. It is possible that she uses "sexual" in her definitions of erogamic as a metonym for vulgar language in general, and more specifically, for the dirty speech of those who delight in "rolling in the mud." The term may thus operate to signify a form of vulgar language without necessitating its reproduction and dissemination, enabling her to maintain the hygiene of her own text.

This engagement with questions of language in relation to the dissemination of sexual knowledge is clearly bound up with an evaluative process that seeks to assert the legitimacy of an "erogamic" discourse of sexuality (in all respects a middle-class property) and the dangers and degeneration associated with a working-class discourse. Yet, in endeavoring to legitimate this discourse, Stopes was not only repudiating the dirty speech of "nasty-minded" maids but also engaging in a dialogue with competing theories of sexuality, primarily psychoanalysis and sexology. As I noted above, one of the ways in which she sought to authorize her own project and position as a woman writing about sex was to assert her departure from what she saw as an unhealthy preoccupation with sexual abnormality or deviance in psychoanalytical and sexological writings. This strategy is clearly in evidence in *Sex and The Young* when she notes that the head of the school would be advised not to allow a large proportion of books dealing with abnormalities and perversions into the staff library:

The "sexologists" have quite unduly emphasised a mass of perversion and nastiness which even the adult members of a school staff may find contaminating. In addition to these some of the works of the "psycho-analysts" are filthy in the extreme, and I should hesitate to put them on open shelves even for adults. Some of these books contain ideas so contaminating that even a strong adult mind trained in sex matters like my own is filled with revulsion and disgust at their obscene suggestions. (Stopes, *Sex and the Young*, 87)

Here, the theoretical discourses of sexology and psychoanalysis are tarred (so to speak) with the same brush as a working-class discourse of sexuality; they are all "filthy" and share the capacity to "contaminate" those who come into close contact with them. Although Stopes was highly dismissive of Freudianism, her debt to works such as Havelock Ellis's *Studies in the Psychology of Sex* is well-documented, and Ellis himself was extremely supportive of her endeavors.[30] In this respect, her attack upon the unmitigated "obscenity" of her contemporaries masks a much closer and more complex relationship to the discourse of sexology. Yet as a rhetorical strategy, her rejection of this body of work is an attempt to assert her own moral authority by casting herself as the protector of moral and sexual health; the "cleanliness" and "beauty" of her erogamic discourse is contrasted with the "filth" and "nastiness" of those studies of the "sexual." There are elements here of the rhetoric of the social purity movement in which (middle-class) women were cast as the guardians of clean-living moral standards, to which men were exhorted to adhere. Although conservative in many ways, deployed in the context of a work of sexual advice, this rhetoric serves to valorize her position *as a woman* writing and campaigning about sexual matters by lending her voice a moral weight denied to her (predominantly male) contemporaries in the fields of sexology and psychoanalysis.

The minting of the term "erogamic" is one significant instance of a wider discernible process in Stopes's work whereby constructions of heterosexuality are constituted and evaluated in relation to social, moral, and cultural hierarchies. The discourse of married love is predicated upon the production of social and moral discriminations that differentiate the erogamic practices of the cultivated classes from the sexual habits of the working classes. In texts such as *Married Love*, *Radiant Motherhood*, and *Enduring Passion*, heterosexual relations are subject not simply to a moral or social evaluation but also to a set of evaluative aesthetic criteria, which are themselves structured according to the social and cultural values of a middle-class constituency.

Bourdieu's analysis in *Distinction* of the intelligible relationships between economic and social hierarchies and forms and perceptions of distinction at the level of taste, lifestyle, and cultural consumption provides an enabling theoretical framework through which to explore Stopes's writings with regards to the intersection of discourses of heterosexuality and perceptions of class, social identity, and sensibility. For Bourdieu, rather than embodying some absolute or universal value, aesthetic distinctions are historically and socially produced and related to social background, economic position, and educational experience; hierarchies of cultural practices correspond to the social hierarchy of consumers. One of his central propositions is that the production of "aesthetic" distinctions is not simply the province of consumers of "culture"— (in the "narrow" sense of the word)—but extends to "the most everyday choices of everyday life" from cooking to home decoration and fashion.[31] It is this argument about the relationship between social class and the attribution of evaluative aesthetic classifications upon a range of objects and cultural practices that is helpful in exploring the class resonances of the aesthetic sensibility characterizing Stopes's discourse of married love, although clearly Bourdieu's work can neither speak to the specific historical and cultural context in which Stopes wrote nor account for the strategies she deployed as a woman struggling to authorize her own voice as a professional in the field of sexual science.

One of the distinguishing features of Stopes's works of sexual advice is the significance she accords to forms of behavior and etiquette beyond the bedroom door, so to speak, in a way that serves to forge a relationship between sexual relations, lifestyle, and social and cultural practices. This operates to bind legitimate heterosexual relations to a middle-class habitus, as Bourdieu describes it, the set of dispositions characteristic of a particular class. For instance, in a chapter of *Married Love* entitled "Modesty and Romance," Stopes advises couples to perpetuate the mystique and the "keenness" of their relationship by avoiding everyday contact and, ideally, retaining separate bedrooms:

In the rather trivial terms of our sordid modern life, it works out in many marriages somewhat as follows: The married pair share a bedroom, and so it comes about that the two are together not only at the times of delight and interest in each other, but during most of the unlovely and even ridiculous proceedings of the toilet. Now it may *enchant a man once—perhaps even twice—or at long intervals—to watch* his goddess screw her hair up into a tight and unbecoming knot and soap her ears. But it is inherently too unlovely a proceeding to retain indefinite enchantment. . . . Hence, ultimately, everyday association in the commonplace daily necessities tends to reduce the keen pleasure each takes in the other. . . . Escape the lower, the trivial, the sordid. So far as possible (and this is far more possible than appears at first, and requires only a little care and rearrangement in the habits of the household) ensure that you allow your husband to come upon you only when there is delight in the meeting. (*Married Love*, 118–19, 121)

Beyond the implicit irony of the advice to couples to see as little as possible of each other in order to maintain a positive relationship, her injunction to "escape the lower, the trivial, the sordid" appeals to a middle-class imagination able to envisage separate bedrooms, or the rearrangement of the habits of the household. These comments are also predicated upon an aesthetic evaluation of the spatial arrangements that structure heterosexual relations, endowing the social and economic privilege enabling a couple to keep two bedrooms with an aesthetic value. As with the coining of erogamic, her advice is founded upon an opposition between the everyday, the commonplace, the merely corporeal and the rare and the "careful." Beauty and "enchantment" are held to be the province of the latter, while what is commonplace is necessarily unlovely, ridiculous, and sordid. This demarcation of the careful and lovely against the sordid and the trivial is bound up with a discourse of taste and discernment for, as Bourdieu argues, notions of taste are predicated upon a refusal of the merely pleasurable: The refusal of what is easy in the sense of simple, and therefore shallow, and "cheap," because it is easily decoded and culturally "undemanding," naturally leads to the refusal of what is facile in the ethical or aesthetic sense, of everything that offers pleasures that are too immediately accessible and so discredited as "childish" or "primitive" (Bourdieu, *Distinction*, 486). Throughout *Married Love*, sexual fulfillment is correlated with the possession or acquisition of certain skills, the conscious arrangement or rearrangement of lifestyle, and the development of an aesthetic sensibility. Stopes divides the proficient lover from the ignorant husband according to their "artistry," describing the path toward married love in explicitly cultural terms; an improved sex life is viewed as a process of acculturation, of learning an art and learning art appreciation, far from a simple pleasure. As she informs her readers, "only by learning to hold a bow correctly can one draw music from a violin" (*Married Love*, 30). And thus: "Only by a reverent study of the Art of Love can the beauty of its expression be realised in linked lives. And even when once learnt, the Art of Love takes time to practise" (38).

The conceptualization of an ideal heterosexuality as a kind of cultural practice also emerges in her writings on motherhood. In *Radiant Motherhood* (1920), she offers advice to prospective mothers on the "*creation of a new and irradiated race.*"[32] The text itself is organized into chapters with titles such as "The Lover's Dream," "Conceived in Beauty," and "The Gateway of Pain," designed to appeal to a romantic literary sensibility. This appeal is further expressed through the epigrams to the chapters, taken from texts by writers such as Spencer, Milton, and Dante Gabriel Rosetti, signs of a cultivated sensibility addressing itself to a cultivated readership. The advice itself posits an explicit relationship between maternity and cultivation as a form of acculturation. Take, for instance, the following advice to women in the early months of pregnancy:

In my opinion, undoubtedly the ideal way of spending the earlier months of coming parenthood is in the form of an extended honeymoon, in which the couple travelling slowly should follow the guide of seasonal beauty or should visit place after place of historic interest or natural charm so that the mother's mind should be fed and stimulated by historic memories, by the exquisite freshness of nature, and the grandeur of man's artistic achievements. (Stopes, *Radiant*, 50)

Here, an ideal motherhood is conceptualized as a process of cultivation aided by an engagement with beauty in a number of forms: nature, the arts, and historical monuments. Again, the emphasis is on a departure from the everyday and the commonplace; the ideal form of cultivation to which all expectant mothers should aspire is hardly easy to achieve. It is certainly not an option open to the majority of prospective parents, although this is possibly the point. The ideal way to behave is characterized by its distinction and difference from the norm, just as beauty and cultivation are the antithesis of the banal and the facile. Stopes acknowledges, however, that not every prospective mother will find herself in a position to take an extended honeymoon, and suggests, in its place, a more accessible form of cultivation: "The mother by reading and conversation can, if she has a kind of trained imagination, vary and enrich the mental environment of her child while it is developing" (50–51). Although this suggestion appears to be more readily attainable, it is still delimited; reading and conversation are posited as forms of cultivation capable of enriching the child's development *in utero* only if the mother "has a kind of trained imagination" (50–51). This transposition of forms of cultural distinction onto the suggested prenatal activities of the prospective mother also extends to other related areas of lifestyle and consumption. Commenting, for instance, on the appropriate style and manner of dressing during pregnancy, she suggests: "the standard of dressing for the prospective mother, whose garments should be of the lightest wool and silk if possible, ... should be so lightly hung that a butterfly can walk the length of her body without tearing its wings" (89). This description of dress fabric offers an image of delicacy and sensitivity that hardly bares translation into the physicality of everyday life. Although the price of such a standard of dress in financial terms is not mentioned, the quality of the fabric insisted upon signifies affluence while the image of the butterfly, delicate wings intact, naturalizes the union between aesthetic value and economic cost. Maternity wear, subject to the scrutiny and particularity of an aesthetic sensibility, becomes another marker of cultural distinction, differentiating the radiant mother from her poorer sister.

∾

AS THIS CHAPTER HAS SHOWN, Stopes's elaboration of the "art of love" moves persistently from the sphere of sexual practice alone to other spheres of lifestyle and cultural consumption, rendering the "perfection" of married heterosexual relations contingent upon an engagement with other forms of cultural activity, from the arrangement of a household and the viewing of historical monuments and works of art to the possession of the finest fabrics during pregnancy. Indissolubly fused with the sensibility and aspirations of a middle-class constituency, certain forms of sexual behavior are imbued with a cultural value, in that the ideal of married love is predicated both upon the development of an aesthetic sensibility and the product of a process of acculturation. Particular practices and discourses of sexuality are thus evaluated in relation to a hierarchy of class and cultural distinctions. For what secures the morality and respectability of the erogamic language and practices Stopes envisions is the sense that they are limited and evaluative, marking the good from the bad, the normative from the deviant, the high from the low, the clean from the dirty, the cultivated from the primitive. Erogamic sexual intercourse achieves its legitimacy as a sign of cultural distinction and as a socially specific practice.

NOTES

1. Margaret Jackson, *The Real Facts of Life: Feminism and the Politics of Sexuality c. 1850–1940* (London: Taylor & Francis, 1994), 129.

2. Paul Ferris, *Sex and the British: A Twentieth-Century History* (London: Mandarin, 1994), 112; Cate Haste, *Rules of Desire: Sex in Britain in World War I to the Present* (London: Pimlico, 1992), 60.

3. Lesley A. Hall, "Uniting Science and Sensibility: Marie Stopes and the Narrative of Marriage in the 1920s," in *Rediscovering Forgotten Radicals: British Women Writers, 1889–1939*, ed. Angela Ingram and Daphne Patai (Chapel Hill: University of North Carolina Press, 1993), 119.

4. Coward's song is quoted in full as an epigram to Annette Kuhn's chapter on Stopes in her *Cinema, Censorship and Sexuality, 1909–1925* (London: Routledge, 1988), 75.

5. See Hall, "Uniting Science and Sensibility," 119, and Kuhn, *Cinema, Censorship and Sexuality*, 77.

6. Samuel Hynes, *A War Imagined: The First World War and English Culture* (London: Bodley Head, 1990), 366, 368–69.

7. See Ellen Holtzman, "The Pursuit of Married Love: Women's Attitudes Towards Sexuality and Marriage in Great Britain, 1918–1939," *Journal of Science History* 16, 2 (1982): 39–51.

8. Hall, "Uniting Science and Sensibility," 122; Sheila Jeffreys, *The Spinster and Her Enemies: Feminism and Sexuality, 1880–1930* (London: Pandora Press, 1985), 120–21; Margaret Jackson, *Real Facts of Life*, 148–49, 155.

9. Jackson, *Real Facts of Life*, 155.

10. Marie Stopes, *Married Love: A New Contribution to the Solution of Sex Difficulties*, 10th ed. (London: Putnam, 1922), 25.

11. Barbara Gates, *Kindred Nature: Victorian and Edwardian Women Embrace the Living World* (Chicago: University of Chicago Press, 1998), 109.

12. As quoted by Ruth Hall, *Marie Stopes: A Biography* (1977; London: Virago, 1978), 261.

13. See Gates, *Kindred Nature.*

14. June Rose, *Marie Stopes and the Sexual Revolution* (London: Faber & Faber, 1992), 77.

15. Stopes, *Married Love*, 15.

16. Ferris, *Sex and the British*, 109.

17. Hynes, *War Imagined*, 366.

18. See Hall, "Uniting Science and Sensibility."

19. *Natural Eloquence: Women Reinscribe Science*, ed. Barbara T. Gates and Ann B. Shteir (Wisconsin: University of Wisconsin Press, 1997), 3.

20. June Rose, *Marie Stopes and the Sexual Revolution* (London: Faber & Faber, 1992), 112.

21. See Marie Stopes, *A New Gospel: A Revelation of God Uniting Physiology and the Religion of Man* (London: Putnam, 1920), for a description of her divine inspiration.

22. Marie Stopes, *Sex and the Young* (London: Putnam, 1926), 4. Subsequent citations are given parenthetically in the text.

23. Marie Stopes, *Enduring Passion*, 6th ed. (London: Putnam, 1936), 14–15.

24. Deborah Cameron, *Verbal Hygiene* (London: Routledge, 1995), 1, 114.

25. Pierre Bourdieu, *Language and Symbolic Power*, ed. John B. Thompson, trans. Gino Raymond and Matthew Adamson (Cambridge: Polity Press, 1991), 113. Subsequent citations are given parenthetically in the text.

26. Marie Stopes, *Truth About Venereal Disease: A Practical Handbook on a Subject of Most Urgent National Importance* (London: Putnam, 1921), 46.

27. See Tony Crowley, *Language in History: Theories and Texts* (London: Routledge, 1996), 168–69.

28. See Carolyn Steedman, *Childhood, Culture and Class in Britain: Margaret McMillan 1860–1931* (London: Virago; New Brunswick, N.J.: Rutgers University Press, 1990), 218–19; Crowley, *Language in History*, 176.

29. See Steedman, *Childhood*, 218; Crowley, *Language in History*, 242.

30. Rose, *Marie Stopes*, 112.

31. Pierre Bourdieu, *Distinction: A Social Critique of the Judgement of Taste*, trans. Richard Nice (London: Routledge & Kegan Paul, 1984), 5–6. Subsequent citations are given parenthetically in the text.

32. Marie Stopes, *Radiant Motherhood: A Book for Those Who Are Creating the Future* (London: Putnam, 1920), 3. Subsequent citations are given parenthetically in the text.

Shift Work

Observing Women Observing, 1937–1945

ROBBIE: And do you do anything else? I have a feeling you work at something.
ISABEL: I observe.
ROBBIE: Yes, I'd noticed that! I do too—when I remember.
ISABEL: No. I observe professionally. When the King abdicated, various people got very interested in the reaction of the masses, in "primitive reactions" as they were called. In measuring them scientifically.
ROBBIE: Primitive reactions—I know all about those!
ISABEL: Yes—so they recruited people to conduct surveys into what the masses were really thinking—by sitting in pubs, standing in bus queues, being amongst them at the races. Mass Observation. Noting everything down they saw and heard. (She smiles.) I do that.

—Stephen Poliakoff, *Talk of the City*

February 1937. London. Isabel is one of a growing number of men and women working for a new social research organization called Mass-Observation (M-O). Robbie is the "mercurial master of ceremonies" of a popular radio variety show, *Friday Night at Eight*. Both sit sipping cocktails in a nightclub waiting for Clive, the brilliant but arrogant producer from BBC Talks. Together, these three will devise a new form of radio documentary to deliver the truth about anti-Semitism in Hitler's Germany to an otherwise anaesthetized British public.

Fast forward to January 1939. Isabel has moved to the Ministry of Information (MOI) where she now interprets the surveys that she once collected. Robbie is being wooed by the U.S. market in the form of Walt Disney. Clive has just returned from Germany with firsthand testimony of the violence directed at Jews by the Nazi regime. By the end of the play, Isabel will lie dead on her bedroom floor, driven to suicide by the failure of the Munich peace accord, the threat of a second world war, and by her role as witness to Clive and Robbie's reenactment of Nazi atrocities. She has been dead for a long time, she says, trapped at the moment in 1918 when she learned that her brother was dead. She "can't watch any more" (124).

Stephen Poliakoff's *Talk of the City* plots one line of institutional hiatus for the documentary movement of the 1930s and a literal death for Isabel and M-O. His feminization of M-O reduces the organization to little more than a vicarious mode of existence, a way for Isabel to generate some semblance of emotion by miming the life that others live around her. Observing lovers in Blackpool for a survey on sexual mores makes her feel sexy (54). Observing immigrants in the customs house "makes her feel their need" (109). Isabel watches: she does not act. While the play supports her contention that "it's not rubbish to try and work out for the first time what the mass of people are thinking, rather than just guessing—or not caring" (37), M-O, it decides, is unhealthy, and, for Isabel, lethal. The play remains faithful to the all too familiar tropes of modernity, then, plotting a solipsistic morality tale of mounting female hysteria, casting Isabel as the sacrificial victim whose figurative death in 1918 and literal death in 1939 punctuate the lives of the men around her. The play projects female identity as a kind of synchronic time out of time, a time of looking and not acting.

But this chapter is not about this particular Isabel. It is instead a study of the women upon whom Isabel is based: the mass-observers, BBC researchers, Post Office workers, market research employees, Home Intelligence operatives, and volunteers who were drawn into the MOI as a network for gauging public morale as the events of World War II escalated. It responds to the guiding questions of Rita Felski's *The Gender of Modernity* (1995)—"How would our understanding of modernity change if instead of taking male experience as paradigmatic, we were to look instead at texts written by women[?] And what if feminine phenomena, often seen as having a secondary or marginal status, were given a central importance in the analysis of the culture of modernity[?]"[1]—by shifting critical attention from the production of forgotten aesthetic objects by women to the frequently invisible labor of women who took notes, learned shorthand, collected and processed information, wrote memos, compiled reports, kept diaries.

The key here is to understand the products of institutional actors like the BBC, MOI, and M-O, or the factory, as what the sociologist Bruno Latour calls "the congealed labor" of the men and women who made them.[2] It is in this sense that my title, "shift work," may be understood. "Shift work" combines two different registers. It refers first to a mode of production that involves successive relays of workers, and so alludes to the division of labor that drew women into the British war machine in World War II. The word "shift" refers also to the concept of "shifters" or deictic markers, "terms from semiotics to designate the act of signification through which a text relates different frames of reference (here, now, I) to one another."[3] "Shift work" foregrounds the centrality of the labor (both literal and discursive) that goes into producing institutional actors and their products. "Shift work" asks us to approach the matter of textuality differently, to understand a report lying on the desk of the cabinet secretary or a radar installation as an investment of men, women, information, matter, and time that links radically separated spheres of action.

Billed as a mode of recovery, a "shift" from the productions of men and a truncated view of aesthetics to consider the everyday productions of women, this essay continues the valuable work of recovery by feminist scholars. Ultimately, however, "shift work" implies a more thoroughgoing response to *The Gender of Modernity*'s guiding questions. The very notion of "recovery," it implies, is inadequate to the task to which Felski enjoins us. For what is at stake is not merely an act of textual recovery but the narrative function of the modern within our histories, and the possibility not merely of assembling a parallel or alternative gendered text of modernity, but of telling an entirely different kind of story. My hope is that by learning to speak not simply of human agents but of texts as the productions of collectives of humans (men and women) and nonhumans (animals, facts, technological objects), we can begin to write the story anew, to imagine a version of the story written outside the terms and tropes of the so-called "Great Divide" of modernist high seriousness and everyday life.[4] As we shall see, it was exactly this last hope that gave impetus also to that most confused and contradictory of enterprises, M-O.

Anthropology at Home

On January 30, 1937, a letter appeared in the *New Statesman and Nation* announcing the arrival of a new social actor on the national scene. "Mass-Observation" was formed by Tom Harrisson, an ornithologist, anthropologist, journalist, and adventurer, Humphrey Jennings, a documentary filmmaker, and Charles Madge, a journalist and surrealist poet, in response to the call for "an anthropology of ourselves" made by Geoffrey Pyke in a letter arising out of the

Simpson affair in 1936.[5] Pyke identified the "sexual scene" of the crisis over the abdication of King Edward VIII as the nation's primal scene, the trigger for a systemwide crisis of representation that revealed the gulf between those who ruled and the mass they governed. It was to this crisis that M-O would minister, offering itself as a kind of surrogate, responding to the loss of faith in the representational mechanisms of the state by representing the voices of the mass to all who cared to listen.

Taking up where Darwin, Marx, Taylor, Breuer, and Freud left off, M-O would "work with a mass of observers" to study everyday culture rather than "primitives and abnormals." Ultimately, it envisaged "a complete plan of campaign," requiring a total of about 5,000 members, who would focus their efforts on, among other things, "Behavior of people at war memorials. Shouts and gestures of motorists. The aspidistra cult. Anthropology of the football pools. Bathroom behavior. Beards, armpits, eyebrows. Anti-Semitism. Distribution, diffusion, and significance of the dirty joke. Funerals and undertakers. Female taboos about eating. The private lives of midwives." The "multitude" of observers would enable the organization to keep a "continuous watch" on the daily press for "popular images" and "symbolism" that might reveal the national "unconscious or repressed," enabling M-O to decide whether, for example "the outbreak of parturition-images in the press last October . . . [was] seasonal or . . . [the result of] some public stimulus." They would "provide the points from which can be plotted weather maps of public feeling during a crisis" (155). The mass of observers would guarantee the objectivity of the data. The objectivity of the data would guarantee the facticity or scientificity of M-O's findings. And these "mass facts" would free the masses from their dependence upon authorized modes of news reporting—the government and the media.

Amounting almost to a psychoanalysis of culture, minus the theoretical self-awareness of the Frankfurt School, M-O proposed to diagnose the masses and prescribe treatment—a self-help version of Freud's talking cure delivered by publications authored not by individuals but by a new collective, "M-O." M-O did indeed go on to analyze all kinds of "problems," producing reports, pamphlets, and books, such as *May the Twelfth* (1937) and *Britain by Mass-Observation* (1939), that pitted the multiple observations of its members against state-sponsored narratives of the coronation of George VI and the state of Europe. At its height, M-O even produced a magazine called *Us*, financed by popular subscription.

In its initial stages, Madge and Jennings recruited what would become known as the National Panel, a group of some 2,000 volunteers "whose first duty was to keep one-day diaries on the twelfth of each month"[6] and also to respond to directives asking them to comment on their attitudes to specific issues, as well as those of their family, friends, neighbors.[7] Harrisson recruited a group of artists, writers, and intellectuals to form a group of "professional observers" to study working-class life and leisure in Bolton and Blackpool. The "Worktown study," as it was called, owed much to Victorian social investigation and the journalistic techniques of George Orwell's *The Road to Wigan Pier* (1937). Together, these very different groups formed the members of M-O's alternative, "democratic parliament."[8] It was their diaries, reports, and responses, which they mailed into M-O on the 12th of every month (in memory of May 12, 1937, the date of King George VI's coronation), that M-O shifted from the everyday world of living rooms, street corners, newsagents, pubs, and factory floors, into the pages of its printed texts.

Within the panel, each observer was understood to be one point in a complex meteorological chart, and represented abstractly as a point in space surrounded by a series of concentric frames of reference that comprise "the social horizon of the observer" (Fig. 16.1). "The innermost circle (1) . . . includes the Observer's family, people in the same employment, regular customers, regular tradespeople, roundsmen, postmen, etc"—everyone that the observer might meet habitually. The second "(2) . . . includes strangers, newcomers, [and] chance acquaintances." The third and "outermost circle (3) consists of people and institutions whose pressure and contact is less direct . . . but no less effective."[9] Responses to directives could be mapped according to this abstract scheme, and statements located in one of the three spheres of action. Additionally, statements could be classed according to a system of powers, "(x1)," "(x2)," or "(x3)," depending on whether the observer "describes himself as: Meeting people, Seeing people . . . [or] Hearing of People, Talking of people . . . [or more convoluted still] Hearing of people known to the person one is talking to but not to oneself, [or] Reading an account by a second person of a third."[10]

At stake in these frames of reference was nothing less than the "objectivity" of the data, M-O's way of shifting the raw material of observation from the world of the everyday into the realm of "mass fact." As Latour observes, "the word for 'reference' comes from the Latin referre, 'to bring back.'"[11] "Reference," he adds, "is not simply the act of pointing or a way of keeping, on the

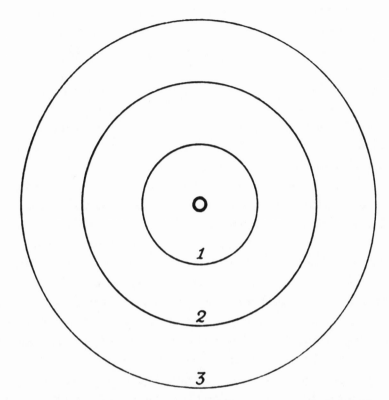

FIG. 16.1. "The Social Horizon of the Observer." *From May the Twelfth: Mass-Observation Day-Surveys, 1937*, ed. Humphrey Jennings, Charles Madge et al. (London: Faber & Faber, *1937*). Reproduced with permission of Curtis Brown Group Ltd, London, on behalf of the Trustees of the Mass-Observation Archive. Copyright Trustees of the Mass-Observation Archive.

outside, some material guarantee for the truth of a statement, rather it is our way of keeping something constant through a series of transformations."[12] "If the chain is interrupted at any point, it ceases to transport truth."[13] It was the security of this chain that M-O's directives sought to maintain. M-O asked its observers to monitor their observations and to record the time, the place, and the signs they decoded, keeping the information stable as it traveled from the act of observing to the moment of sorting and interpretation. If the chains of reference were secure, M-O could represent itself as a purely instrumental or technological object—a camera, or perhaps a radio. "Through M-O," wrote

Harrisson and Madge, "you can already listen-in to the movements of popular habit and opinion. The receiving set is there, and every month makes it more effective."[14] The voice of the collective was out there, circulating through the air. All you had to do was listen.

Critical assessments of M-O have been mixed. On the one hand, the M-O archive has served as an invaluable resource of primary materials for feminist historians, enabling them to reconstruct women's "experience" of World War II. On the other, M-O has fallen foul of Marxism and cultural studies because of its ambiguous relation to the mass it represents. Part of the problem, as Stuart Laing notes, is that the word "mass" has something of a checkered history among left and left-leaning groups. Citing Raymond Williams's conclusion to *Culture and Society*, Laing reminds us that "he saw it as a way of seeing people as objects," as but one further reification of social life under capitalism.[15] The fact that, as the war eclipsed the traumas of the abdication crisis, M-O's information was increasingly used simply, as Penny Summerfield tells us, to "offer guidance on how to wield power more effectively, by telling leaders how to lead, managers how to manage and salesmen how to sell" seems only to confirm Williams's fears.[16] Indeed, James Buzzard reads M-O as little more than one of the false communities that it sought to demystify, a kind of middle-class, left-leaning parody of modernist form. "Volunteers were not so much contributing to some collective project," he writes, "as assisting themselves to rise above superstitions of collectivity."[17] For him, M-O serves as a case study of the limitations of "Weapons of the Weak approaches to the study of popular culture,"[18] a cautionary example of what goes wrong when we fail to appreciate the ways in which "the putative subversions" of the weak may "in the long run shore up rather than fundamentally challenge authority, by siphoning off dangerous energies in trivial or ephemeral protests."[19] M-O, so it would seem, precluded mass resistance.

These are strong reservations. But I suggest that these critics demand too pure a form of resistance. Of course, M-O offered its practitioners "imaginary" ideological compensations for their work; of course, as it developed and began to succeed in its mission, it was conscripted by the mechanisms of the state. What should we expect other than a gradual hegemonic sponsorship and normalization of the kinds of social activism it articulated? We should be careful also not to underestimate the power of M-O's observers to reroute its complex procedures, or to regard their involvement as mere passive consumption of its invitation to observe.[20] M-O was a thoroughly contradictory entity, with as many heads and voices as participants. On the one hand, it asked the mass to "speak for itself"; on the other, it aimed to penetrate working-class culture. Everywhere, it traded in "mass-facts," marketing the discourse of everyday "experience" as a kind of capital, as the very measure of social truth. M-O should be understood neither as a resistance movement nor as a sublation of revolutionary energy, but as a complex chain of references and textual links, maintained by the postal service and at its head office in the form of an archive of materials that far exceeds the sum of the published books and reports it produced. In Latour's terms, M-O was one of those "hybrids of nature and culture," promiscuous joinings of humans and nonhumans, that are the distinctive product of the modern.[21] The modern constitution, argues Latour, insists upon absolute, ontologically distinct zones or dichotomies: nature/culture, world/language, nonhuman/human, hard/soft. It insists on the gap between the two poles, insists on their purity, and yet everywhere produces agents and actors, assemblages or mixtures, that enable the gap to be negotiated or translated. M-O is one of these hybrids, one of these translators. And it is within the chains of reference that it so carefully documented that we discover the ways in which one group of women were inducted into one particular "experience" of modernity.

Shift Workers

Poliakoff's Isabel "observes professionally." But she is hardly typical of the majority of women who volunteered as mass-observers between 1937 and 1945. Meet Muriel Green, one of some 500 diarists who agreed to record the daily events of their lives for M-O during World War II. Reading her diary, we learn all sorts of information about the everyday realities of wartime Britain for a young woman of nineteen working in her father's garage. The Greens "make Yorkshire tea-cakes with yeast now because they have no butter in them like other cakes."[22] "Mother ha[s their] cat Henry Hall shot" (80); Happy, the older cat who "eats so very little," hides and so escapes this fate. Alec the tortoise, "who did not eat anything anyone else could have eaten" (86), dies of natural causes. Muriel visits an aerodrome; goes to Cambridge with her sister for a WEA meeting; the two get angry that none of the bookstores in Lynn stock M-O's publications. Mother is annoyed because Muriel has a "new French correspondent . . . a man . . . and says she knows all Frenchmen are immoral" (88). Jenny "feel[s] particularly bumptious" the day she is described as a "young woman" in an M-O pamphlet. Muriel remains a "garage girl" (89). Both take immense pleasure in the "14 . . . and 25 lines" each has published in "'our' book (We always call it 'ours,'" writes Muriel, "hope M-O doesn't mind, but you see we've never had anything we've written in print before)" (88).

The events that Muriel describes, the scenes of home life, the recipe for tea cakes, the tragedy of Henry Hall, her French pen pal, are signs that we accept as indications of everyday immediacy, of an "ordinariness," that insists upon the transparency of her words. It is frequently tempting simply to quote large passages from such diaries to supplement our understanding of modernity with voices that have long gone unheard. The mere act of naming Muriel Green, a woman whom the founders of M-O never met, already changes the texture of the history we are trying to reimagine. And yet, what is most striking is less this everyday immediacy than the role played by a strange-sounding organization, "good old M-O," as Green calls it, in soliciting her thoughts, in providing her with an implied audience for her text, and so in inducting her into a community of observers whose words it used in its reports and publications, authored not by individuals but a nonhuman agent, M-O itself.

The form this solicitation took was complex. As Penny Summerfield reminds us, "the vast majority of women [who replied to M-O] classified themselves as housewives"[23] from lower-middle-class backgrounds, and were "either single or older married women with grown-up children."[24] Responses to a directive asking observers "Why I joined Mass-Observation" at the end of 1937 demonstrate that the reasons for women's participation in M-O were not reducible to a single set of motivations. Mrs. Grant from Gateshead, for example, became an observer because M-O seemed "fresh . . . human" and because of "the unselfish wish to help clever young men who do things."[25] Mrs. Aldington from Burnley in Lancashire joined in order to hone her observational skills and "gain . . . a power of detachment and an impersonal and accurate way of observing life."[26] Miss Fisher from London maintained that the chief benefits of the organization were for the observers rather than the world at large;[27] her fellow Londoner, and parenthetically self-declaring "(left wing Marxist)," Miss Earnshaw, found that "M-O fills the gap" and made "political activity seem a possibility."[28]

M-O appealed to women for a range of reasons: its focus on everyday life meant that it was compatible with the realities of domestic work and childcare; it was not particularly invasive; nor was it necessarily political or embarrassing. Implicitly valorizing women's everyday life, M-O seemed to invite women to enter the public sphere. The opportunity for anonymous publication in pamphlets and books that circulated nationally offered women the chance to have an impact on national politics, enfranchising their views in a way that voting rights perhaps had not. There was also a subtle understanding of a complex division of political labor. Women produced observations that would become the mass facts of M-O. And this careful, objective process was understood to produce both social change and a cadre of new social actors: "young men who do things." *Talk of the City* puts this gendered division of labor to dramatic effect, casting Isabel as lover, friend, and co-worker to the commanding Clive.

The coincidence of M-O's sponsorship by the MOI in 1939 with the induction of Britain's female population into the British war machine changed the everyday operations of the organization. M-O devolved control of the National Panel, inviting its members to keep undirected, daily diaries (some 500 responded), while professional observers worked directly with the MOI. As the workforce changed, so did M-O's focus. During the first three years of the 1940s, M-O began to focus its attention more squarely on women as a subject for study. In 1939, Harrisson wrote that "women are bearing the brunt in this home-fronted war. I believe that the way they react to the strain may largely determine the outcome. And I see everywhere . . . very little sign that the woman's point of view matters nearly as much as the man's. This war is being led by men and run by men, mostly old men."[29] The rhetorical identification between women and young men as against the old men who were running the war characterized the way M-O conserved its populist agenda. Nevertheless, it worked hard to fashion a united front, producing numerous reports, funded by the MOI, focusing on how the authorities might better appeal to women, and accepting a grant from the department store chain Marks & Spencer that "enabled them to start studying women's lives, particularly those of the woman at home."[30]

Following the introduction of conscription in 1941, M-O was commissioned to undertake a study of women factory workers by Ekco Limited, a manufacturer of radar equipment, and so to deal with the mounting scandal that not all of England's women were exultantly taking their place on the factory floor as the MOI's inspirational posters (Fig. 16.2), adapted from Soviet socialist realism, suggested. The poster depicts a woman, hair tied back and covered, arms outstretched, with her back to the factory in which she works. A

FIG. 16.2. "Women of Britain Come into the Factories." Courtesy of the Imperial War Museum, London.

stream of aircraft passes overhead, and a row of tanks marshals to her right. The poster seizes on the ecstatic moment of production, focusing not on the fact of labor or even on what kind of labor is necessary to produce these planes and tanks. Instead, it presents the woman as herself a kind of product—a product that the women of England must fashion, rerouting their footsteps to the labor exchange and to the factory. The poster represents the structurally invisible labor of the factory in order to produce the swell of patriotic feeling necessary to produce the workforce needed to manufacture the parts for tanks and planes but, more often, for equipment whose purpose was unknown or that was not for immediate use.

Such posters mark only the fine edge of a larger campaign that mobilized the resources of the MOI, leading to inspirational films such as *Millions Like Us* (1943), which Jenny Hartley has used as a metaphor for approaching women's wartime careers. The film tells the story of Celia, who is shifted into factory work. As Hartley observes, "with its recourse to Beethoven symphonies and shots of purposeful workers, the film unashamedly adopts the heroic tone."[31] We discover that "in Celia's factory there seems to be no fatigue or boredom, and as the foreman says, she has the satisfaction of knowing that 'You'll be making something.'" The realities were, of course, quite different: and to middle-class women, especially, "the factories offered nothing but sweat, fatigue and poor pay."[32] Women did not meet the demands made upon them with the same ecstasy of fulfillment as the M-O poster's anglicized Soviet woman, and there developed a significant counternarrative, emblematized best perhaps in Inez Holden's *There's No Story There* (1943), whose title emphatically insists on the anti-narrative basis of factory work. In Holden's factory, "the character who attempts a Mass-Observation study loses his notebook in the snow," and whatever sense of community there is emerges as the result of the suspended routines of a blizzard.[33] The weather, rather than ideology, generates a sense of belonging.

M-O appeared to have both the resources and the analytic ability to address this problem. Ekco Ltd approached M-O, who inserted a "highly trained and experienced Cambridge graduate, married, one child"[34] who had "worked for Mass-Observation for the past four years" into the factory, thereby "short-circuiting normal channels through which information filters." While this arrangement broke M-O's usual practice of employing a "team of trained objective investigators," "owing to the small size of the unit and the difficult problems of security . . . it was decided . . . that the study should be made by one investigator moving about within the framework of the problem" (5, 6–7). The resulting report, written entirely by Celia Fremlin, but listed as authored by "Mass-Observation" and "edited" by Tom Harrisson, was published in 1943 by Victor Gollancz with the title *The War Factory*. While Hartley sponsors an important reattribution within our bibliographies, citing Fremlin as the author, it is imperative that we consider this text not as the work of one person but as a complex combination of different spheres of reference, of human and institutional agencies.

"I found the poems in the fields,/And only wrote them down . . ." the book proclaims in an opening salvo from John Clare, offering itself up as the unmediated, objective results of M-O's trademark mass-observation techniques. But a short prefatory note identifies M-O as a consultant or neutral research team used by "many political, social, commercial and official bodies . . . in peace and war" (5, 2). Gone is the commitment to the mass. Likewise, the dedication page includes this short but revealing note on class terminology: "NOTE: In this book income levels ("class") are indicated by a simple code, thus: A = Rich people. B = 'The Middle Classes.' C = Artisans and skilled workers. D = Unskilled workers and the least economically or educationally trained third of our people." The report proceeds as a typology of working women, using this rudimentary alphabetical code as a guide to understanding the resistance of certain class-marked groups to conscription.[35]

The book transcribes every detail of Fremlin's original report, prefaced with Harrisson's remarks, and footnoted with "the Works and Labor Manager's remarks . . . printed as written on the MSS., and without comment."[36] "They give a view not directly studied in the survey," adds Harrisson, neglecting to tell us that not a single worker in the factory was ever told that a study was under way. Working according to a rhetoric of unattributed quotation, whereby transcriptions of overheard conversation are shifted directly from the factory floor into the text of the report via undocumented methods, the text describes a trajectory through the factory that mimics the arrival of the workers and the realities of a working day. At 8 A.M., "the factory buzzer sounds and a wild scramble starts at the entrance of the machine shop" (23). And so, we learn about the town; find our way to the factory; spend a day in the machine shop. Fremlin records the frenzy of activity as day workers exchange shifts with night workers, and the factory is in movement. Disembodied voices emerge from the hubbub to testify to the confusion of the morning:

"Oh, my lord, my handbag's come open again. Thought I'd lost it that time. OH, my lord, they'll be having the arms off me before they're through!"

"Come on, sister. Give him a shove! You won't get nowhere without you shove for it!"

"Oh, my foot!"

"You shouldn't leave it on the floor, then it wouldn't get trod on." (General laugh from immediate neighborhood.)

"O-ooh! This'll be the finish of me!"   (23–24)

We follow these women to their work; listen into their conversations; watch for "the first signs of slacking off" (27); and follow them into the cloakroom.

In the machine shop, we meet the "machine-shop girls," Hilda, Peggy, Edith, Clarie, Sadie. These are "D-class" girls, Fremlin notes, "with no experience whatever of industrial work, or indeed of any organized work in a community" (31). Hilda "is a heavy girl of about twenty-eight" (32), "Peggy is a lively very good-looking girl of twenty, with lovely naturally-wavy hair" (33), Edith is "a very sweet, gentle girl of twenty-two ... married with two babies" (34), "Clarie is fifteen, though she might easily be taken as twenty" and is "invariably so tired and sleepy it is hard to tell what her real potentialities are" (36), Molly is "a queer old-fashioned looking little thing, with glasses, and a rather childlike voice ... she is the only girl who positively enjoys the work" (37), and then there is Sadie, who "is usually working on one of the hand-presses. She is a slow, very good-natured girl" (40). None of the "girls" have a truly interested relationship to their work. And none work from a patriotic sense of duty. All speak of their relation to the work in terms of an exaggerated sense of time. Hilda doesn't "grumble ... [because she's] got nothing to do weekends" (32) and is looked after by her mother. Peggy is "care-free" but so bored by the work that her "slapdash manner with the machine results in frequent breaking of the drills" (34). Edith's husband is in the services abroad, and so her mind is torn between the drudge of work that she finds "dirtier and more monotonous than she had expected" (36) and the faraway places she reaches via the radio on Wednesday nights. Everyone looks askance at Clarie who is out almost every night with her boyfriend of twenty. Molly is the only one who doesn't "believe in rushing ... You don't get things done any quicker" (37) and maintains that "I'm happy here because I put my heart and soul into it" (40). Sadie can work efficiently when she wants to but "will sit for minutes on end gazing round the room." "It's wicked the hours we work here," she insists. "The day the war ends I'll be first out of this factory. It'll be a race, and I'll be the one to get to the outside of those gates first" (41).

Listening to these working-class girls teaches Fremlin that, "paradoxical as it may seem, life in a twelve-hours-a-day war factory makes one feel further removed from the war than one could in any other type of life" (46–47). She records the "slipping away of all responsibilities . . . [as] from eight in the morning till eight at night life is taken off one's own hands, completely and absolutely." "Is it therefore surprising," she asks, "that, after a few weeks of this sort of life, a girl should begin to feel isolated from the outside world, and lose her sense of responsibility to it?" (47). In effect, Fremlin, whose own class position is hard to measure according to M-O's standards (she's a B-class girl but a Cambridge graduate), discovers exactly what Holden would go on to represent so vividly in *There's No Story There*, that the exaggerated temporality of shift work in the war factory made it impossible to provide these "D-class" girls with sufficient ideological compensations for their work. The challenge that Fremlin and M-O faced was to provide Ekco with the means to reduce the deadening of responsibility that produced the counternarrative that Holden would articulate.

In the published book, Harrisson concludes that there is "underlying the life of young working women to-day . . . a background of aimlessness, irresponsibility and boredom" that amounts to a "dangerous decline in positive citizenship," a "decline that subtly threatens the health of all democracy." It is reassuring then to learn that, in Harrisson's opinion, these women's "hearts still beat in the right place." If Ekco follows M-O's instructions, she thinks, the situation should be improved (9). In two final appendices, the works manager and the labor manager respond to the report as whole, and we discover how M-O's recommendations were implemented. Apparently, "during the period under survey the Machine Shop was largely staffed by female workers in the daytime and male laborers at night" (126). After M-O's visit, the factory instituted a new policy to alternate equal numbers of women between day and night shifts, changing the schedule every month. The results were impressive, and productivity improved. The managers felt sure that it was the combination of glamour and sacrifice that appealed to women on the night shift, but they did not know "[w]hether it will remain so when winter comes."

In a strange postscript to this story of M-O's infiltration of the factory, Harrisson distributed copies of the book to Ekco's workforce.[37] This belated attempt to inform the subjects of the study of M-O's findings, to inform the mass of the same "facts" that M-O provided to their employers, demonstrates how M-O's earlier democratic politics played out against the changing landscape of the war. More important still is that all the while M-O was a tool of the MOI, the National Panel continued to record its observations, maintaining an increasingly undirected and so independent record of wartime experience. In effect, M-O's prewar archiving initiative continued to sponsor a counternarrative of everyday experience even after it was co-opted by the war machine. It is with an entry from one of the diaries from this archive that I should like to end.

Talking Back

For a moment in *Talk of the City*, Isabel imagines an intervention in the world that she hopes might prevent war, not the war to come, but the Great War of memory, the war that served as her traumatic genesis. The play's realist text lapses. Isabel freezes, and mimes the cries of dying soldiers, silently rendering a cacophony of terror that the BBC would never broadcast. "If you could have heard those cries," she says to Robbie, "and then broadcast them"[38] might not they have stopped the war? In good M-O style, Isabel "speaks for herself," but she produces no sound. Instead, she serves as an icon of paralysis, of despairing resistance. I would suggest that rather than searching for a lost immediacy that will, all at once, stop the war or reorient our narratives of modernity, the trick might be to keep an eye on the chains of reference, pause sometimes to reverse them, and see where they lead. By way of an ending, then, I want to reverse the shift work that enabled M-O to produce "mass-facts," and conclude with an entry from a diary at the other end of the chain, a diary that places us with Muriel Green who faithfully responded to M-O's directives and kept a diary for the duration of the war.

March 1940. London is far away, but the radio to which Muriel and Jenny Green have been listening brings it closer:

At dinnertime we had the midday music on the radio in the Oldsmobile in the garage. When at 2 the schools programme was announced Jenny went to switch it off and she gave a wild whoop of delight and yelled, "Listen! Tom Harrisson." I rushed to listen. We always have been very curious about why the cannibals did not eat Mr. Harrisson when he lived with them, so we were very interested in the talk and intend to listen again next week. We also were curious re voice of above, and what on earth sort of a person would go and live with cannibals, so part of the mystery surrounding same was solved as he sounds quite normal and cultured!"[39]

With the whoop of one of Harrisson's cannibals, Jenny yells for her sister. Harrisson is in London. But, at 2.00 o'clock that afternoon, he is in the Greens' garage. Now he is in Muriel's diary, his voice siphoned off into the words "Harrisson," "above," and "same." He has, as M-O headquarters will learn, been the subject of conversation. Muriel Green voices the question that must have been on everyone's minds, if not their lips, "We always have been very curious about why the cannibals did not eat Mr. Harrisson" (he had made an anthropological study of cannibals in the New Hebrides), not to mention concerned about "what on earth sort of a person would go and live with cannibals." Apparently, his voice sounds "quite normal and cultured." He is a gentleman, one of the "young men who do things." The lilt of his voice communicates the class markers of an educated, well-spoken man. The facts speak for themselves.

The challenge we face in responding to the demand for a new narrative of modernity is how to make sense of texts such as Muriel Green's diary, how to understand its relation to a letter to the *New Statesman and Nation* in January 1937, to Harrisson's study of cannibals, or to the sound of a man's voice on the radio in March 1940. While we read Muriel Green's diary all too readily for the indications of immediacy it offers us, we should be careful of this lure to immerse ourselves in the everyday. Muriel Green is not this woman's true name. The protocols that permit me to use her life and words as a text forbid me telling you who she is or where she really lives. The text that "Muriel Green" embodies is the product of a particular technology of observation that assured its participants' anonymity when it shifted their writings into the public sphere. Like women who entered the factory in 1941, Muriel Green is a shift worker, a hybrid of different times and places, her diary the product of a textual web that links radically separated spheres of action. It is to this web, to the institutional actors in faraway places, to Tom Harrisson, London, the New Hebrides, the schools and university where he received his education, that Muriel Green's text responds, cannily talking or, more accurately, writing back, reversing the chain of references that cast her as passive listener to the radio, and representing herself as an active producer of text, and as the critical ear that determines the normalcy of Tom Harrisson, ornithologist, anthropologist, adventurer, and founder of M-O.

The archive of materials that M-O has left us may not "speak for itself." It may not deliver a compensatory truth for the narrative of modernity that Poliakoff's Isabel personifies. But it does provide us with an opportunity to understand the "shift work" of the modern constitution whose technologies Latour defines and whose tropes Felski questions, and so to construct a new kind of story about modernity, a story that may lead us to frame a very different kind of future.

NOTES

Epigraph: Stephen Poliakoff, *Talk of the City* (London: Methuen, 1998), 35–36. Subsequent citations of this source are given parenthetically in the text.

1. Rita Felski, *The Gender of Modernity* (Cambridge, Mass.: Harvard University Press, 1995), 10.

2. Bruno Latour, *Pandora's Hope: Essays on the Reality of Science Studies* (Cambridge, Mass.: Harvard University Press, 1999), 189.

3. Ibid., 310–11.

4. More flexible and inclusive models for this story are suggested by Donna Haraway's *Simians, Cyborgs and Women* (New York: Routledge, 1991) and *Modest_Witness@Second_Millennium.FemaleMan©_Meets_OncoMouse™* (New York: Routledge, 1997), as well as by Bruno Latour's *We Have Never Been Modern*, trans. Catherine Porter (Cambridge, Mass.: Harvard University Press, 1993) and *Pandora's Hope.*

5. Geofrey Pyke, "King and Country," *New Statesman and Nation*, December 12, 1936, 974. Madge replied on January 2, 1937, and his letter chanced to appear on the same page as a poem written by Harrisson titled "Coconut Moon: A Philosophy of Cannibalism, in the New Hebrides." Harrisson, Jennings, and Madge made contact leading to the inaugural letter, "Anthropology at Home," *New Statesman and Nation*, January 30, 1937, 155.

6. Tom Jeffrey, "Mass Observation, a Short History" (Occasional Paper No. 55, Center for Contemporary Cultural Studies, University of Birmingham, 1978), 28. For further information on M-O's origins and methods, see Nick Stanley, "'The Extra Dimension': A Study and Assessment of the Methods Employed by Mass-Observation in Its First Period, 1937–1940" (Ph.D dis., Birmingham Polytechnic, 1981).

7. In the first few months of 1937, M-O recruited 400 or so men and women. By 1939, this number rose to a "total population" of 1,894 men and 953 women between 1937 and 1945. When "'once off' replies are excluded, the male panel descends to merely 680, the female to 415" (Angus Calder, "Mass-Observation 1937–1949," in *Essays on the History of British Sociological Research*, ed. Martin Bulmer [Cambridge: Cambridge University Press, 1985], 121–36).

8. Charles Madge and Tom Harrisson, *Britain by Mass-Observation* (Harmondsworth, UK: Penguin Books, 1939), 8.

9. *May the Twelfth: Mass-Observation Day-Surveys, 1937*, ed. Humphrey Jennings, Charles Madge et al. (London: Faber & Faber, 1937), 348–49.

10. Ibid., 349–50.

11. Latour, *Pandora's Hope*, 32.

12. Ibid., 58.

13. Ibid., 69.

14. *May the Twelfth*, ed. Jennings, Madge et al., 10.

15. Stuart Laing, "Presenting 'Things as They Are': John Sommerfield's *May Day* and Mass Observation," in *Class, Culture, and Social Change*, ed. Frank Gloversmith (Brighton, UK: Harvester Press; Atlantic Highlands, N.J.: Humanities Press, 1980), 153.

16. Penny Summerfield, "Mass-Observation: Social Research or Social Movement," *Journal of Contemporary History* 20 (July 1985): 448.

17. James Buzzard, "Mass-Observation, Modernism, and Auto-ethnography," *Modernism/Modernity* 4, 3 (1997): 10.

18. Ibid., 14.

19. Ibid.

20. I have Meaghan Morris's voice in mind here, as she responds to John Fiske's "Cultural Studies and the Culture of Everyday," in *Cultural Studies*, ed. Lawrence Grossberg, Cary Nelson, and Paula A. Treichler (New York: Routledge, 1992), 165. Morris thinks beyond binarized models of resistance and reminds us of the pioneering work of Michel de Certeau's *The Practice of Everyday Life*, trans. Steven Rendell (Berkeley: California University Press, 1984), in this regard.

21. Latour, *We Have Never Been Modern*, 10.

22. Dorothy Sheridan, *Wartime Women: An Anthology of Women's Wartime Writing for Mass-Observation, 1937–1945* (London: Heinemann, 1990), 79. Subsequent citations of this collection are given parenthetically in the text.

23. Summerfield, "Mass-Observation: Social Research of Mass Movement?" 441.

24. Ibid., 443.

25. Sheridan, *Wartime Women*, 16.

26. Ibid., 22.

27. Ibid., 17.

28. Ibid., 20.

29. Angus Calder and Dorothy Sheridan, *Speak for Yourself: A Mass-Observation Anthology, 1937–1945* (London: Jonathan Cape, 1984), 153.

30. Sheridan, *Wartime Women*, 71.

31. Jenny Hartley, *Millions Like Us: British Women's Fiction of the Second World War* (London: Virago, 1997), 74.

32. Ibid., 82.

33. Ibid., 83.

34. Mass-Observation, *The War Factory*, ed. Tom Harrisson (London: Gollancz, 1943), 6.

35. For a consideration of M-O's class and gender biases in more detail, see Peter Gurney, "'Intersex' and 'Dirty Girls': Mass-Observation and Working-Class Sexuality in England in the 1930s," *Journal of the History of Sexuality* 8, 2 (1997): 256–90.

36. Mass-Observation, *War Factory*, 11.

37. Summerfield, "Mass-Observation: Social Research or Social Movement," 447.

38. Poliakoff, *Talk of the City*, 61.

39. Sheridan, *Wartime Women*, 85–86.

RITA FELSKI

Afterword

Until recently, "modernity" was not a word that rolled easily off the tongues of most literary critics. It sounded too academic, too foreign, too sociological. In English departments, at any rate, people tended to talk about modernism, by which they meant the revolutionary new forms of literature and art that burst onto the European and American scene between the turn of the century and around 1940. Thus scholars of the modern typically organized themselves into tidy groups according to a taken-for-granted division of labor. The sociologists saw themselves as experts on modernization, turning out empirical studies of societies in the throes of rapid economic development or political change. The more theoretically minded also talked about modernity, a capacious concept that allowed them to analyze the dramatic transformations of worldviews and philosophies as well as social systems. Modernity thus meant the whole package of changes that marked the move away from a traditional social order: capitalism and secularization, bureaucracy and the nation-state, individualism and the mass media.

Literary critics, by contrast, were interested in looking at how writers responded to these large-scale transformations of the social world. Here, modernism was hailed above all for its formal breakthroughs and its startling and subversive challenge to established ways of seeing. After all, many writers in the nineteenth century—Balzac, Dickens, Zola, Eliot, Gissing, to list just a few— had already explored the often terrible costs as well as the nascent hopes of a rapidly changing social world. What was distinctive and authentically modern about modernism—what allowed it to subsume the adjective into its own self-naming—was its bold and visionary use of form. For many modern writers and intellectuals, art was a way of shaking up certainty, attacking middle-class complacency, contorting and distending language in order to fashion new modes of perception and apprehension. Exploding Victorian certainties of plot and structure, they plunged the reader into the chaos of the unconscious, reveled in the slipperiness of language, splintered the world into heaps of disconnected fragments.

Thus most scholarly work on the "M" word was carved up between different fiefdoms, with only a few intrepid scholars daring to broach the boundaries between disciplines. To simplify somewhat, sociologists tended to speak of modernity as an all-encompassing social system and ever-tightening web of constraints (Weber's famous "iron cage"); English professors typically saw the iconoclastic gestures of literary modernism as subverting, or even transcending, such constraints. Between the study of social rationalization and the close reading of moments of formal rupture, however, quite a lot got left out of the picture.

For example, scholars paid little attention to the vast repertoire of images, ideas, stories, and objects that made up the everyday experience of the modern world. Sociologists were often inclined to treat culture in rather summary terms as a reflection of the socioeconomic system. This was nowhere more obvious than in the belief that religion was a historical anachronism that would eventually wither away in a fully modernized society. Literary critics, for their part, often showed little interest in popular culture and everyday life except as a foil for the bold experiments of modernist art. Indeed, they often portrayed the artist as a righteous antagonist of the commercialism, soullessness, and vulgarity that had descended on the world. In neither case did we get much "thick description" of the myriad forms, styles, and modalities of modern culture. What exactly did it mean to live in the world of the 1890s, or the 1920s, or the 1940s? How were daily routines, fleeting perceptions, the taken-for-granted sense of self, shaped by the experience of modernity? What did it really mean to be a modern subject?

We are, I've recently argued, seeing a shift to "new cultural theories of modernity" that explore some of these questions.[1] Literary and artistic modernism still plays a vital role in this new work, as one important route by which people learned to make sense of the modern. But there is also a strong interest in exploring other facets of modernity that have been overlooked in previous scholarship. Like the cultural studies tradition on which it draws, this new work is often interested in the mundane, the fleeting, the taken-for-granted. It often looks at modernity from the bottom up rather than the top down. It reminds us that the complex melange of ideas, images, and stories that make up the modern world is not simply imposed from above on a passive mass, that ordinary individuals are not just subject to modernity but also modern, self-conscious, and reflective subjects. Quite simply, these new theories allow scholars to engage seriously with the role of nonelite groups in the formation of modern life.

We should not make the mistake, however, of assuming that everyday life offers us a bedrock of authentic experience that escapes the classifying gaze of the observer. This point becomes clear in Julian Yates's fascinating discussion of the British Mass-Observation movement, a government-sponsored attempt to create an ethnography of the British people in the 1930s. Who or what was to be observed? "Behavior of people at war memorials. Shouts and gestures of motorists. The aspidistra cult. Anthropology of the football pools. Bathroom behavior. Beards, armpits, eyebrows. Anti-Semitism. Distribution, diffusion, and significance of the dirty joke. Funerals and undertakers. Female taboos about eating. The private lives of midwives" (273). This truly surreal list makes it clear that there is no neutral viewpoint from which to record the humdrum events of everyday life. The strangeness of the modern world is discovered, yet in a sense also created, by the randomness and incongruity of such juxtapositions.

The present volume, then, adds to an ongoing conversation that is slowly changing our view of the modern. As many of the essays show, linking women and modernity requires us to look anew at both these terms. Women have not figured as key players in theories of modernization or, with some obvious exceptions, in studies of literary modernism. But thinking about modernity in terms of popular culture and everyday life cedes them a starring role. Indeed, many of the cultural experiences that we think of as distinctively modern—from shopping to sex, from movies to fashion—are closely tied up with the experience of women in the modern world. To think of modernity in this way is to be plunged, in Ann Ardis's words, into reflections on "selling and shopping, travel and world expositions, political and social activism, urban fieldwork and rural labor, and radical discourses of feminine sexuality, as well as experiments with literary form" (1).

At the same time, the meanings of woman and femininity are also in flux. This is partly a question of revisiting and revising old value judgments, such as the once common feminist view that modernity was an unmitigated evil foisted by men onto hapless and helpless women. And it is partly a question of looking anew at many aspects of women's lives—from religion to mothering, from artistic creativity to same-sex love—and seeing them as embedded in the modern rather than outside modernity. We can no longer hold onto a consoling fantasy of women as pure victims and outsiders in an alien milieu. Rather, they are desiring and complicitous agents deeply immersed in the ambiguities and complexities of the modern world.

Feminist scholars, then, are currently expanding our sense of what modernity means. Reading through the preceding essays, I suggest that they are doing so in three ways. First, by rethinking the time of the modern, second, by revising the place of the modern, and, finally, by rethinking the distinction between modern art and modern society. I want to look briefly at each of these ideas in turn.

How we view the dates and times of the modern is strongly influenced by the pull of discipline and national tradition. For example, as someone with a background in comparative literature, I am often struck by the sharp division between Victorianists and modernists among my colleagues in English.[2] This is partly a question of the inevitable specialization that dogs a large field still largely organized by chronological period. But there is also something more fundamental at stake, with Victorian and modern often being seen as antithetical terms. In one sense, this seems odd, given the conservative and backward-looking nature of much of English modernism. Yet while scholars of European literature routinely trace modernism back to Baudelaire and the 1850s, this kind of genealogy is rare in English studies. The Victorians, until recently, were definitely not modern.

One result of recent scholarship, then, is that modernity is being extended back in time. For example, it is now quite common to hear the fin de siècle described as modern. A period once deemed to be conservative, aesthetically uninteresting, and still in the throes of Victorian ideology now has a new face. Thanks to the explosion of work on aestheticism, decadence, New Woman fiction, and suffragette culture, the late nineteenth century now looks much more exciting, innovative, and quintessentially modern than it used to. And as the title of this collection makes clear, modernity is being extended back to the 1870s or even earlier. We need, as Lyn Pykett suggests, to question rather than endorse the temporal schema that caused modernists to define their own endeavor in the language of rupture, crisis, and new beginnings.[3] The dividing line between the Victorians and the moderns is no longer so clear-cut.

A related phenomenon is the disentangling of modernism and modernity, a dawning realization that the modern is not simply a question of radical changes in language and form. As Claire Buck points out, feminist critics have often conflated modernism and modernity, believing that certain writers could not be modern because they failed to be modernist. The common equation of sexual and textual experimentation, the belief that feminist politics was synonymous with an avant-garde feminist poetics, often led critics to occlude or to oversimplify an important array of works by women.

Once we rethink our usual assumptions about what counts as modern, writers such as Alice Meynell become interesting in unexpected ways. Talia Schaffer shows that Meynell's work was a formal and political hybrid, balancing uneasily between different ideals and images of women. The Victorian image of genteel womanhood was not simply an outmoded symbol to be swept away so that women could freely enter the modern world. Rather, she is a figure that haunted, and continues to haunt, women's modernity. The Angel in the House and the New Woman could easily co-exist in the same body. Rather than imagining women's history as a progressive sequence of stages toward ever greater emancipation, we need to recognize that the past remains active in the present and that older ideals of femininity may continue to exercise a powerful pull. The Angel in the House is not so easily laid to rest.

Thus writers such as Meynell, whose genteel femininity grated on modernist sensibilities, may nevertheless have something to add to our understanding of modernity. The same is true of other writers of the modernist period who were not formal iconoclasts. Writers can, of course, tackle modern ideas without deploying modernist form; conversely, experimental styles may be used to express conservative and nostalgic ideas. Works that are modern are rarely modern all at once and in every respect; in most cases, we can speak of a complex melange of the old and the new. Here Radclyffe Hall's *The Well of Loneliness*, as Claire Buck shows, is a demanding test case, a puzzling blend of sexuality and sentimentalism, of tragic bohemianism and nostalgic Englishness, which is not easily classified according to the usual temporal schemas.

To rethink the modern is not just to rethink its rhythms and temporalities, its patterns of progress and succession, of development and change. It is also to look again at the spaces and places of the modern, and to question the once common view that nonwhite, non-Western individuals were belated and backward subjects of modernity, passive beneficiaries of Western largesse. Several essays draw on the idea of hybridity to disrupt oppositions between the modern and the primitive, the progressive and the static. Alpana Sharma suggests that the history of the youthful Indian poet and translator Toru Dutt can be read in this way. Neither authentically Indian nor purely Western, Dutt's work points to the possibilities as well as the risks of in-between-ness. Piya Pal-Lapinski reads Bram Stoker's *Lair of the White Worm* as touching on contemporary anxieties about the decay of English women's wombs and ovaries in the febrile heat of the tropics. The novel, she writes, explores "an Englishness transformed and depleted through its imperial activities," forced to acknowledge "its own 'original' hybridity and lack of internal coherence" (5). Finally, Leslie Lewis's discussion of Pauline Hopkins mounts a powerful critique of notions of racial purity and authenticity. Whereas discussions of African American women writers have often stressed their links to rural and oral traditions, there is now a growing interest in highlighting the modernity of their work, as evidenced in its formal and cultural hybridity.[4]

So, too, in this collection, we see that the work of modernity is carried out in places once perceived as insufficiently or belatedly modern. It makes little sense to think of the Western metropolis as the only source of novelty and change when the global reach of modern development binds together disparate locales in a complex web of dependence and interconnection. Modernity is present in both Olive Schreiner's South Africa and Khun Fa's Thailand. Lynn Thiesmeyer reminds us that the rural labor of women does not take place outside the modern but is often indispensable to the creation of modern nations. Both she and Carolyn Burdett, in her discussion of Olive Schreiner in South Africa, stress the ambivalence of the modern, its often hefty burdens and costs, as well as the new opportunities it unleashes.

Carla Peterson's essay on the novels of Emma Dunham Kelley-Hawkins is an illuminating account of the racial politics of the modern. Peterson shows how the historical convergence of religion, psychology, class politics, and consumption helped to channel racial affiliation. While Kelley-Hawkins's novels do not fit comfortably into a dominant African American canon of social protest literature, they espouse an alternative vision of black modernity that yokes worldly consumerism to Christian piety. Peterson's essay raises interesting questions about differing forms of attachment to racial identity, as well as showing how American religion could serve as a sign of modernity rather than tradition.

Peterson's discussion of an "economy of pleasure" raises another question that defines much of this collection: the aesthetics and politics of consumerism. To say that modern consumerism is as much about art as it is about politics is to recognize that key aspects of the aesthetic—playfulness, imagination, eroticism, loss of self—are often harnessed in a consumer culture to market goods. As a result, some of the conventional ways of distinguishing between art and society become untenable. Even as modernist art defiantly insisted on its own autonomy, aesthetic elements permeated many aspects of everyday life. In a reading of Djuna Barnes's early journalism, Katherine Biers brings out this idea, suggesting that the daily newspaper was a powerful illustration of the power of spectacle, the links between violence and the visual and the ambiguities of gender identification. Modern culture, as Michael North has recently shown, is a deeply aestheticized culture.[5]

This idea is fleshed out in Lucy Burke's discussion of the writings of Maria Stopes. Stopes was, of course, a well-known campaigner for public knowledge about contraception and sexuality. Burke highlights the aesthetic dimensions of her factual as well as fictional writings. Not only did the genre of the marital hygiene manual draw heavily on the conventions of romance fiction, but sexuality itself was portrayed as a lyrical experience transcending the vulgarities of the flesh. By associating sex with the appreciation of beauty and the cultivation of a refined sensibility, Stopes made her ideas palatable to a middle-class audience. What she advocated for her readers, she insisted, had absolutely nothing to do with working-class masturbators, deviant domestic servants, and the sorrowful specimens of Havelock Ellis.

Consumerism and travel are clearly central to women's experience of modernity. As Barbara Green points out, consumption is the key link between the everyday and modernity, the means by which new technologies, products, and images of self are assimilated into daily practice. Rebecca West seems uncannily prescient here in her rejection of what would become left-wing orthodoxy on the evils of consumerism and her defense of female pleasure, appetite, and delight in fashion. Similarly, Ana Vadillo offers an upbeat reading of the history of public transport, arguing that the introduction of London buses and the tube blurred class and gender boundaries and allowed women to gain control of the gaze. Such a questioning of feminist pessimism about male domination of space and the alienating nature of the modern city can be useful.

I want, finally, to make some comments on the idea of the public sphere, a theme touched on in the chapters by James Davis and Barbara Green. In an early book, I sought to make sense of some new genres of women's writing by situating them in the context of a feminist "counter-public sphere." At that time, I still pretty much took it for granted that modernity had progressed along a single and unified path until the flowering of the new social movements in the 1960s and 1970s. Counter-public spheres thus arose from a unique "postmodern" constellation of ideological and social forces. It now seems clear, however, that such a view of the utter uniformity and homogeneity of modernity is much too simple. In particular, the women's suffrage movement seems like an obvious example of a counter-public sphere that was not until recently seen as such.

Part of the reason for this neglect, perhaps, is that suffrage activists strove to have women incorporated in the machinery of the state, as voting citizens and political actors. It is easy to conclude, then, that they sought assimilation rather than difference, incorporation into existing structures rather than resistance to them. Yet recent work on the suffrage campaign reveals that its practices transcend simple oppositions of equality versus difference, that the struggle for votes for women went along with forms of militant action, disruptive performance, and bodily display that were deeply at odds with the dominant norm of civic debate. Expanding the notion of what counted as politics, the suffragettes in particular fashioned a form of activism that was closely linked to advertising, spectacle, and the public display of bodies and emotions.[6]

For the Marxist scholar, of course, this entanglement with consumerism merely confirms the compromised nature of early feminist politics. But we need to rethink the view that a counter-public sphere can only exist outside the institutions of modernity and that commodification is an automatic sign of co-option. Here I agree wholeheartedly with James Davis's observation that "[t]oo tidy an opposition between mass culture and authentic citizenship has overorganized public sphere talk" (201). Francesca Sawaya touches on a related chord in her discussion of the polarity of professionalism and experience that has often dogged feminist debate. While appeals to "women's experience" have allowed the voices of women to be heard, such appeals have often relied on a vision of personal experience as authentic wholeness that transcends the fractures and divisions of modernity. Specialized knowledge is often viewed with distrust. The belief that an authentic political subject can be neither a consumer nor an expert springs from a form of romantic anti-modernism that feminism should not automatically endorse.[7]

Deborah Garfield's discussion of a 1920s best-seller, the purported diary of a six-year-old child living alone in the Oregon forest, raises further questions about the role of nostalgia and primitivism in modern culture. Is the romantic impulse modern or anti-modern? It resolutely pits itself against the institutions and ideas of modernity yet is tightly interlaced with the very reality that it condemns. Can a sympathetic and nuanced rereading of the gender politics of modernity do justice to romanticism, which is often so vehement in its own antagonism to the modern? Alternatively, can we see romanticism as outside or at odds with modernity, as anachronistic or elitist, when nostalgic longings for authenticity, escape, and wholeness permeate not just high art but so much of popular culture and everyday life? Given the crucial role of woman and the feminine in the romantic dream of redemption, such questions seem worth asking.

Reading through this collection of essays, it is clear that these scholars' revision of modernity is fueled by contemporary commitments and passions. Whether we decide to call it a postmodern notion of modernity is perhaps a moot point. It is certainly influenced by contemporary theory and cultural studies, as well as by the new scholarship on gender, race, and sexuality. Yet the inevitable partiality of our perspective on the past should not, I believe, be confused with an approach that simply remakes the past in the image of the present. As much of the work in this volume shows, the experience of modernity in the late nineteenth and early twentieth century is both uncannily like and uncannily unlike our own. It is out of such a dialectical movement, which simultaneously respects and bridges the otherness of the past, that the best feminist scholarship on modernity emerges.

NOTES

1. Rita Felski, "New Cultural Theories of Modernity," in *Doing Time: Feminist Theory and Postmodern Culture* (New York: New York University Press, 2000).

2. There are, of course, important exceptions to this rule, such as the work of Gillian Beer.

3. Lyn Pykett, *Engendering Fictions: The English Novel in the Early Twentieth Century* (London: Edward Arnold, 1995).

4. See, e.g., Carole Anne Taylor, *The Tragedy and Comedy of Resistance: Reading Modernity through Black Women's Fiction* (Philadelphia: University of Pennsylvania Press, 2000).

5. Michael North, *1922: Rereading the Scene of the Modern* (Oxford: Oxford University Press, 1999).

6. See Barbara Green, *Spectacular Confessions: Autobiography, Performative Activism and the Sites of Suffrage 1905–1938* (New York: St Martin's Press, 1997), and Wendy Parkins, "Taking Liberty's: Suffragettes and the Public Sphere 1905–1914" (diss., Murdoch University, Australia, 1996).

7. Feminist cultural studies is an instructive example here. Feminist scholars have by and large recuperated consumption, which they see as linking them to other women, but are often deeply anxious about institutionalization and their own status as "experts," which they see as separating them from other women. See my review article, "Feminist Futures," *International Journal of Cultural Studies* (forthcoming).

∾ ANN L. ARDIS is a professor of English and director of the University Honors Program at the University of Delaware. She is the author of *New Women, New Novels: Feminism and Early Modernism* (1990), co-editor (with Bonnie Kime Scott) of *Virginia Woolf Turning the Centuries: The Proceedings of the Ninth Annual Virginia Woolf Conference* (2000), and author of *Modernism and Cultural Conflict, 1880–1922* (2002).

∾ KATHERINE BIERS completed her Ph.D. in English at Cornell University in 2001. She is currently working on a book about modernism, mass media, and female authorship in the early twentieth century.

∾ CLAIRE BUCK is an associate professor of English at Wheaton College in Massachusetts. She is the author of *H.D. and Freud: Bisexuality and a Feminine Discourse* (1991) and editor of *The Bloomsbury Guide to Women's Literature* (1992), and has published many articles on women's writing. She is currently writing a study of the effects of World War I on prewar paradigms for the literary representation of dissident sexualities.

∾ LUCY BURKE lectures in English literature and cultural theory in the Department of English and American Studies at the University of Manchester. Her main research interest is the relationships between discourses of sexuality, culture, and class in women's writing in the interwar period in Britain. She has written on Storm Jameson, Dorothy L. Sayers, Rebecca West, and Marie Stopes in this context. She is one of the editors of the *Routledge Language and Cultural Theory Reader* (2000) and is currently working on a book on Marie Stopes.

∾ CAROLYN BURDETT is a principal lecturer in English and critical theory at the University of North London. Her research interests are in nineteenth- and twentieth-century literature and culture. She is the author of *Olive Schreiner and the Progress of Feminism: Evolution, Gender, Empire* (2001).

ᦰ   JAMES DAVIS   is an assistant professor of English at Nassau Community College, where he teaches American literature. He is currently writing a book about consumer culture and race in the United States in the late nineteenth and early twentieth centuries.

ᦰ   RITA FELSKI   is a professor of English at the University of Virginia and the author of *Beyond Feminist Aesthetics* (1989), *The Gender of Modernity* (1995), and *Doing Time: Feminist Theory and Postmodern Culture* (2000). She is currently completing *Literature after Feminism*, an overview and assessment of feminist literary criticism.

ᦰ   DEBORAH GARFIELD, a member of the English Department at UCLA, teaches American literature and women's studies. Her published work includes articles on female slavery, Theodore Dreiser, William Faulkner, and American anthropology and child study at the turn of the twentieth century. Along with Rafia Zafar, she is the editor of *Harriet Jacobs* for Cambridge University Press's American Literature and Culture Series, to which she contributed two essays; she is currently finishing a book called *Alternative Origins: Women, Narrative and the Mythology of Beginnings, 1870–1936*.

ᦰ   BARBARA GREEN   is an associate professor of English at the University of Notre Dame and a member of the Gender Studies faculty. She is the author of *Spectacular Confessions: Autobiography, Performative Activism, and the Sites of Suffrage* (1997).

ᦰ   PIYA PAL-LAPINSKI   is an assistant professor of English at Bowling Green State University. Her recent and forthcoming publications include articles on Victorian fiction, hybridity, and medical discourse. She is currently working on a book on the exotic female body in nineteenth-century fiction and culture.

ᦰ   LESLIE W. LEWIS   is an associate professor of English and director of the American Studies program at the College of Saint Rose. She is currently finishing a book focused on racial consciousness and the role of secrets in nineteenth- and early-twentieth-century African American narrative literature.

∾   C A R L A   L .   P E T E R S O N   is a professor in the Department of English at the University of Maryland. She is the author of *"Doers of the Word": African-American Women Speakers and Writers in the North (1830–1880)*. In addition, she has published numerous essays on the nineteenth-century African American writers Frederick Douglass, Frances Harper, Charlotte Forten, and Pauline Hopkins. She is currently working on a book tentatively entitled "The New Negro Novel at the Nadir (1892–1903)."

∾   F R A N C E S C A   S A W A Y A   is an assistant professor of English at the University of Oklahoma. She is completing a book on women writers and professionalism in the United States.

∾   A L P A N A   S H A R M A   teaches postcolonial literature and theory at Wright State University in Dayton, Ohio. She is the editor of *New Immigrant Literatures in the United States* (1996) and has published in the areas of Indian women's literature, postcolonial film, and globalization.

∾   T A L I A   S C H A F F E R   is an assistant professor of English at Queens College, CUNY. She is the author of *The Forgotten Female Aesthetes: Literary Culture in Late-Victorian England* (2000), and she and Kathy A. Psomiades are co-editors of *Women and British Aestheticism* (1999). She has published articles on noncanonical women writers at the turn of the century, the material culture of aestheticism, and fin de siècle writers in *Victorian Poetry, Victorian Literature and Culture, ELH*, the *Henry James Review, Nineteenth-Century Literature*, and various collections.

∾   L Y N N   T H I E S M E Y E R   is an associate professor in the Faculty of the Information Environment at Keio University's Shonan-Fujisawa Campus, where she teaches discourse, social theory, and gender and development. Through her Mekhong Region Development Net/Women and Development Online Information Project, she works with community projects sponsored by government, nongovernmental, academic, and private sector organizations in Thailand and Vietnam. She is a team leader for the 2001 Asia Pacific HIV Impact Research Tool project of the United Nations Development Program and a member of the Board of Advisors for the World Bank's Gender and Development Gateway and its Culture and Development Gateway. Her recent publications on women and Asia include "The West's 'Comfort Women' and the Discourses of Seduction," in *Transnational Asia Pacific: Gender, Culture, and the Public Sphere*, ed. Shirley Lim, Larry Smith and Wimal Dissanyake (1999) and "Identifying and Using Knowledge Sources: Transnational and Trans-sector Cooperation in Southeast Asia" (*Journal of APEC [Asia Pacific Economic Commission] Studies*, Summer 2000). She is currently developing a multilingual website to make available direct information from populations impacted by development schemes in Southeast Asian communities.

∾   ANA PAREJO VADILLO is currently a visiting lecturer at Birkbeck College, University of London. She is the author of a number of articles on fin de siècle women poets and is currently writing a book manuscript entitled "Passengers of Modernity: Women Poets and the Aesthetics of Urban Mass Transport."

∾   JULIAN YATES teaches English at the University of Delaware. He is the author of *Object Lessons from the English Renaissance* (University of Minnesota Press, 2002).